Valuing

Natural

Assets

The
Economics
of
Natural
Resource
Damage
Assessment

Valuing

Natural

Assets

The
Economics
of
Natural
Resource
Damage
Assessment

Raymond J. Kopp and
V. Kerry Smith, editors

Resources for the Future
Washington, D.C.

Cloth: 0-915707-66-7/93 $1.00 + .10
Paper: 0-915707-67-5/93 $1.00 + .10

Printed in the United States of America

Published by Resources for the Future
1616 P Street, NW, Washington, DC 20036

Library of Congress Cataloging-in-Publication Data

Valuing natural assets : the economics of natural resource damage
  assessment / Raymond J. Kopp and V. Kerry Smith, editors.
          p.   cm.
  Includes bibliographical references and index.
  ISBN 0-915707-66-7 (cloth)
  ISBN 0-915707-67-5 (paperback)
  1. Liability for environmental damages—United States.   2. Natural
resources—Law and legislation—United States.   3. Natural
resources—Valuation—United States.   I. Kopp, Raymond J.
II. Smith, V. Kerry (Vincent Kerry), 1945–   .
KF1298.A75V35   1993
346.7303′8—dc20
[347.30638]   92-35479
                                                                CIP

This book is the product of the Quality of the Environment Division, Raymond J. Kopp, director, at Resources for the Future. The project editor for the book was Samuel Allen and the copy editor was Linda Humphrey. The book and cover were designed by Kelly Design. The book was indexed by Shirley Kessel.

∞ The paper in this book meets the guidelines for permanence and durability of the Committee on Production Guidelines for Book Longevity of the Council on Library Resources.

RESOURCES FOR THE FUTURE (RFF) is an independent nonprofit organization engaged in research and public education on natural resource and environmental issues. Its mission is to create and disseminate knowledge that helps people make better decisions about the conservation and use of their natural resources and the environment. RFF neither lobbies nor takes positions on current policy issues.

Because the work of RFF focuses on how people make use of scarce resources, its primary research discipline is economics. However, its staff also includes social scientists from other fields, ecologists, environmental health scientists, meteorologists, and engineers. Staff members pursue a wide variety of interests, including forest economics, recycling, multiple use of public lands, the costs and benefits of pollution control, endangered species, energy and national security, hazardous waste policy, climate resources, and quantitative risk assessment.

Acting on the conviction that good research and policy analysis must be put into service to be truly useful, RFF communicates its findings to government and industry officials, public interest advocacy groups, nonprofit organizations, academic researchers, and the press. It produces a range of publications and sponsors conferences, seminars, workshops, and briefings. Staff members write articles for journals, magazines, and newspapers, provide expert testimony, and serve on public and private advisory committees. The views they express are in all cases their own, and do not represent positions held by RFF, its officers, or trustees.

Established in 1952, RFF derives its operating budget in approximately equal amounts from three sources: investment income from a reserve fund, government grants, and contributions from corporations, foundations, and individuals. (Corporate support cannot be earmarked for specific research projects.) Some 45 percent of RFF's total funding is unrestricted, which provides crucial support for its foundational research and outreach and educational operations. RFF is a publicly funded organization under Section 501(c)(3) of the Internal Revenue Code, and all contributions to its work are tax deductible.

Contents

PART 2: Measuring Natural Resource Damages

PART 3: Two Key Conceptual Dimensions of Damage Assessment

PART 4: Research Implications of Damage Assessment

Tables and Figures

Foreword

Methodological disputes between economists seldom attract attention beyond the halls of academe (and those of research organizations). But when they do, they can generate considerable controversy. This has been the case, for instance, when economists have differed on whether a particular market was competitive or not. Since the initiation and ultimate disposition of antitrust actions can hinge on such definitions, lawyers, judges, and legislators have been drawn into what was once a rarified debate among economists. A similar controversy involving methodologies has erupted in natural resource and environmental economics, and the focal point of that controversy is the subject of this book.

Under the Comprehensive Environmental Response, Compensation, and Liability Act of 1980, Congress gave federal, state, and local governments the right as trustees to sue for damages resulting from the release of harmful materials into publicly owned natural resources such as rivers, lakes, estuaries, oceans, or other aquatic or terrestrial habitats. Some components of these damages—for example, incomes lost by those who derive their living from the damaged natural assets—are relatively straightforward to measure, and their inclusion in legal actions has not been exceptionally controversial. This has *not* been the case with all types of damage, however.

In particular, some recent court decisions have suggested that among the injuries for which trustees might recover damages are those resulting from what are known as lost "existence values" (or "nonuse values")—that is, the values individuals may derive from the mere knowledge that an unspoiled natural area exists. If, as a result of an oil or chemical spill, say, individuals who make no active use of the resource in question nevertheless experience such losses in well-being, and if these losses can reliably be expressed in dollar terms, the potential recoverable damages for such an incident are much larger than if they were restricted to out-of-pocket losses or other relatively easily measured damages. Welcome to the world of natural resource damage assessment and the use of a technique known as the contingent valuation method to measure damages.

In this collection of papers—originally prepared for a conference held by Resources for the Future in 1988, but rewritten several times since then in response to rapidly changing developments—editors Raymond J. Kopp and V. Kerry Smith and a host of contributors introduce the reader to the legal and economic issues surrounding this fascinating public policy problem. The papers in this volume identify the origins of the concept of existence value, discuss the way in which it came to play a role in natural resource damage assessment, explain the history behind the contingent valuation method (which is being used increasingly to measure lost existence values), identify the pros and cons of this technique, review some of the law and federal rulemaking that have evolved from natural resource damage cases, and suggest a research agenda for the future.

Valuing Natural Assets: The Economics of Natural Resource Damage Assessment should appeal to professional economists, members of the environmental bar, environmental and natural resource policy analysts, members of business and environmental organizations, legislators and their staffs, elected and appointed officials, and even the very highly motivated (and somewhat intrepid) lay reader. As with all RFF publications, this book is published in the hope that it will help elevate the debate about an important—and, in this case, controversial—public policy issue.

Paul R. Portney
Vice President
March 1993   Resources for the Future

Acknowledgements

Since 1987, when natural resource damage assessment was the concern of a small number of environmental economists, interest in that subject has attracted the attention of a wide range of theoretical economists and econometricians, as well as several Nobel laureates. Thus this book, which was intended to be an introduction to the issues in damage assessment, has become a vehicle for reporting on established research on the conceptual and empirical issues raised by the litigation-driven demands for increasingly complex natural resource damage assessments. Indeed, the growing research devoted to measuring damages from injuries to natural resources has transformed nonmarket valuation as it has come to be applied in benefit-cost analysis and environmental costing.

A number of people have contributed to our research on natural resource damage assessment at Resources for the Future (RFF) and North Carolina State University (NCSU). The participants in the RFF-sponsored conference in June 1988 that launched these research efforts (see chapter 1) provided an initial sounding board for the preliminary ideas of all the authors of this volume. Special recognition should be given to Charles J. Cicchetti, William H. Desvousges, Baruch Fischhoff, Anthony C. Fisher, and W. Michael Hanemann, who provided written comments on individual research papers on the issues involved in developing damage assessments, and to Nancy Firestone, Allen V. Kneese, and John V. Krutilla, who chaired some of the conference sessions. Marc B. Carey, then a graduate student at the School of Natural Resources at the University of Michigan, prepared an interpretive summary of the discussions at the conference, on which we have drawn for this book. As research progressed, our colleagues at RFF and NCSU were the source of many valuable discussions. Paul R. Portney of RFF provided significant and constructive insights into transforming the collection of papers on research programs into an integrated treatment of natural resource damage assessment.

Initial support for the 1988 conference was provided by the Alfred P. Sloan Foundation, CIBA-GEIGY Corporation, the 3M Company, and the General Electric Company. The Alfred P. Sloan Foundation has continued to support Ray Kopp's research in this area at RFF. Throughout the research period, the NCSU Sea Grant Program provided partial support for Kerry Smith's research on the theory and implementation of nonmarket methods for assessing marine resources, under a series of three separate grants.

Careful and detailed reviews by anonymous readers have had a significant impact on the overall structure of the volume and its chapters. The chapters by Kopp and Smith were prepared, through numerous drafts, by Patricia Flynn and Joy Hall of RFF and Barbara Scott of NCSU. RFF project editor Sam Allen and managing editor Dorothy Sawicki, and copy editor Linda Humphrey, helped to assure a more accessible final product.

Finally, our families—Linda, Kristin, and Kevin for Ray, and Pauline, Shelley, and Tim for Kerry—provided the support and time that sustained our efforts on research, assuring the ultimate completion of this volume.

Raymond J. Kopp and V. Kerry Smith

Contributors

Frederick R. Anderson, Cadwalader, Wickersham and Taft, Washington, D.C.

Gardner M. Brown, Jr., Department of Economics, University of Washington

Richard T. Carson, Department of Economics, University of California, San Diego

Ralph C. d'Arge, Department of Economics, University of Wyoming

A. Myrick Freeman III, Department of Economics, Bowdoin College

Howard Kenison, Kutak Rock, Denver, Colorado

Raymond J. Kopp, Resources for the Future, Washington, D.C.

Kenneth E. McConnell, Department of Agricultural and Resource Economics, University of Maryland at College Park

Robert Mendelsohn, School of Forestry and Environmental Studies, Yale University

Robert Cameron Mitchell, Graduate School of Geography, Clark University

William D. Schulze, Department of Economics, University of Colorado

V. Kerry Smith, Department of Economics and Department of Agricultural and Resource Economics, North Carolina State University

Willie R. Taylor, U.S. Department of the Interior, Washington, D.C.

1

Introduction

Raymond J. Kopp and V. Kerry Smith

1. BACKGROUND

The origin of this volume dates to 1987, when V. Kerry Smith, one of its editors and authors, was serving on an advisory panel for the National Oceanic and Atmospheric Administration's assessment of the damages to New Bedford harbor, Massachusetts, caused by releases of polychlorinated biphenyls (PCBs). Also on the panel were Gardner M. Brown, Jr., and A. Myrick Freeman III, authors of other chapters in this volume. This assessment was part of the first federal suit brought for natural resource damages under Superfund, known formally as the Comprehensive Environmental Response, Compensation, and Liability Act (CERCLA) of 1980. The research team conducting that assessment included Kenneth E. McConnell and Robert Mendelsohn, also among our authors. At about the same time, under state laws Colorado was pursuing a natural resource damage case for injuries to land and to surface and ground waters from mining waste. Lawyers for the defendant in that case organized a simulated trial, allowing their experts and Kerry Smith to present each side's assessment of the natural resource damages. Both the Massachusetts and Colorado activities served to highlight important research issues that were emerging from the interactions among the intentions of the legislation establishing natural resource damage liability, their realization through the rulemaking and litigation processes, and the corresponding demands imposed on natural science and economics. While the questions being raised appeared to be central to economic analyses of the nonmarketed services of natural assets, we did not imagine that damage assessment would emerge five years later as a major influence on economic research associated with the nonmarket valuation of environmental resources.

The Comprehensive Environmental Response, Compensation, and Liability Act and its reauthorizing amendments, the Superfund Amendments and Reauthorization Act (SARA) of 1986, established two types of liability for past and current releases of hazardous substances. The first is associated with cleaning up old and abandoned hazardous waste sites, the second with residual liability arising after cleanup. Damage claims associated with injuries to natural resources are a concern under the second type of liability. Damage awards for injuries to natural resources are intended to maintain a portfolio of natural assets that have been identified as being held in public trust. When injuries to these resources prevent the public from enjoying the services of the resources, provisions under the second type of liability allow compensation for the losses incurred from the time an injury starts until a settlement is reached. Because this compensation is to the public as a whole, the payment is made to a designated trustee and the compensation takes the form of in-kind services, presumably made available because the dollars from an award can be used to acquire or enhance existing natural assets over and above what is done to restore the injured natural resources to their baseline condition. Thus, the damages can include monetary compensation for injuries to the resource sustained prior to and during cleanup, as well as compensation for any residual injuries remaining after sites have been cleaned to meet a human health standard.

CERCLA was not the first legislation to identify injuries to natural resources as compensable damages. States have brought suits *parens patriae* or under the public trust doctrine of the common law, and under the Federal Water Pollution Control Act of 1977 (known as the Clean Water Act). Since CERCLA does not classify petroleum products as hazardous substances, claims for natural resource damages due to oil spills are filed under state common law, provisions of the Clean Water Act, or provisions of the Oil Pollution Act of 1990.[1]

Once aware of the issues, we recognized (as did many other environmental economists) that the methods being used for assessing natural resource damages were drawn from the existing stock of nonmarket valuation techniques used in traditional benefit-cost studies for proposed environmental regulations. Because natural resource damage liability is a residual liability, knowledgeable analysts in the private sector suggested that one could reasonably expect growth in the number of damage cases as the processes of proposing and finalizing assessment rules were completed and as recognition of this residual liability aspect of the CERCLA and SARA statutes widened.

Methods for nonmarket valuation were developed in part to help establish whether the net benefits of a proposed action or activity would be positive or negative. Inaccuracies in this process are usually evaluated in

---

[1]See Breen (1989) for an overview of the evolution of natural resource damage liability.

terms of how they influence conclusions about whether the net benefits meet this test. However, damage assessment dramatically changes the context for applying nonmarket valuation methods. Some single, identified entity (but not anonymous taxpayers) pays damages based on what is measured. Evaluations of those measures take place largely in a courtroom, not in agency meeting rooms. This procedure in itself changes how the measures are presented, received, and defended. Our objective has been to evaluate the process and the research issues it has raised, both for damage assessment and more generally.

In 1988 we approached the Alfred P. Sloan Foundation with the idea of holding a conference that would address the economic issues involved in natural resource damage assessment. In particular, we wished to focus on the interactions between legal and administrative requirements on the one hand and the scientific and economic frameworks that would form the basis of assessments on the other. Our intent was to evaluate the suitability of the available economic theory and tools, as well as the issues involved in implementing the assessments and bringing them before the courts. With the aid of the Sloan Foundation and Resources for the Future (RFF) a workshop was held in Washington, D.C., in June 1988. This conference started the research that resulted in the present volume. Many of the chapters in this volume are revisions to papers presented at the conference.

Over time, most of the authors of chapters in this volume have been involved in damage assessment cases, providing analyses for either defendants or plaintiffs. They have also written for academic journals on damage assessment issues. Their chapters reflect individual research programs that temper the rigorous demands of scholarship with the practical realities of litigation.

It is hard to anticipate how many legal cases will involve natural resource damage claims. The *Exxon Valdez* oil spill focused national attention on the magnitude of damages that can occur from the release of crude oil, and raised public awareness of the damage assessment process and the questions associated with appraising damages. Indeed, when the settlement was agreed upon among Exxon, the federal government, and the state of Alaska, the state's analysis was the focus of a major news story and nonmarket valuation became "news."[2] In addition, recent legal action by the U.S. Department of Justice under CERCLA will seek damages for long-term releases of PCBs into a number of the nation's waterways; a complex array of environmental injuries will be alleged. Because the Environmental Protection Agency (EPA) continues to identify more old and abandoned waste sites, concerns over the cleanup process and the

---

[2]See the *Washington Post*, March 20, 1990.

residual liabilities for natural resource damages are unlikely to be any less important in the future than they are now.[3]

2.   A GUIDE TO THE VOLUME

This brief introduction to the origins of the volume is followed in chapter 2 by a discussion of definitions and concepts concerning natural resource damages that prepares the reader for the more detailed analyses in the ensuing chapters. Chapter 2 suggests that damages to natural resources are best understood when the resources are treated as assets that provide a flow of services to individuals. Given this framework, injuries to natural resources due to the release of hazardous substances or oil are seen to diminish people's valuation of these services; the diminished value is a measure of the economic damage.

Following these introductory chapters, the volume is divided into four parts: part 1 concerns statutes, rulemaking, and practice; part 2 treats the measurement of natural resource damages; part 3 focuses on two key conceptual dimensions of damage assessment; and part 4 discusses the research implications of damage assessment. The parts are largely independent of each other and may be read in any order by those having some familiarity with natural resource damage assessments. Each of the first three parts is prefaced by a brief introduction; newcomers to the field and readers wishing to browse through the volume are directed to these introductions.

Part 1 begins, in chapter 3, with a discussion of CERCLA—the most significant piece of natural resource damage legislation to date—and its place in legal history. Chapters 4 through 7 turn to the implementation of CERCLA and related legislation and what it implies for the manner in which damages for resource injuries claimed under CERCLA are assessed.

Part 2 concerns itself with the economic methods used to assess natural resource damages. The four chapters in this part present and critically evaluate the range of economic methods and models that are employed to measure the value placed on lost use and nonuse services of the resources. Included are both revealed preference methods (often termed indirect methods, and based on travel cost, averting behavior, and hedonic property value models) and direct methods (most notably contingent valuation).

In part 3 attention is turned to two important areas of damage assessment—the role of time in capitalizing past losses and discounting

---

[3]A recent report of the Office of Technology Assessment (1989) indicated that at the end of the first nine months of 1989, EPA had 1,224 sites on its National Priorities List and more than 31,000 sites in the CERCLA inventory system.

future losses (chapter 12), and the theoretical underpinnings for the important category of losses known as nonuse or existence values (chapter 13). Both of these topics have been addressed in recent court rulings.[4]

Part 4 closes the volume with a single chapter that presents our views regarding the impact that natural resource damage assessment will have on the discipline of environmental and natural resource economics in particular and the role of applied welfare economics for public policy in general.

REFERENCES

Breen, Barry. 1989. "Citizen Suits for Natural Resource Damages: Closing the Gap in Federal Environmental Law," *Wake Forest Law Review* 24, pp. 851–880.

U.S. Congress, Office of Technology Assessment. 1989. "Coming Clean: Superfund's Problems Can Be Solved . . . ," OTA-ITE-433. Washington, D.C., U.S. Government Printing Office. October.

---

[4]The role of time in damage assessment was addressed in U.S. District Court, District of Massachusetts, *Acushnet River & New Bedford Harbor: Proceedings Re Alleged PCB Pollution*, Civil Action, No. 83-388201-1, "Memorandum Concerning Natural Resource Damages Under CERCLA," District Judge Young, June 7, 1989. The proper role of nonuse values in quantifying natural resource damages under CERCLA was clarified in the judge's opinion in *Ohio v. The United States Department of the Interior*, 880 F.2d 432 (D.C. Cir. 1989).

2
Understanding Damages to Natural Assets
Raymond J. Kopp and V. Kerry Smith

1. MEASURES OF DAMAGE

1.1 Introduction. Any discussion of natural resource damages must begin with a working definition of what has been damaged. Many will be surprised to learn that a considerable difference of opinion exists regarding what is—and what is not—a damage. Conventional definitions of damages (ignoring issues related to punitive damages) hold that when liable parties are required to pay damages equal to the monetized loss they cause, we can expect that they will take optimal precautions (Shavell [1987], pp. 127–133). When readily produced commodities are injured, the damage estimate is the cost of replacing them, provided the original goods do not have some unique, irreplaceable characteristics. When the commodities have unique characteristics, replacement with a cheaper substitute is not the appropriate definition of damage. Restoration of the original will be required. In contrast, if the damaged party gains exceptionally high levels of utility from the goods, but the cost of replacing them with a perfect substitute is substantially less than the monetized value of that utility, the appropriate damage is often the smaller amount.

There is no mystery to these two situations. The determination of loss requires a judgment about how to provide services equivalent to those that would have been available from the good that was lost, recognizing that uniqueness might contribute to these services from the owner's perspective. However, it is important to recognize that implementation of replacement or restoration in each situation inevitably requires some judgment about the commodities involved. Thus, translating concept into practice with a marketed good is difficult, but substantially more straightforward than measuring the nonmarketed services of natural assets.

The legislation establishing liability for natural resource damages (the Comprehensive Environmental Response, Compensation, and Lia-

6

bility Act of 1980 [CERCLA][1] and the Superfund Amendments and Re-authorization Act of 1986 [SARA][2]), a recent appeals court ruling (*Ohio v. The United States Department of the Interior*),[3] and proposed Department of the Interior (DOI) rules for damage assessment generally specify damages to be equal to the cost of restoring the injured resource and the economic value lost during the period the resource is injured. Problems arise with this measure of damage because restoring the resource that provided the original services is not a straightforward task, even conceptually. Indeed, our understanding of just what constitutes the services provided by natural assets may itself be incomplete.

The end result is that we identify restoration costs as a measure of damages, but clearly recognize that the total bill corresponds to costs for the restoration alternative *plus* the ". . . dollar figure computed for the compensable value of the services lost to the public for the period of the recovery—whether a natural recovery, which might be longer, or an assisted recovery, which might be shorter."[4] Unfortunately, this avoids the basic issue—how do we select an alternative when the original services cannot be restored? Because this is more likely to be the rule in most damage cases, we must consider how the components of damage are defined by the Department of the Interior.

1.2   Lost Value. The services of natural assets are not produced and sold on organized markets. Moreover, natural assets provide a variety of services, some closer to what conventional economic treatments of liability describe as pecuniary commodities and others closer to what are described as nonpecuniary commodities.[5] Because neither type of service has a market-determined price, economic measures of loss attempt to measure the amount of money required to provide the owner of the damaged resource an equivalent level of well-being. The owner in the case of natural resources is the general public. The trustee is simply an agent acting on the public's behalf.

This measure of loss corresponds to the Hicksian concept of compensation. It can be defined using an ordinal description of utility as the

---

[1]42 U.S.C. 9601–9675.

[2]Pub. L. No. 99-499, 100 Stat. 1613.

[3]880 F.2d 432 (D.C. Cir. 1989).

[4]"Natural Resource Damage Assessment, Notice of Proposed Rulemaking," 56 *Federal Register* 19764 (April 29, 1991).

[5]Shavell (1987) defines losses of wealth or produced commodities as pecuniary losses and losses of irreplaceable goods (which he illustrates as land or physical integrity) as nonpecuniary losses. The correspondence to use and nonuse values of nonmarket valuation is not direct, because the use values provided by unique natural environments may be irreplaceable.

characterization of an individual's well-being. With utility specified as a function of both marketed and nonmarketed goods and services, including the services provided by natural resources, we have a conceptual basis for developing money measures of the value provided by the services of nonmarketed resources.[6] This conceptual framework is central to the modern application of applied welfare economics and has resulted in several important advances in valuation methods since the early 1980s (see Freeman [1985], Johansson [1987], and Braden and Kolstad [1991] for overviews of this research).

In implementing these methods of damage assessment, the first step involves describing how the natural asset's services contribute to people's utility and how the injury arising from the release of hazardous substances or oil affects these contributions. This description must specify how each individual's level of well-being responds to the injury-induced changes in the arguments of the utility function. The Hicksian measure of consumer surplus (in this case, the compensation measure) represents the money required to restore an individual's well-being to what it was at the level of the baseline (or pre-injury) situation. By aggregating these monetary measures across individuals who experience the services, we define the lost value.

Since resources are assets, the time profile of lost services will be important in the determination of damage. Damage should include the value of lost services from the date of injury to the date of decision *plus* the smaller of two measures—the economic value of the loss of the resource's services for the indefinite future (or until there is natural recovery) or the sum of loss value and restoration costs for the mix of enhanced and natural recovery.

The first component of this calculation makes the public "whole" in the legal sense for past losses of services, and the second ideally restores the natural asset in equivalent value terms. It is important to recognize that the compensation measures remain a part of the second component because the resource is an asset and restoration may take time and entail future loss of services.

1.3 Restoration Cost. According to the 1989 *Ohio* decision by the Court of Appeals of the District of Columbia, Congress intended that the cost of restoring an injured natural resource to its pre-injury state as the measure of damages to be awarded in cases brought under CERCLA. The proposed revisions to the DOI rules for natural resource damage assess-

---

[6]There is not a one-to-one correspondence between utility changes and Hicksian surplus measures when one maintains that utility can be described only to an ordinal scale. If one uses cardinal descriptions of individual preferences, a one-to-one characterization can be offered for money metric measures of consumer surplus. See Morey (1984) and Johansson (1987) for more details.

ment appear to accept this position, but they actually provide more discretion to trustees so that the measure of damage can correspond to the economist's measure of lost use.

Before discussing this interpretation, we consider first the definition of damages as restoration cost. The logic of the concept may seem compelling. If you want to make society whole, why not just put the injured resource back the way it was? Aside from the technical complexity of actually putting the resource back the way it was, few would argue that society had not been made whole as far as the injured resource is concerned. However, on closer examination, some would argue that society had not been made whole in a cost-effective manner; moreover, when the full resource allocation implications are considered, one might discover that in fact society had been made worse off.

To understand the argument against restoration cost as a measure of damage, consider an example that might arise in a more conventional tort liability case involving injuries to a 1973 AMC Gremlin with 150,000 miles on the odometer, extensive body rust, and worn interior, tires, and brakes. While parked on the side of the road, the Gremlin is hit by a passing motorist. The Gremlin's gas tank ruptures and the car ignites, burning into rubble. If you were required to determine the damage award in the case of the Gremlin, would you award an amount of money necessary to restore the Gremlin to its original condition—rust, worn tires, and all? This would seem to be the literal interpretation of the court of appeals ruling. It would *not* be consistent with the production cost concept as explained by Shavell (1987) for conventional liability situations. At issue is the provision of equivalent services, recognizing the potential requirement for a premium because of the potential for uniqueness of an irreplaceable asset.

Thus we might consider the transportation services provided by the vehicle in terms of remaining service life and ride comfort, fuel economy, and the like. Providing the owner with the ability to purchase the equivalent would be to provide replaccment cost and would be consistent with a service-based restoration concept as defined in the court's ruling. If, however, the owner was in the process of restoring the vehicle, there would be an added burden to assure that payment would allow purchase of a comparably restored vehicle.

The revised DOI rules seem to have captured this concept by recognizing a range of actions that trustees can use to restore the injured resource, from intensive restoration to natural recovery with minimal trustee action. In implementing this concept, it is important to define what constitutes the services provided by resources and to specify their level and quality at the pre-injury or baseline condition.

In comments on the DOI proposed rules, Desvousges and Dunford (1991) argue that the rules offer a confused perspective on restoration. By seeming to require restoration of both the resource and its services, these authors suggest, the rules introduce the prospect of inefficient use of resources. In interpreting this criticism it is important to distinguish between the compensation objectives of the legislative mandate underlying natural resource damage liability and the desire to use efficiently the monetary resources recovered as part of enforcing that liability.

The liability requires some compensation because of a desire to maintain the public's portfolio of natural resources. Desvousges and Dunford (1991) raise the issue of whether the rules' use of restoration cost as the basis for defining that liability would restore the complete loss when the focus is on the services of the asset, rather than on the asset itself. The answer is yes, in principle. With complete descriptions of all the services and authentic restoration we should have the sources of value provided by the asset—provided that the ability to generate these services in the same way the original asset did continues to be maintained.

The logic of the arguments motivated by concerns over either compensation or incentives implicitly maintains that the commodity (or service) involved is readily defined. Under these conditions, evaluating the restoration issue is straightforward. Our point is that often this determination will not be straightforward for injured natural resources. Consequently, it can be this implicit assumption that distinguishes analysts' interpretations of whether damage assessment practices are appropriate. For example, we might be faced with a situation where a free-flowing river without contamination by hazardous substances supports a trout fishery. So also will certain private trout-fishing ponds, but the two recreational experiences are very different. Similarly, in the Eagle River case discussed in chapter 7, the defendant's analysts argued that the services of a groundwater resource used for drinking water could be restored by providing those using the groundwater with bottled water. In both cases, legitimate arguments would arise about whether full and authentic services had been restored.

2.   NATURAL RESOURCES AS ASSETS

Economists generally have described natural and environmental resources as natural assets. However, this description has not had tangible implications for analysis of policies associated with most of these resources. Only in the case of nonrenewable, extractive resources such as mineral deposits, or commercial uses of renewable resources such as forests, has the analysis explicitly connected levels of usage to the capacity of the asset. In other situations, static models have been used, so some type of instantaneous regeneration of the ability to provide services (or levels of use substantially below physical carrying capacities) was assumed. Natural resource damage assessment has changed these implicit assumptions and forced a more careful consideration not only of the services these natural assets provide, but of how alterations in conditions influence the ability of natural assets to continue to provide them. Service flows can take many forms and any one natural asset can provide numerous flows. For example, Yellowstone National Park provides a wide range of recreational activities that includes camping, hiking, fishing, boating, swimming, and animal watching. The Brazilian rain forest provides for atmospheric cleansing of carbon dioxide, generation of oxygen, and growth of timber resources. Further examples include the Rocky Mountains, the Texas plains, and the rolling hills of the Midwest, which provide minerals, crude petroleum, and rich agricultural land, respectively.

Understanding the factors that influence the flow of services from a natural asset is one key to damage measurement. Because service flows are valued by individuals, reduction in the value of these flows due to injuries to natural resources provides the information necessary to calculate damage. For assets that exchange on markets, the existence of these markets provides opportunities for arbitrage (operating on either of two relevant markets to exploit the weaknesses in the other) and, with it, the means to link the asset value and the value of services the asset provides.

Consider the example of a commercial office building. Suppose one were asked to appraise the value of this structure for a prospective buyer. Assume that no comparable office buildings had changed hands recently so no information on the market prices for such buildings was readily available. Nevertheless, we know that the building's value must be related to the anticipated stream of profits that could be earned from renting its space (in other words, the market value of the services it provides). In such a situation, a real estate appraiser would examine the rent that tenants pay to occupy space in the building and subtract the operating costs to arrive at an estimate of the annual rental profit. Given an assumed occupancy rate, often outside the owner's direct control, this annual profit is a measure of the value of the rental services provided by this asset. Next, the appraiser would determine the relevant service life of the building (say, twenty years), estimate how the rental rates and costs of operation might change over this period, and then discount this twenty-year stream of profits to a present value, using the potential buyer's current rate of return on capital as the discount rate. Any residual value (or perhaps appreciation) of the asset at the end of the twenty-year period would also be discounted to the present and added to the discounted present value of the profit stream.[7] The sum of discounted profits and residual value would provide an estimate of the current value of the asset.

Now suppose the building suffers a fire that leaves the upper one-third of the structure smoke damaged. The tenants agree to stay on, but they renegotiate their leases at lower rental payments. The current value of the building is now reduced by the discounted present value of the reduced lease payments. Thus, a formal link exists between the value of the services an asset is capable of providing over time and the value of that asset at any specific date. The existence of markets for both commercial buildings and office space assures that discrepancies between the selling prices for buildings and the discounted profits they can provide will not be great. Otherwise, there are incentives for arbitrage.

With natural and environmental resources, neither the asset nor its services are exchanged on organized markets. Thus, while the economist uses the same approach as the real estate appraiser, there is no market mechanism connecting measures of the value of services to replacement value of natural assets. To implement the process of assessment, the economist first identifies the services provided by the natural asset. Second, he or she seeks to determine how the quantity and quality of those services has been affected and over what time period the effects will take place. Third, the economist places a value on the degradation in each service flow over the relevant time period. And finally, he or she employs a discount rate to turn each of these decrements in service-flow value into present dollars and sum these over the life of the injuries. This summation would be the estimate of the change in the value of the natural asset due to the injury and would serve as the estimate of the natural resource damage.

One might reasonably ask how the measure of natural resource damage defined in terms of the change in the value of the natural asset compares to the definition of damage based on the value of lost services presented in section 1 of this chapter. The answer is that they are equivalent. The change in the value of the asset equals the discounted present value of the change in *all* the service flows, which equals the monetized loss in utility for all affected individuals. The feature that serves to link the two damage concepts is the degradation in the value of the services. Services give rise to both individual utility and the asset's value.

---

[7]The need for a residual value estimate seems to imply some circular reasoning since we are trying to formulate an initial estimate of the value and the residual value must in some way be linked to the initial estimate. This is true, but, owing to discounting, the initial estimate is insensitive to the residual value. For example, the present value of a building providing annual profits of $1 million, discounted at 15 percent for twenty years with a residual value of zero, is $6.25 million, while the value of the same building with a residual value of $10 million is $6.8 million.

3. CLASSIFYING THE SERVICES OF NATURAL ASSETS

Two aspects of the services provided by natural assets offer the basis for a taxonomy. The first aspect is whether we can observe a choice being made to consume or use the service. For marketed commodities, this action corresponds to a purchase on the part of a consumer. Similarly, for firms providing the commodity, the choice can involve the allocation of effort and expenditures to produce or acquire the commodity. Commercial fisherman use a natural resource, the fishery, in the process of generating a marketable output. Recreational fishermen may use the same resource, but the output is more than just the fish caught. Indeed, in some cases, none of the fish caught will be retained. Thus, while the fishery provides input services to both activities, the types of output and approaches for valuing them will be different. In both cases one is able to observe that choices were motivated by a desire to use the services of the resource. To the extent these actions entail costs, there are implicit (if not explicit) transactions taking place that can be used in measuring the value of the services.[8]

A second aspect of a resource's services concerns the degree to which the services are public or can be excludable or appropriated. Are the conditions of access to the service controlled in some way? And does the enjoyment of the service by one individual influence the ability of another person to enjoy it? An absence of control over access does not imply that everyone will value a resource's services. Rather, it eliminates an opportunity to use whatever access conditions exist to recover valuation information.[9]

Consider a hypothetical natural resource, say an unspoiled stretch of the Northern California coast. This natural asset provides commercial fishing and tourism in addition to such noncommercial services as recreational fishing, swimming, boating, hiking, sunbathing, and ocean viewing, as well as wildlife habitat. The value placed on commercial fishing can be determined from knowledge of how the profits of those engaged in the fishing industry respond to the quality of the fishery, while the value of tourism can be determined from a similar type of knowledge about the behavior of the profits of firms in the tourism industry. Not only are

---

[8]We return to this transaction analogy in chapter 7 in developing a framework for describing the logic underlying indirect or revealed preference methods for measuring the values of nonmarketed goods.

[9]Equally important, restriction of access in some way will contribute to defining the feasible aggregate levels of use and, in turn, the value of the asset. For example, a bag limit for fishing or hunting restricts the amount of the service available to any particular user. Similarly, leases for white-water rafting that limit the number and size of rafts to be used during specific time intervals define the capacity for users.

observable choices made, but market prices exist for the outputs involved. To value the resource's services we need only determine how they contribute to these profits. But what about the value of recreational fishing? In the case of nonmarket activities, the value of the services will have to be determined by nonmarket valuation techniques. People make observable choices—to fish or to go on other recreational trips. If the resource is defined as a specific fishery, then we must connect the trip-taking decisions to the status of the services from that fishery.

Commodities can be defined along a continuum from purely private to purely public goods, depending on the excludability and appropriability of the services they provide. In practice, many commodities will fall somewhere in the middle between purely private and purely public goods. These will be described as quasi-private/public services. For these goods there may be opportunities for private consumption, but the decisions of others may well influence in a positive or a negative way the enjoyment realized from that consumption. Boating and hiking are examples of quasi-private/public services. When access is uncontrolled, congestion may cause the enjoyment of the service to decline. Examples of pure public services flows include the nonconsumptive or passive enjoyment of the resource—often associated with existence values. Table 2-1 summarizes the categories we propose to use in grouping a resource's service flows, and highlights some of their characteristics.

3.1   Pure Private Services. Valuing pure private services is reasonably straightforward, provided those services are exchanged in competitive markets where prices and quantities are directly observed. [10] Under these conditions, the total value of the service flows may be approximated by estimation of the relevant demand and supply functions and the calculation of the sum of the producer and consumer surpluses (that is, the economic surplus). [11] Injuries to natural resources that provide pure private services are monetized by measuring the shift in the demand and supply schedules brought about by the injury and measuring the change in the economic surplus between

---

[10]Even in cases in which competitive market conditions do not prevail, techniques for measuring damages from injuries to natural resources providing pure private goods have been developed. For example, Kopp and Krupnick (1987) measure damages to agricultural production due to concentrations of ground-level ozone (an air pollutant causing injury to crops). In this study, the effect of distortions of commodity prices by U.S. agricultural policies was taken into account.

[11]In the case of demand functions some form of behavioral theory, together with a specification of initial conditions, would be used to recover the Hicksian consumer surplus. See Hausman (1981) for a discussion of the issues involved in simple situations in which a single price changes.

Table 2-1.   A Service Flow Taxonomy

Service category	Service flow characteristics
Pure private services	Usually goods are exchanged in normal markets; one individual's consumption excludes others' enjoyment; access to the good can be controlled; quantity of the good or service is directly observable in the market. Example: commercial fishing.
Quasi-private/public services	Usually goods are not exchanged on markets; up to a point one individual's enjoyment does not affect others' enjoyment, but beyond that point congestion reduces the enjoyment of all; access can be controlled but often is not strictly regulated; the quantity of the good or service is inferred from observations on individual behavior. Example: recreational fishing.
Pure public services	Goods are not exchanged on markets; any number of individuals can enjoy the good while not reducing the enjoyment of anyone else; access cannot be controlled; quantity of the good or service cannot be determined by observation or inference. Example: services underlying existence (or nonuse) values.

the pre- and the post-injury states of the resource.[12] While difficulties can arise in determining the baseline demand and supply relationships (due to lack of data on available price and quantity), there is nothing in the character of the service flow that causes conceptual difficulties.[13]

3.2   Quasi-Private/Public Services. The valuation of injuries to natural assets that provide quasi-private/public services proceeds in a manner analogous to that of the pure private services. To the extent possible, the relevant demand functions are estimated.[14] The problems associated with measuring Hicksian welfare losses from quality changes corresponding to the pre- and post-injury states of the resource parallel the issues raised for marketed goods. However, further complications are raised by the assumptions required to define implicit prices for the services involved.

---

[12]As Bockstael and McConnell (1991) demonstrate, there are limits to our ability to measure or bound the value of Hicksian surpluses for changes in resource quality using Marshallian demand functions.

[13]Many releases of hazardous substances may have occurred quite far in the past and therefore little information may exist describing the prerelease or baseline levels of pure private services.

[14]There may be no market-based supply functions in this case, although there may be access conditions that serve a role comparable to that of a supply function. These must be taken into account.

Recreation offers a well-studied example of a quasi-private/public service. In the case of the California coastline, suppose an oil spill occurred and one attempted to measure recreational damages. One would attempt to estimate demand for the coast's recreational services by observing pre-spill recreational use (including types of use, number of persons using the site, and time spent on site) and then developing a measure for the implicit price for use. The measurement of this implicit price is discussed in chapters 7 and 8; here we simply state that the implicit price relies on travel to gain access to the site.

Thus, an important feature that serves to distinguish damage measurement for pure private services from that for quasi-private/public services is the lack of information on both market prices and quantities for the services in question. One can usually find measures for one element in the implicit transaction, but not both. In the case of recreation, one can observe the quantity of the service consumed if one is willing to describe it as trips to a site, but a price must be imputed. In the case of a marketed pure private good, both the price and the quantity consumed are directly observable.

3.3   Pure Public Services. Pure public services of natural resources pose even more difficult problems for determining people's values than do quasi-private/public services. Because they are not excludable or appropriable, there may not be a straightforward mechanism to observe either an implicit price or a quantity. This does not mean valuation is impossible. However, it does limit the opportunities to verify with behavioral choices the assumptions made in developing these estimates.

As we discuss in chapter 7 and McConnell and Schulze summarize in chapters 8 and 10, respectively, there are indirect and direct methods that in some circumstances can be used to estimate the values people place on these services. In the case of the indirect or revealed preference methods, a hedonic property model might be used to gauge the value if the services could be linked to the proximity of the resource in relation to the location of each house or to the conditions of access. This estimate would not include existence values as conventionally defined, but it might capture the value people place on public good services associated with, for instance, a scenic vista, migratory waterfowl, or marine mammals. In the absence of this type of linkage, contingent valuation offers the only approach for estimating those pure public good services we think of as existence services—where no action (or proximity) is required to enjoy the passive consumption values. However, even if an analysis is willing to rely on contingent valuation for measuring people's values,[15] the issue of defining the quantity measure for the services being valued remains.

To highlight the quantity problem, consider the existence services provided by the African elephant, a species close to extinction. There are many individuals in this country who have seen pictures of African elephants and have seen the elephants in zoos, but few have had direct experience with these elephants in the wild. Nonetheless, many if not most people in the United States feel that the remaining herd should be preserved. The presumption here is that individuals who have never undertaken any action to enjoy these elephants in the wild, but feel they should be preserved, are deriving an existence or nonuse value from these natural resources. The service underlying this nonuse value is a pure public good. Any person's enjoyment of these resources does not diminish the enjoyment available to anyone else. No one can be precluded from such enjoyment.

But how would one describe the quantity or changes in the quantity of these services in case of some injury to the natural resource providing nonuse value services? Recall that in the previous cases of pure private and quasi-private/public services the values are determined by constructing estimates of consumer surplus from demand functions, or, in the case of pure private goods, estimates of both producer and consumer surplus from both demand and supply relations. In principle, the same could be done for nonuse services, recognizing that they are quasi-fixed goods entering preferences at levels outside each individual's direct control. However, we are often not sure how to measure the quantity of the services provided.

Do we use the quantity of elephants in the herd as a proxy for these nonuse services? If so, does the level of service increase and decrease with herd size? Suppose we could measure the nonuse value of the elephants in the herd today. Then suppose that next year, due to the ivory trade, the herd size is reduced by half and the herd is closer to extinction. If we were to measure again the nonuse value of the herd, would we expect the value to fall by half? Would we expect it to fall at all, or possibly to rise? Obviously, we do not know the answer, but introspection suggests that the value we place on the herd is not necessarily linked to its size in a

---

[15]The new DOI rules offer a contradictory position on contingent valuation methods and nonuse values. On the one hand, they accept a total value framework, including use and nonuse values, as part of what is defined as compensable value. Yet the rules suggest that when either nonuse value or total value (use and nonuse value) are measured with contingent valuation, the estimates should be regarded as arising from a least-reliable source. Finally, the rules recommend that contingent valuation be applied to measure total value, not nonuse value alone. (56 *Federal Register* 19759 [April 29, 1991].) For further discussion, see Carson, Hanemann, and Kopp (1991).

monotonic fashion—such would be the case if we were only interested in the ivory the animals produce.

The above example was chosen to underscore the difficulty of specifying quantity measures for nonuse services, not to draw attention to the difficulty of measuring them. A related but no less important issue is the question of which people care about these nonuse services. How do we isolate the people who hold values for nonuse services? In the case of pure public services, where behavior offers no insight to value, defining the equivalent of the extent of the market poses problems. Some analysts would adopt ad hoc rules or use the concept of a representative sample to include both those who do and those who do not hold values in the computation of an overall average. In this setting, those who do not value the services would be assigned zeros and all others would be assigned positive values. Scaling by the number in the population is often proposed as the method to aggregate under these conditions. In contrast, one might argue that separating those who care about the services from those who do not care is essential to a correct definition of the empirical extent of the market.

Some authors (notably Rosenthal and Nelson [1992] and Quiggin [1990]) have argued that issues of this kind are unlikely to be resolved in a satisfactory way in the near future. As a consequence, they suggest that nonuse values should not be included in damage assessment. Indeed, according to Quiggin any attempt to develop empirical measures for people's values for public goods (whether pure public goods or mixed goods) is ill advised. These judgments are reminiscent of Eckstein's (1958) admonition that benefit-cost analyses should not include monetary measures of the benefits derived from methods other than market prices. For him, the available method for nonmarket valuation (principally the travel cost recreation demand model) was not sufficiently reliable. The progress of research in the intervening years has demonstrated that Eckstein's concerns were ill founded. The travel cost framework is now widely accepted and has accumulated an extensive record documenting its effectiveness in at least the terms we routinely expect from demand models for marketed commodities.

Would this success and corresponding acceptance have been realized without the policy demands? We think not. A wait-and-see attitude is unlikely to provide the incentives required to understand when the methods will provide reliable estimates of nonuse values. Needed instead is a protocol describing how we will evaluate what we can measure today.

As with the mandates for evaluating public investment projects and the associated requirements for valuation information when Eckstein prepared his treatise on benefit-cost analysis, a recommendation that we avoid consideration of nonuse values does not mean these values will be treated neutrally. Excluding nonuse values from a natural resource damage assessment assigns them a value of zero! In the case of public investments, the decision maker had the option of requiring "generous margins" of net benefits in evaluating development projects that would forgo the amenity services of undeveloped resources. Such margins assign implicit values to the public good services we associate with nonuse values. This type of discretion is unlikely to be present in litigation.

Few critics of the treatment of nonuse values deny their existence. The debate hinges on measurement. The concerns motivating reductions in the intangible components of benefit-cost analyses thirty years ago parallel the court of appeals decision that nonuse values are a legitimate component of compensable values. Both provide stimuli for answers for those concerned with the reliability of methods for measuring nonmarket values. What has changed is the focus of attention from use to nonuse values.

REFERENCES

Bockstael, Nancy E., and Kenneth E. McConnell. 1991. "The Demand for Quality Differentiated Goods: A Synthesis," working paper, Department of Agricultural and Resource Economics, University of Maryland, College Park, Md.

Braden, John B., and Charles D. Kolstad. 1991. *Measuring the Demand for Environmental Quality*. Amsterdam: North-Holland.

Carson, Richard T., W. Michael Hanemann, and Raymond J. Kopp. 1991. "Comments on the United States Department of Interior's Notice of Proposed Rulemaking, 43 C.F.R., Part II, Natural Resource Damage Assessments." Submitted to the U.S. Department of the Interior.

Desvousges, William H., and Richard W. Dunford. 1991. "Comments on the Proposed Revisions in the NRDA Rule Pursuant to the 1989 Ohio vs. Interior Ruling," Natural Resource Damage Assessment Program, Research Triangle Institute.

Eckstein, Otto. 1958. *Water Resource Development: The Economics of Project Evaluation*. Cambridge, Mass.: Harvard University Press.

Freeman, A. Myrick III. 1985. "Methods for Assessing the Benefits of Environmental Programs," pp. 223–270 in *Handbook of Natural Resource and Energy Economics*, vol. 1, edited by A. V. Kneese and J. L. Sweeney. Amsterdam: North-Holland.

Hausman, J. A. 1981. "Exact Consumer's Surplus and Deadweight Loss," *American Economic Review* 71, pp. 662–676.

Johansson, Per-Olov. 1987. *The Economic Theory and Measurement of Environmental Benefits*. Cambridge: Cambridge University Press.

Kopp, Raymond J., and Alan J. Krupnick. 1987. "Agricultural Policy and the Benefits of Ozone Control," *American Journal of Agricultural Economics* 69(5), pp. 956–962.

Morey, Edward R. 1984. "Confuser Surplus," *American Economic Review* 74 (March), pp. 163–173.

Quiggin, J. 1990. "Do Existence Values Exist?" Unpublished paper, Department of Agricultural and Resource Economics, University of Maryland, College Park, Md.

Rosenthal, D. H., and R. H. Nelson. 1992. "Why Existence Value Should *Not* Be Used in Cost-Benefit Analysis," *Journal of Policy Analysis and Management* 11(1), pp. 116–122.

Shavell, Steven. 1987. *Economic Analysis of Accident Law*. Cambridge, Mass.: Harvard University Press.

Part 1
Statutes, Rulemaking, and Practice

Introduction to Part 1: Statutes, Rulemaking, and Practice

Part 1 of this volume sets the stage for the conceptual issues that natural resource damage assessments raise. Chapters by Frederick R. Anderson and Gardner M. Brown, Jr., discuss the legal and procedural foundations for natural resource damage assessments, while the chapters by Howard Kenison and Willie R. Taylor provide both criticism of and additional insights into these discussions.

Anderson (chapter 3) begins with the law, but he takes us beyond the requirements of the Comprehensive Environmental Response, Compensation, and Liability Act (CERCLA) of 1980 and the Superfund Amendments and Reauthorization Act (SARA) of 1986 to the legal context from which they emerged—federal remedial and compensatory legislation. Like Breen in his recent essay,[1] Anderson acknowledges that natural resource damage liability follows a long legal tradition. However, Anderson's goal is not to provide a legal history but instead to offer insight into the court's interpretation of this new type of liability. His arguments provide a legal parallel to Shavell's analysis of the economic rationale for liability as a policy instrument (see chapter 2).[2]

The use of replacement cost as a measure of damage has strong precedent in other situations, provided the commodity lost is not unique to its owner. When the lost commodity is unique to its owner, replacement with the most economical substitute does not totally compensate the damaged party. So it is not surprising that Anderson highlights the question of substitution as an essential element in understanding the court's likely future direction in defining the concept of natural resource damages.

What can we expect from the courts—many or few substitutes? Anderson expects the courts to have more sympathy for the view that many of the resources involved in damage assessments are unique than for the

---

[1]Breen, Barry. 1989. "Citizen Suits for Natural Resource Damages: Closing the Gap in Federal Environmental Law," *Wake Forest Law Review* 24, pp. 851–880.

[2]Shavell, Steven. 1987. *Economic Analysis of Accident Law*. Cambridge, Mass.: Harvard University Press.

view that holds substitutes abound. Under these circumstances, restoration and not replacement will motivate the damage calculations. Thus, even though the newly proposed Department of the Interior (DOI) rules offer trustees broad discretion in how they select an alternative as part of their plan for restoration, rehabilitation, replacement, or acquisition of equivalent resources, Anderson probably would recommend a focus on both pro and con grounds for arguing that any particular resource is unique. (For background on the DOI rules, see chapter 2.)

While Anderson believes that courts will adopt a liberal interpretation of CERCLA as it pertains to the recovery of natural resource damages, and perhaps even provide plaintiffs with an accommodating forum for their claims, Kenison (chapter 4) suggests that state and federal trustees may not vigorously pursue damages. Kenison attributes such potential lack of enforcement to legal uncertainties, funding inadequacies, and political realities. Brown's introduction of the notion of natural resource slander captures the essential role of the subjective elements in determining damages (chapter 5). People are the ultimate arbiters of uniqueness. Unfortunately, the rulemaking process from the initial DOI rules through the decision in *Ohio v. The United States Department of the Interior*,[3] to the newly proposed DOI rules offers more questions than answers on this key element in implementing damage assessments.

A few constant elements have remained throughout the rulemaking process. First, Brown tells us that important linkages exist between what is done to satisfy a cleanup liability and what becomes the residual liability. The residual liability cannot be considered effectively without examining the criteria for defining cleanup, and no clearcut standards tell us where to stop. Equally important, Brown reminds us that defining a compensation criteria does not in itself require that restoration be used in judging what should be done with the damage payments made by potentially responsible parties (PRPs). Complete restoration may not be an efficient use of resources. Finally, all discussions in the rulemaking process have missed some fundamental issues concerning how the discount rate should be selected for these calculations. Decisions regarding damages are not comparable to public investment decisions; Brown suggests that the public opportunity cost—not the private cost—provides the relevant rate. Moreover, in the case of assessing damages at past hazardous waste sites, both capitalization and discounting will, in principle, be necessary. Brown finds no reason for capitalization or discounting rates to differ, but nonetheless this question deserves special consideration. It is discussed among the special topics developed in the chapters in part 3.

---

[3] 880 F. 2nd 432 (D.C. Cir. 1989).

Brown's chapter interprets the Department of the Interior rules from a purely economic perspective—a perspective that evaluates the rules against a standard of efficiency. In Chapter 6, Taylor reminds us that these rules were drafted subject to the constraints of the law, constraints that often force a divergence from efficiency.

A hierarchy of nonmarket valuation methods played a prominent role in the initial DOI rules. Brown tells us (as the *Ohio* decision did) that DOI's concept of the tasks involved in measuring the value of natural resources that provide services outside of markets is "out of touch" with the real circumstances governing access to these services and what we can expect to know about their values from people's choices. In chapter 7, on the practice of damage assessments, Raymond J. Kopp and V. Kerry Smith begin by discussing how the rules connect to the two components of damage assessments (restoration cost and loss of economic value) that must inevitably underlie the development of a formal (type B) damage assessment. Doing it right requires balancing the roles of the natural and economic sciences in determining the monetized value of the injuries associated with the release of a hazardous substance or oil. To provide a tangible basis for understanding the role of coordination and judgment in developing damage estimates, Kopp and Smith close the chapter with a brief comparison of the assessment methods used by economic experts for the plaintiff with those used by the defense in a recent damage case in Colorado.

What can be learned from considering the law, the rules, and practice together? The lessons are familiar to past students of the effects of government involvement on any aspect of economic activity. Law alone rarely provides a credible view of how a prescribed public involvement in private activities will actually take place. Instead, we must look to a more detailed study of rulemaking, especially the practical realities of how a process ultimately works, to identify the issues that must be addressed to make the rules correspond with the legal goals. Equally important, the study of the rulemaking process provides a necessary first step toward understanding how those engaged in the affected activities are likely to respond to intervention. Thus, both the positive analysis of the performance of policy instruments and the normative design of new ones must begin by considering these interactions.

3

Natural Resource Damages, Superfund, and the Courts

Frederick R. Anderson

1. INTRODUCTION

At the beginning of the Environmental Decade of the 1970s, thoughtful students of the new field of environmental law observed an interesting phenomenon. While a homeowner could enjoin a neighbor from harming his or her land and could recover damages for an injury to it, public natural resources lacked a clear champion. The states possessed limited common-law authority to protect public resources, and the federal government had to rely on explicit legislative mandates before acting. Governments lacked broad power to recover damages for injury to public natural resources. Against this background, in a little-noticed provision of the

On June 16–17, 1988, Resources for the Future sponsored a national conference on natural resource damage recovery under Superfund. This chapter was originally a paper prepared for that conference. The author thanks Raymond J. Kopp and V. Kerry Smith for their valuable commentary on earlier drafts.

In addition, the Natural Resources Committee of the Administrative Law Section of the American Bar Association sponsored a symposium focused on this paper on October 14, 1988. Participants included representatives from the Department of the Interior's Solicitor's Office and Office of Policy Analysis, the New York State Attorney General's Office, the National Wildlife Federation, and private law firms. The author thanks the committee chair, Owen Olpin, for organizing the symposium.

A much longer version of this paper appeared in the *Boston College Environmental Affairs Law Review* (vol. 16, pp. 405–457, 1989). In its decision invalidating many of the Department of the Interior's guidelines for implementing Superfund's natural resource damage provisions, *Ohio v. The United States Department of the Interior*, 880 F.2d 432 (D.C. Cir. 1989), the U.S. Court of Appeals for the District of Columbia Circuit relied heavily on the Boston College law review article. This decision, which overtook the publication schedule for this book, required changes in the chapter that acknowledge the altered and uncertain regulatory context. In the footnotes to this chapter, however, the style of the law review article has been retained.

Comprehensive Environmental Response, Compensation, and Liability Act of 1980 (CERCLA), known as Superfund, Congress created the first federal and state resources trustees and empowered them to seek damages for injuries to public natural resources caused by toxic wastes.[1] The purpose of this chapter is to probe into the relationship between Superfund and the common law, to show that Congress does not view traditional common-law doctrines as a limitation on the scope of Superfund's remedial and compensatory provisions.

The Superfund law is not perfect, but it appears to be adequate to the task of obtaining substantial recoveries to be spent on resource restoration and replacement, if the resource damage provisions are fully implemented by the federal government through statutorily mandated guidelines. Already, the federal government and state governments have obtained more than $120 million in natural resource damages in settlements from cleanup cases.[2]

The Department of the Interior (DOI) originally took a conservative approach to implementing the natural resource damage provisions. In particular, DOI maintained that the common law limits the damages that trustees can seek to recover to either (1) lost resource-use values or (2) restoration or replacement costs, whichever is less. A federal court of appeals in *Ohio v. The United States Department of the Interior*[3] invalidated this and other provisions of the federal guidelines, sending them back to DOI for rewriting. DOI's proposed rules conform to the court's ruling and state in unambiguous terms that trustees should seek restoration costs for resources injured by hazardous waste or oil. When implementation of the plan for restoring the injured resources takes a long time, the

---

[1]Comprehensive Environmental Response, Compensation, and Liability Act (CERCLA), 42 U.S.C. §§ 9601–9675 (1980), as amended by the Superfund Amendments and Reauthorization Act (SARA) of 1986, Pub. L. No. 99-499, 100 Stat. 1613 (1986).

Section 101 of CERCLA defines public natural resources as "land, fish, wildlife, biota, air, water, ground water, drinking water supplies, and other such resources belonging to, managed by, held in trust by, appertaining to, or otherwise controlled by the United States . . . , any State or local government, any foreign government, any Indian tribe . . . [or] . . . member of an Indian tribe." Other federal statutes authorizing recovery of damages to publicly controlled natural resources are narrower in scope. See Outer Continental Shelf Lands Act Amendment of 1978, 43 U.S.C. § 1813(a)(2)(C)–(D), (b)(3) (1982); Deepwater Port Act, 33 U.S.C. § 1517(i)(3) (1982); Trans-Alaskan Pipeline Authorization Act, 43 U.S.C. § 1653(a)(1), (c)(1) (1982); Federal Water Pollution Control Act, 33 U.S.C. § 1321(f)(5) (1982).

[2]The Damage Assessment and Restoration Program of the National Oceanic and Atmospheric Administration reports $120.7 million in marine resource damage settlements as of November 1992. This figure does not include damages resulting from the *Exxon Valdez* settlement.

[3]880 F.2d 432 (D.C. Cir. 1989).

services lost because of the injuries are to be valued with consideration of their use and nonuse values. This sum, designated "compensable value," corresponds to the widely accepted standard of total value by which the benefits people receive from nonmarketed natural and environmental resources are measured.

Settlement has played the leading role in the natural resource damage recovery program, as it has for the Superfund remedial program. Courts have not as yet had to order cleanup or compensation, although they have issued scores of decisions clarifying the meaning of the statute. Still, the ultimate decision makers under the statute, the federal district courts, seem likely to give the natural resource damage provisions a broad reading, consistent with the sweeping powers that the courts have conferred upon the federal government through a multitude of decisions on Superfund's waste site cleanup program.

At stake is whether lost or damaged public natural resources will be replaced or restored, so that the enjoyment of natural resources can continue substantially unimpaired. More is threatened than the loss of timber, waterfowl, and harvestable species of fish and shellfish. The loss of songbirds, natural vistas, endangered species habitat, and entire stable ecosystems is also involved. Surely the value of lost songbirds, for example, is not to be measured only by their caged value, or even by the willingness to pay for them that is measured by birdwatchers' purchases of field guides, binoculars, and transportation. The question for trustees, agencies, and the courts is whether Superfund will be used to help meet the cost of maintaining public natural resources at existing levels, not only for their approximate market values, but for their wider use and nonuse and option values as well. The way to ensure this result is greater resort to restoration and replacement of natural resources, measured at the full cost of restoring the uses that the public has lost.

This chapter enters onto treacherous ground, because it attempts to predict how government institutions will behave in implementing an innovative statute. On the one hand, the courts may be tempted to read restrictive common-law concepts governing liability, causation, and damage recovery into the statute. On the other hand, because the natural resource provisions are part and parcel of Superfund, the courts may interpret them no less broadly than they have interpreted the rest of Superfund's provisions, where they have relaxed common-law requirements. This chapter argues that in all parts of Superfund, including its natural resource damage provisions, Congress intended to go well beyond prior requirements of law, fashioning a powerful corrective and compensatory mechanism based on a broad theory of cost internalization, primarily to give the costs of rectification back to the parties who benefited, but also to provide a disincentive for future harmful conduct.[4]

Relaxed liability, broad power to determine cleanup scope and financial responsibility, civil penalties, rebuttable presumptions, and summary administrative and judicial proceedings are frequently included in modern welfare legislation. The courts uphold and even extend such statutes, despite the anti-interventionist bias of the common law.[5]

2. SUPERFUND PROVISIONS AND IMPLEMENTATION, 1980–1988

2.1 General and Natural Resource Damage Provisions. At base, Superfund creates a cleanup program for abandoned and inactive hazardous waste disposal sites and for chemical spills. It is an extension of both the Resource Conservation and Recovery Act of 1976, which created a strict regulatory regime for active hazardous waste disposal sites, and the liability and cleanup provisions of the Clean Water Act of 1977. Federally funded cleanups are the most visible portion of the site cleanup program. They are responsible for the general public perception that the heart of Superfund is direct federal cleanup.[6] Cleanups are subject to a plethora of statutory and administrative rules through the National Contingency Plan (NCP). A National Priorities List (NPL) of sites has first call on the fund and other cleanup efforts.

---

[4]Some members of Congress sought to deter future harmful conduct by imposing risk and cost sharing in Superfund, but clearly the primary purpose of the legislation was to correct hazardous situations at the expense of responsible parties. See generally Shavell, *Liability for Harm Versus Regulation of Safety*, 13 J. of Legal Stud. 357 (1984) for a discussion of the merits of using liability and regulation to reduce risks.

[5]G. Calabresi, A Common Law for the Age of Statutes 32–38 (1982).

[6]Under the 1980 legislation, revenues were to be collected over a five-year period ending in 1985, with $1.38 billion collected from taxes on the manufacture of petroleum products and certain inorganic chemicals and $220 million from general federal revenues. CERCLA, 42 U.S.C. § 9631(b)(2) (repealed 1987). Under the 1986 reauthorization, SARA enlarged the fund to $6.65 billion and extended its life through 1991. The fund is financed by taxes on oil and chemicals, I.R.C. §§ 4611, 4661, 4671 (1986); an environmental tax on corporate income, I.R.C. 59A (1986); and by general appropriations of up to $250 million per year, SARA Pub. L. No. 99-499, § 517(b), 100 Stat. 1613, 1773. Superfund also receives cleanup costs and penalties recovered from responsible parties. See 42 U.S.C. § 9607.

Congress was not willing to approve a Senate-proposed $2.5 billion victim compensation fund. Trauberman, *Compensating Victims of Toxic Substance Pollution: An Analysis of Existing Federal Statutes*, 5 Harv. Envtl. L. Rev. 1, 1 (1981). Recovery for personal injuries was left to the common law, although hearings and debates prior to CERCLA's enactment focused on the compensation issue. S. 1480, 96th Cong., 2d Sess. § 4(a), (c), (n), 126 Cong. Rec. 30,901 (1980).

These reporting, inventorying, and fund-expenditure requirements saddle the federal government with the obligation to see that the sites are cleaned up, but the statute also places ultimate financial responsibility on the parties that used the sites and created the dangerous conditions. The parties potentially responsible for site and spill cleanup in general are the same as the parties responsible for paying natural resource damages. These parties include current and past owners and operators of vessels and facilities; waste generators or other persons who arranged for treatment, disposal, or transport of waste; and transporters who selected a disposal or treatment facility that required a fund response. Once a remedy is specified by the government after a remedial investigation and feasibility study (RI/FS), the government may itself clean up a site and bring suit later to shift the costs to responsible parties, or it may seek to have the responsible parties carry out a cleanup specified by the government. Liability extends to costs incurred by the federal government, state governments, or other persons. Parties are financially responsible, although they may have already paid substantial sums into the fund through the taxes that Superfund imposes. Still, after 1986 it is clear that Congress wants the Environmental Protection Agency (EPA) to negotiate voluntary cleanup with private parties before expending Superfund revenues.

Personal injuries are not recompensable, but restoration, replacement, and damages to natural resources are. The statute comprehensively covers "land, fish, wildlife, biota, air, water, ground water, drinking water supplies and other such resources" owned, managed, held in trust, or otherwise controlled by the United States, a state, local government, or an Indian tribe. Liability includes "damages for injury to, destruction of, or loss of natural resources, including the reasonable cost of assessing such injury, destruction, or loss" resulting from the release of a hazardous substance.[7]

Because resources themselves do not have standing to sue,[8] Congress invented a guardian for the resources—the trustee. Liability is to the federal government or to the states as trustees of the affected natural resources. Most important, to ease the trustee's difficult task, any determination of damages made by the trustee in accordance with natural resource damage regulations promulgated under Superfund has the force of a rebuttable presumption in any judicial or administrative proceeding for recovery.

The natural resource damage regulations are another important innovation that breaks new ground by having agencies and courts share the

---

[7]42 U.S.C. § 9607(a) (C) (1986).

[8]See generally C. Stone, Should Trees Have Standing? (1974); C. Stone, Earth and Other Ethics (1987).

responsibility for establishing cause and harm, and are of paramount importance. The regulations specify standard procedures for simplified assessments, called "type A" assessments, requiring minimal field observation. These typically will be done with a simple computer model. "Type B" assessments address larger impacts on a case-by-case basis and require a significant amount of fieldwork.[9]

The only avenue to recovery of natural resource damages is through private responsible parties, although before the 1986 amendments CERCLA allowed claims against the federal fund. Damages for resource injuries caused before the statute was enacted theoretically are not available, but since 1986 the statute has included the "discovery rule." The states have adopted this rule in increasing numbers in recent years as their statute of limitations on toxic personal injury claims. The discovery rule enables a party to file a claim for harm that is discovered long after exposure to a disease agent—for example, when cancer appears after a long latency period. Thus, actions for natural resource damages must be filed within three years of the later of the date of discovery of the loss and its connection to the release of the toxic substance or the date on which regulations were promulgated. At sites or facilities where remedial action is pending, an action for damages must be commenced within three years after completion of the remedial action.

2.2 The Trusteeship of Natural Resources. The concept of state or federal government acting as a trustee is not new. The concept is similar in function to the trust arrangements made either by legislatures by special enactment or by the courts on an ad hoc basis after a hearing (for example, for the senile or for unborn children in contested wills). The California legislature has even given public-interest organizations standing to sue to protect works of fine art.

More specifically, the states have brought suits *parens patriae* or under the public trust doctrine of the common law to protect natural

---

[9]For convenience, citations to all the relevant rulemaking for the natural resource damage provisions and the type A and type B assessments are set out here. Many of these provisions will have to be promulgated again after the D.C. Circuit Court opinion.

    A. Final type B rules: 51 Fed. Reg. 27,674 (Aug. 1, 1986)

    B. Final type A rules: 52 Fed. Reg. 9,042 (Mar. 20, 1987)

    C. Adjustments for the SARA Amendments: 53 Fed. Reg. 5,166 (Feb. 22, 1988)

    D. Type A corrections: 53 Fed. Reg. 9,769 (Mar. 25, 1988)

    E. Type B Advance Notice of Proposed Rule Making: 53 Fed. Reg. 15,714 (May 3, 1988)

    F. Type A Advance Notice of Proposed Rule Making: 53 Fed. Reg. 20,143 (June 2, 1988).

resources, as well as under certain public trust statutes. Courts have steadily expanded the public trust concept beyond application to submerged lands, the foreshore, and navigable waters to encompass injuries to parks, non-navigable water, air, land, wetlands, ecological values, and water quantity as well as quality. The doctrine retains contemporary vigor, as evinced by the U.S. Supreme Court's decision in *Phillips Petroleum Co. v. Mississippi*, but has roots in early nineteenth century state law.[10] Yet the law still is unsettled as to whether a state suit *parens patriae* will support an action for damages as well as injunctive relief. Perhaps for this reason, approximately 60 percent of the states have authorized actions for money damages for injury to fish and wildlife.[11]

The federal government exercises broad trustlike authority under organic legislation for parks, forests, and public lands, but the only close federal analogy to state trust concepts is the federal legal trusteeship of Indian tribes and lands. Hence, no federal trust doctrine goes as far as Superfund in making money damages available when public natural resources are injured. Because the concept of a trustee of natural resources is specifically legislated by Superfund, with the broad implied fiduciary obligations that accompany the trust relationship as it exists throughout Anglo-American law, one may ask whether the trustee owes obligations toward natural resources—the corpus of the trust—that are not spelled out in Superfund. Bank officials are liable to beneficiaries for their mishandling of trust funds. Similarly, a natural resources trustee's failure to perform fiduciary duties toward resources may possibly be actionable at the instance of private citizens, who are the beneficiaries of the trust. Arguably, Section 310 of Superfund (the citizen's suit provision) affords a basis for such an action.

In the broadest sense, of course, government officials are trustees of any resources that they are charged by statute to administer in the public interest. No special fiduciary duties attach to this routine administration of public natural resources. Standard judicial review of administrative action aside, any cause of action against the federal government for alleged failure to administer public resources properly must be explicitly granted by statute. But Superfund is different: it specifically mentions the trustee, sets up an appointment process, gives the trustee certain duties, and empowers the trustee to bring legal actions to protect the trust corpus. The trustee is not an ordinary government official; a trust is not a routine resource management tool.

---

[10]See Comment, *Phillips Petroleum Co. v. Mississippi: Is the Public Trust Becoming Synonymous with the Public Interest?*, 18 Envtl. L. Rep. 10,200, 10,201 (1988).

[11]Halter and Thomas, *Recovery of Damages for Fish and Wildlife Losses Caused by Pollution*, 10 Ecology L.Q. 5, 9, 10 (1982).

2.3   An Aside on Liability for Non-Lawyers. The meaning of "liability," a concept clear to lawyers, may become more obscure the closer one examines it. Liability is the presence of an obligation to act or behave in a certain manner, but not immediately. The closest synonyms for "liable" are perhaps "obliged," "responsible," or "bound." A person held liable in a legal action ordinarily will have a duty to pay money or behave in a certain manner. Thus, although a disposer, transporter, or site owner has been made liable under Superfund, none owes a duty to pay or clean up until the government exercises its power by administrative order or successful lawsuit. Many are in the condition or status of "potentially responsible party" (PRP) under Superfund, but only some will end up paying for or executing cleanups, paying for lost natural resource uses, executing or paying for restoration, or providing replacement funds.

2.4   Program Implementation. The Superfund program has worked well for quick emergency containment of spills and fires, and the statute has stimulated some good negotiated cleanups at the more stable, older sites. Yet only a handful of NPL sites has been cleaned up to date.

2.4.1   Implementation of the Site Cleanup and Natural Resource Damage Programs. The government's own estimate of future cleanups sets the date by which half of the sites will have been cleaned up past the millennium (at a rate of twenty-five to thirty sites per year), with cleanup of the current list sites to be completed about the year 2020 at a cost of tens of billions of dollars. Federal studies indicate that many more sites may eventually be placed on the NPL, with the result that cleanups may stretch sixty years into the future.

Amendments to Superfund in 1986 were redolent of the tinkering and mid-course corrections that Congress made in other major environmental statutes in the 1980s. In the opinion of some critics, the Superfund amendments failed to address major ambiguities in the liability provisions of the statute, denied funding adequate to correct the abandoned-waste-site problem, and did not effectively alter the schedule for cleanup. Further, many believe that the injection of regulatory standards from other environmental statutes directly into the struggling remedial program may prove fatal to Superfund in the next few years. By defining how clean a cleanup must be by applying regulatory standards from other environmental statutes—standards that arguably should be used only for entire categories of point sources of industrial pollution—Congress may have denied the agency vital flexibility to tailor remedies case by case at the widely varied Superfund sites.

Both the natural resource damage recovery program and the remedial program have moved forward slowly, but for different reasons. While EPA has poured enormous effort into the remedial program, and has obtained favorable judicial precedents for its broad interpretation of strict and joint and several liability, causation, and defenses, DOI has given the natural resource damage provisions comparatively less attention.[12] The remedial program has too many chefs in its kitchen; the natural resource damage program too few.

The Department of the Interior did not draft the rules governing natural resource damage assessments until after the two-year statutory deadline for their promulgation had expired, and the rules were not finished until 1987, four years after the deadline. As has frequently happened with guidelines under other environmental statutes, lawsuits forced production of these rules. Environmental groups and ten states successfully challenged the final rules, alleging that they provide inadequate compensation. Some members of Congress attacked DOI's performance and tried to change it in the 1986 amendments.[13] A suit to recover natural resource damages from the federal fund resulted in a federal circuit court decision rejecting as dilatory the administration's "preauthorization" scheme for processing several billion dollars in natural resource damage claims filed by state trustees. DOI has acted somewhat more quickly in responding with proposed revisions to the type B regulations, reflecting the court of appeals ruling.

2.4.2   Integration and Coordination of Remedies, Removals, and Natural Resource Damage Recovery. The text of Superfund leaves many key problems unresolved, as is usual with complex legislation that delegates implementation to an administrative agency. The rules are partially provided in EPA's National Contingency Plan and by EPA's National Priorities List. DOI's natural resources guidelines were also produced by notice-and-comment rulemaking, that is, through public notice of the department's proposed rules, written public comment on them, and final promulgation of them by the agency.

The process of EPA elaboration of Superfund's meaning has not ended with notice-and-comment rulemaking. EPA has prepared hundreds of pages of informal Guidance Memoranda, which spell out EPA's program plans and expectations in exhaustive detail. It taxes the abilities of Superfund lawyers to keep track of what guidance has been proposed, finalized, withdrawn, or awarded in this gray world of agency policymaking.[14] Whether these materials are law is a less settled question, although

---

[12]U.S. General Accounting Office, Natural Resource Damage Claims and Assessment Regulations Under Superfund 4 (GAO/RCED-84-196) (1984).

[13]See 132 Cong. Rec. S14,930 (daily ed., Oct. 3, 1986) (colloquy between Senators Stafford and Baucus); *accord*, 132 Cong. Rec. H9612-13 (daily ed., Oct. 8, 1986) (statement of Congressman Jones of North Carolina).

[14]Anderson, *Negotiation and Informal Agency Action: The Case of Superfund*, 1986 Duke L. J. 261, 287–297.

the final product of notice-and-comment rulemaking is just as much a law as a statute is.

The relationship of the natural resource damages program to the dominant removal and remedial programs is governed by the NCP, DOI's guidelines, and EPA Guidance Memoranda. EPA and DOI implementation policy for the natural resource damage provisions of Superfund seems at first to be comprehensive. Federal action under the removal and remedial programs and actions under the natural resource damage program begin more or less together, but then they gradually diverge. First, EPA must notify the trustee if a potential natural resource injury exists. Likewise, if the trustee first learns of the potential injury, the trustee must notify EPA. In a remedial situation, based largely on data in the RI/FS, the trustee conducts a "preassessment screening" to see if a full assessment is necessary.[15] The trustee must verify that ordinary response actions would not adequately remedy the natural resource injury. If a full assessment is necessary, an assessment plan covering assessment costs and scientific and economic methodologies is prepared. The potentially responsible parties must be advised and invited to help define and participate in the assessment. The trustee is to coordinate with the lead agency under the National Contingency Plan.

In the assessment plan, the trustee must establish that injury in fact did occur and that it was caused by the responsible party's discharges or releases. The standards for discharge, release, and causation appear generally to parallel the generous standards of the removal and remedial programs, as they should. In quantifying the damage, the trustee is instructed to determine the decrease in the "level of services" the resource provides by comparing the service level before injury to that which will exist after the response is completed. Before the opinion in *Ohio v. The United States Department of the Interior*, the trustee was told to seek either cost of restoration or replacement or diminution of use values, whichever is less. Before the opinion, DOI's regulations also made clear that only injury to public, not private, interests were recoverable (although economists find the distinction artificial); that damages are compensatory, not punitive; and that any recovery is only for harm beyond that remedied in a Superfund response action.

Proposed revisions of type B regulations reaffirm that the damages are for injuries to resources held in public trust. Use and nonuse values must now be reflected in compensable value. While restoration cost re-

---

[15]43 C.F.R. § 11.23(a). This two-step process is strongly reminiscent of the threshold determination of whether or not to prepare an impact statement under the National Environmental Policy Act of 1969 (NEPA) and is just as likely to cause controversy in the future. D. Mandelker, NEPA Law and Litigation § 8:46 (1984).

mains the principal basis for assessing damages, the rules provide trustees broad discretion in interpreting how the costs of a restoration plan are to be evaluated in relation to the monetary damages associated with the injured natural resource. Indeed, the numerical interpretation of "grossly disproportionate" that some attributed to the court of appeals decision was rejected in the multifaceted criteria DOI proposed for this comparison.

Two observations should be made regarding the administrative implementation of the natural resource damage provisions. First, by now it should be clear that damage to natural resources alone will not cause EPA to place a site on the National Priorities List. Health risk is at the core of NPL status. NPL status is, however, necessary for top-priority federal attention. The statute does not require a site to be on the NPL for natural resources trustees to seek damages, but trustees will face tremendous obstacles if their target sites are not on the list. Indeed, there has been litigation over the ability of responsible parties to recover costs from others where the expenditures were incurred prior to NPL status or were arguably incurred in a fashion inconsistent with the National Contingency Plan.

Second, because natural resource damages may be tacked on to NPL sites, they may not receive adequate attention. According to lawyers for responsible parties, EPA has had difficulty getting the trustees to formulate damage assessments in a timely manner. Personnel for resource damage assessments are limited. The fund cannot be used to pay for natural resource damage assessments after the 1986 amendments. Where RI/FS costs may approach $1 million, only a few thousand may be available for determining natural resource damages. Finally, observers report that in some instances resource damage claims appear to have become an expendable chip in bargaining over cleanup settlements.

A possible conclusion is that the remedial and natural resource damage programs should proceed quite separately from each other. This view contradicts the current approach of close administrative coordination. To an extent, it also contradicts both logic and intuition, but administrative realities may in fact confound both from time to time.

3. SUPERFUND WITHIN THE CONTEXT OF FEDERAL REMEDIAL AND COMPENSATORY LEGISLATION

Congress has not been as eager to enact remedial and compensatory environmental measures as it has preventive environmental regulatory statutes. Still, Superfund is part of a federal paradigm for remedial and compensatory legislation that has been gradually emerging for a number of years. If the agencies and courts interpret and implement the natural resource damage provisions of Superfund consistently with this basic paradigm, recoveries will be easier to obtain and will span a variety of injury types. This is so primarily because the paradigm assumes the relaxation of standards of liability, proof, and procedure that otherwise would apply under the common law and traditional norms of the judicial process.

3.1 The Recent Emergence of Federal Remedial and Compensatory Legislation. It is not an overstatement to say that historically all environmental law was common law. If substantial problems of proof and legal action could be overcome, courts would award money damages to compensate a private person for environmental harm or would prevent potential injury by awarding a prohibitive injunction. By the twentieth century, as part of a wider movement promoting legislative solutions to social problems, the federal government and state governments had put in place a few rudimentary statutes to prevent environmental harm. The common law had proved too narrow to deal comprehensively with the community-wide disruptions typical of environmental degradation.[16] These early statutes addressed future harms and redressed public rather than private wrongs. By the 1970s, Congress and state legislatures had enacted sweeping precautionary environmental protection measures. The common law has been reduced to providing interim relief, pending likely regulation.

The statutory displacement of the damages remedy has occurred at a much slower pace than displacement of the preventive injunction. Legislatures have been slow to provide remedial funds or compensation to wronged parties, whether from the public treasury or through a government-supervised transfer of funds from the persons responsible for

---

[16]Most commentators agree that the common law is a seriously flawed system for providing general environmental redress. A minority thinks that there are distinct advantages in having common-law judges decide environmental cases. See Furrow, *Governing Science: Private Risks and Private Remedies*, 131 U. Pa. L. Rev. 1403, 1456–64 (1983).

   The movement from common law to statute that has taken place in recent decades throughout the American legal system has implications far beyond the confines of environmental law. See G. Gilmore, The Ages of American Law 95 (1977). As one well-known judge noted, "The hydra-headed problem is how to synchronize the unguided missile launched by the legislatures with a guiding system of common law." Traynor, *Statutes Revolving in Common Law Orbits*, 17 Cath. U. L. Rev. 401, 402 (1968). Yet the possibilities for a fruitful, creative tension between common law and statute have been noted and encouraged by several outstanding scholars of jurisprudence. See Friendly, *The Gap in Lawmaking—Judges Who Can't and Legislatures Who Won't*, 63 Colum. L. Rev. 787 (1963); Landis, *Statutes and the Sources of Law*, in Harvard Legal Essays 213 (1934); Pound, *Common Law and Legislation*, 21 Harv. L. Rev. 383 (1908); Stone, *The Common Law in the United States*, 50 Harv. L. Rev. 4 (1936). Searching for a role for courts in a statute-dominated era, Calabresi has explored the question of whether courts should take it upon themselves to invalidate outmoded statutes that no longer fit within the wider fabric of American law. See G. Calabresi, A Common Law for the Age of Statutes 163–166 (1982).

harm. The main reason is the reluctance of legislatures to supplant the fault- and cause-based civil law system. Yet legislatures have become less reluctant to act where harm is broadly diffused and its causes equally widespread and uncertain. In recent years legislatures have deliberately relaxed the strict common-law requirements for fault and causation in order to fashion broad redistributive corrective and compensatory programs that supplant the common-law tort compensation system.

Congress has acted frequently enough in recent years to establish a rough paradigm or template for federal ameliorative, restorative, and compensatory legislation. Superfund is not the first statute to fit the emerging template, nor is it the first to provide funds for repair and compensation for natural resource damages. For those who believe Superfund to be unprecedented, a look at these statutes is instructive. Indeed, sections 104(a) and 106 are taken virtually verbatim from earlier legislation. Superfund's funding mechanism is not unique; the pattern for this provision was established years earlier in the oil spill liability and abandoned mine reclamation legislation. Another of Superfund's features, suits against responsible parties to recoup response costs when the conduct giving rise to the liability occurred before enactment of the law, is also found in the Asbestos School Hazard Detection and Control Act of 1980.

Superfund may appear to be a potpourri of elements invented or borrowed from other models in the corpus of federal legislation. It draws upon all the basic legislative strategies used by Congress thus far to legislate on environmental problems. One hardly need be reminded that Congress has primarily relied on command-and-control regulation to control pollution. In Superfund, Congress did not initially require EPA to set ambient or performance standards specifying the degree or type of cleanup required at the sites. However, in 1986 at EPA's request Congress did specify that site remedies must meet all legally "applicable or relevant and appropriate" standards required by the other environmental regulatory statutes. This brief language makes Superfund much more like the Clean Water and Clean Air acts, although this onerous requirement flies in the face of the need for individually tailored cleanup at most sites. Conversion of Superfund to a quasi-regulatory statute more like the Clean Water and Clean Air acts was perhaps inevitable, because EPA is a quintessential regulatory agency. Its basic mission and raison d'etre is regulation. If one uses a hammer often, everything begins to look like a nail.

Other hallmarks of federal environmental regulation are shared responsibility with the states and action-forcing deadlines. In Superfund, Congress did delegate limited authority to obligate federal funds, to participate financially (usually 10 percent), and to settle claims. Yet, in Superfund, Congress dropped all pretense of sharing basic responsibility with the states by refusing to delegate to them the implementation of federal standards. The usual action-forcing deadlines were conspicuously absent from Superfund in 1980, but as agency projections of the time needed to complete the cleanup task reached into the next century, Congress disciplined EPA in 1986 by putting it on a schedule of quotas for cleanup.

Superfund also is a multibillion dollar public works program. In this respect it recalls the approach of the Clean Water Act, which combines industrial point-source category regulation with massive funding for municipal sewage treatment plants. The Clean Water Act also attempts to internalize costs to industrial dischargers to publicly owned treatment works, but leaves the municipalities to shoulder most operational costs. Still, the Clean Water Act provides for future water purification only, passes the funds to the states, does not authorize direct federal construction projects, and does not recover full costs from the broad array of water polluters.

Parallels to federal spill and disaster legislation over the years are much closer, although it is striking how little attention these resemblances have received from courts, legislators, and policy analysts. New Deal programs such as the Civilian Conservation Corps and the Tennessee Valley Authority foreshadowed Superfund. Congress also adopted a number of Superfund-like federal relief acts over the years to permit the federal government to assist state and local governments in responding to disasters. In the past fifteen years federal programs specifically designed to attack hazardous conditions that cannot be ameliorated except by direct cleanup action have proliferated.

Environmental legislation rarely is self-executing, that is, rarely does a federal environmental law state a broad environmental protection standard and entrust its interpretation and enforcement to the courts as do, for example, the Michigan Environmental Protection Act or the Sherman and Clayton antitrust acts. Large agencies interpret and apply detailed environmental standards in the first instance, with courts playing a limited backup role. Superfund is no exception to any of the preceding. Superfund contemplates deferential judicial review of policymaking, provides for judicial enforcement if administrative enforcement fails or is challenged, preserves individuals' common-law remedies for damages, and provides (as do most environmental regulatory statutes) for an immediate resort to the courts by the government when an imminent and substantial endangerment threatens.

Superfund is like other environmental statutes in other respects. Superfund copies the reporting and information disclosure requirements of other environmental laws, especially since the imposition in 1986 of the public-right-to-know requirements in the wake of the Bhopal disaster in India. In its National Contingency Plan and National Priorities List, which bring out the systematic and comprehensive side of the statute, Superfund appears much like such environmental planning statutes as the National Environmental Policy Act of 1969, the Federal Land Policy Management Act of 1976, and the National Forest Management Act of 1976.

Congress did not do a very good job of spelling out its approach in Superfund. The federal courts, however, spurred by EPA and Department of Justice arguments that the statute had to be given the broadest possible reading, have completed the task.[17] Not since the National Environmental Policy Act have the federal courts played such a seminal role in shaping a statute into a coherent and powerful tool to carry out federal environmental objectives. Their aggressive role has obvious implications for the future implementation of Superfund's natural resource damages provisions.

3.2 The Elements of Federal Remedial and Compensatory Legislation. The emergence of a general federal approach to ameliorative and compensatory legislation has ramifications reaching far beyond the scope of this chapter. Further, the elements of the paradigm are not equally applicable to an analysis of Superfund's natural resource damage provisions. The basic elements are listed below. Of these elements, the first, fourth, and fifth are of primary concern in analyzing Superfund's natural resource damage provisions.

3.2.1 Liability Standards. In the federal paradigm, strict and joint and several liability are mainstays. Liability without regard to fault is widely acknowledged as vital to the theory of modern accident injury compensation.[18] Interestingly, Superfund does not expressly mention either strict liability or joint and several liability. Relying on legislative history, the courts have inferred that both apply to Superfund. Superfund borrowed the strict liability standard from the oil and hazardous substances cleanup program of the Clean Water Act. However, the Clean Water Act did not expressly mandate strict liability; the courts inferred liability without regard to fault into the statute to fulfill congressional intent. Likewise, neither Superfund nor the Clean Water Act expressly adopted joint and several liability; the courts again had to spell out congressional intent. Predecessor statutes providing for oil and hazardous substance cleanup in deepwater ports, along the route of the trans-Alaska oil pipeline, and over the continental shelf and other submerged lands impose the same liability standards.

3.2.2 Funds and Fees. Federal cleanup funds were established by the Clean Water Act of 1972, the Deepwater Port Act of 1974, the Oil Spill

---

[17]Glass, *Superfund and SARA: Are There Any Defenses Left?* 12 Harv. Envtl. L. Rev. 385 (1988).

[18]See generally G. Calabresi, The Costs of Accidents (1970).

Fund of 1978, and the Trans-Alaskan Pipeline Authorization Act of 1973. In general, Congress imposed fees on the hazard generators to create and replenish the funds. These funds were to clean up future spills, yet Superfund largely addresses past conduct. In this regard it more clearly resembles the black lung benefits and abandoned mine reclamation programs. The former requires coal mine operators to pay into a federal fund to compensate pre-1974 injuries and also makes them liable to miners who discover that they have the disease after 1974, while the latter imposes a fee on the current coal mining industry for cleanup of abandoned mines.

3.2.3 Government-Initiated Remediation. Superfund's predecessors also placed on the federal government the burden of taking direct action, but only if prompt private remediation was not possible. Private parties with a defense could often recoup their remediation costs from other responsible parties. Subrogation and contribution were preserved in these earlier statutes more clearly than in Superfund.

3.2.4 Administrative Decision Making and Fact Finding. We live in an "administered" society.[19] Under the paradigm statutes, federal agencies carry out study and cleanup; they control the apportionment of responsibility between states and the federal government; they write regulations defining hazard, responsible parties, remediation and compensation eligibility, and remediation priorities. Finally, they largely determine the role courts will play through guidelines and agency enforcement policies. Under Superfund the courts make the final money damage awards, but the statute authorizes DOI to write regulations that provide the district courts with guidelines about the sufficiency of evidence or proof necessary to prevail in a natural resource damages suit. This is but one instance of how under the emerging paradigm the courts' traditional decision-making processes are subtly redefined to make the courts more like administrative tribunals than traditional common-law courts.

3.2.5 Shifting the Burden of Proof. Regardless of whether it is coupled with agency regulations, the practice of shifting the burden of going forward with the evidence to the hazard generator is a well-established part of Congress' overall strategy.[20] Legislatures and courts create pre-

---

[19]Anderson, *Human Welfare and the Administered Society: Federal Regulation in the 1970s to Protect Health, Safety, and the Environment*, in Environmental and Occupational Medicine (W. Rom, ed. 1983).

[20]The phrase "burden of proof" loosely refers to three separate burdens that must be discharged by a traditional proponent in a court of law: the burden of pleading, the burden of production (or going forward with the evidence), and finally the burden of persuasion. The second and third burdens are more important than the first. Once allocated, the burden of persuasion (the risk of nonpersuasion) never shifts, but the burden of

sumptions to shift the burden of proof to correct an imbalance resulting from one party's superior access to the evidence, to favor certain claims for social and economic reasons, and to facilitate the prompt resolution of claims.[21] Superfund's predecessor statutes included the rebuttable presumption as a means of easing the burden of proof, which to a claimant may pose a redoubtable barrier if scientific causation is difficult to establish between a hazard generator and a victim, or if the measure of damages is subject to scientific debate over evaluation techniques.

4.   SUPERFUND AND THE COMMON LAW

The relationship between the common law and the natural resource damage provisions of Superfund is vital. Modern social welfare legislation takes the common law as part of its "deep background."[22] Although Superfund in important respects draws upon public works legislation, command-and-control regulation, and disaster and spill programs, the most important source of law with respect to interpretation of the natural resource damage provisions has become the common law. This is the case in part because the courts are presumed to know and apply the common law, and in part because DOI has at least partially viewed the common law as a limitation on how broadly natural resource damage regulations can be written.

If Superfund was heavily based on traditional common law, the common law might act as a brake on full natural resource damage recovery. But if the statute is not constrained by traditional common-law doctrines, trustees may succeed in obtaining larger awards, which can then be applied to natural resources enhancement. In fact, in Superfund, Congress enacted provisions that go well beyond the common-law background. Indeed, the awkward attempt by Congress to proceed beyond traditional common law has in the past eight years been fully executed by the federal courts.

---

going forward with the evidence may shift. M. Graham, Federal Rules of Evidence, § 301.3 at 43–44 (1987).

[21]"In the creation of presumptions, a reasonable judgment of probabilities is the most important consideration. This plays a strong part in the establishment of presumptions to aid the claimant injured by hazardous wastes to meet his burden of proof in a compensation proceeding. In certain recurring fact situations, proof of fact A renders inference of fact B so probable that it is sensible and time-saving to presume the truth of fact B until the adversary disproves it." See Superfund Section 301(e) Study Group, 97th Cong., 2d Sess., Injuries and Damages from Hazardous Wastes—Analysis and Improvement of Legal Remedies at 205. See also id., pt. 2 at 312–339 (Appendix M-1).

[22]W. Rodgers, Environmental Law I § 3.1 173 (1986).

4.1   Strict Liability. The courts and the Environmental Protection Agency today maintain that potentially responsible parties are strictly, jointly, and severally liable for cleanup or its costs.[23] This is as true for natural resource cleanup, restoration, and damages as it is for site and spill cleanup on private property.

Common-law strict liability and Superfund strict liability are similar, but only up to a point. The salient attribute of common-law strict liability is that a defendant will be found liable even if he has not violated any standard of care and even if he is not morally blameworthy. Through common-law strict liability, the defendant is forced to internalize the costs of damages that result from his activities by incorporating those costs into the price of goods or services.[24] Strict liability is not a theory for shifting loss to or for punishing a wrongdoer, but rather is a means for determining who will ultimately bear the risks associated with activities that actually in the broader scheme of things may be socially desirable.[25]

Up to this point, the two versions of strict liability agree. Beyond this point, however, there are differences between what Congress saw in strict liability and what the trained common lawyer sees. First, common-law courts have considerable discretion to decide which activities are hazardous. They may balance injury against the value of the activity to the community in deciding if strict liability is appropriate. But, in Superfund, Congress chose an agency to designate which wastes were hazardous and did not provide that high social utility would excuse any category of responsible parties. Second, in common law a plaintiff must prove injury or imminent irreparable harm of a substantial nature. Superfund dispenses with this requirement and adopts the preventive and precautionary endangerment standard that Congress has placed in most environmental regulatory legislation.

Third, the common law requires the plaintiff to show that the defendant's conduct proximately caused injury. But in a radical departure from

---

[23]See, for example, *United States v. NEPACCO* 810 F.2d 726 (8th Cir. 1986); *United States v. SCRDI*, 653 F. Supp. 984 (D.S.C. 1986); *United States v. Conservation Chemical Co.*, 619 F. Supp. 162 (W.D. Mo. 1985).

[24]"The doctrine of strict liability at its core reflects the judgment that even if some harm is inevitable, the social value of some enterprises is greater than their costs, but if an enterprise's benefits exceed its costs, fundamental fairness requires at least that profits be net of any harms inflicted." F. Anderson, D. Mandelker, and A. D. Tarlock, Environmental Protection: Law and Policy 636–637 (1984).

[25]The Senate seemed to say that waste disposers had not been morally culpable or negligent in adopting prior waste disposal practices. Discussing the S. 1430 strict liability scheme, the Senate Committee Report remarked that often the choice of a responsible party is not between an innocent victim and a careless defendant, but between two blameless parties. In such cases the costs should be borne by the one whose acts instigated or made the harm possible. S. Rep. No. 848, 96th Cong., 2d Sess. 33–34 (1980).

common-law norms, Superfund does not require proof that the waste that was generated, transported, or otherwise handled by a responsible party be the very waste that created a hazardous condition necessitating response activities. Thus, after incurring response costs consistent with the National Contingency Plan, a plaintiff seeking reimbursement need only prove that the defendant is in the class of parties identified by the statute. It does not require the plaintiff to prove that the defendant's waste was, for example, leaching into the groundwater—only that the defendant's waste was present at the site that was cleaned up. Hence, Superfund liability may be more like enterprise or market-share liability than traditional strict liability. The explanation for the difference in causal analysis is that Superfund provides a remedy for hazardous conditions and does not fix liability for ultrahazardous or abnormally dangerous activities.

Fourth, a common-law plaintiff may be subjected to a variety of defenses, including contributory negligence, assumption of the risk, the public duty of the defendant to engage in the activity, the plaintiff's unusual sensitivity, and the intervening acts of others. Superfund defenses under the reimbursement provisions are exclusive and different. Finally, Superfund imposes financial liability limits unknown to the common law.

A statutory doctrine embedded in a modern administered welfare statute, strict liability under Superfund departs significantly from the common law. Common-law balancing, causal requirements, defenses, and the like have no place in the statutory scheme. Certain sections of CERCLA affirmatively support imposition of a unique legislative type of strict liability. Yet a judge trying to find specific statutory text indicating congressional intent to impose broad strict liability can only grasp at a few fragments; Congress left its texts incomplete and in what must be called a mess.

Section 107 does declare forthrightly that four classes of responsible parties shall be liable for the cleanup costs associated with hazardous waste sites and for certain damages to natural resources. Section 107 does not establish a standard of care for responsible parties, nor does it or its legislative history contain any suggestion that proof of reasonable care, or even utmost care, would absolve an astonishingly diverse array of parties—including those with extremely tenuous connections to sites—from the cost of cleanup. The defenses that are available to responsible parties—acts of war, God, and certain third parties—are not typical of the defenses that would be available if the plaintiff had to prove negligence. For example, if the standard of liability were negligence, one would expect that contributory negligence or assumption of the risk would constitute defenses. Yet Section 107(b) precludes such defenses. A standard of negligence is involved in Section 107 (b)(3), which provides that an otherwise responsible party shall not be liable when the actual or threatened release is the result of "an act or omission of a third party other than an employee or agent of the defendant, or than one whose act or omission occurs in connection with a contractual relationship . . . with the defendant (except where the sole contractual arrangement [is with] a common carrier by rail), if the defendant establishes . . . that he (a) exercised due care . . . and (b) took precautions against foreseeable acts or omissions." The mention of a single fault-based defense for a common carrier contractor for waste shipment by rail shows that strict liability is the rule, not the exception. The third-party defense of Section 107(b)(3) relieves disposers of responsibility for the consequences of the conduct of parties unrelated to them either by contract, agency, or employment, unless their acts or omissions were foreseeable. The common-carrier-by-rail exception is the only time the defendant's due care will be available as a defense where privity exists. Plausible policy reasons for exempting defendants from liability for shipments by rail but not by truck were not offered. In short, Section 107 creates unique statutory liabilities and defenses.

Because Superfund was hastily passed and inartfully worded, and perhaps because the congressmen involved were not particularly well trained in the common law, a few problems still exist with this interpretation. Nowhere does the statute plainly state that responsible parties are liable without regard to fault for the cost or execution of cleanup. Indeed, language to this effect was removed from earlier versions of the statute. "Any person who caused or contributed to the release or threatened release shall be strictly liable for such costs, damages and losses. . . . Such liability shall be joint and several with any other person who caused or contributed to such release.[26]

Another CERCLA predecessor, S. 1480 as introduced on July 11, 1979, also contained specific mention of strict, joint, and several liability. Section 4(a) read, in pertinent part, ". . . any other person who caused or contributed or is causing or contributing to such discharge . . . shall be jointly, severally and strictly liable. . . ."[27] Instead, CERCLA declared that the standard of liability under the act should be the same as that which applied under Section 311 of the Clean Water Act (CWA). Although Section 311 of CWA did not, by express terms, establish a standard of strict liability, it has been so interpreted by the courts. The legislative history indicates that Congress perceived that it was adopting a standard of strict liability for parties that were held responsible under the act.

Some legislative history indicates that Congress wanted to adopt the standard from the common law. For example, Congressman Albert Gore

---

[26]H.R. 7020, 96th Cong., 2d Sess. § 3071(a)(1), 126 Cong. Rec. 26,779 (1980). H.R. 7020 was passed by the House on September 23, 1980, with § 3071 intact. 126 Cong. Rec. 26,799 (1980).

[27]S. 1480, 96th Cong., 2d Sess., 125 Cong. Rec. S17,991 (daily ed., July 11, 1979).

discoursed extensively on the history and reasoning behind strict liability, beginning with *Rylands v. Fletcher* (1868) continuing on the Restatement (Second) of Torts (1977) through the applicability of strict liability to the modern-day problem of hazardous wastes. Still, a wider view of the statute's purpose and its legislative history suggests that Congress borrowed the phrase simply to explain that the Superfund scheme was not fault-based and that enterprises that benefit from hazardous waste disposal will be expected collectively to internalize the costs of cleaning up past disposal. Nothing more, nothing less. If Congress meant anything more than this, it failed utterly to say so.

Also, the rationale offered for removing express strict liability was to leave the common law undisturbed. But this seems to be an afterthought, offered up to obscure the real reason the phrase was removed: the bill's opponents could be placated to some extent by making the statute less explicit, a classic gambit used to secure passage of controversial legislation, no matter how much it may vex the justices. As we have seen, the common law was modified in five important aspects in Superfund.

Congress's plan for implementing the statute would be disrupted if the government had to meet traditional common-law standards regarding balancing, injury, causality, and defenses each time it brought an action. Superfund's strict liability reflects a unique statutory policy. The federal district and circuit courts seem almost unanimously to have endorsed this view.[28]

4.2   Joint and Several Liability.   An intriguing example of the interplay of common law and legislation also exists in Congress's handling of joint and several liability in Superfund. Joint and several liability and strict liability both followed virtually identical paths of legislative evolution. Congress was again unclear as to its intentions in applying a common-law concept *sub silentio* in a complex environmental cleanup statute. On the one hand, Congress seemed to want joint and several liability to follow traditional and evolving principles of common law. On the other hand, the active participants in the legislative process appeared to be completely unaware of the confusing diversity of common law on this point. Perhaps sensing this, the chief House sponsor indicated that the bill would encourage the development of a federal common law of joint and several liability.[29] Those following the debate sensed that the courts would allow the

---

[28]Cadwalader, Wickersham and Taft, *Significant CERCLA Decisions During the Past Year*, at 1–2 (1987) (unpublished memorandum on file with author).

[29]126 Cong. Rec. H11,787 (daily ed., Dec. 3, 1980) (remarks of Congressman Florio). The policy motivations identified by the congressman were "to insure the development of a uniform rule and to discourage business dealing in hazardous substances from locating primarily

government to collect its expenses or impose cleanup tasks on one or a few responsible parties and exit the case. There was no discussion of apportionment, that is, whether and to what extent each responsible party's share could be easily identified. These parties apparently would obtain court-supervised contribution from the remaining parties.

The state law weaves a tangled web, despite facile reference to black-letter rules contained in the Restatement of Torts by some federal district courts in Superfund cases. One surmises from the debates that many members of Congress would have been surprised to learn that under the common law most applicable to the waste site cleanup problem—the state court nuisance decisions—as recently as thirty years ago no joint and several liability was generally allowed; the court would have to apportion liability. Some jurisdictions still insist that courts must apportion independently caused nuisance damages according to each defendant's share, stoutly maintaining in a triumph of reason over experience that in all cases the nuisance theoretically is no more or less than the sum of its discrete parts, and that the court must isolate each part, despite the practical problems of proof that often arise.

Debate over the fine points of state common and statutory law governing joint and several liability and contribution may traditionally have been reserved to law students and professors, but for a long time after CERCLA was enacted, practitioners and government lawyers spoke of little else. Had the federal district courts applied the existing state common law of joint and several liability, apportionment, and contribution in deciding reimbursement and cleanup cases, chaos would have resulted. Instead, Congress kept the common law in the deep background.

5.   ADMINISTRATIVE DECISION MAKING AND FACT FINDING UNDER SUPERFUND

Superfund contains a provision that on close analysis may prove to be the most salient example in federal law of the alteration (some might say the corruption) of evidentiary standards to serve a legislative policy goal. The law authorizes the Department of the Interior to write regulations that, in effect, direct the courts to give extra weight to evidence on natural resource damage that is computed in a particular manner using approved methodologies.

DOI's regulations could become a sort of primer or scientific evidentiary manual instructing federal judges on how to understand

---

in states with lenient laws." Of course, a federal common law of cost allocation for abandoned and inactive sites would have no incentive effect with respect to the problem at hand.

and apply complex technical natural resource injury assessment methodologies. This provision, make no mistake, is highly novel. Courts are accustomed to reviewing agency actions to determine if they are within the law, if the agency has based formal decisions on the substantial evidence in the agency's record, or if more informal determinations are reasonable and may not be said, in the ritualistic phrase, to be arbitrary and capricious. But it is quite another thing to authorize a federal agency to give a federal judge detailed directions as to how to think about expert testimony in a plenary trial court action for damages. Some judges may become confused, even a little truculent. They may feel that they know a thing or two about how to find facts in a trial on the evidence. If Congress wanted the agency to determine the facts, judges may reason, then it could have vested the decision in an agency tribunal. On judicial review, the court then would gladly defer to the agency.

Exact statutory precedents apparently do not exist for the natural resource damage regulations. Yet Congress has considered authorizing agencies to write regulations that give evidentiary weight to federal agency endorsement of particular personal injury etiologies and methodologies. This author made such a proposal in testimony to Congress in 1978; the twelve-member congressional study commission on toxic injury compensation endorsed the concept in 1982; and similar proposals appear in model state statutes and articles.[30] The heart of such proposals are federal agency regulations, variously called "criteria documents," "presumption documents," or "carcinogen catalogs," which would analyze the literature on toxic substances and would certify to the trial court that a toxicant's disease-causing characteristics merit generous statutory presumptions and burden shifts, which the court would apply in finding the facts and determining awards.

The parallel between the Superfund's natural resource damage regulations and the rebuttable presumption is exact. The substantial problems natural resources trustees encounter in proving substantial but difficult-to-measure environmental harms to public natural resources warranted both assistance for the courts by an expert agency, on the one hand, and presumptive, preferential evidentiary weight for the agency's determinations, on the other hand, even if Congress chose to vest the final word in the courts and not in the agency.

---

[30]Trauberman, *Statutory Reform of "Toxic Torts": Relieving Legal, Scientific, and Economic Burdens on the Chemical Victim*, 7 Harv. Envtl. L. Rev. 177 (1983); Rosenberg, *The Causal Connection in Mass Exposure Cases: A "Public Law" Vision of the Tort System*, 97 Harv. L. Rev. 849 (1984); Note, *Tort Actions for Cancer: Deterrence, Compensation, and Environmental Carcinogenesis*, 90 Yale L. J. 840, 855 (1981).

6. BURDEN OF PROOF AND THE REBUTTABLE
PRESUMPTION

A procedural innovation can have an equal or greater impact on the outcome of a trial than can a doctrinal shift, as common-law judges realized long ago. Borrowing from the courts, legislatures have mandated burden-shifting in modern welfare statutes to promote policy objectives. In adopting the device of shifting the burden of proof, however, legislatures have sometimes strayed quite far from the burden-shifting that courts first employed in jury trials. As with the doctrines of strict liability and joint and several liability, Congress in Superfund adopted a burden-shifting rebuttable presumption that travels far afield from traditional procedural devices for allocating power to the judge and jury.

Ordinarily, the plaintiff bears the burden of going forward with the evidence at every point in a trial. But the courts, and later modern legislatures, created rebuttable presumptions to shift the burden of proof to correct the imbalance resulting from one party's superior access to the evidence, to facilitate the prompt resolution of claims, and to favor certain claims for social and economic reasons. Furthermore, the chief reason for reallocating the burden of going forward with the evidence was to reallocate power between judge and jury. In a jury trial, the rebuttable presumption ordinarily has the effect of getting the claim to the jury more rapidly and under more favorable jury instructions than would otherwise be the case. The intent of Congress in adopting a rebuttable presumption in Superfund seems simply to give the trustees a better chance of prevailing in cases involving difficult-to-prove ecological damage. At base, the presumption instructs courts to give heavy weight to the expert opinion reflected in DOI's damage regulations. The presumption is Congress's imprimatur on federal administrative determinations of methodology and fact.

Superfund departs significantly from the current rules applicable to rebuttable presumptions in general. Under the current federal rule of evidence applicable to rebuttable presumptions, the intent (or certainly the effect) of the rule is to increase the number of cases decided by a jury. The policy of the rule is to increase the power of the jury to decide factual controversies by reducing the power of the judge, who by applying presumptions may try to keep a controversy from the jury or may try to require the jury to decide the case in a particular way.

Yet under Superfund it is unlikely that trials will be by jury, despite the recent decision of the Supreme Court in *Tull v. United States*,[31] and despite nonbinding dicta in a recent Eighth Circuit decision to the effect

---

[31] 17 Envtl. L. Rep. (Envtl. L. Inst.) 20,667 (1987). See also Slavitt, *Jury Trial Rights Under CERCLA: The Effect of Tull v. U.S.* 18 Envtl. L. Rep. (Envtl. L. Inst.) 10,127 (1988).

that natural resource damages are legal in nature and therefore require a jury trial.[32] No court has permitted a jury trial as yet in an action for Superfund response costs. The reason is that cleanup costs are equitable in nature, that is, they are restorative and restitutive, and do not penalize conduct so as to trigger a constitutionally guaranteed jury trial. Further, all damages recovered under Superfund, even damages for lost use between the time of injury and the time a final judicial determination is made, must be spent on repair or replacement of the lost natural resources. These statutorily required expenditures fulfill the traditional equitable purpose of restitution. This result is also supported by recent Supreme Court cases holding that where Congress has created modern statutory public rights, these rights do not fall within the category of rights the founders intended to be protected by jury trial at the time the Bill of Rights was adopted.[33]

Finally, Superfund itself implies that a jury trial will not be available, because the statute authorizes the rebuttable presumption not only in claims brought to court, but also in administrative determinations, on which no jury ever sits.[34] The availability of the presumption in administrative proceedings is also further evidence that Congress did not have in mind traditional presumptions, with their emphasis on judge–jury interactions, when it enacted the natural resource damage presumption.

Draft Superfund legislation also included a rebuttable presumption favoring the personal injury claimant. The personal injury provision was removed at the last moment. Significantly, the bill listed more than a dozen types of injury for which damages would be recoverable, in addition to natural resource damage. The rebuttable presumption was to facilitate recovery for medical expenses. Only natural resources survived the final triage, probably because natural resource damage recovery was popular with state governments. Victim groups were not well organized at the time.

The personal injury damage award provisions of federal statutes shed light on how courts may interpret Superfund's provision for a rebuttable presumption favoring the natural resources trustee's claim, and on how DOI might revise its natural resource damage regulations. A close reading shows that these provisions ensure that a wide variety of personal injuries are fully compensable and make the claimant's burden quite light in most

---

[32]*Continental Ins. Cos. v. Northeastern Pharmaceutical & Chem. Co.*, 842 F.2d 977, 986–987 (8th Cir. 1988). See also *United States v. Northeastern Pharmaceutical & Chem. Co.*, 810 F.2d 726, 729 (8th Cir. 1986) (holding that since government's effort to recover response costs did not involve legal damages, defendants had no right to a jury trial).

[33]See *Commodity Futures Trading Comm. v. Schor*, 478 U.S. 833, 847–858 (1986); *Thomas v. Union Carbide Agricultural Prods. Co.*, 473 U.S. 568, 584–593 (1985); *Northern Pipeline Constr. Co. v. Marathon Pipeline Constr. Co.*, 458 U.S. 50, 62–76 (1982).

[34]42 U.S.C. § 9607 (f)(2(C).

instances. Congress focused the provisions directly on the difficulties that a claim at common law would create. The effect is to move beyond the strictures of common-law recovery, to the point that critics now claim that if Congress continues to replace traditional tort law causation and fault requirements with no-fault recovery funded by entities with only a tenuous connection to the injury, economic incentive and affordable insurance will disappear.

The expansive purpose of modern legislative burden-shifting can perhaps be best illustrated by a close look at the 1970 federal legislation to compensate victims of black lung disease (pneumoconiosis), a respiratory condition that afflicts miners and others who have breathed coal dust for long periods of time. The Secretary of Health and Human Services defines black lung disability by regulation, just as the Secretary of the Interior issues natural resource damage regulations under Superfund. Five rebuttable presumptions favor a claimant seeking recovery for death, black lung disease, or respiratory impairment, just as a natural resources trustee enjoys a rebuttable presumption if the claim for damages is made under DOI's regulations. For pre-1974 injuries, black lung claimants could proceed against a federal fund analogous to Superfund (and taxed to the mining industry). After 1986 natural resources trustees must proceed directly against potentially responsible parties. Beginning in 1974, black lung claimants must usually recover damages under state worker compensation laws or from mine operators, the analogues to Superfund's potentially responsible parties. For recovery of damages from operators, claimants must use the procedural provisions of an older and yet more sweeping federal compensation statute, the Longshoremen's and Harbor Workers' Compensation Act, a strict liability, employment-based statute providing for death benefits, permanent total and partial disability, and medical services. This statute also calls for regulations; further, if a claimant merely establishes the fact of injury, a statutory presumption arises that all other relevant requirements for compensation have been met. Only substantial evidence to the contrary can rebut the presumption.

7.   APPLICATION OF THE NATURAL RESOURCE DAMAGE PROVISIONS BY THE AGENCIES AND THE COURTS

The preceding discussion shows that Congress intended a wide interpretation when it enacted Superfund. At least, the courts have clearly indicated that they believe a broad interpretation is appropriate. The courts have held that Superfund made potentially responsible parties even minimally involved with waste sites and spills individually and collectively liable, without regard to fault for all aspects of an agency-designed cleanup, regardless of who performed it, and whatever the cost.[35] In this light Superfund is a federal bill collector's statute, which identifies such a broad group of debtors that one might ask if Congress had not reached the limit of the constitutionally required rational nexus that must exist between the objectives of legislation and the scheme adopted to achieve them. Traditional fault-based theories of liability, defenses, causal requirements, measure of damage limitations, and procedural limits do not apply.

If Congress intended for the natural resource provisions to incur these limitations, it gave no such indication. Before the November 1980 elections, Congress was moving toward a simple and inclusive theory for Superfund legislation: for every site or spill, complete remediation; for every injury already sustained by public or private property or persons, compensation. After the election, all damage compensation provisions were dropped—except damages to public natural resources. For them, the inclusive approach of the statute was retained.

7.1 Department of the Interior Interpretation of the Natural Resource Damage Provisions. The Department of the Interior moved slowly and cautiously toward implementation of the regulations for damage recovery. Relying upon what it believed to be the common-law rule, the department initially interpreted the statute to limit damage awards to either the diminution in value of a resource, or the cost of replacing or restoring the resource, whichever is less.[36] In addition, damages would be awarded for harm incurred from the date of injury to the time an award for diminished use or restoration or replacement is made.

The department's "either/or" rule severely constricted the natural resource damage recovery program, and a federal court has invalidated the rule as inconsistent with the Superfund statute's emphasis on environmental restoration. The rule completely precluded the trustee from pursuing restoration or replacement costs when lost use was small. Under DOI's initial rule, if a lost resource has a value to citizens who do not use it but value its existence, or who want future use reserved as an option for future generations, these nonuse values cannot be included in the damage assessment. These limitations upon full recovery also were invalidated by the court. The rule also precluded mixed solutions—for example, some lost-use compensation, some restoration, and some replacement—but this issue was not addressed in the recent decision. With the proposed revision,

---

[35]Glass, *Superfund and SARA: Are There Any Defenses Left?*, 12 Harv. Envtl. L. Rev. 385 (1988).

[36]43 C.F.R. 11.35(b)(2) (1987). When restoration or replacement of the damaged resource is not "technically feasible," damages are to be measured by diminution in use values only. 43 C.F.R. 11.35(b)(3) (1987).

it appears that the rule will be more tolerant of mixed solutions. While continuing to profess that damages will correspond to restoration cost, the new regulations acknowledge that there may be considerable time involved in restoration. For example, the proposed rule suggests that ". . . the measure of damages under the proposed revision would be the estimated cost of the selected alternative for restoration, rehabilitation, replacement and/or acquisition of equivalent resources, plus the compensable value of the services that will be lost to the public through the period of recovery to the baseline conditions existing before the discharge or release."[37]

Even with existence and option values included, as they now must be, the techniques for computing lost-use values are beset with conceptual difficulties and measurement uncertainties. Thus lost-value damages may still be awarded after the court's decision, because restoration and replacement may seem grossly disproportionate to the dollar value of the lost uses. The techniques themselves also tend to undervalue lost natural resources.[38]

The primary methodologies focus on lost consumptive uses (such as lumber, fish, and game birds) and nonconsumptive uses (such as backpacking, scuba diving, and bird watching) of public natural resources. Private markets may provide damage measures, either because private resources identical to the public resources are also traded privately or because inferential market appraisals can be traded privately or because inferential market appraisals can be made. But individually and collectively, resources in situ may exceed the surrogate prices that might be observed for them in available private markets. For example, values for the fish, shellfish, plants, and coral in the live reef cannot be adequately reflected in the prices charged for them by laboratory suppliers or by owners of shell and curiosity shops.[39] Consumer behavior will not produce prices if resources are not directly traded in markets, which is often the case with resources for which damages under Superfund may be recovered.

---

[37]56 Fed. Reg. 19756 (Apr. 29, 1991).

[38]E. Yang, R. Dower, and M. Menafee. The Use of Economic Analysis in Valuing Natural Resource Damages: An Overview (Envtl. L. Inst. 1983); Yang, *Valuing Natural Resource Damages: Economics for CERCLA Lawyers*, 14 Envtl. L. Rep. (Envtl. L. Inst.) 10,311, 10,314–10,315 (1984); Frishberg, *Computing Natural Resource Damages*, Calif. L. Bus., June 6, 1988, at 1, col. 1.

[39]See *Developments—Toxic Waste Litigation*, 99 Harv. L. Rev. 1458, 1570–1572 (1986), and the discussion there of the "absurd" measure in *Puerto Rico v. The SS Zoe Colocotroni*, 628 F.2d 652 (1st Cir. 1980); see also Breen, *CERCLA's Natural Resource Damages Provisions: What Do We Know So Far?* 14 Envtl. L. Rep. (Envtl. L. Inst.) 10,304, 10,309–10,310 (1984).

Economists have developed methods to establish the money value of such resources. Aggregated travel expenses, entrance fees, the opportunity cost of the travel time invested, and similar travel-related costs may be taken as the value (willingness to pay for) of the natural resource visited. Travel cost studies, however, while the most widely used measure of outdoor recreation demand, apply only if travel is a large factor in access to the resource. The method suffers also from researchers' inability to gather accurate data and from conceptual problems in valuing travel time, isolating the damaged resource from undamaged ones, and establishing the pre-injury baseline resource condition. Another indirect method, hedonic price valuation, does not fare better. This method tries to capture the value of a nonmarketed resource as a measurable component of a marketed resource; for example, where polluted air lowers housing prices and wages, price and wage differentials between clean and dirty air areas are taken as the value of the damages to the air resource. Yet, isolating declines in public natural resource value as *the* cause in wage and price differentials is exceedingly difficult except in a very few instances. Further, wages and prices for many key public natural resource users will not be affected. Indeed, many natural resources, such as marshes, natural parks, and forests, are in part highly valued because they have few nearby neighbors.

Another methodological line of attack, contingent valuation, depends on directly asking interviewees what they would pay to maintain a resource in its present condition. This method depends on an accurate description of the resource and on the interviewees' ability to imagine that money actually changes hands. Critics charge that strategic responses may skew these expressed preferences (as opposed to preferences revealed by actual market behavior), but methodological innovation has blunted this criticism.

At the heart of these methodologies is the concept that a use cannot be counted as lost and its money value counted as damages if a substitute resource is available that provides the same services. Valuation techniques fix the money value of the lost resource uses on services that cannot be provided by the next-best alternative. For example, damages at a destroyed lobster fishery would be measured by the added cost of access to a substitute fishery, differences in market value between the two fisheries' lobsters, and other indications of the value the public formerly owned or controlled but has since lost. Likewise, recovery for damage to a recreational beach would be limited to the money value of attributes unique to that beach: its accessibility, swimming opportunities, suitability for sunbathing, and the like. In more precise economic terms, trustees would recover lost economic rents. In the above examples, these rents are measured by the money value of the extra effort a lobster fisherman or beach visitor would have to make to receive the same price (lobster) or satisfaction (beach) at a substitute, next-best lobster fishery or beach.

The problem at the heart of this economic framework is substitutability. Perfect substitution is a conceptually contentious concept from the outset, even among economists. Federal district court judges are not likely to be clearer headed or more sympathetic. Many would argue that traditional notions of fungibility that may apply, say, to cars, clothes, and houses, simply are inapplicable to many natural resources. Comparative degrees of less-than-perfect substitutability for marshes, bays, beaches, forests, scenic overlooks, birding sites, aesthetic formations, and scenic rivers are no less daunting than perfect substitution. Defendants will argue perfect or close substitutability, while trustees will argue uniqueness. Each will marshal their economic experts, but courts will probably be most impressed by the conceptual difficulty of comparing resources and of valuing lost resources with the techniques and frameworks offered. "Soft" aesthetic and recreational values have usually been undervalued in similar circumstances.

All of this brings the focus back to Superfund's alternative measures of damages—that is, diminution of use values, and the cost of restoration or replacement. Yet if the trustee could focus on the real costs of restoration or replacement from the outset, the result would more nearly conform to the overall congressional purpose in enacting Superfund—restoration of contaminated sites as near as possible to their prior condition. (In any event, the statute requires that any and all damages recovered be spent on cleanup or replacement. Forced resort to lost-use values as the measure of damages would simply reduce the total amount available for ameliorative measures.)

Restoration and replacement are easier to estimate than diminution of use values. Instead of approximating lost uses, estimators would compute the expense of, say, dredging contaminated soil, containing and immobilizing wastes too extensive to relocate, and reintroducing plant and animal species. The problem is similar to that facing the preparers of RI/FS at ordinary Superfund sites, and the expertise garnered in this process may prove useful in estimating restoration of damaged natural resources. Admittedly, ecologists, botanists, biologists, and other scientists may disagree over the adequacy and feasible extent of restoration or replacement, although progress has been made recently in the new field of restoration ecology.[40] But at least compari-

---

[40]The Breakdown and Restoration of Ecosystems (Holdgate and Woodman, eds., 1978); Ecology and Reclamation of Devastated Land (Hutnik and Davis, eds., 1969); Aber and Jordan, *Restoration Ecology: An Environmental Middle Ground*, 35 Bioscience 399 (1985).

sons can be made in kind between the biological character of the resource before the injury, its scenic value, and the services it rendered and the same attributes as provided by the restored resource or its replacement. Reduction of lost values to suspect dollar sums is unnecessary, except when restoration or replacement may be grossly disproportionate to the destroyed resources reduced to dollars. Lost use, option, and existence values, whatever their dollar equivalent may be, are restored to the extent restoration or replacement is successful. To require restoration, that is, to restore the supply of a lost resource without limiting it by considering demand, is possibly to open the door to hugely expensive restoration projects. Benefit and cost must be kept in proportion, but surely techniques for doing so are well within the talents of economists, perhaps the same economists who developed the travel cost, hedonic, and contingent valuation methodologies.

The Department of the Interior—the federal trustee *primus inter pares*—should wish to preserve for itself the broadest possible scope of action under Superfund's natural resource damage provisions, if the statute permits. And the statute does seem to permit a much broader reading, as the court concluded. The statute authorizes recovery for injury, destruction, and loss, and it mentions replacement value and lost use as relevant to determining damages. It states that the measure of damages "shall not be limited by" restoration or replacement cost. DOI's initial interpretation contradicted the legislative history of sections 4 and 6 of S. 1480, the Senate Superfund bill. The traditional common law appears to require that in general the measure of damages is the lesser of the value of lost uses or the cost of replacement or restoration. DOI inferred that Congress intended to adopt this conservative concept of damage measurement in the absence of "clearly expressed congressional intent to deviate"[41] from the common law. Some cases suggest, however, that the diminution-in-value measure of damages that governs damage to private property should not restrict recovery for injury to public natural resources.[42] Still, an Idaho federal district court applied the restrictive version of the common-law rule in a natural resource damage case that predated DOI's regulations and that

---

[41]Natural Resource Damage Assessments, 51 Fed. Reg. 27,705 (1986).

[42]Traditionally the courts have favored diminution in value, but the recent trend is toward awarding restoration costs. Although courts favor awarding the remedy that costs less—usually diminution in value—this is not an absolute rule. The courts in some cases involving crop damage have awarded the cost of reseeding and the rental value of the land during restoration. See D. Dobbs, Handbook on the Law of Remedies, 312–318, 325–327, (1973); Halter and Thomas, *Recovery of Damages for Fish and Wildlife Losses Caused by Pollution*, 10 Ecology L.Q. 5, 10 (1982). See especially *Puerto Rico v. The SS Zoe Colocotroni*, 628 F.2d 652, 673–674 (1st Cir. 1980).

was filed under state common law as well as the Superfund.[43] In fact, one wonders if a state trustee would have had a stronger case without DOI's guidelines, under state *parens patriae*, public trust and public nuisance doctrines.[44]

The preceding analysis has shown that modern social legislation liberalizes traditional legal concepts that bar or impede ameliorative action and compensation. Traditional common-law concepts have all been exten-

---

[43]*Idaho v. Bunker Hill Co.*, 635 F. Supp. 665 (D. Idaho 1986). The state brought suit under CERCLA and the common law against the present and former owners of a mine for natural resource damage caused by mining wastes. The state contended that a value-based measure of recovery is appropriate under this concept, that is, the value of the natural resources as they exist after the damage or injury has occurred will be subtracted from the value of the resources as they existed prior to the damage (considering all uses, aesthetic value, and economic value). The defendants contended that the measure of recovery is the cost of assessing the damages and the cost of restoration or rehabilitation. *Id.* at 675–676.

The court cited remarks by Senator Simpson during a colloquy with Senator Stafford, chief sponsor of the final Superfund bill. In the judge's paraphrase, "[Senator Simpson] noted that methods of measuring resource damages are in the stage of early development. However, he suggested that traditional tort rules for calculating damages should be observed as appropriate. He commented by way of example that the law awards the difference in value before and after the injury in some cases and where the injury can be restored to its original condition for less than the difference in value, the cost of restoration is the appropriate measure." *Id.* at 676, citing 126 Cong. Rec. 30, 986 (1980). The court concluded that damages could be calculated both ways and that "the calculation which provides the least recovery in terms of dollars is the appropriate measure of damages." *Id.* No other sources for the holding are cited.

Senator Stafford, the Senate's chief Superfund sponsor and floor manager, merely responded to Senator Simpson that damages for injury to natural resources could not be pursued until a restoration plan was developed and that rehabilitation and replacement of natural resources had to be accomplished in the most cost-effective manner possible. Thus he simply did not respond either to Senator Simpson's concern that the statutory definition of natural resources covered "a very broad array of economic and aesthetic values," *Id.*, or to his support for traditional tort recovery.

The wider colloquy between the two senators shows something of the art of Senate legislative history-making. Senator Simpson was attempting to induce Senator Stafford to narrow the scope of Superfund or even deny that Superfund created strict joint and several liability. Senator Simpson was a strong opponent of the bill and dissented from the Senate report, on the grounds that the bill required natural resources to be restored. Senator Stafford did state that the words "strict, joint and several" did not appear in the bill, and that beyond the liability standard in the Clean Water Act § 311, the bill did not embody "other forms of no fault liability or innovative federal intrusion into the law now developing within individual State jurisdiction." *Id.* Senator Stafford had sidestepped the issues. Whatever else this meant, CERCLA has been interpreted to create strict, joint, and several liability. Chancellor Bismarck would have admired Senator Stafford's sausage-making ability.

[44]See Carlson, *Making CERCLA Natural Resource Damage Regulations Work: The Use of the Public Trust Doctrine and Other State Remedies*, 18 Envtl. L. Rep. (Envtl. L. Inst.) 10,299, 10,302 (1988); Atkeson and Dower, *The Unrealized Potential of SARA: Mobilizing New Protection for Natural Resources.* 29 Env't., 6, 8 n.5 (1987).

sively modified or superseded by Superfund. In particular, the natural resource damage provisions abandon the conservative common-law approach mandating damage recovery that is least costly to the defendant.

Further, the provision requiring the government to write regulations that specify damage assessment methods was designed to assist trustees, not arrest their efforts at the threshold by codifying conservative common-law doctrines that favor defendants. These doctrines have forced the courts to dismiss as speculative and insubstantial claims for damages for health, aesthetic, and environmental harms that are widely acknowledged as important today.[45] In Superfund the government was given the task of preparing natural resource damage recovery rules so that its expertise and technical specialization could be brought to bear on the complex task of measuring loss of aesthetic, conservational, recreational, and environmental values. The government's expertise is not needed if the court is merely to apply familiar rules to rather obvious types of injury, such as the deaths of ducks and geese brought about by toxic spills on salt water. It appears that Congress intended the regulations to function like criteria or presumption documents, which would ease the claimant's burden in personal injury cases. Trustees have no need for regulations that are merely declaratory of the common law.

More likely, the rebuttable presumption was placed in the statute specifically in anticipation that the government would adopt regulations that would press well beyond traditional damage awards. The rebuttable presumption facilitates recovery for difficult-to-quantify, difficult-to-characterize injuries that would not be compensated under the traditional common law. Trustees claiming under liberal damage guidelines would need not only the prestige and assistance of government expertise, but also the potent procedural device of shifting the burden of persuasion to the defendant. While DOI's proposed revision accepts the court's interpretation of the state of benefit measurement for natural resources, DOI implicitly maintains the same concern over reliability that presumably motivated its exclusion of nonuse values from the initial set of rules. Now the revision would include nonuse values in the compensable value and admit that contingent valuation methods offer the only way to estimate nonuse values, but classify them in "the least reliable category" of nonmarket valuation methods. Thus, there is a mixed set of assistance offered by the proposed revisions to the type B rules.

An attorney dare not tread into the tribal kingdom of the Econ, particularly to quarrel with the Micro caste.[46] But the temptation is great

---

[45]For a recent example, see *Sterling v. Velsicol Chem. Corp.*, 18 Envtl. L. Rep. (Envtl. L. Inst.) 20,978, 20,985–20,990 (6th Cir. 1988).

[46]Leijonhufvud, *Life Among the Econ*, 9 W. Econ. J. 327 (1973).

to comment on the perception that the rule DOI adopted was generally sound from an economic viewpoint, especially when this opinion is encountered in a law review.[47]

The problem has not so much to do with the conceptual framework—trying to define and capture for the public its lost economic rents; rather, the difficulty is that, as suggested earlier, environmental damage computations and selection of damage assessment methodologies involve great uncertainty. Lost-use value is a difficult concept to define even qualitatively, but it is even more difficult to quantify the lost values. Small resource damage recoveries where the lost resource values are actually very large seem inevitable, because the trustee and court are forced under the guidelines both to ignore existence and option values and to accept tightly circumscribed lost-use values instead of replacement or restoration costs, if they want to apply the rebuttable presumption.

In its draft guidelines, DOI clearly acknowledged this problem and carved out an exception to its general policy limiting recovery to lost-use value when restoration or replacement costs exceeded lost-use value—but this exception was limited to "special resources," that is, resources set aside by statutes (such as wildlife preserves, but not national forests or public lands) that reflect a political judgment that the value of such resources exceeds their measurable use value.[48] DOI dropped the exception from the final guidelines. Later, DOI flatly rejected the approach, but offered to continue to consider it. Perhaps the concept of special resources will be resurrected when DOI issues new guidelines after the *Ohio* decision.

Arguably, Congress had special resources particularly in mind when it enacted the natural resource damage provisions. The uncertainty pervading computation of "soft" lost uses (for example, nonmarket values such as gene pools and bird watching, existence values, and option values) on state and federal wetlands, forests, and public lands suggests two critical changes in DOI's approach to conform it to the purposes of the law. As a result of the *Ohio* court's "gross disproportionality" dictum, the statute can be read to permit restoration or replacement even where economists cannot yet accurately compute the myriad of intangible but very real use values involved in natural resources.

In theory, the cost of replacement or restoration may be astronomical, but DOI itself once proposed an approach, acceptable to courts although untidy to economists, of not allowing restoration costs (greater than lost-use costs) to be recovered even for special resources if the costs would be grossly disproportionate to the benefits gained.[49] Basically,

---

[47]*Developments–Toxic Waste Litigation*, 99 Harv. L. Rev. 1458, 1570–1572.

[48]50 Fed. Reg. 52,154 (1985).

[49]*Developments–Toxic Waste Litigation*, 99 Harv. L. Rev. 1458, 1570 (1986).

therefore, by endorsing "gross disproportionality" analysis, the court adopted a line of reasoning suggested by DOI itself but discarded before the first rules were issued.

7.2   An Approach to Judicial Interpretation. In light of the foregoing, what can be said about how the courts will interpret and apply Superfund's natural resource damage provisions? The statute lodges the ultimate authority to make damage awards in the federal district courts. State and federal trustees enjoy a special status as statutorily designated guardians of resources, and DOI has a large say about which injuries are compensable and how much can be recovered, but in the end the courts must decide. Their decisions ultimately will determine if the Superfund natural resource damage recovery provisions will be a potent remedy or an insignificant satellite of the spill and disposal site programs.

The District of Columbia Circuit Court has already decided essentially that resource damage provisions deserve the same broad interpretation the federal courts have accorded the removal and remedial programs. This chapter has shown that modern remedial and compensatory legislation follows a congressional paradigm that moves far beyond the common law. Despite their historic tendency to construe statutes narrowly when they derogate from the common law, the courts have accepted Congress's objectives and have even supplied missing elements and rationales where Congress acted hastily or indecisively. Superfund is undoubtedly the best recent example.

Liability under Superfund has been held to be strict and joint and several. It is hard to imagine now that the courts would define liability for natural resource damage any more narrowly. Causal requirements under the remedial program have been relaxed to an extent unimaginable in common law. Causation of resource damage is not likely to be more narrowly construed by the courts simply because natural resource injury is involved. To the contrary, one would expect the courts to recognize that establishing the cause of ecological and environmental injury is difficult to accomplish and that cause must be generously inferred if injuries are to be compensated for by their most likely agents.

Under the remedial program, the federal government has wide latitude to specify the remedy to be effectuated virtually without cost constraint. Some site cleanup costs already have reached tens and hundreds of millions of dollars. Yet despite judicial reaffirmation of EPA's plenary authority to obtain the cleanup it wants—even costly, near-perfect restoration—the agency has moved very slowly and has not in practice exerted its full legal authority. Court resources damage awards large enough to permit the return of uses as close as possible to the status quo before the injury seem very likely, subject to a rule of reason and a

$50 million upper bound. EPA would not order responsible parties to clean up the Chesapeake Bay.[50]

Courts also seem likely to agree with the District of Columbia Circuit Court that by making the rebuttable presumption available, Congress wanted to ease the trustee/plaintiff's difficult task of demonstrating environmental damage. The courts are likely to grasp that by conferring guideline-writing authority on DOI, Congress wanted the department to enhance the trustee's chances with the courts by endorsing complex natural resource injury valuation methodologies that otherwise might have been viewed skeptically by a nonscientific court of general jurisdiction. Hence the rebuttable presumption provision and the guideline-writing provision go hand in hand: together they help persuade a court to award full resource damages in situations where the court would otherwise be reluctant to act.

The Department of the Interior's redrafted guidelines will eventually be available for application by trustees and district courts in determining actual resource damages in individual cases. What will happen at this second level? Some courts undoubtedly will apply the departmental guidelines and the rebuttable presumption. Yet if other courts are persuaded that Congress did intend even more liberal damages than the federal guidelines permit, they have the option of accepting the trustees' evidence without the benefit of the rebuttable presumption. If the courts do accept the trustees' arguments, they may award additional damages under the statute.

The difficulty of course is that the trustees must try to succeed without the benefit of the rebuttable presumption. Still, some federal district court judges may resent being tutored by a federal agency on what evidence to accept or reject in a plenary action for damages. Some courts conceivably could accept the broad interpretation given to strict liability, joint and several liability, causation, defenses, and restoration costs by other federal courts under Superfund, but reject narrower approaches to acceptable evidence of resource damages that may be embodied in DOI guidelines. Such courts would proceed to assess independently the trustees' claims in light of Superfund's overall remedial and compensatory policy.

8. CONCLUSION

This chapter suggests that the courts will be sympathetic to the natural resource damage provisions of Superfund. In the end the question for the

---

[50]Superfund establishes a $50 million liability limit per responsible party per release or incident, with certain exceptions. 42 U.S.C. § 9607(c).

future of the natural resource damage provisions in the federal courts may come down to this: will the district courts accept the Department of the Interior's guidance on permissible damage recovery, or will they take an independent tack and fashion their own approach? The courts may conclude that Congress intended larger resource damage awards in particular cases than DOI's guidelines permit.

The rebuttable presumption is available at the election of the trustee. State trustees are free to ignore it and put before the courts methodologies and lost values that DOI has elected to pass over. And is a departmental trustee fulfilling his or her fiduciary duty toward resources if he or she fails to go beyond the employer's guidelines when it appears that a larger recovery can be won? Department of Justice lawyers may soon be faced with the dilemma of whether their obligation as counsel is to plead in the alternative: guidelines and presumption but a lesser claim; no benefit of guidelines and the presumption but a greater claim.

Federal district courts are accustomed to vigorous prosecution of site cleanup cases by EPA and the Department of Justice. They may resolve conflict over resources claims by following the lead already established by courts in the remedial program, by listening carefully to the more enthusiastic state trustees, and by permitting private intervenors to enter cases where the federal trustee seems constrained by overly cautious federal policy. All of these possibilities exist because the thrust of the new federal paradigm for remedial and compensatory legislation authorizes and perhaps even compels the courts to go beyond the strictures of the common law in correcting the unprecedented environmental problems facing modern society.

Admittedly, if courts strike out on their own, they may have to hear the arguments not only from biologists and engineers about restoration or replacement of a damaged resource, but also from economists about how certain difficult-to-quantify use and nonuse values will be measured despite DOI's description of contingent valuation methods. This will involve more work for already overburdened federal district court judges. Some judges may prefer to let DOI do the thinking for them, partly to save time, partly to shorten technical presentations, and partly to honor the intent of Congress that the Department of the Interior play a role. But federal judges are a bright group, the type of individuals who would enjoy the challenging philosophical and policy issues bound up in valuing vistas, songbirds, endangered species habitat, and ecosystem stability. Many would be quite interested to hear what economists have to say in their courtrooms.

4
Uncertain Legal Issues: Comments on Chapter 3

Howard Kenison

1. INTRODUCTION

Will courts render broad opinions construing Superfund's natural resource damage provisions, consistent with the past decade's liberal judicial interpretations of the cost-recovery provisions? Frederick R. Anderson believes they will. In chapter 3 of this volume he argues that courts "seem likely to give the natural resource damages provisions a broad reading, consistent with the sweeping powers that the courts have conferred upon the federal government . . ." He further argues that the legislative history of Superfund—the Comprehensive Environmental Response, Compensation, and Liability Act of 1980 (CERCLA)[1]—the aggressive enforcement requirements imposed on the federal government by the Superfund Amendments and Reauthorization Act of 1986 (SARA),[2] an arsenal of legal weapons given to government enforcers, and the legal precedent already established by courts under Superfund's cost-recovery provisions lead inexorably to this conclusion.[3]

Anderson is correct that as a matter of public policy Congress probably intended that cleanup of hazardous waste sites, for which it showed strong preference, should be followed by assessment and recovery of natural resources. However, it is uncertain that recovery of natural resource damages can be pursued by resource trustees as successfully as Superfund cost-recovery actions are by federal and state enforcement

[1]42 U.S.C. 9601–9675.

[2]42 U.S.C. 9601–9675.

[3]Superfund's cost-recovery provisions are found in CERCLA § 107(a)(1–4)(A) and (B); the natural resource damage provisions are in CERCLA § 107(a)(1–4)(C). The statutory schemes for recovery of costs and damage differ.

agencies. Court decisions subsequent to the writing of Anderson's chapter lead us to the conclusion that in natural resource damage actions, unlike cost-recovery actions, a causal link between the release and the resource's injury must be established, and that courts are imposing a higher standard of proof for natural resource damage actions. This likely will make natural resource damages more difficult to pursue and prove. The causation requirement together with complex economic theories for measuring damages, the public's desire for cleanup, and political issues may make enforcement of natural resource damage actions a secondary choice of Superfund enforcers.

2. DISCUSSION

There are several reasons why federal and state resource trustees may find the courts less inviting for enforcement of natural resource damage actions than for prosecution of cost-recovery cases. They include legal uncertainties, political and practical realities, and strategic enforcement decisions. CERCLA gives resource trustees compelling powers, but it will take creative enforcement, judicial resolution of uncertainties, adequate funding, and a concerted expression of political will by state and federal trustees to achieve the goals of Congress.

2.1 Superfund's Health-Based Goals. A review of reported CERCLA cases and settlements makes clear that government enforcers have not given the same attention to restoration, rehabilitation, and replacement of injured natural resources as they have to cost-recovery efforts. The fundamental reason can be found in Congress' goals for Superfund—namely, that protection of public health and remediation of hazardous substance releases are CERCLA's paramount objectives.[4]

There is considerable public support for Superfund site cleanup. This provides a solid political base for government regulators to pursue site cleanups. Effective government efforts to remediate hazardous waste sites alleviate the public's primary fear—the threat to health and physical safety from a neighborhood toxic waste site. For example, contaminated drinking water in a residential neighborhood bordering a chemical facility will cause immediate public reaction and pressure for government action. However, that same neighborhood can be mollified if clean drinking water

---

[4]U.S. Congress. House. Committee on Interstate and Foreign Commerce. 1980. *Environmental Response Act* (to accompany H.R.7020). H.R. Rep. No. 96-1016, 96 Cong. 2d sess., reprinted in *U.S. Code Congressional and Administrative News*, 1980, vol. 5, pp. 6119–6125.

is provided. It is likely that resource trustees would not feel the same public pressure to recover damages for the injured natural resource—the groundwater aquifer.

Superfund's natural resource damage provisions codify an important but abstract common-law principle: that the nation's natural resources are in the public domain and as such are held "in trust" for all citizens and all generations. Recovering damages for injury to the nation's natural resources requires resource trustees to have a commitment to, and to clearly communicate, the long-term cross-generational benefits of the public trust doctrine. Public support for recovery of natural resource damages might be difficult to maintain after an immediate health threat has been removed.

Environmental enforcement agencies may be as confounded as the public by the complex conceptual nature of resource damages and be less willing to tackle these concepts in court. Also, once site remedies are achieved, especially if the remedial action plan would in effect restore injured natural resources, there may be less incentive for government attorneys and trustees to prosecute resource damage actions. In practice, many environmental enforcers may view the natural resource damage provisions as a strategic bargaining chip by which to obtain more effective remedies. As Anderson states, natural resource damages are often "tacked on" to Superfund cost-recovery actions.

2.2   Legal Uncertainties. Resource trustees must also overcome several legal requirements not encountered in cost-recovery actions. Litigation to define the scope and extent of the natural resource damage provisions is in an embryonic stage—similar to the cost-recovery litigation of the mid-1980s. Many issues have yet to be resolved. However, trends are now emerging that point to less judicial "activism" in natural resource damage actions.

2.2.1   Causation. Anderson states that "causation of resource damage is not likely to be more narrowly construed by the courts simply because natural resource injury is involved. To the contrary, one would expect the courts to recognize that establishing the cause of ecological and environmental injury is difficult to accomplish and that cause must be generously inferred if injuries are to be compensated for by their most likely agents."

However, Section 107(a)(4)(C) of CERCLA states that a responsible party shall be liable for "damages for injury to, destruction of, or loss of natural resources, including the reasonable costs of assessing such injury, destruction, or loss *resulting from* such a release" (emphasis added). The language in Superfund's cost-recovery liability provision does not contain a similar causal element of proof. Under the cost-recovery section, a state or the United States recovers *"all costs* of remedial or removal action incurred" (emphasis added). The courts have interpreted this to mean that responsible parties are strictly liable for response costs without regard to fault *or* causal links:[5] "A literal reading of the statute [42 USC § 9607(a)(1–4)(B)] imposes liability if releases or threatened releases from [a responsible party's] facility *cause the plaintiff to incur response costs;* it does not say that liability is imposed only if the [responsible party] causes actual contamination of the plaintiff's property" (emphasis added).[6] Thus, the government need only show that it incurred costs when responding to a release of a hazardous substance in order to impose liability on a potentially responsible party (PRP). No link between a particular PRP's release of a hazardous substance and the injury to the environment need be shown.

However, the "resulting from" language requires a resource trustee to show that actual damage occurred, *and* that the damage to the resource *resulted from* the PRP's release of a hazardous substance into the environment. Thus resource trustees must establish a causal and factual link between the injury, destruction or loss of natural resources, and the release of a hazardous substance. As a further indication that Congress intended a less expansive basis for recovery, for "threatened releases" of hazardous substances the government (and private parties) may recover only the response costs incurred.[7] Recovery of natural resource damages is limited to actual releases of hazardous substances.

In fact, courts faced with the issue of causation in natural resource damage cases have held that there must be a causal link between the actions of a responsible party and the damage. In *State of Idaho v. Bunker Hill Company*,[8] the court found that to recover under Superfund's natural resource damage provisions, the damages must be tied to the defendant's release. Because there is "admittedly strict liability" under CERCLA, the state's attorneys argued, there was no need for causation in a resource damage case. The *Bunker Hill* court disagreed: "Strict liability does not abrogate the necessity of showing causation. . . . the damage for which recovery is sought must still be causally linked to the act of the defen-

---

5See *Violet v. Picillo*, 648 F. Supp. 1283 (D.R.I. 1986); *United States v. Chem-Dyne Corp.*, 572 F. Supp. 802 (S.D. Ohio 1983); *City of Philadelphia v. Stepan Chemical Co.*, 544 F. Supp. 1135 (E.D. Pa 1982).

6*Dedham Water Company v. Cumberland Farms Dairy, Inc.* 889 F.2d 1146 (1st Cir. 1989) at 1152.

7The phrase "from which there is a release *or* threatened release which causes the incurrence of response costs, of a hazardous substance," (modifying paragraphs [1]–[4] of CERCLA § 107[a]) limits liability for threatened releases solely to response costs. See *Dedham*, footnote 4, p. 1151, for an excellent explanation of a "printer's error" in the placement of this phrase.

8635 F. Supp. 665 (D. Idaho 1986).

dant."[9] The court further noted that the word "resulted" ties the damages to the releases and concluded that "[t]he proof must include a causal link between releases and post-enactment damages which flowed therefrom."[10]

The requisite causal link in natural resource damage actions was also addressed by the court in *Dedham Water Company v. Cumberland Farms Dairy, Inc.* The court, in a footnote, contrasted the private cost-recovery and resource damage causation requirements by stating that "the statutory requirements are clearly distinct. In the former situation [a natural resource damage claim] there must be a connection between the [responsible party] and the damages to natural resources; in the latter situation [a private cost recovery] there must be a connection between the defendant and the *response costs* (and no mention is made of any damages at all)" (emphasis added).[11] When undertaking to recover damages for injury to natural resources, government trustees have a statutory limitation that has been judicially supported. The early judicial trend is toward more restrictive causation requirements for damage cases than for cost-recovery actions.

2.2.2 Burden of Proof. The "not inconsistent with" language in the National Contingency Plan (NCP), in CERCLA's Section 107(a)(1–4)(A), has been judicially interpreted to mean that potentially responsible parties in a cost-recovery action bear the burden of proving, on the administrative record, that the government's remedy selection was arbitrary and capricious.[12] The government must present a prima facie case of its consistency with the NCP, but need not affirmatively show that it acted properly unless challenged.[13] SARA Section 113(j)(2) codifies this early judicial interpretation, providing that the "objecting party must demonstrate on the record that the decision was arbitrary and capricious." The natural resource damage provision of Superfund does not contain similar language and SARA did not address the question of which party in a natural resource damage action bears the burden of proof.

It is arguable that the phrase "resulting from" places the burden of proof in a natural resource damage action squarely on the resource trustee. Of course, if a trustee follows the Department of the Interior (DOI) regulations, the trustee gains a rebuttable presumption that operates, as a practical matter, to shift the burden of proof to the defendants. However,

---

[9]Ibid.

[10]Ibid.

[11]889 F.2d 1146, 1154 (footnote 7) (1st Cir. 1989).

[12]See *City of Philadelphia v. Stepan Chemical Co.*

[13]See *U.S. v. Hardage,* 733 F. Supp. 1424 (W.D. Okla. 1989).

in light of the potentially restrictive damage measures in the DOI rules, many state trustees may choose not to follow the rules and will forgo the presumption. These state trustees will presumably bear the burden of proof.

2.2.3 Standard of Proof. In addition to providing direction regarding causation, the courts have recently addressed the standard of proof in natural resource damage cases. In *U.S. v. Montrose Chemical Corp.,*[14] the court dismissed the government's complaint for failing to show that the defendants' release was the sole or a *"substantially* contributing factor" in damaging natural resources. An amended complaint has been filed. Another federal court has stated that the government meets its burden of proof if it can establish that the defendant's release was merely a "contributing factor" to injury of natural resources.[15] There is obviously a difference in the standards of proof established by these court decisions. It is uncertain whether the appellate courts will adopt the substantial standard or the less restrictive standard. Thus resource trustees are confronted with a legal uncertainty and another requirement that may reduce their ability to prosecute natural resource damage cases.

2.2.4 Evidence. Another legal uncertainty is whether certain economic valuation methodologies, especially those that determine nonuse values (a key element in the measurement of natural resource damages), will be admissible in court. Defendants will undoubtedly argue that nonuse value methods and results, especially those based on opinion surveys, are highly speculative. One federal court denied a defendant's pretrial motion to limit or deny admission of an opinion survey. The court held that the defendant's concerns went to the credibility of the evidence, not to its admissibility. However, the court denied the motion without prejudice, leaving the defendant PRP the opportunity to renew its objection to admissibility at trial.[16] Since there are no reported trials of a natural resource damage case, it will be some time before there are rulings on the admissibility of the methodologies for measurement of damages.

This uncertainty works to the disadvantage of responsible parties as well as resource trustees. Multimillion-dollar damage assessments, using the most liberal assessment methodologies, may be a strategic weapon for resource trustees to negotiate for more effective, higher-cost remedies or to achieve negotiated pretrial consent decrees for damages. Potentially

---

[14]*U.S. v. Montrose Chemical Corp.,* DC Calif., No. CV90-3122-AAH.

[15]*In re Acushnet River & New Bedford Harbor.* 722 F. Supp. 893, 897 (D. Mass 1989).

[16]*Colorado v. Gulf & Western,* U.S. District Court, Colorado, Civil Action No. 83-C-2387.

responsible parties may be unwilling to risk admissibility of multimillion-dollar assessments, preferring instead to resolve natural resource damages out of court. Of course, if this results in earlier "restoration" of injured natural resources, Congress' policy goals will be met.

2.2.5 Bifurcation. Natural resource damages are "residual" to cost-recovery actions.[17] As discussed above, cost-recovery actions and natural resource damage actions differ in terms of causation standards and other legal requirements.[18] Thus, courts have chosen to bifurcate remedy and damage actions.[19] Resource damage trials will follow the remedy trial. The practical effect may be to increase the focus on remedy actions and decrease the effect of natural resource damages as an enforcement threat.

2.2.6 Public and Private Interest. CERCLA provides that liability for natural resource damages "shall be to the United States Government and to any State for natural resources within the State or belonging to, managed by, controlled by, or appertaining to such State."[20] CERCLA defines "natural resources" to be those resources "belonging to, managed by, held in trust by, appertaining to, or otherwise controlled by the United States . . . or any State."[21]

In pretrial arguments, one state—Colorado—has argued that these provisions establish a public interest in all natural resources "within the State."[22] The defendants countered by arguing that the state must own (or directly control or maintain) the natural resources before a cause of action arises for the state. The issue was left unresolved when the parties reached a negotiated settlement.[23]

Colorado reasoned that there is an underlying *public interest* in all natural resources regardless of whether the resource is publicly or privately owned, and therefore a government resource trust may recover damages if this public interest is injured. For example, assume that the state owns a piece of land. If the land is injured by the release of a

---

[17]"Department of the Interior's Proposed Natural Resource Damage Assessments," 56 *Federal Register* 19752 (April 29, 1991).

[18]*Dedham Water Company v. Cumberland Farms Dairy, Inc.*

[19]See *State of Colorado v. Idarado Mining Co.*, 707 F. Supp. 1227 (D. Colo. 1989).

[20]42 U.S.C. 9607(f)(1)(a).

[21]Ibid.

[22]Plaintiff's Reply Brief on the Issue of the State's Role as Public Trustee, *State of Colorado v. Cotter Corp.*, U.S. District Court, Colorado, 83-C-2389, filed May 22, 1986. See also Supplemental Brief of Cotter Corporation pursuant to Order of Court dated Feb. 3, 1986, *Colorado v. Cotter Corp.*, filed April 10, 1986.

[23]Final Consent Decree, Order, Judgement and Reference to a Special Matter, *State of Colorado v. Cotter Corp.*, U.S. District Court, Colorado, Civil Action No. 83-C-2389. Approved by the court, April 4, 1988.

hazardous substance, the state resource trustee clearly has a cause of action to recover damages under Superfund.[24]

Colorado went further, arguing that there may be an underlying public interest for which damages may be recovered in a privately owned resource. For example, assume that a privately owned wetland is injured by the release of a hazardous substance. The wetland's contribution to the local and regional ecosystem is arguably a public interest damaged by the release. The wetland may have provided services such as wildlife habitat, recharge to groundwater aquifers, or support to biota and aquatic life. The injury to the public interest may also include the government's inability to use (by zoning) the wetland as open space, the lost visual amenity associated with the wetland, and any lost recreational use. Colorado's resource trustees maintained that if this underlying public interest in a privately owned resource is injured, lost, or destroyed, it is compensable under Superfund.

While public interest in privately owned property may be difficult to define and damage troublesome to measure, natural resource economic theories and common-law public trust concepts as codified in Superfund may provide a theoretical basis to argue for recovery of damages to a public interest in privately owned natural resources.

2.2.7 Other Issues. Further, the statute states that no damages can be recovered "where the damages and the release of a hazardous substance from which such damage resulted have occurred wholly before December 11, 1980."[25] The court in *Bunker Hill* found that both the release and the resulting damage had to have occurred prior to enactment of CERCLA for this statutory bar to apply.[26] If the release and resultant damage occurred after enactment, the bar does not apply. And if the release occurred prior to enactment, but the resultant damage occurred after enactment, recovery is not barred by Section 107(f).[27] The court in *In re Acushnet River & New Bedford Harbor* found that in cases where natural resource damages are indivisible and damages *and* releases that caused the damages occur after enactment, plaintiffs can recover for nondivisible damages in their entirety. However, damages incurred prior to enactment are barred. Additional damages after enactment may be recovered.[28]

---

[24]Kenison, H., C. L. Buchholz, and S. P. Mulligan. 1987. "State Actions for Natural Resources Damages: Enforcement of the Public Trust," *Environmental Law Reporter* 17 (November): pp. 10434, 10439.

[25]CERCLA § 107(f).

[26]*Bunker Hill*, p. 674.

[27]Ibid., p. 675.

[28]*In re Acushnet*, p. 686.

2.3   Department of the Interior Regulations. The Department of the Interior's regulations governing natural resource damage assessments were originally promulgated in 1986.[29] Several states challenged the regulations as limiting the ability of trustees to collect for injury to natural resources.[30] The DOI regulations "manage[d] a very difficult and complex task by simplification and arbitrary limitation" and would have biased damage assessments downward.[31]

The states challenged major provisions of the regulations, such as the limited definition of injury, the restrictive damage measurement requirements (for example, limiting recovery to committed and public uses and allowing consideration of nonuse or intrinsic values only as a substitute for use values), and the arbitrary preference of damage measurement methods. It was argued that strict compliance with the DOI regulations would not have protected "the natural resources trust corpus."[32]

DOI's revisions to the regulations in conformance with court order were issued on April 29, 1991. The revisions "*just* implement the court decision" (emphasis added).[33] DOI intends to wait for public comment— and possibly more court orders—to make further revisions to the regulations.

The revisions allow a trustee to recover "the value of the services lost to the public until the lost services are returned to baseline levels."[34] Direct and indirect costs are included under restoration costs and are as broadly defined as direct and indirect costs allowed the government in cost-recovery actions.[35]

Computation of use and nonuse values falls under DOI's revised definition of "compensable value." The term is meant to "encompass all of the public economic values associated with an injured resource, including use values and nonuse values such as option, existence and bequest values."[36] Nonuse values are defined as "the difference between compensable value and use value."[37] The revisions also delete the economic valuation hierarchy and permit a trustee to choose among or use a combination of economic methodologies.

---

[29]43 C.F.R. § 11 (1986).

[30]*Ohio v. United States Department of the Interior,* 880 F.2d 432 (D.C. Cir. 1989); *Colorado v. the Department of the Interior,* 880 F.2d 481 (D.C. Cir. 1989).

[31]Kenison, Buchholz, and Mulligan, "State Actions for Natural Resources Damages."

[32]Ibid., p. 10439.

[33]56 *Federal Register* 19753 (April 29, 1991).

[34]Ibid.

[35]Ibid., p. 19758.

[36]Ibid., p. 19759.

[37]Ibid.

As Anderson notes, the revised guidelines will eventually be available for application in natural resources damage actions. Federal court judges will likely have an opportunity to hear considerable evidence in the field of natural resource economics. If DOI's regulations are followed, they may, as Anderson points out, become scientific evidence "primers" for the courts. State trustees will accept the new assessment regulations if use of the assessment rules does not limit the recovery for injured resources or bias the results downward. Application of the regulations' procedures and economic valuation methodologies to an injured public resource will be the ultimate test of their acceptability to state trustees. Federal trustees, of course, are required to use the regulations. It will, as a practical matter, be state application that determines whether Congress' broad intent is met.

2.4 Political Considerations. In addition to legal uncertainties, there are political considerations that may affect resource trustees' actions. States have been slow in appointing state trustees as required by SARA. Colorado, for example, has recently appointed a board of resource trustees. The board is comprised of the executive directors of the state departments of health and natural resources and the state attorney general. The effectiveness of the board approach remains to be seen. Where, as in Colorado, the board members are from opposing political parties and have markedly different public constituencies, the result may be enforcement paralysis or compromised restoration settlements.

In Colorado, the funds used to prosecute several state natural resource damage cases were appropriated from the state's General Fund. However, for political and state fiscal reasons, the appropriating statute declared that any funds recovered by the state acting as trustee for natural resources were to be placed in a "CERCLA Recovery Fund." This fund was then available for "any lawful purpose" of the state legislature, including (for example) education or highways.[38] This state legislative assertion of fiscal authority raises a key issue of federal preemption under Superfund. For example, when a state has appropriated money from its general funds to prosecute under a natural resource damage case and uses the federal Superfund as its cause of action, is it bound by the "restoration, replacement, and rehabilitation" requirements if damages are recovered? The DOI regulations say that recovered damages must be used for restoration, replacement, or rehabilitation. Can the recovered damages be used to fund resource assessments and litigation at other sites with injured natural resources?

---

[38]Colorado Revised Statutes § 25-16-104.6.

5

Economics of Natural Resource Damage Assessment: A Critique

Gardner M. Brown, Jr.

1. INTRODUCTION

Natural resource damage assessment is a joint product of law and economics. The economic content of the Comprehensive Environmental Response, Compensation, and Liability Act of 1980 (CERCLA) would be different if the law prior to 1980 had been different. Existing law, not to mention political considerations, constrains the design of economic procedures.

What status should legal constraints have in evaluating the resulting economic policies, particularly if the law rules out efficient, first-best policies or procedures? This is an age-old problem for social scientists. While acknowledging here the exogeneity of the law, for the most part I criticize the damage assessment procedures, assuming that in the fullness of time, good economics will triumph. If nothing else, this perspective gives the rulemaker something to shoot for.

The damage assessment procedures under consideration in this chapter are largely those put forth by the Department of the Interior (DOI) in August 1986, hereafter referred to simply as the DOI rules.[1] Because rulemaking is an evolving process, challenges to these rules have required some revisions to the rules. I will incorporate in my discussion some comments on the implications of the April 29, 1991, proposed revisions to the rules. The rules are intended to specify procedures for both the scientific quantification of injury to a natural resource (that is, physical alterations in the resource due to the release of hazardous substances or oil)

Willie Taylor, an economist at the Department of the Interior responsible for interpreting damage assessment procedures, helped the author to better understand the rules guiding those procedures. However, any misinterpretations are the author's responsibility.

[1]Type A rules are specified in 52 *Federal Register* 9042 (March 20, 1987). Type B rules are specified in 51 *Federal Register* 27674 (August 1, 1986).

and the quantification of damage to the resource (monetization of the value lost as a result of injury). In this chapter I focus attention on the rules that provide guidance for the quantification of damage.

Although evaluation of damage assessment procedures is the main task of this chapter, there is also some discussion of the Environmental Protection Agency's (EPA) mandated role in the CERCLA cleanup process; that role is to protect health, welfare, and the environment at hazardous waste sites.[2] Damage assessment procedures under CERCLA are implemented after EPA has specified the cleanup liability at a site. To the degree that cleanup occurs in a timely fashion and remedies remove all injury to the resource, the scope for residual natural resource damage is reduced. How substantial the remedies should be depends on EPA's estimate of the impact of the injury on the citizenry. EPA establishes criteria for cleanup based on assessments of risk to human health and other activities. The procedures for implementing the risk analysis require making a string of assumptions, many of which greatly magnify the implied risk compared to the risk found under alternative assumptions made in similar settings. Increased cleanup liability and decreased residual natural resource damage follow from higher estimates of risk. Because of this interdependence, risk analysis and EPA's policies and procedures can often establish the domain of damage assessment. Thus, these decisions establish the extent of the problem as a residual liability to be evaluated with a natural resource damage assessment.

Damage assessment is controlled either by type A or type B rules. Type A rules are greatly simplified and are used for small losses. Type B rules are more comprehensive and are designed for the economically most important incidents. Procedures based on type B rules receive the most attention in this chapter. The damage assessment procedures are described in section 2 of the chapter, and are followed in section 3 by a critical evaluation of selected features. Two recent court decisions, *Ohio v. The United States Department of the Interior* and *Acushnet River & New Bedford Harbor*,[3] along with DOI's response, will change the way damage assessments are conducted; these modifications are discussed and evaluated where appropriate. Conclusions are presented in section 4.

Readers may find the following guide to the subsections of the critical evaluation (section 3) of use. Section 3.1 attempts to show that the

---

[2]Comprehensive Environmental Response, Compensation, and Liability Act of 1980, 42 U.S.C. 9601–9675.

[3]*Ohio v. United States Department of the Interior*, 880 F.2d 432, (D.C. Cir. 1989), hereafter cited as *Ohio*; U.S. District Court, District of Massachusetts, *Acushnet River & New Bedford Harbor: Proceedings Re Alleged PCB Pollution*, No. 83-3882-y, "Memorandum Concerning Natural Resource Damages Under CERCLA," District Judge Young, June 1989, hereafter cited as *New Bedford*.

major flaw in the economics of public hazardous waste management occurs in the Superfund response. This charge has been diluted, however, because the *Ohio* case gives primacy to the use of replacement cost as the monetary measure of economic damage, as discussed in section 3.3.

Individual citizens who have suffered damage or loss through release of hazardous substances seek private remedies in civil suits. Since CERCLA legislation covers public losses, the law must distinguish between private and public loss. However, from an anthropocentric perspective all economic loss can be seen as change in the utility experienced by private individuals. Section 3.2 discusses how the law has still not correctly understood the private-public distinction.

The DOI rulemakers encountered difficulties trying to define a hierarchy of valuation methods and a hierarchy of types of damages based on use and nonuse values. These are discussed in sections 3.4 and 3.5, respectively.

Under CERCLA, injury refers to the physical or natural manifestation (impact) of a hazardous waste or oil spill on the environment. Damage is the monetary value of injury. Economic loss depends on how individuals respond to and perceive changes in their environment. Natural scientists have been trained to identify physical injuries, but there is no reason why private individuals should see the world or interpret phenomena in the manner of scientists. When a discrepancy between scientific and private perception arises, as it has, society bears economic loss, as discussed in section 3.6. The loss arises because the law has omitted the perceived injury associated with the economic loss.

Problems with a poor choice of discount rates (discount rates affect the total present value of loss) are discussed in section 3.7. Restricted views of future use (loss) and past losses are treated in section 3.8. Past damages and indivisibility of damages are considered in section 3.9, and bias against private land purchases in section 3.10.

2. REMEDIAL INVESTIGATION AND DAMAGE ASSESSMENT

2.1 Superfund Response Policy. Natural resource damage assessment can be understood well only if it is placed within the CERCLA process. Damage assessment is the final chapter of CERCLA, written by a different author than earlier chapters, or so the economic tone and intent would suggest. The practical importance of damage assessment depends on quite separate activities, which largely have preceded the damage assessment in time.[4] The agencies or trustees responsible for the damage assessment differ

---

[4]A good summary of the CERCLA process and how natural resource damages are measured may be found in Desvousges, Dunford, and Domanico (1989).

from and do not legally impinge on the agencies and entities making cleanup response decisions that profoundly affect hazardous waste sites. EPA is responsible for designing cleanup procedures and seeing that response actions are taken to protect health, welfare, and the environment. The trustee of each natural resource is responsible for damage assessment. EPA may inform the trustee, who assesses the damage while EPA conducts the remedial investigation.[5] However, the procedures for assessing damages follow after and are partly dependent on the choices of alternative remedial measures EPA has promulgated. The remedial activities undertaken can in large measure determine the size of the damage estimates. Only damages net of remedy are relevant. Thus, the importance of damage assessment depends inversely on the comprehensiveness of the removal and remedial programs adopted and on how they affect the resource's ability to provide services equivalent to those available in the prerelease baseline state. These programs are likely to be quite comprehensive.[6]

Economists will find the language in the Superfund Amendments and Reauthorization Act of 1986 (SARA) very instructive. Whenever there is a substantial threat "or actual release of any hazardous substance," EPA must design a removal and remedial program that protects "the public health or welfare or the environment" (SARA, § 9604[a]). EPA does this by conducting a remedial investigation and feasibility study, which the cognoscenti know as an RI/FS. Interim remedial activities can be and usually are undertaken during the investigation if they will be useful in preventing further degradation of the site. The intention behind the RI/FS is to ensure that remedial actions meet any legally applicable or relevant and appropriate requirements (ARARs) at the state or national level.[7]

Alternative responses developed in the remedial investigation and feasibility studies are evaluated in terms of three guiding criteria: effectiveness in achieving protection; implementability, including technical feasibility; and cost (EPA [1987]). What these criteria imply and the

---

[5]The Superfund Amendments and Reauthorization Act of 1986 (SARA) (42 U.S.C. 9601–9675) also requires coordination with and notification of trustees as part of any negotiations with potentially responsible parties for the costs of cleanup in the event those negotiations would affect liability for natural resource damages.

[6]It is important to note that natural resource damage assessments under CERCLA may take place at sites that are not designated Superfund sites. Examples include New Bedford Harbor outside of Boston and San Pedro Bay in Los Angeles. Both sites have suffered polychlorinated biphenyl (PCB) contamination and are the object of suits under CERCLA, but they are not Superfund sites.

[7]See SARA § 9621. Among the statutes that must be satisfied are the Clean Air Act (42 U.S.C.A. § 7410), the Clean Water Act (33 U.S.C.A. § 1251 et seq.), the Solid Waste Disposal Act (15 U.S.C.A. § 2601 et seq.), the Toxic Substances Control Act, and the Safe Drinking Water Act (42 U.S.C.A. § 300f et seq.).

tradeoffs among them are discussed more precisely in section 3.1 of the chapter. Generally, SARA instructs EPA to rank remedies more highly if they reduce toxicity, mobility, or volume than if they merely prevent exposure. Removal and incineration of material therefore rank higher than capping hazardous material at a site. SARA instructs EPA to prefer permanent solutions "to the maximum extent possible" (EPA [1986]).

If there are no ARARs, a preliminary goal for dealing with carcinogens is to reduce the extra risk to between 1 in 10 million (1×10^{-7}) and 1 in 10 thousand (1×10^{-4}). Reducing risk to 1×10^{-6} might be regarded as a focal point since the instruction for conducting an RI/FS requires one alternative response designed to treat all groundwater and soil to the 1×10^{-6} level. Of all the remedial alternatives that protect health, welfare, and the environment and that are implementable and permanent solutions, EPA should choose the one that is most cost-effective (SARA § 9621).

2.2   The Damage Assessment Process. A natural resource damage assessment begins when the agency or agencies identified as the trustee for a natural resource are informed that hazardous wastes may have injured the natural resource.

2.2.1   Type A Assessment, for Small Losses. If the injuries are relatively moderate, a set of simplified procedures—type A rules—can be used in coastal or marine environments. Investigators obtain a damage estimate by submitting incident-specific data, requiring minimum field observation, to a computer model that has physical, biological, and economic components.[8] Thomas Grigalunas and James Opaluch wrote and have described the economic features of the computer model. The submodel for economic damages produces estimates based on reduced in situ use values (Grigalunas and Opaluch [1987]). The simplified approach to damage assessment is motivated by the sensible desire to keep the expenses of investigation under the cost of damages of an event. This reasonable criterion has not been met in some cases. In one such example approximately $1.6 million was spent investigating the losses from the oil spill from the *ARCO Merchant* off the coast of Massachusetts in 1976, but little economic damage was discovered (Grigalunas and Opaluch [1987]).[9] More recently, the Washington State Department of Ecology spent ap-

---

[8]The regulations for type A assessments are available in 52 *Federal Register* 9042 (March 20, 1987).

[9]CERCLA and SARA do not provide liability for oil spills, only for releases of hazardous substances. Oil is not categorized as hazardous. The legislation is important for oil spills, however, because language in CERCLA directs the president to promulgate rules for the assessment of damage to natural resources resulting from the release of hazardous substances *or* oil. These rules are the DOI rules.

proximately $240,000 studying the oil spill from the *ARCO Anchorage* off the coast of Washington on December 21, 1985, to determine $32,930.03 worth of damages (WDOE [1987], p. 93).

While there may be many instances for which the type A regulations are useful, larger oil spills or releases of hazardous waste have a greater economic impact, and require the more substantial type B assessment, to which we now turn.

2.2.2   Type B Assessment, for Larger Losses.   When the discovery of an oil spill or hazardous waste release creates an immediate threat to health, welfare, or the environment, the federal and/or state trustee, acting as if it is the owner of the affected natural resource, determines the nature and extent of the natural resource injury by following the DOI rules.[10] An injury to a natural resource is defined by physical or biological researchers in terms of physical or biological phenomena.[11] Defining resource injury in this manner is critical, as we shall see in the evaluation portion (section 3) of this chapter. During the course of quantifying the injury to natural resources, researchers are required to establish baseline conditions. These are the qualities and quantities of natural resources that would have existed in the past or in the future had there not been any oil spill or hazardous release, given both natural processes and human activities.[12]

A trustee develops a natural resource damage assessment plan ensuring that damages can be estimated at a reasonable cost.[13] Plans are reviewed and revised if warranted. During the actual assessment of damages, a trustee, following the DOI rules, would choose the smallest cost produced by the three methods identified in the rules for developing monetary measures of damages—the restoration cost, replacement cost, and diminished use value methods.[14] The ruling in *Ohio* on challenges to the DOI rules has changed this protocol. This ruling argues that the Department of the Interior misunderstood the intent of Congress in specifying a "lesser-of" rule for measuring damages. Such a mandate runs against the statutory grain to prevent recovery by trustees of the full cost of restoration unless restoration is not feasible or "the cost is grossly

---

[10]51 *Federal Register* 27734, § 11.61 (August 1, 1986).

[11]51 *Federal Register* 27734–780, § 1162 (August 1, 1986).

[12]51 *Federal Register* 27744–747, § 11.72 (August 1, 1986). While CERCLA instructs the president to promulgate rules for natural resource damage assessment, the law does not require the trustee of the injured resource to follow the rules. However, if the rules are followed, the injury and damage estimates presented by the trustee carry the force of rebuttable presumption. The nature and advantage of rebuttable presumption is discussed by Frederick R. Anderson in chapter 3 in this volume.

[13]51 *Federal Register* 27702, § 11.30(c) (August 1, 1986).

[14]51 *Federal Register* 27750–751, § 1184(g) (August 1, 1986).

disproportionate to use value." Future case law will determine what the crucial term "disproportionate" means, but some guidance may have been provided by footnote material in *Ohio* in which the ruling suggests that the costs of restoration might be limited to three times the amount of use value.[15] As in traditional benefit-cost analysis, restoration options must not be technically inferior. Options must be cost-effective, achieving a given level of restoration at the least cost (measured in terms of present value).[16] Naturally, restoration alternatives must be legally acceptable at the federal and state level.[17]

The Department of the Interior's proposed revision to the type B rules eschews any numerical definition of "grossly disproportionate" in comparing restoration costs with the benefits from any proposed restoration/replacement plan. The rules now call for multifaceted criteria including technical feasibility, relationship of costs to benefits, cost-effectiveness, results of actual or planned response actions, potential for further injury from any proposed actions, time for natural recovery, ability of the resource to recover without intervention, ability to acquire replacement land, and consistency with federal laws.

Under the new proposed DOI rules, damages are equal to the estimated loss in consumer's and producer's surplus from a decrease in use, as well as in any nonuse value due to injury to the services of natural resources.[18] Some of this loss might be loss of fees or loss of economic rent accruing to a private individual because the public owner of the resource did not charge for use.

The proposed revisions to the rules recognize a resource's services as "all of the functions performed by that resource for and/or to the public and to other resources and the interactions between them" (p. 19757). Moreover, passive and nonconsumptive functions are recognized. With this *Ohio*-mandated recognition of the services underlying nonuse values, DOI has defined the relevant valuation concept as compensable values, to include "all of the public economic

---

[15]See *Ohio*, footnote 7.

[16]51 *Federal Register* 27749, § 11.82(f) (August 1, 1986).

[17]See Kopp, Portney, and Smith (1989) for a discussion of the *Ohio* decision and an interpretation of the court's ruling regarding the "lesser-of" concept.

[18]51 *Federal Register* 27749–750, § 11.83(b) (August 1, 1986). A useful way for non-economists to understand consumer's surplus is to identify it with getting a bargain. It is the extra value one gets "above" the price paid. Producer's surplus has a similar meaning. It is the extra value a producer gets when selling a product for more than the cost of production plus a normal profit.

Damage theoretically exists when the unit value of use falls but the quantity demanded remains unchanged. This possibility occurs when there is complete unresponsiveness of the supply of quality or quantity of services due to a natural resource injury.

values associated with an injured resource, including use values and nonuse values such as option, existence and bequest values."[19] Use values are defined as "values to the public of recreational or other *public* uses of the resource" (emphasis added)[20]—language that confuses economists.

2.2.2.1   Market and nonmarket procedures. Originally, the Department of the Interior established two sets of valuation procedures—identified as market and nonmarket approaches—for type B assessments. If there were a competitive market for the resource, then the diminished value occasioned by a spill or release was to be captured by the price change. When market prices would be inappropriate (as determined by the trustee), the next best procedure would be appraisal.[21] When neither of these approaches was appropriate, nonmarket procedures could be used. The court of appeals ruling rejected the notion of a hierarchy, and DOI was forced to remove it, acknowledging that "the mere presence of a competitive market does not, however, ensure the price will 'capture fully' the value of the resource."[22]

Nonmarket procedures include:

• Estimation of the contribution the natural resource makes to the production of marketable goods—that is, the value added.

• Travel cost or regional travel cost models, in which differences in travel costs incurred by those living in various places are associated with differences in rates of use of recreation facilities in a systematic way. These observed or assumed differences lead to an estimation of the demand for a site. Damages are estimated in the above two methods by comparing values with and without the natural resource injury in the traditional manners.

• Hedonic pricing techniques, in which the market price of a composite good such as a home is partitioned among housing attributes, including the quality of enviromental amenities, using appropriate statistical procedures. The value of changes in environmental amenity produced by the resource injury is then estimated from these procedures.

• The contingent valuation procedure, in which hypothetical markets are set up to discover individual use values, nonuse values, or both,

---

[19]56 *Federal Register* 19757, 19760 (1991).

[20]51 *Federal Register* 27749–750, § 11.83 (August 1, 1986).

[21]Using appraisals, damages are calculated by "the difference between the with- and without-injury appraisal value determined by the comparable sales approach as described in the Uniform Appraisal Standards." 51 *Federal Register* 27719–722 (August 1, 1986).

[22]56 *Federal Register* 19759 (1991).

which are designated the compensable values for a quality or quantity of a natural resource.[23]

• Preassigned unit (dollar) values for relevant recreational or other experiences by the public.

• Other nonmarket procedures based on willingness to pay. These procedures elicit use values and are cost-effective.

Estimates of damages arising from nonuse values can only be measured through the contingent valuation method. While DOI eliminated the hierarchy of valuation methodologies, the proposed rules make clear that this does not imply that "all valuation methods are equally reliable or applicable".[24] Moreover, the new proposed method for measuring compensable value recognizes that only the contingent valuation method can estimate nonuse values, but that when it is used the CV estimates should be regarded as in the "least reliable" category.

2.2.2.2   Past and future damages. Traditionally, benefits and costs of federal water projects have been estimated on a with- and without-project basis. This reasoning carries forth in the context of natural resource damage assessments. Future damages are estimated as the difference between the value of baseline economic activities without the spill or release and the estimated value of economic activities with the injury to natural resources. The original DOI rules provided an important guide for determining future activities, limiting them to committed uses. These are uses for which there is "a documented legal, administrative, budgetary, or financial commitment established before the [injurious event]."[25] The *Ohio* decision does not meddle with the concept of committed use, but reduces its force by giving primacy to restoration or replacement values.

The clearest way to understand past damages is to specify when they do not exist. Past damages do not exist when the natural resource injury occurred wholly before passage of CERCLA on December 11, 1980, and the resulting damages occurred wholly before that time.[26] Thus damages

---

[23]Nonuse values include existence and option value. Existence value refers to the value associated with knowing that a natural resource, presumably in an unsullied state, will be available in the future for oneself and perhaps for others. Economists have no unified definition of option value. In chapter 13, A. Myrick Freeman treats the topic in detail. A modal professional view of option value is that it refers to what one is willing to pay now for the availability of a natural resource of given quality in the future. Such a value is not picked up in the traditional use value studies described here. The definition here is the one specified in the rules. 51 *Federal Register* 27692 (1986).

[24]56 *Federal Register* 19759 (1991).

[25]51 *Federal Register* 27727, § 11.14(h) (August 1, 1986).

[26]42 U.S.C. § 9607(f).

can be recovered if the release stopped before passage of CERCLA but the economic costs of the release continued after December 1980.[27]

However, District Judge Young in the *New Bedford* decision established a different definition of past damages, drawing the line at the date of enactment. The controversial case arises when the injury and related damage occurred prior to enactment of CERCLA. Judge Young ruled that recovery for damages applies for the period after enactment (*New Bedford*, pp. 15–17). Damages incurred before December 1980 are not compensable according to Judge Young's decision but were compensable under the original interpretation of the law.

One point of clarification from Judge Young's decision is helpful. Losses due to injury that are reflected in property sales consummated before December 1980 are not recoverable. Losses due to injury on property sales consummated after December 1980 are compensable, as are losses due to injury "on property which still has not changed hands since the contamination of the Harbor because the latent damages these properties have incurred will occur at some as yet undetermined time, but definitely after enactment" (*New Bedford*, p. 21).

Judge Young also addressed the problem of "indivisibilities." Suppose an injury occurred prior to 1980 and an individual suffered a loss of economic welfare at the time of the injury and the loss endures to this day. Moreover, the individual cannot divide or apportion the loss. In that instance, "the sovereigns can recover for such non-divisible damages in their entirety" (*New Bedford*, p. 20). The meaning of this is still ambiguous and will be discussed in section 3.8 below.

2.2.2.3 Discounting. The procedures simply state that the discount rate of 10 percent should be used to calculate the present value of damages in the future or past. This rate follows the recommendations of the federal Office of Management and Budget (OMB [1972]).

2.2.2.4 Other procedures. Investigators are warned not to double count, not to choose worst-case assumptions,[28] not to count secondary effects, to treat uncertain outcomes explicitly by considering the probability of different outcomes when this is important, and to compute the expected (average) value.[29] Different natural resources can be treated differently. Investigators are cautioned to take economic interdependencies into account, recognizing, for example, that levels of activity utilizing one resource can impinge on the quality, hence the value, of experience arising from enjoyment of other resources.

---

[27]See also 51 *Federal Register* 27692 (1986).

[28]51 *Federal Register* 277721 (August 1, 1986).

[29]51 *Federal Register* 27750, § 11.84 (August 1, 1986).

2.2.2.5   Efficiency. Key passages of the old DOI rules make clear that damage assessment was to be governed by principles of economic efficiency and cost-effectiveness. Damages were estimated as the lesser of diminution of use values and restoration or replacement costs. If the costs of restoration or replacement were higher than the estimated value of foregone uses, "it is rational to base compensation on the lowest value."[30] On this matter, common law and economics are in agreement.[31] The proposed revisions to the DOI rules include the comparison of costs with benefits and cost-effectiveness. However, seven other factors are listed as factors the trustee should consider in selecting the most appropriate alternative, and therefore in determining restoration costs. Thus the prospects for economic efficiency governing the assessment and restoration process now seem less likely. Nonetheless, it is worthwhile to make four points of clarification here.

First, if the damage assessment procedures were governed by principles of cost-effectiveness, only the least-cost restoration or replacement strategy for some given non-economically determined level of damage reduction would be computed. However, the DOI original damage assessment rules take the next giant step in public policy analysis by considering opportunity costs for baseline goods and services damaged and by setting a standard of economic efficiency. The procedures require trading off additional costs of restoration or replacement against additional forgone use benefits. Thus the DOI damage assessment procedures follow the thirty-five-year-old tradition of benefit-cost analysis for federal water resource projects—a tradition that requires economic efficiency.[32] In the

---

[30]The purpose of damage assessment is compensatory, not punitive. 51 *Federal Register* 27680.

[31]51 *Federal Register* 27690, 27705 (1986). However, G. J. Johnson (1987) says that common law generally pays the cost of restoration when the damage to property is temporary. Economists have no comparative advantage in discussions about what common law holds. In one of the cases Johnson sites to make his point, the court argued that an owner ought to be compensated for repairing a backyard garden even though the market price of the house would not have reflected the changed value of the garden. There is no tension between economics and common law or between what Johnson believes economists should estimate and what they would estimate following the damage procedures. Economists would not argue that damages are zero in this case. They would argue for the lesser of forgone use value or restoration costs, just as the court argued. See *Regal Construction Co. v. West Lanham Hills Citizens Assn.*, 256, Md. 302, 260 A.2d 82 (1970).

[32]Whether or not the damage assessment procedures meet efficiency criteria from a broader perspective when the uncertainty of future hazardous releases is treated explicitly turns on theoretical and empirical considerations that take us well beyond a critique of damage assessment techniques. When the dischargers are risk-averse and cannot insure against cleanup and damage liability, requiring full liability as the DOI regulations do can place the burden or cost of uncertainty (not the actual cost) inefficiently on those who would

context of water development, projects are designed until incremental benefits equal incremental costs. In the case of damage assessment, incremental restoration costs are balanced against incremental forgone use benefits. After this point, compensation matches residual damages.

Second, adopting the criterion of economic efficiency is consistent with the view that "owners" of natural resources do not have a right to the physical quality and quantity of natural resources prior to the spill or release. They have a right to the economic value of the natural resource. Figure 5-1 draws the visual analogue. In response to EPA's criteria for cleanup liability, suppose the site is cleaned up to level Q_1, which restores total benefits of E to users of the site. However, Q_1 is less than Q_0, the quality or quantity of the resource before the release occurred. Therefore damage assessment establishes that the users are to be compensated by the incremental amount $F - E$ for the economic loss in quality $Q_0 - Q_1$. It would be economically silly to spend any more than C at this site on replacement or restoration activities because the extra costs of cleanup would not be worth the extra benefits recaptured in use value. The excess compensation ($F - E$) over actual cleanup costs is available for replacement expenditures elsewhere and might even be sufficient to provide services elsewhere in excess of $F - E$, the foregone use value at the site in question.

Third, restoration and replacement actions and costs need not exclude foregone use values. The least-cost situation can entail using replacement for some injured acreage or sites, and partial restoration for other injured acreage or sites. This then creates some residual loss of use value. In all cases, however, the legislation requires that funds collected are to be used for restoration or replacement of related natural resources, regardless of the technique used to compute compensation.

Fourth, the damage assessment procedure together with the compensation features illustrate the economics profession's prescription for managing externalities—that is, charge the social opportunity cost for the use of natural resources to those private decision makers using the resources. This induces them to properly take into account (internalize) the otherwise unvalued consequences external to their firm, municipality, or any decision maker in general.

---

bear less of the burden if risk markets were perfect. See Segerson (1987) for an instructive treatment of liability. Thus, conclusions about efficiency in the context of uncertainty depend on the way in which the researcher constructs (or estimates) the second-best model. An unknown number of major hazardous waste producers have liability insurance. The actual liability of the insurance companies currently is under litigation in a very large hazardous waste case. If risky events can be insured, full liability is an efficient regulation policy.

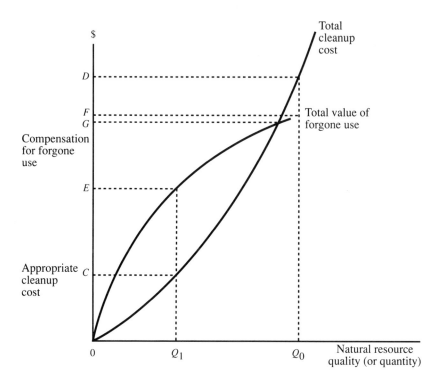

Figure 5-1. Compensation, a combination of cleanup costs and use values sacrificed

Suppose that the appropriate concept of cost or damage recovery is replacement costs; the replacement or restoration costs in this example are D in Figure 5-1, an amount necessary to put the site back to its initial quality. This level of cost is to be compared with the economic values of F lost by the injury. The magnitude of economic loss bears no relationship to the magnitude of restoration cost. In this case, the measure of economic inefficiency is $D-F$, which may be billions of dollars or hundreds of dollars, depending on the tastes and technology underlying the benefit and cost relationships.

The District of Columbia Circuit Court of Appeals ruling in *Ohio* has required changes in DOI's rules for type B assessments. In particular, the lesser-of component that underlies these efficiency arguments has been replaced by one that uses restoration cost as the sole measure of damages, except in cases where restoration is technically infeasible or these costs are judged to be grossly disproportionate in relation to economic measures of the total value (including use and nonuse values) of the services lost as a result of the release. DOI's proposed revision to the rules will greatly expand the discretion available to trustees in responding to the court's requirement that restoration cost be the measure of damages.

3.   CERCLA'S SHORTCOMINGS

3.1   Early Cost-Effectiveness Plus Zeal: A Prescription for Economic Waste. The following is an economist's understanding of how CERCLA works.[33] Imagine that a hazardous waste discharge occurs or is discovered. It comes as no surprise to one familiar with public policy rhetoric that "defensive actions should begin as soon as possible to prevent, *minimize* or mitigate threats to the public health or welfare of the environment" (emphasis added).[34] Two sections later, doubts about the economist's role fade as one learns that cleanup should be "fully sufficient to minimize or mitigate threat" to the trinity of health, welfare, and the environment.[35] The mere existence of a potential threat to health, welfare, and the environment is sufficient cause for removal.[36] In practice, this means that public health standards, including drinking water standards, are met or exceeded even when the water is not an existing or prospective supply of drinking water.

Remedies, including removal of hazardous waste, should be cost-effective. Cost-effective means choosing the cheapest alternative actions that minimize threat to health, welfare, and the environment. There is no discussion about trading off extra costs for extra benefits, with one extreme exception. It is possible to exclude some remedial alternatives if they "far exceed the cost" of other options and they do not "provide substantially greater public health or environmental protection." Lest this be misconstrued, *all* options that meet environmental requirements, by definition, do provide sufficient protection to be considered. In all cases, the public health standards must be met.

Any economist who has experience with hazardous waste sites knows that phrases like "minimize threats," when combined with no budget constraint, have provided a license for many dubious remedial decisions. The discrepancy between likely benefits and costs of remedies

---

[33]Hazardous waste laws, rules, and regulations are obscure. Boland and Milliman (1987) helpfully point out that CERCLA is the umbrella piece of legislation. "Superfund" refers to Title II of the act, in which certain trust funds are created. The National Contingency Plan has been described by Kenison, Buchholz, and Milligan (1987) as CERCLA's implementing regulations.

[34]National Oil and Hazardous Substance Pollution Contingency Plan, 40 C.F.R. § 300.65 (1986).

[35]40 C.F.R. § 300.55.

[36]40 C.F.R. § 300.65.

is exacerbated by the extremely conservative assumptions underlying EPA's risk analysis procedures, which translate hazardous exposures into consequences for health (Nichols and Zeckhauser [1986]).[37] The results, in turn, dictate the remedy.

One possible response to the requirements of the National Contingency Plan to minimize threat might be to remove all contamination. Then there is no need to collect data or do analysis that estimates the benefits of the remedy at the time the remedy is selected. It is sufficient to know that the mitigation reduces threats to health, welfare, or the environment. In this case there would be no way to know if millions are being spent to provide thousands of dollars worth of benefits because there is no requirement for benefits to be calculated. The National Contingency Plan should be amended to replace the term "cost-effective" with a phrase such as "economically efficient."

3.2   Values Restricted to Public Use of the Resource. Damage assessment is limited to public resources because there are other well-defined legal procedures for remedying losses arising from injury to private resources. It is natural for an economist to think of a trustee acting as if he or she is the owner of the public natural resource, and it is correct to do so up to a point. However, the line between compensable and noncompensable damages is blurred. Consider the following example. Suppose all agree that an injury to a groundwater aquifer has occurred. Users of the aquifer include a family that pumps water for a garden whose produce is for home use; a family that pumps water for a small garden whose produce is sold at a roadside stand; and a farmer who irrigates thousands of acres of crops for commercial purposes. All are hurt by the contaminated aquifer. The large farmer's losses are excluded from the damage calculation because he has a "private cause of action."[38] The family that can no longer apply groundwater to its garden has suffered a compensatory damage that should be estimated. I do not know about the damages incurred by the family whose garden produce is sold at a roadside stand. Profit is being earned.

The rules attempt to distinguish (though this is admittedly vague in the specific language provided) between lost income and those rents attributable to access to the natural resource in its baseline condition.[39] The rents can be recovered as part of natural resource damages. They will not,

---

[37]Carson and Navarro (1988) contains a very good discussion about determining the level of injury when there is uncertainty. Choosing maximum measures of uncertainty—a strategy attributed to environmentalists—leads to "gross overpayment," they conclude. Carson and Navarro argue that the technically correct measure is computed from properly computed expected values.

[38]51 *Federal Register* 27720 (1986).

[39]51 *Federal Register* (August 1, 1986).

in general, correspond to either losses in private income or profit. Moreover, because rents can accrue to private parties for a variety of reasons, the task of separating out the component attributable to the resource under specified quality conditions promises to be challenging.[40]

3.3   Reliance on Cost of Restoration: A Prescription for Ineffi-ciency.   The points were made in section 2.2.2 that the "lesser-of" provisions in the DOI regulations are good from the criterion of efficiency and that the ruling in the *Ohio* case will result in inefficiency. Why did the court give primacy to restoration costs and DOI add to the trustee's discretionary ability and thereby offer greater prospect for inefficient solutions?

First, the court reasoned from a review of the legislative history that it was the intent of Congress to have the costs of restoration paid (*Ohio,* pp. 37–52). Economists in general, and I in particular, do not have a comparative advantage in fathoming the true intent of Congress from a legislative history. Typically, there are contradictory statements in the history, so one has to pick a set of weights—value one senator or congressman more highly than another—in order to reach a definitive answer. Another court could have chosen different weights and reached a different decision.

Second, in support of the "lesser-of" rule, DOI originally argued that "it is economically inefficient to restore a resource whose use value is less than the cost of restoration." The court then asserted that Congress "soundly rejected" this premise (*Ohio,* p. 47). The court is free to debate what were and were not the premises of Congress, but economics is the profession that passes judgment about economic inefficiency, and the court has got it wrong. The Department of the Interior would be correct in its reasoning, provided the resource was valued reflecting all sources of value—use and nonuse. Economic efficiency involves a balance between demand and supply, whereas restoration cost has nothing to do with demand or value.[41]

The real motivation for adopting restoration costs seems to be that the court fundamentally does not trust economists to get the job of damage assessment done the way the court thinks Congress would like to see it done. The court concludes that Congress "was skeptical" of measuring the "true 'value' of a natural resource" and the court then in support of this position quotes the pronouncements only of non-economists (*Ohio,*

---

[40]This interpretation of the rule is most sensible. For a view that foregone rent should not be included, see 51 *Federal Register* 27696 (1986).

[41]I therefore do not know what to make of the statement that "Congress did intend CERCLA's natural resource provision to operate efficiently" (*Ohio,* p. 50), particularly when the next sentence in support speaks about cost-effectiveness, which differs from economic efficiency, and an earlier sentence views "lesser-of" as benefit-cost analysis, which, in turn, seems to be a dangerously bad idea.

pp. 50, 51). The sources are professionally inappropriate. The devil can cite scripture for his purpose, to put it succinctly.

Unfortunately, DOI's proposed revisions do not help matters by expanding the range of factors available to trustees in selecting an alternative as the best restoration, replacement, rehabilitation, or acquisition combination. Damages are now defined to include these costs plus "a dollar figure computed for the compensable value of the services lost to the public for the period of the recovery—whether a natural recovery, which might be longer, or an assisted recovery which might be shorter."[42] Thus, the distinction between compensation for reductions in the value of the nation's public natural resource assets and efficient uses of the recovered damages have been dropped. It would seem we will both reduce the compensation possible and increase the inefficiency with which these resources can be allocated.

3.4   The Old Hierarchy of Damage Valuation Methods. There are two issues worth discussing regarding the priority given to valuation methods in the damage estimation procedures, even though the court and DOI have removed most of the hierarchy. First, the wording of the original DOI rules certainly sounds as if appraisal procedures should be used if resource markets are not reasonably competitive.[43] One might ask, Why should appraisers know what perfectly competitive market prices would be in the absence of such markets? If the values that appraisers know, when markets are imperfect, are based on observable phenomena, then these data should be identified and studied in a systematic way. Oil spills and hazardous waste often cause economic losses by changing air or water quality. How these qualitative aspects impinge on property values is much more difficult to intuit than the way in which property values change due to quantitative variations across properties, such as number of rooms, bathrooms, and so forth.

Second, the change in market price, given competitive markets, is not in general a good measure of a loss of consumer and producer surplus from market goods. It is a good measure of loss only if the environmental insult is insignificant.[44]

In the following example it is useful to imagine a demand for a resource-related service of a given quality (see figure 5-2). The natural

---

[42]56 *Federal Register* 19764 (1991).

[43]Logically there could be reasons other than imperfect competition, unnamed in the final rule, that warrant jettisoning market price.

[44]Pathological cases of completely elastic supply functions and completely inelastic demand functions, or parallel shifts in the demand function and completely inelastic supply functions, are disregarded.

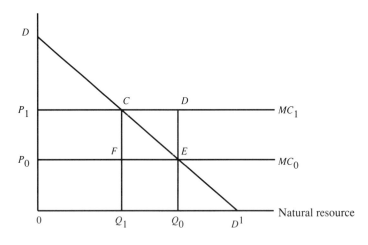

Figure 5-2. Economic damages

resource injury changes the quantity or quality of the natural resource. This in turn makes it more difficult, or more costly, to purchase the same quality or quantity. Technically, the injury drives up the marginal cost function. For example, groundwater contamination drives up the cost of purchasing water of baseline quality. Beach or fishing site closures due to injury make it more expensive to swim at a beach of the same quality or to harvest fish of the same quality or quantity. Obtaining a bird- or mammal-viewing experience of the same quality is more costly. Wind-blown tailings make it more costly to keep houses painted and cleaned and make it more expensive to achieve a given quality of health.

As shown in figure 5-2, if the injury to the natural resource drives the unit cost of the resource-related service up from P_0 to P_1, the loss of consumer surplus is $P_0 P_1 CE$, the demand curve is DD_1 and the supply curves before and after the injury are MC_0 and MC_1 respectively. Loss based on price and quantity change, $(P_1 - P_0)(Q_0 - Q_1)$, bears little relationship to the actual loss unless all the units in the market affected by the price change are used in loss calculations.

It is easy to think that the magnitude of the oil spill or the hazardous substance release determines the magnitude of the damages. Magnitude of the physical effects can matter. However, it is imperative to distinguish between physical and economic effects. An environmental insult with immense results on natural or biological scales might have a trivial economic consequence, either because the organism affected makes an insignificant economic contribution or because there are close substitutes for the resource in question. Groundwater contamination in an aquifer for which there is no existing or anticipated withdrawal is an extreme example of the latter circumstance. Less extreme would be the case in which current and future uses of groundwater have a very-low-cost alternative water supply, say by purchases from a local public water purveyor.

Another example occurs when oil settles on the ocean floor and kills benthic organisms. The loss of tons of benthic species or other organisms at the lower trophic level is not likely to be valuable economically because energy conversion up the food chain is rather inefficient. According to a rule of thumb drawn from ecology, there is an order-of-magnitude loss of energy from one trophic level to another. This means, for example, that it takes 100 tons of sea worms to produce 1 ton of commercially valued predators such as shark or halibut, which eat bottom fish, which in turn eat sea worms.[45]

The judge in the *Ohio* case rightly ruled that economists should draw from the menu of damage assessment procedures available those most appropriate for the particular natural resource injury in question (*Ohio*, p. 66). It was further argued that the Department of the Interior was led into the hierarchy of assessment methods because of its "crabbed interpretation of CERCLA." DOI was also reminded not to make "a fetish [of market value] since that may not be the best measure of value in some cases" (*Ohio*, pp. 64, 66, quoting *United States v. Coors*, 337 U.S. 325, 332 [1949]).

3.5 Use Values or Nonuse Values. One of the most troubling features of the Department of the Interior rules for economists was the exclusion of nonuse values in those circumstances in which use values are estimated for any given resource. Nonuse refers to option and existence values. There was no formal economic reason for such an exclusion. Not only might some people derive satisfaction from using a resource while others derive option or existence value, but, in addition, an individual who uses a resource can derive an option and an existence value from the same resource simultaneously. Resources might have use value today and an option or existence value in the future.[46] Since it is quite reasonable for preferences (which determine value) to vary over time and since for one person use and nonuse may not be mutually exclusive, the motivation for the exclusionary feature of the law must have been on grounds of expe-

---

[45]Of course, the benthic species could be on the endangered list or the intermediate or ultimate predators could have immense value and no substitute food sources. But these are special, not general, cases.

[46]Many economists discuss bequest value, the value one obtains from knowing the resource will be available for future generations. Either DOI believes that bequest value is part of existence value, or bequest value is a category of value inadvertently left out. This oversight easily can be corrected. A more difficult issue arises in distinguishing ex ante and ex post value concepts. Option values arise as one measure of the importance of this distinction. See chapter 13 for further discussion.

diency. The Department of the Interior recognizes that normally economists simultaneously add use and nonuse values to obtain the total value of a resource. The revised rules now follow that norm.

It is fair to acknowledge that the distinctions between the ex ante and ex post perspectives on valuation as well as between use and nonuse values are subtle and depend on how economic models portray people's behavioral decisions. While many professional economists defend the ability of contingent valuation methods to measure them, many other respectable economists disagree. However, it is imperative to emphasize the distinction between a concept and its measurement. The profession agrees that the nonuse values exist; that is, existence value and a measure of behavioral response to uncertainty, under appropriate circumstances, are positive.

A point of clarification is in order before turning to the next concern. There is substantial disagreement about what economists mean by option value. This is not the place for a careful treatment of option value (but see chapter 13). Yet it must be said that most economists believe that option value bears on the sum one is willing to pay in the present for the right to use a resource in the future. The sum depends on what the future holds. No one argues that option value depends on one's desire not to use a resource. Thus in those cases where use values do not exist, litigious lawyers for the responsible parties will argue that since the trustee's estimates of option values are use values, they ought to be thrown out. Lawyers should work with economists to straighten out the legal language regarding future values, making sure to avoid expressions that can lead to double counting. DOI's proposed revisions recognize this potential problem,[47] but offer no insight into how trustees should seek to resolve it.

3.6 Natural Resource Slander. It is natural to reason that if a resource has been injured by an oil spill or by a hazardous substance discharge, the figurative owner of that resource should be compensated for the damage. It is natural to reason that if a resource has not been injured, there is no need for damage assessment. Yet it has troubled many economists for at least a decade that this reasoning systematically rules out the recovery of certain significant economic losses.

The problem may first have come to the attention of professional economists during the National Oceanic and Atmospheric Administration's economic evaluation of the *Amoco Cadiz* oil spill off the coast of Brittany in 1978. For about 240 miles along Brittany's coast, the chemical, physical, and visibility qualities of natural resources were measurably

---

[47]56 *Federal Register* 19760 (1991).

changed adversely (U.S. Department of Commerce [1983]).[48] Another approximately 250 miles of the coastline was not injured by the oil spill. There is substantial evidence that hundreds of thousands of summer vacationers from outside and inside France who would have come to the uninjured section of the coastline did not come because they believed that all of the coastline had been affected by the oil spill. These potential tourists suffered hundreds of thousands of dollars of economic loss either because they paid the same for this vacation but chose second-best, inferior vacation plans or because they paid more to obtain the same quality of vacation elsewhere. Such losses are not damages under CERCLA because if there is no resource injury as defined by CERCLA—as there was not, outside the spill area—there can be no damage.

What is to be done about this great chasm between a legal dictum, which sees no damage without scientifically established injury, and the economic reality of observed, measurable economic losses? In principle, there is a simple solution. The rule's definition of injury should be broadened. Well-intentioned people decided arbitrarily in advance to let the injury to natural resources be defined by biologists, chemists, geologists, air and fisheries specialists, and other non-social scientists.[49] Publications now are devoted to discussing how injuries to specific resources are determined and how to establish the pathways from the sources of pollution to the natural resources injured.[50] There is no prima facie reason why social scientists should not have been included in the original process of defining natural resource injury, in specifying the behavioral and natural pathways from discharge to damage.[51]

There is another way to view the controversy about whether the ultimate user of resources should participate in the definition of injury. Sampling procedures specified in the DOI rules permit investigators to conclude in a statistical sense that hazardous contaminants are present in certain places and at certain concentrations, when in fact the true location and true concentration are different. There is nothing unusual about this discrepancy between statistical truth and reality. Information is costly and

---

[48]These are the words that define injury in the regulation. 51 *Federal Register* 27679 (1986).

[49]These physical and natural scientists lack the expertise to identify all the ways in which people directly or indirectly value natural resources.

[50]51 *Federal Register* 27734–748, § 11.61–11.79 (August 1, 1986).

[51]Judge Young argued that damages occur when expenses are incurred due to the injury (*New Bedford*, p. 13). Can it then be argued that damages occur if expenses are incurred but injury, as defined in the legislation, has not yet occurred? That is, could one engage in costly averting behavior because one perceived that an injury had occurred or would occur, when the injury does not occur, as measured by the scientists?

researchers necessarily must use some form of inference to build a bridge from incomplete information to the workable truth of the situation. However, it is odd that the rules, in effect, prohibit the consumer from making any errors in inference. A resource user making a decision such as choosing a vacation spot might process all the available information about a release (including inaccurate news reports) and might avoid a site that in fact is clean. This is known as a Type I error in statistics: rejecting a hypothesis (the site is clean) that in fact is true. The damages truly are incurred by a consumer but the rules exclude them, thus placing the onus of making the Type I errors completely on the consumer. On the other hand, the rules for establishing injury permit "scientific" researchers to make Type I errors.

Broadening the definition of injury could be achieved by calling on researchers from such appropriate disciplines as psychology, communications, and economics to define injury according to the characteristics the damaged parties use. Including human definitions of injury solves the disturbing discrepancy between the rules and the economist's understanding of economic damage.

The issue of slander provides the closest analogy to existing legal categories and the phenomenon of perceived loss. Oil spills and hazardous waste slander certain natural resources. The courts have found ways for individuals to recover damages for slander, including discovering criteria for distinguishing between slander and everyday bad-mouthing. The legal profession can develop sensible rules for defining recoverable economic damages due to natural resource slander, given the charge to do so.

3.7 Discount Rates: Compounding and Discounting. It will be recalled that future damages are to be estimated in terms of present values and discounted at a 10 percent rate.[52] The Office of Management and Budget document supporting this position states that 10 percent represents the "average" real rate of return on foregone private investment before taxes (OMB [1972]).

The discount rate is just another term for a particular kind of opportunity cost, one that expresses what a particular decision maker is willing to give up (or receive) in one period in exchange for a payoff (or payout) in the next period. The decision maker under CERCLA is the public trustee of a natural resource. Therefore, the public opportunity cost, not the private opportunity cost, is the relevant interest rate to choose. When the damage occurred the trustee could have financed the restoration or replacement (or equivalent) activities with tax-free bonds at some real

---

[52]51 *Federal Register* 27750 (1986).

(inflation-adjusted) rate of interest.[53] The average risk premium reflected in a public agency's rate of interest for bonds may not equal the riskiness of the natural resource damage stream. How precisely risk should be handled is a separate matter, more appropriately discussed by Ralph d'Arge in chapter 12.[54] Real rates of interest reflecting social time preference are closer to 5 percent or less than to 10 percent.[55]

Using a lower rate of interest increases the present value of a "sum certain" paid presently by a polluter as compensation for future damages. There is, of course, economic symmetry. A higher rate of interest increases the compounded value of damages incurred up to the present time. The interest rate used to discount future damages should be the same rate used to compound past damages unless there is some issue of equity or a fundamental change in the future of society's time preference for productive investments between the past and present. I am unaware of a preponderant professional opinion that future real private or public rates of discount are likely to differ from those of the past.

A separate issue is prejudgment interest added in SARA.[56] It refers to interest on the claim trustees make to the responsible parties. Prejudgment interest on damages begins from the later of the date the payment is demanded or the date the expenditure is incurred. The rate of interest is the rate on Superfund, approximately 6 percent in 1991. The Department

---

[53]Boland and Milliman (1987) argue that the social, not the private, rate of time preference ought to be used to value the natural resource and that the rate "would be unrelated to income taxes levied in the private sector." No academic economist, to my knowledge, publicly has supported the DOI regulations on the discount rate. This may be one of the few times in recent history that all, or nearly all, academic economists are on the same side of a discount rate argument.

[54]The Department of the Interior treats risk or uncertainty by emphasizing variations in benefits and costs, not by choosing a discount rate that reflects the appropriate level of uncertainty. DOI requires "a range of probability estimates for the important assumptions used to determine damages." 51 *Federal Register* 27750, § 11.84(d)(2) (August 1, 1986). This approach is a plausible way to treat uncertainty and follows the Water Resources Council's guidelines (Water Resources Council [1979 and 1983]). As Boland and Milliman (1987) point out, if uncertainty is treated properly in this manner, the risk embedded in the bond rate of interest suggested above should be netted out to avoid double counting.

[55]Real interest bonds had interest rates of between 3.5 and 3.8 percent during the last week of April 1988. These are British Treasury bonds with maturities from the years 2003 to 2024, whose nominal yields are linked to the British consumer price index. They are reported in the *London Financial Times*. Real yields in the United States and in the United Kingdom will be about the same, differing by imperfections in the market for hedging the exchange rate and restrictions on flow of funds. Martin Feldstein (1988) estimates real interest rates at about 4.3 percent, the difference between 10-year Treasury bonds yielding 9.3 percent and the "consensus" forecast of about 4.3 percent inflation over the next decade.

[56]SARA § 9607. See 53 *Federal Register* 5169 (1988).

of the Interior allays the fears of responsible parties by noting that the interest on damages incurred before settlement "will generally begin to accrue from the time of the written demand, since by their nature, the emergency actions will be taken early in the assessment process not at its conclusion."[57]

3.8 Past Damages and Indivisibility. Originally, a potentially responsible party (PRP) had to pay for damages that occurred before 1980. That is, a PRP was held financially responsible for actions that were legal at the time, but were subsequently declared to be illegal. One economic effect of this interpretation is to tax future decisions or make them less profitable. That is, if PRPs think the future will be like the past, they will, in response to CERCLA, anticipate that in the future policies will be enacted that will make decisions in the present less profitable. The economic effect of an expected increase in future cost is to reduce investment and entrepreneurial activity in economic areas where future disadvantageous public policy is expected. The *New Bedford* decision by Judge Young reduces but does not remove the disincentive effect.

To understand why the tax is not completely removed and why liability for actions taken prior to the date of CERCLA's enactment remain, suppose that the PRP causes an injury to a natural resource before 1980 that continues after 1980. If the damage associated with this injury is indivisible, and the damage occurs after the enactment, then the nondivisible damages can be recovered in their entirety (*New Bedford,* p. 20).

Exactly what Judge Young means by indivisibility of damages is not clear. The most likely interpretation arises when economic damage behaves irregularly, jumping to some value after injury has exceeded some threshold value. But this is not an economic indivisibility. Suppose that in 1979 I suffered an unquestionable instantaneous lump sum loss of $1,000 as a result of an injury to a natural resource occurring in December 1979, one year before CERCLA's enactment in 1980. The injury continues for one year after, until December 1981. One could argue that the loss occurred before 1981 and that therefore it is not compensable. One could also argue that there are two dollar payments (losses)—one in 1980, the other in 1981—the sum of which is equivalent in a welfare sense to the lump sum figure. Economists believe there is always some intertemporal substitution captured by an interest rate or rates, which can convert a stock into a flow and remove the indivisibility. Following Judge Young's reasoning, I should be compensated for the second year's loss but not for the first year's loss. There may be a visible jump in the loss but it can be "divided" into a flow.

---

[57]53 *Federal Register* 5169 (1988).

There are an analogous problem and solution on the producer side. Suppose one lobster fisherman, to use Judge Young's example and numbers, in response to a natural resource injury incurred in the area before the date of CERCLA's enactment, borrowed funds to buy a boat to fish in a location where there was no natural resource injury. The fisherman pays back the loan at the rate of $60 per day. According to Judge Young, "from enactment day forward, the proper recovery is $60.00 per day" (*New Bedford,* p. 16, note 11). Suppose another lobster fisherman paid cash in 1979 for an equivalent boat and avoided the $60 per day charge both before and after the day of enactment. What is proper recovery in this instance? Is it zero because no observable dollar outlay takes place after 1980? Is it the full sum because it is indivisible in the sense of a lump sum? Or is it the flow equivalent of $60 per day after 1980? It is to be hoped that future courts will make pragmatic use of the notion of opportunity cost when they interpret Judge Young's decision. The proper recovery would seem to be $60 per day after enactment. Proper recovery should be independent of the means of financing the costs of doing business.

3.9 Future Use of Natural Resources. The stream of damages in the future is confined to current or planned "committed" resource uses documented by "legal, administrative, budgetary, or financial commitment established before the discharge of oil or the release of a hazardous substance."[58] This is another case of choosing the most extreme solution that effectively minimizes damages. Boland and Milliman (1987) suspect that this clause effectively removes all future uses from consideration. They reason that if a resource is not in use now, it is because there is insufficient demand now. Since planning and commitment in the present to use resources in the future is costly, prudent decision makers will postpone such expenditures until an appropriate time in the future. In most instances, therefore, one would not expect documentation of public commitment in a quantitative sense to the future use of a natural resource, even if future use is certain.

The exceptional discrimination against future use is illustrated by reminding ourselves of what commitment seems to entail in the case of a groundwater aquifer. It would not be sufficient for a small town or a city to make a quantitative forecast of future water demand. The town also would have to study the cost of developing alternative future supplies of water. These studies would have to be completed with sufficient precision to enable one or more decision-making bodies to commit to use the particular aquifer in question and perhaps also to commit to use it at a particular time. Would it be necessary to have specified the location and

---

[58]51 *Federal Register* 7727, § 11.14(h) (August 1, 1986).

the depth from which the water will be drawn? The rulemakers seem to have defined committed uses too narrowly. They were willing to accept "reasonably probable" future uses but wanted to rule out "uses in the realm of possibility."[59] There are more reasonable measures of acceptable future use than legal commitment. Some of these surely meet the legitimate concerns of the rulemakers. For a start, why not admit expected future use?

Boland and Milliman (1987) further point out that the "committed use" condition makes little sense in the realms of wilderness recreation, visual amenities, and the like until perhaps congestion has set in and rationing rules must be devised. How does one make a legal commitment to an unknown number of viewer days of eagles in the year 2005 or to an unknown quantity of sport-caught lobsters in 1995? Or in the year 2000 commit the commercially valuable bottom fish to eat the sea worms if they are not contaminated? Finally, the very idea of committed use and nonuse values driven by bequest or existence values seems to be a contradiction in terms.

However, in cases where hazardous substances have reduced the quality of natural resources for years, there is every rational reason not to plan in a documented way for future use until steps toward restoration are in sight (Kenison, Buchholz, and Milligan [1987], p. 10438). In a final criticism, Boland and Milliman (1987) point out that the committed use clause in CERCLA removes, in one stroke, the important damages it was designed to recover: those incurred by anonymous individuals lacking cause of action under tort law who might use a reservoir in the future or who would use it now if it were available.[60]

All of these criticisms of the committed use concept remain theoretically valid after the *Ohio* and *New Bedford* cases. However, the practical consequence of the idea has been reduced to quarrelling about what constitutes committed use between the date estimated damages are first computed and the date of restoration or replacement.

The interpretation of committed use will take on substance in those cases in which restoration or replacement is not practical. Ironically, according to Kopp, Portney, and Smith (1989) the impracticality of restoration or replacement turns on its cost relative to the value of future, present, and past foregone uses, if the footnote material regarding disproportionate cost in the *Ohio* opinion is followed (*Ohio*, footnote 7, pp. 21 and 22).

---

[59]51 *Federal Register* 27750, § 11.84(b)(2) (August 1, 1986).

[60]Perhaps this criticism is exaggerated in the case of groundwater. In chapter 6, Willie Taylor points out that the Environmental Protection Agency has classified aquifers and that this may constitute a sufficient documentation for some aquifers.

3.10 Bias Against Private Land Purchases. There is a paragraph in CERCLA so strange that one can only imagine it was introduced to placate the farthest right wing of the Reagan administration. We learn that not another acre of land is to enter federal hands unless this is the "sole viable method" to achieve restoration or replacement.[61] This ideological crumb will be very expensive in some cases. Imagine a large hazardous waste site on undeveloped land where the geology is such that there are no underground pathways. The least-cost solution, by millions of dollars per acre in some cases, is to cap the surface and purchase substitute habitat elsewhere. One must make sure that the substitute habitat purchased would have been bull-dozed for development had it not been purchased, otherwise the system will end up with a net loss of habitat. The alternatives are likely to be surface restoration after excavation and incineration or transportation to remote sites for storage—very expensive alternatives.

The curious consequence of this paragraph in CERCLA is that the private enterprises who are the responsible parties will have to pay for the more expensive solutions dictated by the advocates of private property beavering away in the Department of the Interior.

4. CONCLUSION

It is appropriate for an evaluation of the natural resource damage assessment provisions to be critical because evaluation establishes the scope for revision. However, if CERCLA's damage assessment procedures are compared with similar federal evaluation schemes, as they should be to provide a sensibly broad perspective, we see that the approach in CERCLA has much to commend it.

Except for the restoration/replacement cost provision in the *Ohio* decision, economists should applaud these damage assessment procedures for the most part and the framers of these rules can take pride in their work. It would not be easy to find real benefit-cost procedures in the regulations of other countries that have as much sophisticated economic content as these regulations have. Probably no country can come close in the specific area of hazardous waste management. Viewed along a timeline, a comparison of these damage assessment procedures with procedures for evaluating water resource projects set forth more than thirty years ago in what is known as the Green Book (Subcommittee on Benefits and Costs of the Federal Inter-Agency River Basin Committee [1950]) would show that the United States has come a long way in developing sophisticated applied benefit-cost analysis.

---

[61] 51 *Federal Register* 27748, § 11.81(e)(2) (August 1, 1986).

Basically the Department of the Interior has incorporated many of the procedures for evaluating water resource projects that have been adopted and refined throughout the years by the Water Resources Council. Specifically, it is remarkable that the Department of the Interior procedures have reflected the criterion of maximizing producer's and consumer's surplus. Can technical economic language equal to that be discovered in the comparable legislation of any other country? What other federal agencies even mention willingness to pay, let alone discuss the distinction between willingness to pay and willingness to sell? Where in the world are there agency personnel knowledgeable enough even to draft paragraphs about hedonic analysis, contingent valuation, and so forth? It is a long way, typically measured by decades, to go from the material one reads in contemporary professional journals to legislative guidelines. The Department of the Interior deserves special credit for its precocity.

The Department of the Interior explicitly rules out secondary benefits in damage assessment (secondary benefits are those service forms that stem from and are induced by the direct benefits and costs of the projects). That is no small achievement, as anyone knows who is at all familiar with typical, contemporary economic evaluation studies designed to guide decisions made by state agencies. In fact, many federal agencies use secondary benefit arguments about added workers and wages in the intermediate product and consumer goods and services sectors to justify their investment projects, as did the major water resource development agencies years ago.[62]

In this chapter, I have taken exception to DOI's choice of a discount rate. Nevertheless, we should realize that in reality it is advanced to introduce any discount rate at all. Many federal and state agencies in the United States do not use any discount rate in the analyses that guide their decision making.

It is relatively easy for an economist to find fault with public policy. It is far more difficult to make practical recommendations for revisions. In general, public policy is governed by a broad set of criteria, among which economic criteria play only a part, sometimes an insignificant part. Elements of public policy may violate economic good sense, but satisfy other imperatives. If certain policies exist because of an oversight, then simply pointing out the oversight is all that is necessary to guarantee a revision. However, one has the feeling that the policy features discussed in this chapter did not arise from simple oversight, but are the result of distributive objectives held by politically powerful parties.

---

[62]Secondary benefits could be included in evaluating project proposals under Senate Document No. 97 (see U.S. Congress. Senate [1962]). When a regional, state, or local perspective ("accounting stance") was adopted in the calculations of secondary benefits, an additional benefit-cost ratio was to be computed.

Relevant recommendations flow from a good theory of public decision making, which I do not have. Thus the recommendations and observations that follow can be regarded as speculative. Three elements of damage assessment may be relatively susceptible to revision or may be relatively unimportant.

The first is the preeminence of market methods for estimating damages over the nonmarket method and the preference for using appraisers, as discussed in section 3.3. In fact, damage estimation is sufficiently subtle and difficult that the task is likely to be done by professional economists. The nature of the particular damage will dictate the proper technique. The adversarial environment of litigation will guarantee that the proper technique is used. The exact wording of the rule is not likely to be important in practice. The *Ohio* decision corrects for this flaw, and it appears that the proposed rules go a long way toward eliminating it.

The second is the fact that legitimate nonuse values are excluded under the rules unless there are no use values—an exclusion that has greatly disturbed economists (see section 3.4 for discussion of the original rules). The exclusion would only be important when the nonuse values are large and the use values are also large but not too large to make it worthwhile for the trustee to abandon the advantage of the rebuttable presumption and litigate on other grounds. The revised rules have eliminated the conceptual problem, but place estimates of nonuse values or total values including them in the "least-reliable" category.[63]

The third is the prohibitions on land purchases for the purpose of replacement or restoration, which may be an economically insignificant restriction. If replacement or restoration are very costly, the responsible parties will make the magnitude of the excess costs known and regulations can be expected to respond, since economic punishment is not a purpose of the damage assessment procedures.

Turning to more important shortcomings, there has been a good deal of professional concern that damages based on future uses of natural resources are confined to uses for which there has been a legal or financial commitment prior to discharge. As discussed in section 3.9, fiscally responsible planners know that since commitment to future use in the sense of CERCLA is costly, it should be postponed until necessary, even if future use is certain. CERCLA should not create an incentive for premature commitment to future resource use. CERCLA should also recognize that committing injured resources to future use before the advent of

---

[63]This designation reflects agreement with some professional economists who think that the contingent valuation method and nonuse values have been raised to a higher pedestal of legitimacy than current measurement techniques can justify. See, for example, Phillips and Zeckhauser (1989).

CERCLA does not make good economic sense, in general. Yet they might well have been used in the future had there been no injury. A practical revision is straightforward. Carson and Navarro (1988) recommend that the damage assessment procedures in the regulation should specify which potential types of future use are acceptable, and should provide guidelines for estimating future levels of use.

Other problems may not be so easily remedied. Defining damages as restoration/replacement cost in the *Ohio* decision is a giant step backward and reflects an exceptional disregard of public policy history, and the proposed DOI revisions make matters worse. It took decades of painful and costly experience for federal natural resource agencies to learn what elements of benefit-cost analysis work, not only in terms of what makes sense to economists but also in terms of the interplay of economics and political considerations. This interplay resulted in excising the most egregiously wasteful elements in applied benefit-cost analysis. Putting a practical constraint on the magnitude of replacement cost is one lesson painfully learned. If benefits are to be measured by alternative costs (because the benefits are thought to be too difficult to measure) we must be assured that the alternative would, in fact, be undertaken in the absence of the project in question. Even more to the point, the judge in the appeal of *Puerto Rico v. The SS Zoe Colocotroni* rightly rejected the cost of replacing 92 million biological organisms and the cost of 23 acres of container-grown mangroves as the proper measures of damages, arguing that these alternatives would not be undertaken (and in fact they were not).[64] Finding a way to limit the application of replacement cost and constraining its magnitude when the concept is employed cannot occur too soon.

I suspect that the discount (and compounding) interest rate provisions are the most serious shortcomings of the damage assessment procedures and the least likely to be revised satisfactorily. For as long as federal agencies have conducted economic analysis of natural resource values, economists have argued without much success for the use of proper discount rates. Why should we be successful at this time? There is a practical revision in the discount rate provisions, but it may not be politically feasible. SARA specifies a prejudgment interest rate equal to the interest rate on investments in the Hazardous Substance Superfund (SARA § 960).[65] Since the rate is approximately 6 percent now and is unlikely to

---

[64]*Puerto Rico v. The SS Zoe Colocotroni,* 628 F.2d 652 (1st Cir. 1980).

[65]Note that this is a nominal, not a real, rate of interest so its bias varies with the expected rate of inflation. Moreover, the rate is determined from yields of short-term Treasury bills, not long-term rates, which would be more appropriate for application to damages occurring in future or past years.

exceed 10 percent very often, it is a step in the right direction and would make the interest rates in related legislation consistent with each other. Moreover, EPA has said that, in many instances, 10 percent may not reflect the accurate opportunity cost and that another rate should be chosen (Environmental Protection Agency [1983], p. 15). Pleas for consistency and greater accuracy may attract congressional votes.

The limited view of injury discussed in section 3.6 above is another very serious shortcoming in the procedures. I take the widely held anthropocentric view as a starting point. Rational, keenly calculating people respond to their own best estimates of the nature, location, extent, and expected impact of a hazardous waste discharge. Their damages should be compensated. Rather than limiting damages to the dollar equivalent of resource injury stipulated by physical and natural scientists, the rules' stipulation of acceptable procedures for estimating damages should be broadened to include the elements the public uses to define injury. Responsible social scientists could help revise the rules.

The next serious problem concerns the cleanup liability provisions, not damage liability. Requiring dischargers of hazardous substances to pay for remedies when risks are one cancer (or less) per one million exposed sets a standard of safety inconsistent with other federal standards governing risky situations and is inconsistent with much observed human behavior in the face of risk. The requirement is all the more exceptional since the risk calculations are obtained from models that make extremely conservative assumptions. I am not sanguine about the prospects for major revisions in the cleanup liability provisions. However, there is one constructive revision that would not change contemporary outcomes: cleanup would still be based on present procedures but investigators would have to calculate expected risks using moderate risk models. The cost of remedies necessary to reduce risk to a given level using each of the risk calculations would enable reviewers to see the extra cost of adherence to the extreme value approaches. The revision could be promoted as the cost of an added margin of safety. Making the expected value calculations merely makes the procedure consistent, if only suggestively, with those used by the federal government for other natural resource studies.

Hazardous waste legislation is important because the stakes are large. Proper legislation will ensure that people are adequately protected. Improper legislation will make us poorer in real terms if it calls for allocating resources from one valuable use to a noble but less valuable use.

REFERENCES

Ames, Bruce N., and Lois S. Gold. 1988. "Carcinogenic Risk Estimation," *Science* 240 (May 20) p. 1047.

Boland, John J., and Jerome W. Milliman. 1987. "Overview of CERCLA Natural Resource Damage Procedures: Uses and Misuses of Economic Theory," report prepared for Association of Environmental and Resource Economists and the American Economic Association, Chicago, Ill., December.

Breen, Barry. 1984. "CERCLA's Natural Resource Damage Provisions: What Do We Know So Far?" *Environmental Law Reporter* 14 (August) pp. 10304–10310.

Carson, Richard T., and Peter Navarro. 1987. "Special Interests and Ideology in the Dispute Over Natural Resource Damage Assessment," discussion paper, Department of Economics, University of California, San Diego.

Carson, Richard T., and Peter Navarro. 1988. "Fundamental Issues in Natural Resource Damage Assessment," discussion paper, Department of Economics, University of California, San Diego.

Desvousges, W., Richard Dunford, and Jean Domanico. 1989. "Measuring Natural Resource Damages: An Economic Appraisal," final report prepared for the American Petroleum Institute, Washington, D.C.

Environmental Protection Agency (EPA). 1983. "Guidelines for Performing Regulatory Impact Analysis." Washington, D.C.

Environmental Protection Agency (EPA). 1986. "Interim Guidance on Superfund Selection of Remedy," Guidance Memorandum 9355.0-19. Washington, D.C.

Environmental Protection Agency (EPA). 1987. "Guidance for Conducting Remedial Investigation and Feasibility Studies Under CERCLA." Washington, D.C.

Feldstein, Martin. 1988. "Halving the Pain of Budget Balance," *The Wall Street Journal,* May 25, p. 24.

Grigalunas, Thomas, and James Opaluch. 1987. "Assessing Liability for Damages Under CERCLA: A New Approach for Providing Incentives for Pollution Avoidance?" unpublished manuscript. University of Rhode Island.

Johnson, Gordon J. 1987. "Assessing Natural Resource Damages: Flawed Regulations May Limit Recoveries," *Toxics Law Reporter* 9 (September) p. 432.

Kenison, H., Carolyn L. Buchholz, and Shawn P. Milligan. 1987. "State Actions for Natural Resource Damages: Enforcement of the Public Trust," *Environmental Law Reporter* 17 (November) pp. 10434–10440.

Kopp, Raymond J., Paul Portney, and V. Kerry Smith. 1989. "An Economic Appraisal of the D.C. Appeals Court Ruling on the DOI Regulations for Natural Resource Damage Assessments," Discussion Paper QE90-08, Resources for the Future, Washington, D.C.

Nichols, Albert L., and Richard J. Zeckhauser. 1986. "The Perils of Prudence: How Conservative Risk Assessments Distort Regulation," *Regulation* (November–December) pp. 13–24.

Office of Management and Budget (OMB). 1972. "Circular A-94 Revised," April 3. Washington, D.C.

Phillips, C., and R. Zeckhauser. 1989. "Contingent Valuation of Damage to Natural Resources: How Accurate? How Appropriate?" *Toxics Law Reporter* 4 (October) pp. 520–529.

Segerson, Kathleen. 1987. "Risk-Sharing and Liability in the Control of Stochastic Externalities," *Marine Resource Economics* 4(3) pp. 175–192.

Subcommittee on Benefits and Costs of the Federal Inter-Agency River Basin Committee. 1950. *Proposed Practices for Economic Analysis of River Basin Projects: Report to the FIARBC.* Washington, D.C.

U.S. Congress. Senate. 1962. "Policies, Standards and Procedures in the Formulation, Evaluating and Review of Plans for Use and Development of Water and Related Land Resources." Senate Document No. 97, prepared by the President's Water Resources Council, 87th Cong., 2d sess., May 29, 1962.

U.S. Department of Commerce, National Oceanic and Atmospheric Administration. 1983. *Assessing the Social Costs of Oil Spills: The Amoco Cadiz Case Study.* Washington, D.C.

Violette, Daniel M., and Lauraine G. Chestnut. 1983. "Valuing Reductions in Risk: A Review of the Empirical Estimates," prepared for the Environmental Protection Agency.

Washington State Department of Ecology (WDOE). 1987. "Marine Resource Damage Assessment Report for the *Arco Anchorage* Oil Spill, December 21, 1985, into Port Angeles Harbor and The Strait of Juan de Fuca," WDOE Document No. 87-4.

Water Resources Council. 1979. "Procedures for Evaluation of National Economic Development (NED): Benefits and Costs in Water Resource Planning (Level C), Final Rule," 44 *Federal Register* 72892.

Water Resources Council. 1983. *Principles and Guidelines for Water and Related Land Resource Implementation Studies.* Washington, D.C.: Government Printing Office.

6

Economics of Natural Resource Damage Assessment: Comments on Chapter 5

Willie R. Taylor

1. INTRODUCTION

Chapter 5 by Gardner M. Brown, Jr., addresses the natural resource damage assessment regulations within the overall context of federal hazardous waste management activities. The paper correctly points out that the natural resource damage assessment regulations are but one part of the overall requirements of the Comprehensive Environmental Response, Compensation, and Liability Act of 1980, as amended (CERCLA, also known as Superfund).[1] Most of the other requirements are found in the National Contingency Plan (NCP).[2] These regulations can only be understood within the context of the NCP and CERCLA. Chapter 5 points out, correctly in my opinion, many of the problems with the overall hazardous waste management program of the federal government.

I am pleased that chapter 5 addresses some of the beneficial aspects of the natural resource damage assessment regulations. I agree with Brown's discussion on these aspects of the regulations. The regulations

---

All comments expressed are those of the author and are not the official position of the U.S. Department of the Interior.

[1]42 U.S.C. 9601–9675. Type B regulations are found at 51 *Federal Register* 27674 (Friday, August 1, 1986). Amendments to these regulations can be found at 53 *Federal Register* 5166 (Monday, February 22, 1988). Type A regulations can be found at 52 *Federal Register* 9042 (Friday, March 20, 1987). Technical corrections to type A regulations can be found at 53 *Federal Register* 9769 (Friday, March 25, 1988). Brown addresses type A and type B regulations in section 2.2 of chapter 5.

[2]The National Contingency Plan can be found at 55 *Federal Register* 8666 (Thursday, March 8, 1990).

attempt to combine economics, law, and the biological, chemical, and physical sciences. This attempt is quite possibly a first of its kind. The marriage of economics and law, along with the biological and physical sciences, was not easy. To no one's surprise, the marriage reflected in the regulations has not completely pleased any of the professions.

Brown points out that his critique is solely from an economic perspective. This is as it should be, and his hope that "in the fullness of time, good economics will triumph" is laudable. Unfortunately, in preparing a regulation one finds exogenous legal constraints that are binding. Many of my criticisms of Brown's analysis stem from his search for an unconstrained optimum and the statutory imperative to determine a constrained optimum. His critique is useful in helping to articulate the value of those constraints.

Chapter 5 deals almost exclusively with the type B regulations; therefore, my comments will also deal with only those regulations. However, I think that more attention should be paid to type A regulations. The current procedures encompass only coastal and marine environments.[3] The Department of the Interior (DOI) will be expanding the coverage of its type A regulations.[4] Current and future type A procedures will provide simplified procedures for conducting natural resource damage assessments. As such, their use may eventually become more widespread than procedures under type B regulations.

As Brown notes, the rules have been the subject of legal challenges. In *Ohio v. The United States Department of the Interior,* several issues pertaining to the type B rules were challenged;[5] and in *Colorado v. the Department of the Interior* two issues pertaining to the type A regulations were challenged.[6] A three-member panel of the Circuit Court of Appeals for the District of Columbia unanimously upheld in part and invalidated in part aspects of the type A and type B rules. Those aspects of the court's decisions that directly relate to economic issues are described in section 3 of this chapter.

2. DISCUSSION

Chapter 5 correctly recognizes the so-called public/private dichotomy as one of the major controversies associated with type B regulations. This area was left unaffected by the court's decisions. The distinction between

---

[3]See 52 *Federal Register* 9042 (Friday, March 20, 1987).

[4]See 53 *Federal Register* 20143 (Thursday, June 2, 1988).

[5]880 F.2d 432 (D.C. Cir. 1989).

[6]880 F.2d 481 (D.C. Cir. 1989).

public and private values is difficult for an economist to understand. However, if one reads the history of the legislation that preceded CERCLA, CERCLA itself as enacted, and common law, or examines the potential problems with the government's recovery of damages that should accrue to individuals, it is evident that some type of distinction is necessary.

Three major bills preceded CERCLA: H.R. 7020, H.R. 85, and S. 1480.[7] Each of these bills can be interpreted as an attempt to have businesses internalize all or most of the costs of a discharge of oil or a release of a hazardous substance to the responsible party.[8] It is notable that in CERCLA as finally passed many of these types of damages were deleted, thereby removing the implication that it was an attempt to internalize all, or even a majority of, these costs.

From an economist's standpoint a host of issues are raised when considering the distinction between public and private values (Dower and Scodari [1987]). Clearly, transactions costs, in the form of law suits and the gathering of data for those suits, might be minimized if the trustee could combine all claims into one for the purpose of obtaining compensation. This would save resources and help the economy. However, there are distributional and legal problems with this. For example, Section 107(f)(1) of CERCLA, as amended, requires that "sums recovered by the United States Government as trustee under this subsection shall be retained by the trustee, without further appropriations, for use only to restore, replace, or acquire the equivalent of such natural resources." Therefore the trustee could not compensate the individual for damages. While most economists might argue that the payment to the individual is not crucial to the achievement of Pareto optimality, there may still be questions on this issue (Rowley and Peacock [1975], chapters 2 and 8).

The legal questions that arise when considering the distinction between public and private values are many and varied. Should the trustee be in the position of determining losses for individuals? If the entire damage amount is not granted by the court, how should claims be apportioned? If the trustee recovers damages for individuals, have those individuals lost any private causes of action to recover for damages that the government did not include in its claim? Would collection by the trustee preclude other recoveries for the same discharge or

---

[7]H.R. 7020, 96 Cong., 2 sess. (1980); H.R. 85, 96 Cong., 1 sess, (1979); S. 1480, 96 Cong., 2 sess. (1979).

[8]For example, S. 1480, as introduced, included provisions for out-of-pocket medical expenses, compensation for lost wages or personal income, and capital loss due to the destruction of agricultural products from chemical contamination.

release?[9] Brown's example of groundwater injury is a good one. The question, for the cases he mentions, is: When is the damage compensable to the trustee? I would suggest that the damage to the family that sold its produce in the private market was not compensable to the trustee. Unfortunately, each determination may have to be made on a case-by-case basis. This is clearly a legal standard, not a standard based on economics.

Chapter 5 correctly points out that the regulations set out a hierarchy of economic methodologies that may be used to determine damages. The hierarchy started with methodologies for resources that were traded in a market, using market prices and then appraisals; only if these methodologies were not applicable would the trustee move to the other methodologies, for resources that are not traded in a market—that is, to travel cost and hedonic pricing. Brown points out that in some cases market prices are not an adequate measure of damages. I agree and note that the Technical Information Document that accompanied the regulations makes a similar point (Department of the Interior [1987]).

Brown suggests that reliance on appraisal methods may be misplaced, since "more evidence needs to be found than now generally exists to demonstrate the appraiser's superior ability to penetrate to the truth obscured by market imperfections, compared to other analytical or even ad hoc valuation procedures." I leave it to appraisers to defend their profession; however, I will observe that appraisers have attempted to standardize procedures for performing appraisals (Department of Justice [1973]; Eaton [1982]). While one can criticize some of the standards used by appraisers, it must be said that they have attempted to formalize their procedures and provide ground rules as to what constitutes a good analysis.[10]

The hierarchy of market and nonmarket resource methodologies was an artifact of the regulations, not of CERCLA per se, and was thought to be consistent with the principles of common law. The court has struck down the required hierarchy of economic methodologies. Trustees will be free to select among the methodologies listed in the rules as long as double counting does not take place.

The issues of option value and existence value have vexed the economics profession as well as the promulgation of the regulations (see

---

[9]The Oil Pollution Act of 1990, discussed in section 4 below, expands the liability of spillers to include several types of damages that might be thought to be primarily private in nature. However, these damages are not part of a trustee's natural resource damage claim.

[10]In fact, much of the discussion of economics in the many briefs used in the *Ohio* case can be traced to the lack of a centralized store of good practices for conducting empirical economic analyses for nonmarketed resources.

chapter 13 by A. Myrick Freeman). Contrary to Brown's claim, the regulations did not assume that "the expected value of option [value] and existence value is zero, when use values exist." The preamble to the regulations stated that "ordinarily, option and existence values would be added to use values."[11]

Far from assuming a zero value, the Department of the Interior gave its reasons for limiting the use of option values and existence values. Brown correctly lists those reasons, given in the preamble to the regulations, as (1) the fact that use values are specified in the law; and, more important, (2) the facts that option values and existence values were less well defined and that more uncertainty surrounds their measurement. The preamble stated that "because of these reasons, their [option values and existence values'] *current* use, if the authorized official acting as trustee wishes to obtain a rebuttable presumption, is limited" (emphasis added).[12] Thus, as the results obtained from measurement techniques became more certain, the concepts of option and existence could be added.

The discussion on the applicability of nonuse values in a natural resource damage assessment may now be moot, given the *Ohio* ruling. The court has stated that all reliably calculated values can be included in damage assessments. As such, option values and existence values may become part of all damage claims.

Chapter 5 raises an interesting concept in section 3.6, "Natural Resource Slander." Brown argues that the definition of injury is wrong because injury need not be limited to characteristics of natural resources "defined by biologists, chemists, geologists, air and fisheries specialists, and other non-social scientists." I would carry his argument a step further. From an economist's standpoint, I see no reason why injury in a physical sense is required prior to the calculation of a damage amount. Generally, economists deal with individual and group behavior or perception. There is no obvious reason why the perception of injury would not be sufficient to generate a damage (Dower and Scodari [1987]). Brown's argument is not quite as strong as the argument used by other economists that there is no need for biologists and physical scientists. However, carried to its logical conclusion, his argument would agree with this argument.

From a public policy perspective, I would be uncomfortable in awarding damages based on perceptions, when *no* physical harm could be determined. Congress may have made Brown's argument moot when it stated that "the term 'damages' means damages for injury or loss of natural resources . . ."[13] Furthermore, the legislative history of CERCLA

---

[11]See 51 *Federal Register* 27719 (Friday, August 1, 1986).

[12]See 51 *Federal Register* 27719 (Friday, August 1, 1986).

[13]See CERCLA § 101 (6).

suggests that injury should be related to deleterious physical or chemical changes or changes in viability.[14] The language of the statute and its legislative history would seem to imply that before determining damages (1) a discharge or release that is covered by CERCLA, or by the Clean Water Act of 1977,[15] has occurred; (2) physical injury to a resource has occurred; and (3) it is likely that the injury resulted from that discharge or release. Only then can damages be determined for that injury. The regulations mirror this causal chain. Therefore, while it may be possible for economists to determine injury without a requirement of actual chemical, physical, or viability change, CERCLA seems to require the finding of such change as a prerequisite to the determination of damages.

The regulations use the discount rate established in Office of Management and Budget (OMB) Circular A-94 (1972). That rate is currently 10 percent. Brown notes that "no academic economist, to my knowledge, publicly has supported the DOI regulations on the discount rate. This may be one of the few times in recent history that all, or nearly all, academic economists are on the same side of a discount rate argument." I cannot speak to the unanimity of academic economists; however, I believe that a review of the comments on the rule indicate that at least some non-academic economists have favored the 10 percent rate. Moreover, OMB recommended the use of that rate. As stated in the preamble to the regulation, "the 10 percent rate was selected after extensive interagency consultation and has been retained in this final regulation."[16]

It is interesting to note that any discount rate is a two-edged sword (see chapter 12 by Ralph C. d'Arge). A discount rate is used to "deflate" future values, but it is also used to "inflate" past values. As Brown correctly points out, CERCLA states that "there shall be no recovery under the authority of subparagraph (C) of section (a) [natural resource damages] where such damages and the release from which such damages resulted have occurred wholly before the enactment of this Act [December 11, 1980]." Thus it seems that if the release and damages continued after December 11, 1980, potentially responsible parties are liable for damages from the beginning of the release. In the case of some mining wastes, this could go back to the early 1900s.

In *Ohio*, the court upheld the use of the concept of discounting, and the Department of the Interior's discretion to select the OMB discount in particular. However, Brown's suggestion of using, at a minimum, the discount rate that is applied on the Superfund account is a good one and should be

---

[14]For a legislative history, see U.S. Congress (1980), which recounts the difficulty in proving that a particular exposure to a pollutant is in fact the cause of injury.

[15]33 U.S.C. 1251 et seq.

[16]51 *Federal Register* 27722 (Friday, August 1, 1986).

addressed in the biennial review of the rules. However, any fixed rate may cause problems. In the future, a discount rate formula should be considered.

Brown argues that the concept of "committed use" limits the types of claims that trustees can file. I agree. Committed use is defined in the regulation as ". . . either: a current public use; or a planned public use of a natural resource for which there is a documented legal, administrative, budgetary, or financial commitment established before the discharge of oil or release of a hazardous substance is detected."[17] In its preamble, the DOI noted that only future uses need be documented.[18]

The committed use concept is an artifact of the regulations, not of CERCLA per se. However, the legislative histories of CERCLA and common law indicate that some definition was intended to foreclose speculative damages. In determining damages, one must know what uses and services the resource would have provided if the release or discharge had not occurred. The definition of committed use removes speculative uses from the analysis. It should be noted that the requirement of a committed use does not seem to be onerous. Something as simple as zoning might apply. In addition, if no plans for the resource's future have been made, it is not unreasonable to assume that the resource would be used in the future in the same way it is currently being used.[19]

Brown's argument that one cannot make a legal commitment for "an unknown number of viewer days of eagles in the year 2005" seems to miss the point. The committed use concept requires that the resource currently be used or that future resource uses be documented. If the viewing of eagles is the current use of the property (or the biological resource of the property is eagles), no further documentation is needed. The concept of committed use does not require that a particular level of activity be predetermined and documented. The level of activity is the subject of the damage determination, after the uses and services of the injured natural resource are determined in the quantification phase of the assessment.[20]

Finally, Brown addresses the bias in the regulations against adding lands to the federal estate. Again, this bias against increasing the federal estate is an artifact of the regulations, not of CERCLA. I would agree that this provision could add to the potential cost of compensation for injuries to federal natural resources. The explicit reason for this bias given by the Department of the Interior, after extensive consultation with federal

---

[17]51 *Federal Register* 27727 (Friday, August 1, 1986).

[18]51 *Federal Register* 27695 (Friday, August 1, 1986).

[19]Brown should note that EPA has a groundwater classification system for aquifers, not that all aquifers have been classified according to this system.

[20]Thus the guidance in the quantification section of the regulations provides information on the determination of the level of future uses.

agencies, was to limit the expansion of the federal estate. The federal government currently owns or controls approximately one-third of the land in the nation. It was determined that CERCLA should not be used by federal trustees as a vehicle to further expand this land base.

3.   COURT REVIEW

Section 113 of CERCLA provides that any member of the public may petition the Court of Appeals of the District of Columbia Circuit to review any regulation promulgated under CERCLA. A number of parties have filed such petitions for the court to review the natural resource damage assessment rules. The rules were challenged in two separate but parallel cases. In *Ohio,* petitioners challenged a total of twelve issues pertaining to the administrative process and the type B procedures established in the rules. In *Colorado v. Interior,* petitioners challenged two issues pertaining to the type A procedures.

The D.C. Court of Appeals unanimously upheld in part and invalidated in part certain aspects of the administrative process and the type A and type B procedures. For the purposes of this discussion, the important points decided by the court were:

• The rule must use restoration costs as the preferred measure of damages, rather than take the lesser of restoration costs or economic value as the measure of damages. However, there may be times when this preference is outweighed by other concerns, such as technical feasibility or costs of restoration that are grossly disproportionate to benefits.

• The Department of the Interior's definition of reasonable costs— the amount of money that may be recovered for the cost of performing the assessment—did not contradict the statute.[21]

• The acceptance criteria for determining injury to biological resources were consistent with the statute.[22]

---

[21]The definition of reasonable cost requires that: the injury, quantification, and damage determination phases must be well coordinated; anticipated increment of extra benefits (in terms of the accuracy of estimates) obtained by using a more costly injury, quantification, or damage determination method are greater than the anticipated increment of extra costs of that method; and the anticipated cost of assessment is less than the anticipated damage amount.

[22]The acceptance criteria are as follows: a biological response is often a result of exposure to oil or hazardous substances; exposure to oil or hazardous substances is known to cause this response in free-ranging organisms; exposure to oil or hazardous substances is known to cause this response in controlled experiments; the biological response measurement is practical to perform and produces scientifically valid results.

- The department's definition of committed use, given the court's decision on restoration costs, was consistent with the statute.
- The use of the contingent valuation method to determine damages was consistent with the statute's requirement to use the best available procedures.
- The department's authority to require a restoration plan after the award of damages was consistent with the intent of the statute.
- All "reliably" calculated values (including option values and existence values) could be recoverable, with no specific hierarchy of methods stipulated to calculate values.
- The department should clarify the extent to which the rules apply to natural resources not owned by the trustees.

The court also stated that the department could use a computer model to determine damages under its type A rules; however, these rules should be consistent with the court's decisions on the type B procedures.

In response to the court's decision, the department is currently revising the regulations. Proposed type B rules were published on April 29, 1991.[23] DOI has reviewed comments on the proposed rules and hopes to publish final type B rules late in 1992. It will take the department longer to promulgate type A rules, since considerable research is needed to determine "representative" restoration costs.

The first type A rule was developed for coastal and marine environments. The rule incorporates the Natural Resource Damage Assessment Model for Coastal and Marine Environments (NRDA/CME). In preparing the NRDA/CME, DOI tried to find examples of restoration costs to incorporate into the model. Given the relatively small amount of data available at that time, the department was unable to find adequate restoration costs. However, it is hoped that there are now sufficient data to incorporate restoration costs into the NRDA/CME (as well as into the model currently under development for the Great Lakes environment [NRDA/GLE]).

4.   THE OIL POLLUTION ACT OF 1990

On August 18, 1990, President Bush signed the Oil Pollution Act of 1990 (OPA).[24] OPA addresses a wide range of issues, including the creation of a comprehensive regime for preventing, responding to, and paying for the cleanup resulting from oil spills, and the setting of new standards for vessel construction, crew licensing, and contingency planning, among other things.

---

[23]56 *Federal Register* 19752, April 29, 1991.

[24]33 U.S.C. 2701 et seq.

OPA changed the rules of the game for natural resource damage assessments for oil spills. At least four important changes have been made in this area. First, an Oil Spill Liability Trust Fund was created, which may pay for cleanup and damages not paid for by the spiller. Natural resource damages were originally compensable from Superfund, but authority for expending funds for these damages was explicitly excluded in the 1986 amendments to CERCLA.

Second, OPA provides that the costs of initiating natural resource damage assessments may come from the fund. The ability of trustees to perform natural resource damage assessments has been limited by the lack of seed money. While the fund will pay only the costs to initiate natural resource damage assessments, this may be the boost that trustees need to get over initial funding problems.

Third, OPA (§ 1002) substantially increases a spiller's explicit liability for damages. Spillers are liable for loss of natural resources; loss of real or personal property; loss of subsistence use; loss of taxes, royalties, rents, fees, or net profit shares by governmental entities; loss of profits and earning capacity; and changes in the costs of providing public services. This substantial increase in explicit liabilities seems to correspond to the areas addressed in Senate bill 1480, discussed above.

Finally, OPA provides for natural resource damage assessment rules for oil spills in navigable waters to be developed by the under secretary of commerce for oceans and atmosphere, particularly the subsidiary National Oceanic and Atmospheric Administration (NOAA), in consultation with, among others, the U.S. Fish and Wildlife Service of the Department of the Interior. If a trustee's natural resource damage assessment is performed in conformance with NOAA's rules, it receives a rebuttable presumption.

OPA mandates that natural resource damage assessment rules are to be promulgated by August 1992. Section 6001(b) of OPA provides that any rule in effect under a law replaced by OPA will continue in effect until superseded. Thus it would seem that DOI's rules will remain in effect for oil spills until NOAA's rules are promulgated as final. After NOAA's rules are published as final, the DOI rules would cover spills of hazardous materials under CERCLA. DOI and NOAA are working together to ensure that their respective natural resource damage assessment rules will be as consistent as possible.

5.   CONCLUSION

Chapter 5 provides a good critique of the type B natural resource damage assessment regulations. It points out many of the good aspects of the regulation, as well as some of its perceived shortcomings. That chapter correctly puts the natural resource damage assessment regulations into the context of the government's overall hazardous waste program, and thereby provides a good perspective for the reader. In the context of this overall program, the natural resource damage assessment regulations are a small, albeit controversial, part of a very large program.

I disagree with only a few points made by Brown in chapter 5. Among them are the characterization of committed use and the issue of natural resource slander. The basis for much of my disagreement is not the economic analysis provided by Brown, but the fact that he ignores the legal and statutory constraints facing the Department of the Interior in preparing the rules. CERCLA, its legislative history, and common law all form binding constraints on the application of several economic principles.

The *Ohio* suit will result in changes to the rules. In particular, restoration costs will become the preferred measure of natural resource damages under CERCLA, and all reliably calculated lost use values of injured natural resources will be recoverable, with no specific hierarchy of methodologies required of natural resource trustees in conducting those valuations.

In implementing the court's ruling on the preference for restoration costs, some of the economic efficiency alluded to in chapter 5 will be lost. However, the court recognized that there will be some occasions when restoration costs will not be the preferred measure of damages. In determining those instances, benefits and costs (among other things) will have to be addressed, thereby regaining some of the balance Brown seeks.

The Oil Pollution Act of 1990 created a potential for different rules for natural resource damages, dependent only upon the substance released. The Department of the Interior is working closely with NOAA to ensure the coordination of parallel processes for damage assessments, whether they result from releases of hazardous substances or discharges of oil.

The success of any natural resource damage regulations will depend on how they are used—or not used—in actual damage assessments. It is probably too early to tell whether the DOI regulations will be useful. It should be noted that one of the major uses of the regulations is to provide a framework for negotiated settlements of natural resource damage cases. As such, the regulations provide a much needed basis for discussion between trustees and potentially responsible parties, which may lead to a decrease in litigation.

In any event, by statute the regulations must be reviewed and revised as appropriate every two years. This provision should help to ensure that the regulations will keep pace with advances in science and economics. The topic of natural resource damage is an important one to the public in general and to economists in particular. The regulations can only benefit by review and comment from the widest possible audience.

REFERENCES

Department of the Interior. 1987. *Type B Technical Information Document: Techniques to Measure Damages to Natural Resources.* PB88-100136. Washington, D.C.

Department of Justice. 1973. "Uniform Appraisal Standards for Federal Land Acquisition," Interagency Land Acquisition Conference. Washington, D.C.

Dower, R. C., and Scodari, P. F. 1987. "Compensation for Natural Resource Injury: An Emerging Federal Framework," *Journal of Marine Resource Economics* 4(3) pp. 155–174.

Eaton, J. D. 1982. *Real Estate Valuation in Litigation.* Chicago: American Institute of Real Estate Appraisers.

Office of Management and Budget (OMB). 1972. Circular No. A-94 Revised, April 3, 1972.

Rowley, C. K., and Peacock, A. T. 1975. *Welfare Economics: A Liberal Restatement.* New York: John Wiley & Sons.

U.S. Congress. Senate. Committee on Environment and Public Works. 1980. "Six Case Studies of Compensation for Toxic Substances Pollution: Alabama, California, Michigan, Missouri, New Jersey, and Texas. A Report Prepared Under the Supervision of the Congressional Research Service of the Library of Congress for the Committee on Environment and Public Works." S. Rept. No. 96-13, 96 Cong., 2d. sess., pp. 168–521.

7
Implementing Natural Resource Damage Assessments

Raymond J. Kopp and V. Kerry Smith

1. INTRODUCTION

This chapter discusses the practice of measuring damages to natural resources. These assessments must respond to multiple influences—the statutes defining natural resource damage liability, suggested guidelines for
damage measurement from the Department of the Interior (DOI), established practices in science for measuring injuries and in economics for
valuing nonmarketed goods and services, and past court decisions and
case settlements. These damage assessments are complex evaluations;
even the simplest of them must make a set of assumptions about what is
important and what is not.

Measuring natural resource damages usually involves two assessments. The first, a preassessment, determines whether the situation warrants a second, full-scale assessment.[1] Limited resources are available to
trustees to undertake the analysis and litigation required to recover damages. At the early preassessment stage the trustee (or trustees—there can
be more than one agency with responsibilities) must narrow the range of
uncertainty in evaluating whether the damages justify undertaking the
required analysis and prosecution of a particular case and whether the
trustee can effectively prove the damages. Ultimately this is a strategic
decision, based on considerable information that extends well beyond
early assessments of damage. Our concern in this book is with damage
assessment in general, and we will have little to say about the decision to
prosecute any particular case.

Because this book is about actual damage assessments and the research issues they pose for resource and environmental economics, an

---

[1]In the case of catastrophic events such as the *Exxon Valdez* oil spill, a preassessment
is superfluous.

118

examination of the current practice must consider the context of existing statutes, rules, and precedents in order to describe accurately the assumptions made by analysts in developing damage assessments that might have a special influence on the results of those assessments. In section 2 of this chapter we briefly summarize how the DOI rules and two court decisions about them have influenced current assessment practices. We then discuss the preassessment and the full-scale assessment (section 3).

In section 4 we address the issue of the relationship between science and economics. While it is recognized that a monetary estimate of damage provided by economists is intended to be used in gauging the importance of the physical injuries defined and measured by natural scientists, the two (injuries and damage) are not necessarily well connected in current assessments. Section 4 attempts to draw attention to some of the tensions and misunderstandings that exist between the social and natural science components of damage assessment.

Section 5 provides a brief overview of the current methods economists employ to value injuries. These techniques will be considered in detail in subsequent chapters; however, to appreciate the discussion of an actual case and assessment, a brief introduction to these techniques is useful. Section 6 places our discussion of actual practice in focus by summarizing an analysis undertaken for a damage case involving the Eagle Mine near Minturn, Colorado. This abandoned mine and its tailings ponds and roaster piles released hazardous wastes into the Eagle River and contaminated local aquifers. For this reason, the site qualified for litigation under the Comprehensive Environmental Response, Compensation, and Liability Act of 1980 (CERCLA).[2] Section 7 concludes the chapter with a discussion of potential future damage assessment practices.

2. THE DEPARTMENT OF THE INTERIOR'S ASSESSMENT PROCEDURES

Administrative law envisions that legislation will be implemented in an orderly fashion. The rulemaking process translates legislative intentions into procedures designed to meet certain objectives. Under such legislation, Congress or the president designates an office in the executive branch to assume the responsibility for undertaking the rulemaking tasks, and the courts act as "gatekeepers" who evaluate whether procedures are

---

[2]The case was actually initiated under state law with the state of Colorado as the trustee for the resource. Because information about the approaches taken by the plaintiff's and the defendant's experts are available, we can use the case to illustrate how analysts' judgments influence damage estimates.

consistent with intent. The activities defined by this process usually evolve over time.

While the mandates for a natural resource damage liability can be traced to 1973, researchers' experience with the process is very limited (Breen [1989]). The Department of the Interior's first set of rules for assessing damages to natural resources was initially issued in 1986, and the Court of Appeals of the District of Columbia ruled on challenges to them in 1989. A new set of draft rules was announced and public commentary was being reviewed as this book went to press. Despite these qualifications, the economic logic underlying DOI's initial rules was impressive (as Gardner Brown's critique in chapter 5 suggests). We highlight the primary elements in the revised rules below, and in the closing chapter of this volume comment on their implications as part of our discussion of future research.

Once the relevant trustee has been notified of a hazardous substance release that has the potential to injure a natural resource, a preassessment screening is undertaken to determine whether full assessment is warranted. Scientific criteria provide the basis for defining whether a release has injured the natural resource. The DOI protocol for damage assessment requires that (1) injuries to natural resources be determined, (2) injuries be linked to the substances released, and (3) the substances be linked to a potentially responsible party (PRP) before any monetary assessment of the injury takes place.[3]

When these conditions are satisfied, the damage assessment develops values for any past losses arising from reductions in the flow of services provided by the resource as a result of the injury. These damages are broken down into the cumulative loss from the date of the injury to the present, the loss from the present until recovery is initiated, the loss during the period of recovery, and finally the loss into the infinite future of any service not fully restored. The procedures by which the trustee accomplishes these tasks are the focus of the DOI rules and the two court rulings concerning them. Table 7-1 (pp. 122–123) summarizes the key elements in the assessment process that were affected by the courts' rulings and describes how the proposed revisions to DOI's rules respond to them.

Economic measures of past, current, and future damage require the analyst to specify how the scientifically defined injuries affect the services the resource has provided and could provide in the future. While initial DOI rules limited consideration to what might be described as in situ use (known as "use value" in economic jargon), the D.C. Circuit Court of

---

[3]This establishes the pathway by which a hazardous substance associated with the activities of a PRP could cause the injury identified.

Appeals ruling allows nonuse values to be included, describing them as a form of nonconsumptive use. The proposed revisions to DOI's rules accept this position by defining the compensable value for natural resource services as including all use and nonuse values.[4]

No direct market transactions occur in the in situ uses and, of course, nonuse services do not leave a behavioral trail in market choices.[5] Because of this, the nonmarket valuation methods developed for benefit-cost analyses of environmental policies have become a key focus in applying economics to damage assessment.

Given that values can be measured, the basic structure of an amended DOI damage assessment process would be consistent with a compensation principle. That is, if designated natural resources are held in public trust as assets, and if private actions reduce their value, then the appropriate compensation is the reduction in the value of the natural asset held in trust. The D.C. Circuit Court of Appeals ruling goes beyond this economic interpretation by implying that using a monetary value to compensate for a public asset may consistently understate its social value. Hence, the ruling favors the cost of restoring the resources to baseline (that is, prerelease) conditions over an economic valuation of future loss, unless restoration would be impossible or would impose costs completely inconsistent with (grossly disproportionate to) the resource's value.

In principle, the court's favoring of restoration and the economist's notion of compensation are not necessarily at odds. The loss of future asset value defined by the economist is equivalent to the value of services restored if restoration is complete.[6] Thus, in situations in which the restoration costs are less than the cumulative value of the resource's services, restoration will provide a natural asset with the ability to sustain services. The amount of compensation to the public is the same under both views. However, the cost of restoration (the amount of the damage award levied on the defendant) can exceed the value of the services. In these cases, basing damages on restoration costs may be inefficient from an economic perspective.

The proposed DOI revisions do not substantively modify this aspect of the court's ruling and avoid offering a numerical scale for grossly disproportionate costs. Instead, the proposed rules argue that ten factors

---

[4]Compensable value is defined as encompassing "all of the public economic values associated with an injured resource, including use values and nonuse values such as option, existence, and bequest values." 56 *Federal Register* 19760 (April 29, 1991).

[5]This does not preclude analysts from assuming linkages with the specification of preference functions that associate environmental services with market goods in ways that are not intended to represent uses. This is the logic underlying Larson's (forthcoming) proposed method for estimating existence values.

[6]Both use and nonuse values must be considered.

Table 7-1. Key Elements of Type B Damage Assessment

Issue	DOI final rules for type B (August 1, 1986)	D.C. Circuit Court of Appeals ruling (July 14, 1989)[a]	*Acushnet River & New Bedford Harbor* ruling (June 7, 1989)[b]	Proposed revision to DOI rules (April 29, 1991)
Timing of past damages	Vague. The only specific direction is for releases initiated and completed before CERCLA (1980), because they are not subject to natural resource damage liability.		For divisible damages, establishes date of passage of CERCLA (1980) for releases with continuing effects; for indivisible damages, full amount of damage is to be used.	
Hierarchy of valuation methods	Establishes hierarchy with "prices" for the natural resource.	No hierarchy of methods intended; recognizes that nonmarket valuation is likely to be the only feasible basis; affirms contingent valuation method as a "best available methodology."		Exhibits a contradictory position; acknowledges court's ruling; removes hierarchy, but describes contingent valuation as the least reliable method in most situations, such as measuring compensable value or measuring nonuse value.

Lesser-of rule[c]	Natural resource damages associated with the current and future status of the injured resource should be measured as the lesser of the restoration cost, the replacement cost, or the discounted use values lost as a result of the injury to the resource.	Rejects lesser-of rule; damages correspond to restoration cost unless restoration is technically infeasible or cost is grossly disproportionate in relation to discounted total value (including use and nonuse values) lost as a result of injury. In these cases, damages would be the discounted value.	Leaves determination of "grossly disproportionate" to the direction of the trustee; offers no useful guidance on how to gauge when restoration costs would be too great in comparison with values provided; does not acknowledge that situations without restoration or replacement will occur.
Committed use	Defined as either a current public use or a planned public use for which there is documented legal, administrative, budgetary, or financial commitment before the release.	Removes restriction on nonuse values; defines committed use as a requirement to avoid highly speculative future uses.	

[a]*Ohio v. The United States Department of the Interior*, 880 F.2d 432 (D.C. Cir. 1989).

[b]*Acushnet River & New Bedford Harbor: Proceedings Re Alleged PCB Pollution*, Civil Action No. 83-388201-1, "Memorandum Concerning Natural Resource Damages Under CERCLA," District Judge Young, June 7, 1989.

[c]DOI rules required a 10 percent real rate in calculating present value of future losses; the D.C. Court of Appeals ruling maintained this requirement.

123

should be considered together in selecting alternatives for restoration, rehabilitation, replacement, or acquisition of equivalent resources. They include: technical feasibility; relationship of expected costs of proposed actions to expected benefits from restoration, rehabilitation, replacement, or acquisition of equivalent resources; cost-effectiveness; results of actual or planned response actions; potential for additional injury resulting from proposed actions, including long-term and indirect impacts; the natural recovery period; ability of the resource to recover with or without alternative actions; acquisition of equivalent land; potential effect of action on human health and safety; and consistency with federal and state laws.[7] These same factors are to be jointly considered in judging whether costs are grossly disproportionate to the value of the lost services.

3. DAMAGE ASSESSMENTS

As discussed above, two assessments must be performed to establish natural resource damages; the first determines whether the second is warranted. In order to proceed with a detailed evaluation of the damages from injuries attributed to releases of hazardous waste or oil, the trustee must have reasonable prospects for recovering damages. While the science establishing the link between the substance released and injuries to natural resources is crucial in this process, it cannot be the exclusive basis for determining whether to proceed. The magnitude of this damage depends on what has been injured, what will be lost without restoration, and how much this matters to people. If the injuries do not matter, any expenditure for restoration could be regarded as grossly disproportionate to the value of the natural asset involved.

For these reasons, the likely magnitude of damages is usually appraised as part of the deliberations leading to the initiation of each case. In fact, after a case is filed, the same process will be undertaken by prudent PRPs. Unfortunately, the importance of this first step is often not fully appreciated. By identifying what is known about the economic magnitude of the damages, the first assessment should structure the analysis required in the more complete evaluation undertaken by each trustee. Similarly, a careful evaluation of what can reasonably be established identifies the

---

[7]The Oil Pollution Act of 1990 promises to complicate the damage assessment process. It requires that the National Oceanographic and Atmospheric Administration, in consultation with the Environmental Protection Agency (EPA) and the U.S. Fish and Wildlife Service, develop a separate set of rules for damage assessments involving natural resource injuries from oil spills. The process of developing these rules is still under way. In fact, the proposed revision to the DOI rules outlines procedures for coordinating development of these rules with those offered by DOI.

areas of contention and the research required for any PRP's defense. The defense does not usually involve an independent, full-scale damage assessment. Rather, it establishes the range of physical and economic effects on the systems involved. Based on this information, analysts must estimate the magnitude and duration of the effects and judge the trustee's ability to establish them in a convincing way.

In evaluating the research associated with these preliminary assessments and the full-scale appraisals, it is important to describe some of the ways in which they differ from ordinary benefit analyses for nonmarketed resources. First, they are strategic analyses. As a consequence, the assumptions made in developing estimates will combine economic and scientific judgments with legal strategy. Because of this influence, one important issue to be considered in evaluating any proposed economic research on damage assessment is its role in narrowing the range of estimates that can be produced by the assumptions motivated by each side's legal strategy. In effect, can analysts offer tests or modeling alternatives that isolate how much of a damage estimate is attributable to specific assumptions?

Second, a small number of parties will make payments based on the damage assessments. Errors made in assessing these damages can have a significant impact on the economic well-being of the defendants. In contrast, when methods for nonmarket valuation are used in benefit-cost analysis, some error (bias) can be tolerated in the benefit estimates as long as the direction of bias is known in advance. For example, in discussing public investment decisions involving the preservation or development of unique natural environments, Krutilla and Fisher (1975) suggested a strategy that focused on what could *not* be measured. Often this related to some or all of the benefits associated with the decision to preserve a resource. By calculating the net benefits from developing an existing natural area (excluding the opportunity costs posed by forgoing preservation), one would have gauged the size of the preservation benefits required in order for a benefit-cost rule to signal indifference. What could be measured was biased. Nonetheless, knowing the direction and source of the bias would focus attention on where information and judgment were required.

Third, a damage assessment focuses on natural resources as assets. As we discuss in section 4, the crucial issues for interaction between science and economics arise from the relationship between how the analysts characterize the injuries to the asset's services and how those injuries are perceived and valued by people. This orientation has several implications. It implies that a detailed description of the affected natural resource is crucial to an authentic characterization of the interrelationship between the services provided by one or more natural assets (from both scientific and economic perspectives). This sort of detail is rarely found in a benefit-cost study. Consider the definition of restoration. A coastal wetland has numerous services, including: providing habitat for a wide range of species, offering a nursery for various fish populations, contributing to maintenance of the salinity balance in coastal groundwater deposits, and reducing coastal erosion. When such a wetland is contaminated, a restoration plan must balance these services, reflecting both their natural interdependencies and their relative values. If the analysis defines the natural asset as coastal groundwater deposits or as the fisheries supported by the wetland, different aspects of the services will be identified. Ideally, the ultimate appraisal of damages should be consistent with all the services provided by a resource.

Finally, we must address the issue of selecting discount and capitalization rates for measuring the present value of past and future damages, to gauge how much the monetary value of the natural asset has been influenced by the injuries. These calculations differ from those associated with public investment decisions, and thus selecting rates to discount and capitalize these annual damages may also vary, as Ralph d'Arge discusses in chapter 12.

4.   BALANCING THE NATURAL AND ECONOMIC SCIENCES IN DAMAGE ASSESSMENT

Platitudes could be offered in describing the conceptual basis for a coordinated damage assessment identifying unique roles for the natural sciences, engineering, and economics. However, it is important to explicitly state what is very likely apparent to most observers of these interactions: the plan for coordinated research has conceptual and practical dimensions. At a practical level, it is a struggle over disciplinary turf. It is impossible to escape the direct connection between problem definition and allocation of budgetary resources.

In most cases, the economic analyses of damage and the engineering/economic estimates of restoration costs are the key information defining the boundaries that must be litigated in damage assessments once the connection between PRP, substance release, and injuries has been established. This last qualification is crucial: without the connection, there is no basis for seeking damages. However, the requirement to establish the connection does not imply that the natural scientist's description of the affected resources, measurement of injured services, experiments, and data collection will be useful in the economist's efforts to measure damages. More often than not, the economist will require particular types of scientific information—information not collected—to support the pathway and injury determination phases of the damage assessment.

To understand why this is important, we must describe the economist's perspectives on monetizing the damages from injuries to the services provided by natural assets. The economist's notion of damage is based on an anthropocentric value system that implies that the damage resulting from injuries to a resource reflects the value people hold for the resource and the loss in this value that people attribute to the perceived injuries. While much research must be undertaken to fully understand human perceptions of service losses, current research into natural resource damages has already uncovered some important components.

People perceive natural resources on a more general level than do natural scientists. For example, when considering the injuries to a marine environment, a biologist may identify a wide range of injuries that includes all life forms along a complex food chain, from benthic organisms to fish populations to birds and marine mammals. However, a non-biologist may view this marine environment in terms of a single dimension, perhaps as a wildlife sanctuary. The "average" individual might think of injuries and lost value associated with the resource only in terms of this sanctuary notion. He or she may be incapable of valuing the lost benthic organisms; in that case, no damage would be assigned to them on an individual basis unless it was derived from a coordinated model that describes how the other linked resources contribute to the services that people can enjoy.

From an economic perspective, if damages to natural resources are to be based on human values they must be defined in a manner consistent with human perceptions. But in determining what is required to restore the resource, the analyst's specification must be consistent with the relevant natural constraints defining how these resources interact and support each other's functions. Perceptions alone are not enough in planning restoration; however, this scientific consistency requirement does not mean that people have to understand and provide separate values for each of the constituent elements. Natural and economic scientists must balance their analyses and find mechanisms for linking people's perceptions of a resource's services to scientific evaluations of the physical activities affected by any injury to the resource.

This process is further complicated by the fact that perceptions of injury to a resource's services are not necessarily smooth, continuous functions of the physical measures of injury. When analysts connect a dollar measure of damages to a physical index of the injury, the relationship may appear discontinuous. Because estimates of economic damages incorporate the way people perceive the change in a resource's services, the connection to some physical characteristic of the resource may not be a smoothly rising function with damage rising as the extent of injury increases.

One possible pattern of the relationship between a dollar measure of damages and a physical index of injury is illustrated in figure 7-1. The dollar value of damage is plotted on the vertical axis, and a physical measure of injury is plotted on the horizontal axis. The graph suggests that the damage function may be a step or threshold function, implying that injuries below some threshold may be assigned zero value by individuals. However, the transition can be abrupt. Beyond a threshold there is a clear loss in value, but the magnitude remains relatively unaffected over some range of values for the physical index. Then at some stage it again increases. For example, a small amount of oil washed onto a beach may not deter anyone from visiting the site, but a greater amount will deter all individuals; however, greater amounts of unprecedented magnitude may have no additional effect. Similarly, people may perceive a small number of birds killed as slight damage. But the report of a few more losses extending the number beyond some implicit tolerance level will trigger perceptions of great loss. Once this threshold is reached, doubling the loss

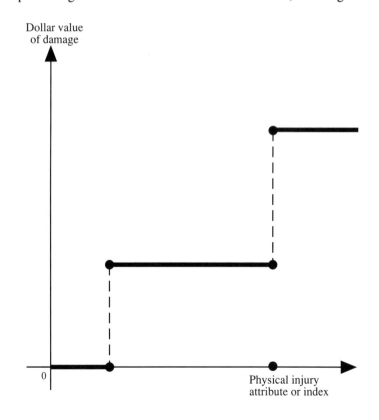

Figure 7-1. A hypothetical damage-injury relationship

of birds may not increase the perception of loss, and thus damage. The attributes of injury on the horizontal axis can take many forms. As stated, they may include the number of birds killed by a substance release or perhaps the number of bird species affected.

If the threshold model of injury and damage accurately reflects people's perceptions, it has significant implications for scientific investigations of injury. One important concern relates to efforts to narrow the range of scientific uncertainty around point estimates of natural resource injuries. If people's perceptions of reductions in the quality or amount of services available from a natural resource after an injury adhere to the threshold function, then refining estimates of the exact magnitude of the injuries may well have no effect on monetary estimates of damage. The thresholds for changes in perceived impacts must be identified for each resource. Then the extent of injury can be estimated in relationship to these thresholds.

Figure 7-2 illustrates on a single dimension the physical index of the injury (that is, the horizontal axis given in figure 7-1). Using this scale, consider a preliminary estimate of the injury index, I_0, corresponding to a confidence interval, $I_0 \pm k$. Refining this estimate by enhanced scientific experiments, data collection, or modeling designed to narrow the confidence bounds will not influence damage estimates in this case. If the thresholds are at a and c, scientific effort to narrow the uncertainty about I_0 will not influence people's perceptions of injury. If the lower threshold

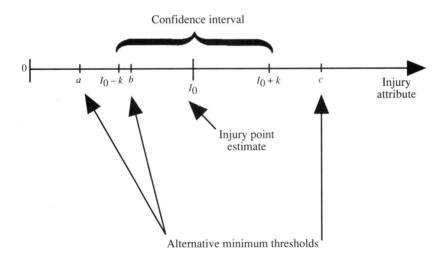

Figure 7-2. Scientific versus economic criteria for estimating injuries to natural resources

for perceiving reduced damage were at b instead of a, then increased scientific resources should be devoted to evaluating the degree to which we can confidently conclude that the injuries exceed b. This is what a coordinated assessment giving equal status to natural and economic considerations would require. The changes in the services or quality of resources that people feel are important, combined with knowledge of the natural interdependencies in the processes that sustain these resources, would define how initial estimates of the injuries to these resources are refined in the assessment process.

5. VALUING THE SERVICES OF NATURAL RESOURCES

Damage assessment is undertaken to estimate how the value of one or more natural assets injured by hazardous waste or oil has changed due to those injuries. This estimated value has two components—the interim damages between the initial onset of the injury and any permanent damages to the extent restoration is incomplete. While the newly proposed DOI rules may seem to make this distinction less clear by identifying the possibility of natural recovery, the basic principles are comparable.

Responding to this mandate involves two tasks that are conceptually linked, but for ease of exposition we treat them separately. The first task is to estimate the value a typical person places on the resource's services under different conditions of perceived injuries, while the second task is to determine how many people hold this value.

Let us first consider the task of quantifying the value. Ordinarily, the economic measure of the real value of anything is expressed by a tradeoff. How much of some good is a person willing to give up to acquire one more unit of something else? This is the marginal rate of substitution. The basic concept is no different for the services of natural resources. The differences arise in measuring these values. For the case of commodities available on markets (at fixed prices), the assumed behavior underlying people's choices allows us to conclude that relative prices (under ideal conditions) reveal these incremental values. When the commodities are available largely outside markets, it becomes more difficult to infer what tradeoffs people would be willing to make (and in some cases do make) to acquire the resource's services. The approaches available to estimate the value of nonmarketed resources have received considerable attention over the past thirteen years since Freeman (1979) assembled the first complete description of the theory, methods, and practice involved in using them.

The second task involves determining who experiences the damage. This problem bears a striking resemblance to evaluating the extent of the market for a commodity available through markets (see Scheffman [1990]). Nonetheless, there are some differences. Most important, people may experience the services of a natural resource in different ways. If they primarily use the resource on site, then determining the extent of the market parallels the processes required to specify the geographic extent of any marketed commodity. Of course, the signals indicating people who hold (or would hold) positive use values require specialized detective work. Nonetheless, people who would realize benefits from using a restored resource can be assumed to take some action that involves implicit, if not explicit, costs. In contrast, when people can experience the resource's services as a nonexcludable public good that does *not* require any specific actions on their part, the task is more difficult.[8]

Most discussions of the approaches used to measure incremental values for nonmarketed resources identify four methods: travel cost models (whether demand or discrete choice), hedonic price models, household or firm production models, and contingent valuation (or survey) methods. The first three methods are usually described as indirect or revealed preference techniques; the fourth is considered a direct approach. The first three use information on the observed choices of people (or firms), combined with a conceptual framework that describes what is hypothesized to motivate those decisions. The goal is to estimate the elements that would be routinely observed in a market transaction—quantity consumed and the price or marginal value (cost) for the service. The specific assumptions used to recover these estimates vary with the approach and the information available about choices. Nonetheless, the strategy in each case is comparable. The elements in a transaction hypothesized to take place because people make specific choices are used to recover a behavioral model that permits value estimates for the resource's services under different conditions. Of course, in practice the analyst must specify the ways that the changes in services are connected to the factors influencing observable choices.

Because chapter 8 by Kenneth E. McConnell and chapter 10 by William D. Schulze review the indirect and direct approaches for measuring the value of nonmarketed resources' services, here discussion about method is limited to what is needed to explain the specifics of the Eagle River case in section 6 of this chapter.

Among the indirect methods, the travel cost model is probably the most straightforward. It relies on a simple insight. Visitors pay an implicit price for the use of a recreation site because they must incur travel and time costs to gain access to the site. While there may be admission fees and parking charges at some sites, they are usually small in comparison to the travel and time costs required to get there. By observing the differences in the usage of a recreation site by users at various distances from it, this method has proved to be a robust approach for estimating the demands

---

[8]This is the case encountered when attempts are made to measure nonuse values.

for a wide range of different types of recreation sites. (See Bockstael, McConnell, and Strand [1991] and Smith [1989] for reviews.)

Early travel cost studies were based on aggregate use levels, often treating the visitation rates from counties (that is, visits relative to population) around a site as measures of the representative individual's "rate" of use. With the availability of micro-level information from on-site surveys, analysts have been able to consider how users' characteristics and constraints influence their demands for recreation sites. Nonetheless, these new data have raised a new set of issues. Because the data describe users only and provide no information on those who choose not to use the site, analyses based on these data do not provide insight (without relying on a priori theory and the restrictions inherent in a given demand specification) into the decision to use the site.

The second indirect approach for estimating the value of non-marketed resources is the hedonic model. When applied to housing, this model relies on two key assumptions. First, it assumes that market participants clearly recognized some technical association between the non-marketed good or service to be valued (or a reliable proxy variable assumed to represent the commodity) and the locations of the properties whose prices are being analyzed to detect the locational tradeoffs participants are willing to make. Second, the model assumes the housing market is open enough for housing trades to continue until the prices provide no more incentives for buyers or sellers to change conditions.

Arbitrage combined with information assures that the set of prices for a closely related collection of heterogeneous commodities (the houses) will define the equilibrium. In practice, this set is usually assumed to be large enough to be approximated by a continuous price function. The derivative of the price function with respect to each nonmarketed commodity (assumed to be available at continuous increments) provides an estimate of the marginal rate of substitution between the commodity and money. Because the commodity is durable, this value is a present value of the person's anticipated value for the commodity over a defined time horizon. With a further set of assumptions, these estimates of marginal values can be used to estimate the incremental value for the nonmarketed good (see Palmquist [1991]).

The remaining indirect approaches relying on some type of production function model—the factor income and averting behavior frameworks—use maintained assumptions linking features of the production, cost, or profit functions to the nonmarketed good to recover estimates of the implicit value of the good as increased output, avoided cost, or increased profits. (See Smith [1991] for a review of applications of this logic to household-averting decisions.)

The contingent valuation or survey methods are described as direct methods because they involve direct activities to collect information about how people would value, respond to, use, or (in some consistent behavioral context) react to the specific nonmarket commodity being valued. Direct and indirect approaches differ in several important ways. First, indirect approaches for the most part rely on records of past actions to value a nonmarketed commodity. Moreover, in the case of natural resource damage assessments, the valuation task is focused on a change in the services provided by the resource. This may be expressed as a change in the conditions of access or in some aspects of the resource's quality. It may be attributed to a proxy variable such as distance to areas where hazardous substances have been released. In contrast, direct approaches face the task of describing how the release and injury relate to survey respondents and then eliciting their responses to questions that can be linked to a consistent behavioral model. Second, the indirect methods are based on actual responses to past conditions of the resource of interest (or closely related ones), while the contingent valuation method must rely on responses describing how the individual would react to (or value) the hypothetical change.

While knowledge and perception influence both approaches in estimating nonmarket values, their impact is usually harder to evaluate when applying the indirect methods and must rely on creative assumptions imposed by analysts. This information can be acquired as part of the surveys. However, it is important to recognize that the survey itself may not be neutral in its influence on the information and perceptions of respondents.

Choice among the potential methods for nonmarket valuation is often based on the context of each problem and the information available. This is as it should be. Also, at this early stage in the history of natural resource damage assessments, there are no ready-made data sets, models, or estimates on which to base assessments. Even when past surveys can be used, they often must be supplemented with additional information. In most situations, data collection (including both economic data and scientific information associated with establishing injuries) is an essential component of the damage assessment.

We will never know the "true" values people place on anything— whether it be a marketed commodity or a nonmarketed service of a natural resource. Because of the evidence of repeated transactions where people's behavior shows that they will pay a certain amount for a marketed good, analysts have confidence that the good in question is at least worth the price paid. Of course, we can observe that people use beaches; engage in fishing, boating, or swimming; select homes in areas with less air pollution; and generally make choices broadly consistent with the values we attribute to the services of natural resources. However, the linkage between the action and a payment is not as specific as in a market transaction. Similarly, there is considerable evidence that people do what they say they will do, but this is not as specific as a payment made to purchase something. Because both the indirect and the survey approaches do not observe actual payments for specific commodities, we must rely on other methods to evaluate how well they measure people's values. Four methods will be discussed—simulation studies, experimental techniques, comparisons, and meta-analyses. All of these approaches provide insights, but some compromise is required to address the question of performance.

Simulation studies parallel the use of Monte Carlo methods to evaluate statistical estimates or test statistics. In this context, the analyst defines a utility maximization problem including a specific characterization of preferences and constraints, specifies the way random errors influence observed outcomes, and uses the results of the choices implied by the "true" model as data. The relevant methods are used to analyze the data, recognizing that when analysis is undertaken to value a nonmarketed resource or characteristics of a property site the "true" value is known.

In the case of methods based on travel cost, Kling's (1988) and Kling and Weinberg's (1990) sampling studies found that the performance of travel cost demand estimates or random utility model (RUM) estimates (as approximations of some unknown underlying set of preferences) will depend on the nature of people's decisions as reflected in the samples involved. For example, the average error as a fraction of the true measure for consumer surplus ranged from 9 to 107 percent. The performance of any method depended on exactly how it was applied and on the proportion of corner solutions in the sample providing data for the recreation demand or RUM models.

Cropper, Deck, and McConnell's (1988) analysis of the performance of alternative specifications for hedonic price functions in estimating the marginal prices for housing characteristics exhibits a more widely dispersed range of errors when compared with the marginal values of these attributes at the equilibrium assignments of houses to people (that is, from under 1 percent to more than 150 percent as the ratio of the average error to the mean true marginal price). Of course, the appraisals accept the analyst's description of behavior and, as in the case of sampling studies for other estimators, may be sensitive to the functional forms and parameter values selected to characterize the "true" state of affairs.

Experimental methods attempt to simulate the actual conditions of a choice and use these actual decisions to evaluate one of the other nonmarket valuation methods. Bishop and Heberlein's (1979) pioneering research with hunting permits was the first application of this strategy. Most subsequent research has used this approach to evaluate the performance of contingent valuation responses in comparison with the "actual" markets.[9]

It is important to acknowledge that the method being evaluated and the standard (usually prices for the simulated markets or a demand function based on actual transactions) are both estimates that can be used to infer a person's value for the commodity. Thus, proximity between them does not in itself evaluate the performance of the method being scrutinized. For the case of contingent valuation, most studies have found reasonable proximity between simulated and hypothetical markets. However, sources of discrepancy between the results have always occurred. Nonetheless, these discrepancies have usually been smaller than those observed in comparative evaluations of contingent valuation and one indirect method's measures of the value of some resource. (See Brookshire and coauthors [1982]; Seller, Stoll, and Chavas [1985]; and Smith, Desvousges, and Fisher [1986] as examples.)

Comparisons across methods used for recreation resources with a common database indicate comparable magnitudes for the differences between consumer surplus estimates derived from travel cost demand, hedonic travel cost, and random utility models. (See Bockstael, Hanemann, and Kling [1987] and Smith and coauthors [1992] as examples.)

The most recent approach for evaluating methods for nonmarket valuation uses meta-analyses to describe estimates across different applications of a method and attempts to associate a measure related to the value of a nonmarketed resource with the type of resource, assumptions made in developing the estimate, and other features of the empirical application. To the extent the variations are connected to features of the resources being valued, this method would suggest a broad level of consistency with expectations. Applications of the method for travel cost demand studies using the consumer surplus per unit of use (Smith and Kaoru [1990a,b]) and hedonic property value estimates using both the marginal rate of substitution with respect to air pollution and elasticity measures for the marginal rate of substitution (Smith and Huang [1991]) suggest that these types of consistencies do exist across studies.

Based on what is known to date, no clear-cut ranking has been established for these different methods of nonmarket valuation. This should not be surprising. All methods are not equally relevant to all resources. Each requires a number of detailed assumptions. We can expect that these maintained assumptions will be violated in some applications and that the importance of such inconsistencies will vary by case. Because

---

[9]Bishop and Heberlein (1979) included the travel cost model in their evaluation, and a significant aspect of their conclusions concerned the sensitivity of its consumer surplus to the treatment of the opportunity costs of time.

there are so few replications of evaluations of nonmarket methods, it is not possible to separate the influence of the situation selected for the evaluation from the methods' comparative performance. This is clearly one of the insights derived from the meta-analysis of travel cost models: key modeling assumptions do have important influences on valuation estimates. Thus, inconsistencies in the maintained assumptions of both direct and indirect methods as they were applied to each of the problems considered in comparative evaluations would seem to be sufficient to account for any observed differences between them.

6.   ALTERNATIVE PERSPECTIVES:
THE EAGLE RIVER CASE

Developing estimates of the values people place on natural resource services combines information derived from observed behavior (or behavioral intentions) with maintained hypotheses that describe how these responses are linked to people's preferences. Equally important, using such a model (even one specifically developed for measuring the natural resource damages associated with a specific case) requires judgments. Because these judgments can take many forms, we have selected an actual case involving a mining site to illustrate the effects of such decisions.

The case was initiated before the DOI type B rules were announced and was settled before the D.C. Circuit Court of Appeals ruling on the proposed revisions to DOI's rules. The case involved the Eagle Mine and a five-mile section of the Eagle River between Gilman and Minturn, Colorado (see figure 7-3). The trustee (the State of Colorado) for the natural resources involved (public lands adjoining the river, the Eagle River, and groundwater aquifers near this section of the river) contended that past operations of the mine had resulted in releases of hazardous substances into the river and the groundwater. Although the mine was no longer operating, the disposal of mine tailings and the condition of the old mine allowed continued releases to take place, with alleged injuries to the natural resources.

Comparison of how the plaintiff's and the defendant's analysts estimated the natural resource damages from these releases illustrates the importance of judgment by analysts in applying valuation methodologies. Neither side attempted to develop comprehensive damage estimates for each of the natural resources alleged to have been injured by the releases, although the defendant's analysis is easier to associate with the two primary resources—the river and the groundwater. We will consider each side's analysis in turn.

The plaintiff's analyst conducted two household mail surveys, one for the residents of Eagle County and the other for the entire state. The

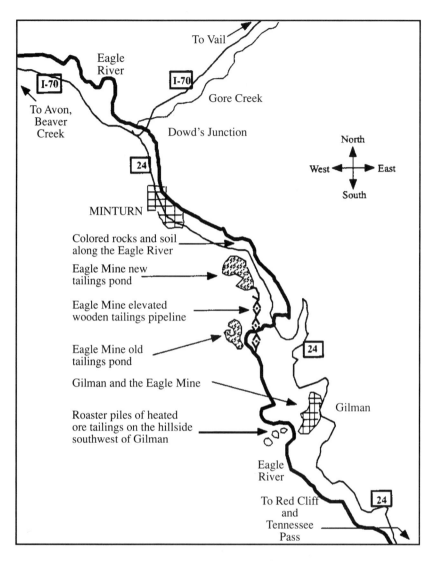

Figure 7-3. Location of the Eagle Mine and Eagle River

county survey collected information to implement three methods for measuring components of the damages. It asked:

- how many days each respondent would spend in fishing and nonwater-based recreation activities if the section of the river (identified on the map in figure 7-3) was restored to its "pre-mine" condition;

• how much each respondent would be willing to pay annually for ten years to clean up this section of the Eagle River; and

• if respondents were homeowners, what the purchase price for their homes and the date of purchase had been. A brief description of the housing characteristics was also asked for.

To estimate per-person annual use values, responses to the first question were combined with measures of current participation in water-based and nonwater-based activities and the U.S. Forest Service's unit-day values for these activities.[10] Responses to the second question provided estimates per person of ex ante use and presumably nonuse values as a composite. The information on housing prices was used only for those individuals living within 25 miles of the river; a hedonic price function (using deflated prices) was estimated. A qualitative variable indicating location within 6 miles of this section of the river was assumed to reflect the effects of the releases into the river. Thus, in terms of the taxonomy of methods described earlier, the plaintiff's analysis involved three different methods. Use values relied on the stated river usage (if restored to baseline conditions) less the previous year's participation in these activities. Increased use levels were valued with the unit-day values.

At the same time these were being measured, two different estimates of use and nonuse values were developed from the contingent valuation questions on the Eagle County and statewide surveys. Both estimated those values as a composite. This strategy was consistent with the revision of DOI's rules for type B assessments. The statewide survey attempted to distinguish the value for restoring the Eagle River to baseline conditions from the values of other sites in Colorado, while the county survey focused exclusively on the river. The hedonic analysis relied on "sales prices" collected with the county survey and limited the market to a 25-mile area around the river. It illustrates the problems involved in establishing the link between the effects of hazardous waste on the resource and the site attribute included in the hedonic price equation. Distance to the impacted area of the river was used to measure these effects, and a somewhat

---

[10]Unit-day values have been developed by a variety of agencies. They were intended to represent experts' judgments about a representative person's average willingness to pay for a day of a specific type of recreation activity. A range of suggested values is proposed by a resource agency and analysts can use them as approximations for the values associated with the relevant activities at specific resources. Unfortunately, the process of developing these values has varied widely and their relationship to a theoretically consistent measure can also be questioned. Some agencies developing unit-day values have relied on entrance fees at private facilities. The U.S. Forest Service undertakes periodic reviews of the travel cost and contingent valuation literature to estimate a consumer surplus per day. None of the approaches for estimating these values provides a theoretically valid measure of the marginal value of a unit of the activity.

arbitrary threshold of 6 miles was used to represent the distance at which the damage to the river had no effect on the property.

The analyst for the defendant (Gulf-Western Industries) developed a travel cost recreation demand model using the U.S. Fish and Wildlife's 1980 survey of hunting and fishing decisions. A subsample of individuals using fishing sites within a five-county region around the mine site was used to estimate the model. While the specific estimates of demand functions were not present in the defendant's report on damages, sufficient information was reported to highlight several aspects of this strategy. Two important assumptions in the defendants' analysis followed from implicit assumptions in their sample and their characterization of how the release would affect potential fishing on this section of the river.

First, by combining all the fishermen using sites anywhere in the five-county area around the mine, they implicitly assumed that all the sites in this area were perfect substitutes for each other. Second, the analysis maintained that when there is damage to the river's ability to support fishing, recreationists will go to the next-best alternative—the river above the mine site. This would imply traveling a maximum of 5 miles further each way. Thus, the loss of the site was described as a price change. However, the key assumption was that the choke price equalled the implied travel cost to what was treated as a "perfect substitute" site.[11]

By contrast, the plaintiff's analysis tended to highlight the uniqueness of the site by asking county residents about their increased use of it without asking where the increased use would come from and whether it represented new recreational trips. The valuation measures implied for site services (per unit) by each side's model were actually quite comparable. The unit-day values (in 1985 dollars) for water- and nonwater-based activities were $14 and $9 per day, respectively, while the consumer surplus from the defendant's travel cost demand models for each type of activity were actually higher, at $21 and $32 per day.

Comparisons of the annual values from the willingness-to-pay (WTP) component of the survey were also quite similar—with the county survey's contingent valuation estimates of $73 per year for water-based and $51 per year for nonwater-based activities. The defendant's model estimated 6.18 days of fishing per season and 10 days for nonwater-based activities. Applying each to the average of the annual consumer surplus from fishing and nonwater-based activities, the defendant's analysis would imply values that *exceed* the contingent valuation estimates. However, the characterization of what was lost from the release is what distinguished the analysis at the level of an individual recreationist.

---

[11]The choke price is the price at which there will be no more demand for use of the resource.

By treating the release as requiring recreationists to use the next best alternative and incur *only* a price increase equivalent to traveling 10 miles further, the per-individual loss from the defendant's travel cost model became $1.35 per day for fishing and $.55 per day for nonwater-based activities (in 1985 dollars). What may be more surprising is that these estimates would still exceed the per-person annual values estimated by the plaintiff from the second contingent valuation survey, which was intended to be representative of the state population's valuation of the river's services. This second survey progressively focused the valuation tasks, first asking annual WTP for cleanup of all 200 potential problem sites (again for each of ten years), then the percentage to be assigned to seven sites (including the Eagle River mine) specifically identified and described in the survey, and finally a percentage of that amount for the site identified as most important.

The average annual per household values from the plaintiff's state-wide contingent valuation survey included use and nonuse values. This estimate ($5.60) was less than the annual use values implied for fishing by the defendant's analysis ($1.35 × 6.18 days = $8.34) and very close to those for nonwater-based activities ($.55 × 10 days = $5.50).

Nonetheless, these comparisons offer a misleading impression of the disparity in each side's estimates of the present value of future losses if restoration did not take place. The plaintiff's estimates ranged from $15 million to $45 million, depending on which method was used to estimate per-person losses and the treatment of nonuse values. Even the lowest end of this range was approximately 100 times the size of the defendant's estimate of $139,500 for fishing and nonwater-based activities. The difference cannot be attributed to the inclusion of nonuse values because these were already removed when the lowest estimate was selected. Moreover, the differences in discount rates, time horizon, and real growth of these values do not explain this large disparity.

The disparities arise from one strategic assumption—each analyst's assumption about the extent of the market for the Eagle River. The plaintiff's analysis assumed that the market corresponded to every household in Colorado, on the grounds that their statewide survey was intended to represent this group. The defendant's analysis implied that the recreationists assumed to be currently involved in fishing and nonwater uses of the area would experience a gain (in the form of the reduced price) from restoring this section of the river.

This observation is important because it establishes that the wide disparity between each side's estimates arises from differences in assumptions and not from inherent variability in valuation estimates across methods. In fact, there is remarkable consistency between the two sides' estimates when they attempt to value the same thing. In some respects, each side exploited the incomplete nature of economic research on those issues associated with defining the extent of the market for the services provided by nonmarketed natural resources.

7. FUTURE IMPLEMENTATION OF DAMAGE ASSESSMENTS

The legislation and regulations governing natural resource damage assessments remain in flux, and they are likely to remain so for some time to come. There will be reactions to DOI's revised rules. The revised rules involve changes that extend beyond the D.C. Circuit Court of Appeals ruling on the earlier rules and will no doubt be subject to comments. Further judicial action may well result. Nonetheless, some aspects of the assessment process seem likely to be permanent regardless of how the revised rules fare in the near future.

First, oil spills will be treated differently from Superfund sites. The Oil Pollution Act of 1990 mandates a new set of regulations for their damage assessment and sets some federal liability limits. However, beyond these statutory distinctions, the substance of the issues involved appears to differ. Oil spills have a clear beginning—the date of the spill. Moreover, information, even if it is informal, is likely to be available about the condition of the resources involved before the spill. People will have had some experience with them, and there may exist records describing how this experience translates into patterns of use. At sites with hazardous waste releases, the beginning of a release is often unclear. It may be decades in the past. No one may be familiar with prerelease conditions.

DOI's proposed revisions to the type B rules seem to make releases of hazardous substances from old sites especially difficult to evaluate. Data are unlikely to be available on people's responses to hazardous substance releases and injury occurring long in the past. Thus contingent valuation (CV) surveys are more likely to be used in these damage assessments. However, here the rules reveal what is a pervasive distrust of CV methods. The new rules note that:

> When CVM is used to quantify use values alone, it is judged to be just as reliable as the other nonmarket valuation methodologies. When CVM is used to quantify use values alone, the survey population would normally consist of actual users of the resource. Use value estimates based on general population surveys would be considered in the least reliable category when survey respondents are asked to allocate a portion of their bid to nonuse values. When CVM is used to quantify either nonuse

alone or use plus nonuse values, it is in the least reliable category of the other nonmarketed valuation methods. [12]

In situations in which injuries have precluded use for some time (so there is no group of users), the rules offer no means to develop reliable estimates of damages. There is no pattern of past behavior to analyze, and contingent valuation methods must be directed to a general population survey. The CV literature agrees that total value should be the focus of surveys (as the DOI compensable value implies), but DOI then claims that contingent valuation methods are a least reliable method of estimation. Equally important, large discrepancies in damage estimates in most of the cases we have been able to review arise from questions related to the extent of the market, as the Eagle Mine case illustrated. Answers to these questions cannot in general be derived without conducting population surveys. At issue is when a person becomes a user. Thus, the rules seem to invite strategic resolution of the issues rather than systematic use of survey methods.

A related issue in the DOI rules concerns the selection of restoration alternatives. The ten attributes listed above imply that the criteria for selecting a restoration, rehabilitation, or replacement plan are so vague as to be useless. The trustee is faced with the requirement of restoration, but is given wide latitude in defining grossly disproportionate costs. Combinations of partial restoration with the "promise" that natural systems may do the rest of the work seem likely. Yet, natural recovery may be infeasible. The very persistence of the substances from early releases is likely to reinforce this conclusion. Multiple contaminants, including pollutants that are not covered under the legislation governing damage assessments, may be involved. The rules, even as amended, offer little or no guidance on these issues.

The second aspect of damage assessment that will in all likelihood be with us for some time is restoration and its cost. Judgments about restoration costs will be a permanent feature of all descriptions of the damage assessment process. Missing, however, will be a description of what these expenditures really buy—that is, what restoration actually means. How does restoration relate to the services provided by the injured natural resources? This question is not answered in any of the treatments of damage assessments to date. The scale and complexity of some sites seem likely to ensure that cost cannot be the exclusive basis for damage assessments. Some notion of the value of what has been lost is unlikely to be removed from the process. Indeed, there is always the possibility that people will be asked to value (in the CV framework) what they perceive to

---

[12]56 *Federal Register* 19762 (April 29, 1991).

be derived from alternative restoration plans. This seems especially likely when the plans focus on restoring primarily the important technical features of an injured resource's services and not those features people perceive to be important.

Third, damage assessment will remain a strategic process, and as such assessments will be ongoing processes. Periodic reappraisals of the damages that can be estimated at each stage will be used to evaluate the importance of the next steps. Measurement will serve to identify those areas in which theory is least clear-cut. For it is in these cases that judgments must be made. Their implications for each site will likely be explored differently than in academic research. Strategic elements may well influence such judgments, but this will only occur where there is ambiguity in the prescriptions of theory.

Fourth, the natural sciences will continue to have perhaps too great an influence on the design of damage assessments. Those scientific criteria that are important to establish the extent and severity of injuries to natural resources may not be important to people's perceptions of resource services and, in turn, to the damages suffered as a result of any injuries to the resource. Some balance in these roles in implementation seems essential.

If the assessment process is to yield replicable evaluations of damages to natural resources, the process must seek improvements in the methods for valuing their services, defining their markets, and evaluating the plausibility of judgments where data and theory are incomplete.

REFERENCES

Bishop, Richard C., and Thomas A. Heberlein. 1979. "Measuring Values of Extra Market Goods: Are Indirect Measures Biased?" *American Journal of Agricultural Economics* 61 (December), pp. 926–930.

Bockstael, Nancy E., W. Michael Hanemann, and Catherine L. Kling. 1987. "Estimating the Value of Water Quality Improvements in a Recreational Demand Framework," *Water Resources Research* 23 (May), pp. 951–960.

Bockstael, Nancy E., Kenneth E. McConnell, and Ivar E. Strand. 1991. "Recreation." In *Measuring the Demand for Environmental Quality*, edited by John B. Braden and Charles D. Kolstad. Amsterdam: North-Holland.

Breen, Barry. 1989. "Citizen Suits for Natural Resource Damages: Closing a Gap in Federal Environmental Law," *Wake Forest Law Review* 24, pp. 851–880.

Brookshire, David S., Mark A. Thayer, William D. Schulze, and Ralph C. d'Arge. 1982. "Valuing Public Goods: A Comparison of Survey and Hedonic Approaches," *American Economic Review* 72 (March), pp. 165–177.

Cropper, Maureen L., Leland B. Deck, and K. E. McConnell. 1988. "On the Choice of Functional Form for Hedonic Price Functions," *Review of Economics and Statistics* 70 (November), pp. 668–675.

Freeman, A. Myrick, III. 1979. *The Benefits of Environmental Improvement: Theory and Practice.* Baltimore, Md.: The Johns Hopkins University Press for Resources for the Future.

Kling, Catherine L. 1988. "Comparing Welfare Estimates of Environmental Quality Changes from Recreation Demand Models," *Journal of Environmental Economics and Management* 8, pp. 331–340.

Kling, Catherine L., and Marcia Weinberg. 1990. "Evaluating Estimates of Environmental Benefits Based on Multiple Site Demand Models: A Simulation Approach." In *Advances in Applied Micro-Economics*, vol. 5, edited by V. Kerry Smith and Albert N. Link. Greenwich, Conn.: JAI Press.

Krutilla, John V., and Anthony C. Fisher. 1975. *The Economics of Natural Environments.* Baltimore, Md.: The Johns Hopkins University Press for Resources for the Future.

Larson, Douglas M. 1990. "Measuring Willingness to Pay for Nonmarket Goods," paper presented at American Agricultural Economics Meetings, Vancouver, British Columbia.

Palmquist, Raymond B. 1991. "Hedonic Methods." In *Measuring the Demand for Environmental Quality*, edited by John B. Braden and Charles D. Kolstad. Amsterdam: North-Holland.

Scheffman, David. 1990. "Statistical Techniques for Market Delineation in Merger Analysis," unpublished paper presented at Allied Social Science Meetings, Washington, D.C.

Seller, Christine, John R. Stoll, and Jean-Paul Chavas. 1985. "Validation of Empirical Measures of Welfare Change: A Comparison of Nonmarket Techniques," *Land Economics* 61 (December), pp. 926–930.

Smith, V. Kerry. 1991. "Household Production Functions and Environmental Benefit Measurement." In *Measuring the Demand for Environmental Quality*, edited by John Braden and Charles Kolstad. Amsterdam: North-Holland.

Smith, V. Kerry. 1989. "Taking Stock of Progress with Travel Cost Recreation Demand Methods: Theory and Implementation," *Marine Resource Economics* 6, pp. 279–310.

Smith, V. Kerry, William H. Desvousges, and Ann Fisher. 1986. "A Comparison of Direct and Indirect Methods for Estimating Environmental Benefits," *American Journal of Agricultural Economics* 68 (May), pp. 280–289.

Smith, V. Kerry, and Ju Chin Huang. 1991. "Meta Analyses for Nonmarket Valuation: Can Hedonic Models Value Air Quality?" Presented at the National Bureau of Economic Research Conference (December). Resource and Environmental Economics Program, North Carolina State University.

Smith, V. Kerry, and Yoshiaki Kaoru. 1990a. "Signals or Noise: Explaining the Variation in Recreation Benefit Estimates," *American Journal of Agricultural Economics* 72 (May), pp. 419–433.

Smith, V. Kerry, and Yoshiaki Kaoru. 1990b. "What Have We Learned Since Hotelling's Letter? A Meta Analysis," *Economic Letters* 32 (March), pp. 267–272.

Smith, V. Kerry, Raymond B. Palmquist, Yoshiaki Kaoru, Jin Long Liu, and Paul M. Jakus. 1992. "A Comparative Evaluation of Travel Cost Methodologies for Valuing Quality in Marine Fishing: The Albemarle-Pamlico Estuary," draft paper under revision, Resource and Environmental Economics Program, North Carolina State University.

Part 2
Measuring Natural Resource Damages

Introduction to Part 2: Measuring Natural Resource Damages

The diverse reactions to the Department of the Interior's proposed rules defining reliable methods for measuring people's valuations for non-marketed resources might lead newcomers to believe that the methods are quite new. However, the primary methods for nonmarket valuation, both indirect (revealed preference) and direct (stated preference), were proposed more than forty years ago.[1] This does not mean that empirical research on methods has accumulated systematically since then, but it does mean that the methods for valuing nonmarketed resources are only about a decade younger than the more widely accepted empirical demand models for marketed goods.[2]

Our consideration of methods for measuring natural resource damages begins in chapter 8 with Kenneth E. McConnell's comprehensive review of the indirect methods. McConnell poses four key questions: How does the researcher link resource injury to behavioral change? How does the researcher measure the index of resource injury? How does the researcher determine the number of people who would value the resource's services under baseline and under injured conditions? and, How does the model used to describe these values incorporate their temporal evolution over the recovery period? McConnell then discusses how these questions can be addressed by models for hedonic property value, travel cost recreation demand, random utility, and averting behavior. While he finds strengths and weaknesses in each method, McConnell concludes by observing that "the hedonic model is most subject to the rigors of the market and seems the most likely to

---

[1]The travel cost and contingent valuation methods were both proposed in 1947 by A. Hotelling and S. V. Ciriacy-Wantrup, respectively. Hedonic approaches for describing heterogeneous goods and understanding people's preferences toward them can also be traced to about that time. See Roy, A. D. 1950. "The Distribution of Earnings and of Individual Output," *Economic Journal* 60, pp. 489–505; and Tinbergen, Jan. 1956. "On the Theory of Income Distribution," *Weltwirtschaftliches Archiv* 77, pp. 155–175.

[2]In tracing efforts to develop empirical demand models, we follow Schultz, Henry. 1938. *The Theory and Measurement of Demand.* Chicago: University of Chicago Press.

reflect informed optimizing behavior." Of course, this judgment assumes that information about injuries to natural resources is consistent with important attributes of housing sites *and* that there is available a reasonably clear measure of the injury exhibiting variation over the properties used to estimate the price function.

Indeed, as a whole, McConnell's review suggests that the specific circumstances of any damage assessment are likely to determine which methods can succeed. Moreover, as he acknowledges, all of these approaches will yield incomplete results to some degree because the revealed preference strategy is, by definition, one that employs observable uses to infer people's values; thus these methods largely describe use values and do not measure nonuse values.

Robert Mendelsohn's reaction (chapter 9) to this summary contends that we can do better at prescribing methods for damage assessment than McConnell would imply. In the scientific analysis required to establish the causal link between substance release and resource injury, the DOI rules allow controlled experiments as alternatives to direct observation. In economic damage assessment there is no equivalent to the scientist's laboratory. Nonetheless, Mendelsohn suggests, the timing of the events associated with a release or spill, coupled with controls for unrelated but potentially influential events, can often provide sufficient variation in conditions and behavioral responses to supply the valuation information for damage assessment. Mendelsohn uses his application of the repeat sales methodology in the *New Bedford Harbor* case to support his argument.[3]

We believe there is room for differences between analysts who agree with McConnell's cautious discussion of the assumptions, judgments, and characteristics of revealed preference methods, on the one hand, and those more willing to argue that revealed preference methods are robust. For the latter, McConnell's caution could be misinterpreted as faint praise for the indirect methods. By contrast, Mendelsohn argues that the indirect approaches are the preferred approach to nonmarket valuation.

William D. Schulze's chapter (10) on the direct or stated preference methods begins (as the newly proposed DOI rules do) by observing that contingent valuation (CV) methods provide the ability to recover estimates of both use and nonuse values. Schulze makes clear that direct methods must address the same four questions that McConnell posed for the indirect. Schulze cautions that because the analyst

---

[3]Mendelsohn, Robert, Daniel Hellerstein, Michael Huguenin, Robert Unsworth, and Richard Brazee. 1992. "Measuring Hazardous Waste Damages with Panel Models," *Journal of Environmental Economics and Management* 22 (May), pp. 259–271.

can ask questions that apparently describe and control the measure of a resource injury, and the link proposed between that injury and people, does not mean that survey respondents accept the information completely. When people have experience with the resource services (whether use or nonuse), he suggests, they are likely to have "crystallized values." In short, they understand what the services mean to them. Consequently, their responses to CV questions are less likely to exhibit sensitivity to the framing of questions.

This conclusion requires the assumption that the variations in question content do not include changes in the availability or amounts of other commodities (nonmarketed or marketed resource) that could induce important income or substitution effects. While this condition may seem obvious as a basic tenet of demand theory, it is one of the issues that underlies the Kahneman-Knetsch critique of contingent valuation,[4] discussed in chapter 14 and treated by Schulze in terms of part/whole effects. When the changes being proposed in CV questions are new, Schulze advises us, we should expect framing effects. This does not mean abandonment of the contingent valuation method. Rather, "a much larger burden is placed on the survey design to provide a complete, realistic, and clear context for the formation of values."

Richard T. Carson and Robert Cameron Mitchell's view of CV (chapter 11) contrasts dramatically with that of Mendelsohn. Nonetheless, just as Mendelsohn suggests that indirect methods can be more effectively used than McConnell implies, so Carson and Mitchell argue that Schulze may be too cautious in advocating CV for damage assessment and evaluating the feasibility of controlling framing effects. From Carson and Mitchell's perspective the methodologies to control these effects exist, *but they are costly.*

Serious efforts to estimate the damages from releases of hazardous substances or oil require avoiding low-cost survey research strategies. They also require careful attention to the details that ultimately represent contingent valuation's answers to McConnell's four questions. In Carson and Mitchell's view, these precautions are not likely to dramatically change damage estimates but they are likely to reduce "the risk of obtaining a grossly aberrant estimate . . . and the courts appear to place great weight on minimizing such a possibility." Of course, the trustee's lawyers will share these concerns because such estimates can call into question the quality of all of the evidence underlying a damage assessment. Do we

---

[4]See Kahneman, Daniel, and Jack L. Knetsch. 1992. "Valuing Public Goods: The Purchase of Moral Satisfaction," *Journal of Environmental Economics and Management* 22 (1), pp. 57–70.

have the accumulated experience from either direct or indirect methods to perform assessments based on existing estimates? Probably not! Can we move in that direction? Perhaps. What seems to be missing in the discussions in these chapters (so we return to these omissions in the closing chapter) is some description of how to begin moving in that direction and, equally important, some examination of the prospects for combining both revealed and stated preference strategies in damage assessment.

8
Indirect Methods for Assessing Natural Resource Damages Under CERCLA

Kenneth E. McConnell

1. INTRODUCTION

In the economic and legal system of the United States, many competing interests have open access to natural resources. The uses of these common properties sometimes are incompatible. When natural resources assimilate hazardous substances, other uses may be curtailed. Under the Comprehensive Environmental Response, Compensation, and Liability Act of 1980 (CERCLA),[1] the trustees of the natural resource may sue responsible parties for damages caused by release of hazardous substances.

In assigning liability for release of hazardous substances, CERCLA represents a considerable departure from past approaches to environmental policy, a departure that many economists have long recommended. CERCLA has the potential for improving resource allocation. Public and private planning will have to account for the liability for damages from injury to natural resources. The allocative effects of CERCLA, however, will not emerge without successful lawsuits. The success of these suits depends in part on the ability of economists to convince participants in the legal proceedings of the magnitude of the damages from the release of hazardous materials.

Techniques for estimating damages to natural resources fall broadly into two categories: indirect methods (discussed in this chapter) and direct or survey methods (see chapter 10 by William D. Schulze). Indirect

The author thanks Rick Freeman, Ray Kopp, Doug Larson, Rob Mendelsohn, Lisa Shapiro, and Kerry Smith for many helpful comments on earlier drafts.

[1]42 U.S.C. 9601–9675.

methods utilize assumptions of optimizing behavior to organize observations on behavior and to deduce measures of economic well-being. Direct or survey methods seek to ascertain estimates of economic damages directly through the interview process by posing hypothetical questions to sampled respondents. The researcher engaged in damage assessment through direct methods imposes two kinds of assumptions: the first is that the person being interviewed attaches the meaning to hypothetical valuation questions intended by the researcher; the second is that responses to hypothetical questions are comparable to responses to actual circumstances. The debate continues over the advantages of each method; this chapter discusses rather than advocates indirect methods. In practice, it may be good strategy to combine various aspects of direct and indirect methods.

This chapter describes how indirect methods of valuing natural resources can be used to calculate damages from the release of hazardous substances. Indirect methods use observations of individual behavior (market and nonmarket) to infer economic values, and thus to infer damages. The release of hazardous substances injures natural resources. Individuals perceive this injury and change their behavior. This change in behavior causes a reduction in their welfare. Indirect methods take their theoretical structure from models of optimizing behavior and take their empirical content from observations of individual behavior. The principal paradigm of modern economics is a model of behavior based on the view that individuals make themselves as well off as possible, subject to their perception of financial and resource constraints. This paradigm pertains to the measurement of damages. Only individuals, through constraints on their behavior and diminution in the value of their assets, can incur damages. Hence indirect methods relate the release of hazardous substances to damages to individuals.

The procedural guidelines for damage assessment are determined in part by CERCLA and the Superfund Amendments and Reauthorization Act (SARA) of 1986 and in part by Department of the Interior guidelines. Ever since the decision in *Ohio v. The United States Department of the Interior*,[2] in which the Department of the Interior (DOI) guidelines issued in August 1986 were struck down, damage assessment has operated within a broad outline. The procedural guidelines are covered by Gardner Brown in chapter 5.

The focus in this chapter is on the substantive economic problems of damage assessment rather than constraints and contradictions within CERCLA, and the concern here is with the kinds of issues that economists are likely to confront under most conceivable guidelines.

---

[2]880 F.2d 481 (D.C. Cir. 1989).

1.1 Economic Value. The notion of economic value is based on models in which rational individuals make the best use of opportunities and resources. These models assume that individuals respond predictably to perceived changes in their circumstances, such as changes in product prices, wage rates, financial endowments, and the natural environment. Economic value relates to the number of dollars an individual will pay to avoid or accept a change in these external circumstances.

Two closely related concepts are involved in economic value: compensating variation and equivalent variation.[3] Compensating variation is the minimum amount of money that an individual will voluntarily accept for an unfavorable change in his external circumstances or the maximum amount an individual will pay for a favorable change. Equivalent variation is the maximum amount of money that an individual will pay to avoid an unfavorable change in his external circumstances or the minimum amount he will accept in lieu of a favorable change. These measures depend on whether the standard of reference is an individual's well-being before the change or after the change. In the compensating case, the standard of well-being depends on circumstances before the change, so that an individual will be compensated for a decline in circumstances and will pay for an improvement. The compensation, paid or received, will leave him no worse off than he would be without the change. In the equivalent case, the standard of well-being is the level achieved after the change in circumstances. In CERCLA cases, it appears that compensating variation is the appropriate concept. The intent of the law is compensatory, although in successful suits only the public at large is compensated.

When measuring economic value by indirect methods, the distinction between compensating and equivalent variation is not especially important. For theoretical reasons, the two concepts are frequently close. (See Just, Hueth, and Schmitz [1983] for evidence in the case of price changes and Bockstael and McConnell [1987] for evidence in the case of changes in the quality of goods.) Consequently, this chapter equates economic value with consumer's surplus, an approximate measure of value that is typically close to and bounded by compensating and equivalent variation. However, when evidence suggests a significant difference between compensating and equivalent variation, consistency with CERCLA requires the compensating measure.

1.2 Damage Assessment and the Economic Value of an Asset. Public natural resources are economic assets that provide service flows of economic value. The essence of damage assessment is to determine the

---

[3]On occasion, when quantity adjustments are not possible, the corresponding surplus measures may be appropriate. See, for example, Foster and Just (1984).

change in the value of these economic assets when the release of hazardous substances injures the resource. The application is simple in concept. Individuals, in their market or nonmarket behavior, utilize a publicly owned resource. Their utilization may be vicarious, as in reading about a wilderness area, or it may be active, as in fishing in an estuary. The vicarious enjoyment is called nonuse value, and the active enjoyment is use value. Individuals, discovering that the resource has been injured, change their behavior, reflecting their reduced valuation of the resource and at the same time leaving footprints for researchers. Analysis of these footprints leads to observations of behavior toward the publicly owned resource in its impaired and unimpaired states. Indirect methods of damage assessment use these observations to estimate the behavioral functions that indirectly yield the loss in consumer's surplus from impairment of the resource. It is almost always the case that this consumer's surplus is use value.

The contrast between the economist's use of individual observations on private behavior and CERCLA's concern over public natural resources warrants explanation. The principal characteristic that makes a resource public is that the resource is held in trust for the public by government agencies. The natural resource is an asset held in the public interest, but it yields valuable services to individuals in their private activities. The individual behavior affected by the quantity and quality of the public resource may be a strictly nonmarket activity, as in recreation. Or it may be fully market-oriented, as in commercial fishing, where harvesters exploit the publicly owned fish stock for market transactions. In all cases, it is useful and valid to conceive of the value of the publicly owned natural resource. This resource enhances the value of private actions. In the economic framework accepted by most economists and implicitly embraced by CERCLA, social value is the sum of individual values. Hence the resource enhances social value, and injury of the resource from hazardous substances causes social damage.

To complete the calculation of damages from release of hazardous substances, one must account for the fact that hazardous waste was released at some time in the past and will likely persist indefinitely into the future. Damages calculated for a period of one year do not measure the total damages of the release. To calculate the total damages, one must consider the natural resource as an economic asset. This asset has an annual dividend equal in value to the increment in consumer's surpluses provided to all users by the resource. The value of the asset is the present discounted value of the dividends. The present discounted value depends on the time stream of benefits and the discount rate. (These topics are discussed in depth by Ralph d'Arge in chapter 12.) The natural resource damages can be calculated as the change in the value of the publicly owned asset induced by the release of hazardous substances. The computation entails knowledge of how long the impairment will last as well as the annual damages, discount rate, and time horizon for the resource itself.

Some of the temporal aspects of damage assessment are determined by the Department of the Interior regulations and bear on the use of indirect methods. Damages are incurred partly from loss of economic services from the legally determined time of initial injury up to the court's decision to recover damages. Damages also depend on the loss of economic services expected from the date of the court decision up to the date of restoration or some other reasonable horizon. Consequently, the timing of restoration is an important element in damage assessment.

One may also distinguish between public and private damages. Public damages are compensable under CERCLA, while private damages are recoverable under private lawsuits. Presumably any damage that cannot be compensated privately is a public damage. The spirit of the recent *Ohio* decision seems to support this view.

2. THE PROBLEM: DAMAGE ASSESSMENT UNDER CERCLA

The assessment of damages to natural resources appears deceptively easy. The researcher simply has to know the economic activity (market or nonmarket) complementary to the resource prior to and following the release of the hazardous substance. The practice of damage assessment involves some hurdles, however, caused primarily by the peculiar characteristics of hazardous releases.

The peculiar characteristics of hazardous substances and their release constrain damage assessment under CERCLA in ways that do not ordinarily affect the assessment of nonmarket goods. First, there is the problem of the perception of resource injury. Hazardous substances may injure resources in ways that can be measured by scientific methods but are not directly perceptible by individuals. For example, the presence of dioxin in soil can be determined only by laboratory tests. Consequently, individuals may have to rely on information from secondary sources. Also, these substances may be released in settings that attract other undesirable pollutants that may not by covered by CERCLA.

The perception of resource injury thus involves a person's judgment about which pollutants injured the resource as well as whether the resource is in fact injured. Where there are several pollutants, people may find it easy to judge the resource to be injured, but may have considerable difficulty in deciding which pollutant injured the resource. When facing the formidable task of sorting out the different effects of different pollutants, people may simply use one pollutant as an index of resource quality.

This element of the perception of resource injury becomes a critical issue when one considers indirect methods. Perception of resource injury from any pollutant may induce behavioral changes and hence economic damage, yet CERCLA damages pertain only to a specific hazardous substance.

A second problem with assessing damages concerns the time over which the release occurred. In many cases, hazardous materials have been released over such a long period of time that it may be quite difficult to establish the baseline service flows and the value of the natural resource. One example might be a hazardous waste site established so long ago that one could observe the level of economic activity complementary to the natural resource in its impaired state but not be able to determine the level of such activity in its unimpaired state. Damages are defined as the value of the asset without injury less the value of the injured asset. The absence of knowledge of the activity complementary to the resource in its unimpaired state makes damage assessment considerably more difficult because it requires extrapolating behavior to conditions that have not been observed. This problem is inherent in CERCLA because the most common case of hazardous substance release is the chronic release case, in which the substance has been discharged over a long period of time.

The problems of the perception of injury and the potential for long-term release of hazardous substances may be addressed jointly. Together, they present the problem of determining the link between injury to the resource and damages incurred. The Department of the Interior guidelines are quite specific about the steps and evidence required to establish injury to the resource but are mute about the link from physical injury to damage. These two problems suggest the need for a strategy to pursue indirect methods of damage assessment. At the heart of this strategy to link damage to injury there must be a plausible story about how people first learned of the resource injury and how and why they have changed their behavior in response. The plausibility of the story is crucial to the development of the strategy because direct testing of the relationship between resource injury and behavior change is rarely feasible.

A crucial ingredient in the modeling strategy is a careful description of the resource injury. The type of injury determines the range of plausible behavioral responses. A complete taxonomy of the types of resource injury is of no particular use, but in practice a modeling strategy will typically conceive of the resource injury as a change in the quantity or quality of the resource.[4] A quantity change may occur in a variety of

---

[4]While DOI guidelines discuss the possibility of a change in the price of the resource, it seems unlikely that there would be a price, since the resource, being publicly owned, is

ways. For example, a hazardous substance may reduce the carrying capacity of a lake to support a fish stock. Or, the quantity change may be created, for example, by a ban on fishing in a contaminated stream. A change in quality may occur because the resource is aesthetically impaired or because it appears risky to a user. The uncertainty of this link in the case of quality changes makes damage assessment under CERCLA more than a routine application of benefit estimation. Modeling the resource injury as a quantity or quality change involves a tactical choice by the researcher and is part of the strategy of constructing a plausible story about the link from injury to damage.

While linking resource injury to behavioral change is perhaps the most important element of strategy of damage assessment, there are other important ingredients. To formalize the strategy of estimating damages, any valuation function can be written $v_i(\theta,t)$, where i is the ith individual, v is the stream of economic value from the resource in period t, and θ is a vector of parameters reflecting perception of the injury to the resource. For example, θ could be moments of the probability distribution of contaminants, such as mean and variance. Or it could be an indicator variable, with 1 being "no release" and 0 being "release." We could get $v_i(\theta,t)$ from a number of different approaches: from an expected utility maximization problem, from the area under a Marshallian demand function, or from any function that shows the consequence of hazardous substance release on behavior and value through θ. All indirect approaches can be reduced to the problem of estimating and utilizing a $v_i(\theta,t)$ function. We can calculate damages for a year by evaluating $v_i(\theta,t)$ in the "no-release" state θ_0 and the "release" state θ_1, and then by subtracting and summing across all individuals:

$$D(t) = \sum_{i=1}^{n_0} v_i(\theta_0,t) - \sum_{i=1}^{n_1} v_i(\theta_1,t),$$

where n_i is the number of individuals receiving services from the resource when $\theta = \theta_i$. A modeling strategy is a set of assumptions and a plausible story about the assumptions that allows one to calculate the present discounted value of annual damages $[D(t)]$ with the resource injury. The story and assumptions must deal with the following issues: What is the link from resource injury to behavioral change? How does the researcher proxy for θ, the index of resource injury? How does the researcher determine n_0 and n_1, the number of people who value service flows? How does

---

not traded on a market. However, were one able to observe the resource price changing, then, barring divergences caused by taxes, one could equate resource damage to resource price change.

the model handle the temporal evolution of v_i (θ,t)? When the hazardous substance simply eliminates access to the resource, θ_1 signifies no access, and θ_0 access. In that case one need only measure the value of access under the uncontaminated case. But where θ qualifies the conditions of access, the problem is more complicated.

Consider the link from resource injury to behavioral change. The link should provide a way for individuals to come in contact with the pollutant and also a way for individuals to learn about the pollutant. This link in the valuation model should bear some relation to the pollutant. For example, one would not model the effect of airborne toxic substances in the same way as contaminated groundwater. Both the kind of model (such as expected utility function, expenditure function, or indirect utility function) and the nature of the exogenous variable (such as extent of hazardous release or distance from a hazardous facility) must be specified. The specification of the valuation or behavioral function must be sufficiently flexible to allow one to discriminate between the passage of time (and the many influences implied by that) and the change in an individual's perception of injury to the resource.

Given a valuation model and an exogenous variable representing hazardous releases, a researcher needs a mechanism for assigning values to θ. When the rules of access remain unchanged, valuation is provided by changes in individual behavior induced by changes in the quantity or quality of the resource. In models of consumer sovereignty, the mechanism ought to be consumers' perceptions of θ. Consumers' perceptions of θ forge the link between hazardous substances and changes in individual behavior, which in turn change the resource's service flows.

The role of information is crucial because in many cases hazardous substances that increase risk are imperceptible. In reacting to impairment of the natural resource through contamination by a hazardous substance, or responding to remedial effects, the public typically uses secondary information about the resource. Direct sensory perception of changes in the quality of the resource is not possible. For example, while there is apparently clinical evidence that polychlorinated biphenyls (PCBs) are carcinogenic, people must be informed about PCBs in a secondary way. Also, pesticides in water wells pose a threat to health that can only be determined by a chemical analysis of the water. Individuals learn of the contamination through various sources: friends, neighbors, newspapers, television, and the like. How people learn about θ will affect their judgment about it.

The substantial role of perceptions in damage assessment must be faced squarely. Occasionally the formation of expectations about a resource may lead people to perceive an injury to a resource as serious when in fact it is negligible. For example, Swartz and Strand (1981), in a study of a kepone spill in the James River in Virginia, found a decline in regional demand for all oysters, not just those harvested from James River estuaries. This decline in demand was associated with newspaper coverage of the kepone spill. The literature on consumer's assessment of risk is rich in examples of erroneous subjective probabilities (see Schulze and coauthors [1986] for references). This misperception, called natural resource slander by Gardner Brown in chapter 5, induces behavioral change. It is reasonable that the strategy for damage assessment include the damages implied by natural resource slander. They are real and are induced by resource injury.

The difficulty of direct sensory observation of injury to natural resources does not invalidate damages, but it does suggest the need for special care in modeling the demand for the resource and the distribution of information about hazardous substances. People are likely to hold diverse opinions about the state of the resource and, in contrast to price expectations, there are no market outcomes to penalize those who hold extreme views. Further, people are likely to form their opinions at different times and revise their opinions at different rates. Whether a particular user knows about the release of the hazardous substance, how he learned about it, and how long he has known are important data for the modeling process. The problems that arise in modeling the formation of expectations about injury to resources will be one component of the CERCLA research agenda.

Indirect methods proceed by estimating behavioral models. Each model requires measures of θ, whether explicit or not, for the estimation process. Proxies for θ can have a big impact on both the estimation process and benefit calculation. For example, suppose in a housing market one uses distance from a hazardous facility as a proxy for risk. How accurate is this proxy? Is it also potentially a proxy for other relevant influences not connected with hazardous substances? Each method must address the problem of proxies, although of course the problem is much more severe in a case in which θ appears explicitly.

The problem of determining the number of people to factor into the sum of damages is simply the problem of determining the extent of the market. How widespread is the effect of the release of hazardous substances? As an example of this problem, suppose we currently observe behavior toward a water-based recreational facility that is contaminated by hazardous substances. We can calculate v_i (θ_1, t), the current flow of services, and n_1, the number of users. It may be straightforward to estimate v_i (θ_0, t). But the most difficult problem of estimation in this example is to predict the number of people who would be induced to use the resource in its unimpaired state. This problem is especially difficult because it requires predicting the effect of hazardous substances on the number of users. As Kopp and Smith (1987) demonstrate, rival estimates of damages are likely to disagree more on the extent of the market than on the value of service flows per individual.

Finally, there is the problem of calculating benefits over time. One faces the standard problems associated with planners' uncertainty: the coefficients of v_i (θ,t) are estimated and hence uncertain; the exogenous variables are unknown and must be forecast; the horizon may be debatable. The previous DOI regulation handles this uncertainty by specifying that damage estimates should be an expected net present value figure. But more important for damage assessment under CERCLA is the question of how one handles θ. Psychologists have argued that people's preferences over small risks are unstable. And many have argued that the subjective probabilities for risks for new health threats are typically quite a bit higher than objective risks. (See, for example, the discussion in Schulze and coauthors [1986].) When the injury to the resource persists over long periods of time, and the realized incidence of health effects substantially differs from the subjective assessment, people will probably revise their opinions.

There is a small but expanding literature on the revision of subjective risk. Viscusi and O'Connor (1984) developed a model of workers' revisions of on-the-job risk based on new, objective information. There is evidence of such revision in the short run, for example in the work of Swartz and Strand (1981), showing how (apparently erroneous) responses to oyster contamination declined over several months. Lipton (1986) showed how consumers' fear of mercury contamination in swordfish declined over several years without additional scientific evidence on the risks. Foster and Just (1989) have estimated a model that allows the risk threats from heptachlor in milk to decline. Work on the valuation of subjective risk from observed behavior and the revision of subjective risk will play a crucial role in damage assessment.

Damage assessment using indirect methods under CERCLA is thus much more than the simple task of estimating behavioral responses to resource injury. It involves a complex set of assumptions by the researcher that tell a plausible story about the links between resource injury and damage. Where direct evidence is likely to be weak (as in determining the effect of resource injury on behavior change), assumptions must be strong and less subject to empirical testing. Where there is more research experience (for example, in determining the implications of market behavior for economic value), assumptions may be correspondingly weaker. Section 3 reveals the nature of various assumptions in specific indirect methods.

3. BEHAVIOR-BASED METHODS OF DAMAGE ASSESSMENT

In this section I discuss four methods of damage assessment that base their analysis on models of individual behavior and their empirical results on observations of individual behavior. One method, the hedonic model, relates primarily to housing market transactions. Two methods, the travel cost model and the random utility model, deal with recreational behavior. The fourth method, the averting behavior model, analyzes direct individual actions taken to avoid the effects of the hazardous substance. The intent of this section is to consider the research issues that will arise as these indirect methods are applied to CERCLA settings. Surveys of each method are legion and references are given in passing. For each method, I give a brief synopsis of the workings of the model and address the questions most likely to arise under CERCLA.

3.1 The Hedonic Model. The hedonic model, a concept initially formulated by Rosen (1974), is a model of the equilibrium outcomes of a market for a good with several attributes. The hedonic model is frequently applied to the housing market, but it fits other markets, such as the labor or automobile markets, where the good has significant quality characteristics that influence the market price. There are many complete expositions of the hedonic model, including Bartik and Smith (1987), Rosen (1974), and Freeman (1979).

The hedonic model is a standard model of supply and demand for a commodity, except that the commodity has characteristics that cannot be unbundled. These attributes are discernible by market participants. Examples are horsepower in automobiles, sugar content of oranges, location of a seat at the opera, or bedrooms in a house.

In such a market buyers and sellers come together, each seeking to maximize his own welfare. Equilibrium is achieved when variations in the price of the good reflect variations in its quality in such a way that neither buyer nor seller can do better by making another deal. The relationship of equilibrium between the price of the good and the characteristics of the good is the hedonic price function. The shape of the function reflects all of the characteristics of buyers and sellers. The hedonic model for the housing market is characterized by the buying and selling of one unit at a time.

The hedonic market for housing can be characterized formally. Sellers maximize profits (or the utility of profits) from the sale of houses with attributes $z_1, \ldots, z_m$ where m is the number of attributes. Buyers maximize the utility from purchasing a house with attributes z, allocating their budgets among housing and other goods. The equilibrium hedonic price function is given by

$$p = h(z;\gamma), \tag{1}$$

where p is the price of a unit of housing, z is the vector of attributes, and γ is a vector of parameters describing the shape of the function, which depends on the number and nature of buyers and sellers.

The hedonic price function is an equilibrium relationship that may not have a closed-form solution as equation (1) suggests. But empirical hedonic models assume that the market outcomes can be approximated by the best fit of the equation

$$p_i = h(z^i) + \epsilon_i, \tag{2}$$

where p_i is the sales price of the ith house, h is a function of unknown form to be estimated, z^i is the vector of attributes for the ith house, and ϵ_i is a random term. While best-fit methods are used to estimate $h(z;\gamma)$, one needs a model of household decisions to interpret it.

In the housing market, the equilibrium set of prices emerges as buyers bid for a fixed stock of houses. In equilibrium, the owner or renter of the house can be viewed as having maximized the utility of that house subject to a budget constraint. Let the utility function be

$$u = u\,(x,z;\beta), \tag{3}$$

where x is a Hicksian bundle, z is a vector of the house's attributes, and β is a vector of parameters describing tastes and the functional form of u. When y is income and the price of the Hicksian bundle is 1, the household's budget constraint is

$$y = x + h(z). \tag{4}$$

Maximizing utility subject to the budget constraint induces optimal conditions for each attribute:

$$\partial u/\partial z_i = \lambda \partial h/\partial z_i \qquad i = 1, \ldots, m, \tag{5}$$

where λ is the marginal utility of income. The marginal conditions in equation (5) help account for the attractiveness of the hedonic model. The derivative of the hedonic price function with respect to a particular attribute equals the marginal value of the attribute. Simulation work by Cropper, Deck, and McConnell (1988) provides some evidence that allocating housing stock among buyers by maximum bid or by the solution of an assignment problem yields equilibrium conditions approximating the marginal value conditions of equation (5).

Economists have considerable experience in applying the hedonic model to the housing market. There is impressive evidence on the role of attributes in the hedonic price function. Consider two types of attributes: attributes of the house and lot—numbers of rooms, bathrooms, square footage, lot size, type of construction, air conditioning, and the like; and, attributes of the neighborhood—density, median income, schools, access to amenities and disamenities, and environmental quality. Evidence about the first kind of attribute is quite strong. Estimated hedonic price models routinely show convincing numerical marginal prices for the major attributes of houses. Evidence on the second kind of attribute is more mixed. Well-known and easily discernible attributes typically show up as expected. But smaller attributes, whose value may be slight, are more problematic, and tend to show up less significantly in hedonic price equations.

Welfare measurement in hedonic markets is surprisingly complicated. Calculation of the exact welfare measure—the compensating variation of all participants—involves consideration of the extent of the market, the degree to which the housing market at issue is open or closed, the heterogeneity of housing owners and occupants, and the relative ease of changing lot size. To determine the extent of the market one must find out how many houses are in the zone of influence of the hazardous substance. The answer is empirical and depends on how the link from resource injury to perception of injury is conceived. The housing market is open if in-or-out migration maintains well-being in the community at a fixed level. It is closed when the magnitude of migration relative to the size of the housing market is so small as to have no effect on the utility or well-being of the market participants. In the short run, when consumers as occupants do not adjust to the change in the attribute, the welfare measure is the area under the consumer's marginal bid function. The simplest long-run case occurs when the city is open, residents are homogeneous and lot size is fixed. In that case, welfare change at each affected site can be predicted from the hedonic price function. In the more general case, in which consumers are heterogeneous and lot size changes, the price change predicted by the hedonic price function serves as an upper bound for the welfare change (see Bartik [1988] or Kanemoto [1988]).

The most intuitive welfare measure is derived when households remain in the same house. When that happens a correct measure of the household's change in well-being is based on the utility function. The compensating variation (cv) for a change in attributes for z to $\hat{z}$ is defined implicitly as

$$u(y - h(z) - cv,\hat{z};\beta) = u(y - h(z),z;\beta).$$

This is a short-run measure of welfare and requires knowledge of the βs. However, the problem of estimating the βs caused by the simultanity in equation (5) are severe. Hence, welfare measures must proceed with information from the hedonic function but without information on the structure of preferences.

In damage assessment for CERCLA, the most appropriate and workable assumptions for hedonic models appear to be an open city with variable lot sizes and heterogeneous consumers. For this case, I use the change in the hedonic price as predicted by the injury to the resource as an approximate welfare measure. The predicted change in hedonic price is

$$cv \approx h(\hat{z}) - h(z) \tag{6}$$

where $\hat{z}$ is the attribute vector in the no-release case and z the attribute vector in the release case. Expression (6) is the (positive) number that represents the loss. It will be an upper bound of the damages that occur in the long run when housing markets adjust. To calculate aggregate damages, the predicted change in the price is summed over all potentially affected houses. In choosing the number of potentially affected houses, one can see the importance of a plausible story about the link from resource injury to damage. This story, which is based in the analyst's judgment and not in statistical evidence, ought to determine the extent of the market effect of the hazardous substance.

Damages under CERCLA are the present discounted value of the annual flow of losses from the hazardous release. The way in which hedonic models can provide such a measure is not obvious and deserves careful consideration. Under ideal conditions, when markets are working perfectly and taxes and other influences cause no wedges between private opportunity costs and discount rates, the change in the housing price reflects the present discounted value of the damage. This is because the house is an asset that provides an expected stream of returns over time. While DOI guidelines for CERCLA stipulate a 10 percent rate of discount, there are arguments for using personal discount rates or the social rate of time preference, which might be higher or lower than 10 percent. Nevertheless, the choice of discount rate is an explicit part of the strategy of damage assessment.

Several forces can cause the service flow from housing amenities to be discounted differently from the chosen public rate of discount. First, when people bid for houses, they must implicitly discount the expected future returns. Two forces here are relevant. One is the potential for differences in personal rates of discount. The other is the potential for differences in the expected rate of service flow from disamenity created by the injury to the natural resource. But even when the housing market works strictly as an asset market, in which people anticipate the future resale price correctly, in equilibrium the market will enforce the market rate of return on the asset, implicitly discounting the service flow at the market rate. The housing market is further distorted by the tax-exempt status of interest payments and the ambiguous tax status of capital gains on residential real estate. Thus, while one may question whether private discounting has been greater or less than the public rate of discount, it is clear that change in the price of housing as a measure of damage will only by accident reflect discounting of future services at the public rate of discount.

Welfare measurement in hedonic models is inexact. Both the nature of the housing markets and econometric problems associated with the hedonic model prevent development of precise measures of damages per household. But special care ought to be given to determining the extent of the market, that is, the number of houses affected by the injured resource. If care is taken with the welfare computations, the principle problem of using hedonic models under CERCLA appears to be in determining how well the market, and hence the hedonic price function, reflects injury to the natural resource.

The primary question about the use of the hedonic market for damage assessment under CERCLA concerns the precise role of exposure to hazardous substances. Here models that reflect decisions under uncertainty are relevant. In the most likely case—an impact on housing markets—the release of hazardous substances increases perceptions of health risks. In such a case the problem of consumer's choice can be cast as a problem of expected utility maximization:

$$\max_{z,\,\pi} \ \pi u_1[\,y - h(z,\pi),z] + (1 - \pi)u_2[\,y - h(z,\pi),z], \tag{7}$$

where $1 - \pi$ is the subjective probability of having one's health impaired, u_2 is the health-impaired utility function, and u_1 is the "healthy" utility function. In expression (7), the housing market has accounted for the risk by incorporating π into the hedonic function. This problem is formulated with state-dependent preference functions because there are convincing arguments that utility functions are dependent on the state of one's health. (See Viscusi and Evans [1988] for approaches to estimating these functions for labor market risks.) The optimal choice of risk involves the tradeoff

$$\partial h/\partial \pi = [u_1 - u_2]/E\lambda, \tag{8}$$

where $E\lambda = \pi\lambda_1 + (1 - \pi)\lambda_2$ and λ_i is the marginal utility of income in state i. Damage assessment under CERCLA involves welfare calculations of an exogenous change in π (or in a more complicated model, moments of the distribution of the risk).

The welfare loss from exposure to hazardous wastes is the ex ante payment that leaves the individual with expected utility with the risk and compensation equal to utility without the risk. This is given implicitly by

$$\begin{aligned}
u_1[\,y - h(z),z] &= \pi u_1[\,y - h(z,\pi) + cv_A,z] \\
&\quad + (1 - \pi)u_2[\,y - h(z,\pi) + cv_A,z]
\end{aligned} \tag{9}$$

where $h(z)$ is the price of a house with attribute z and no risk.[5] Here cv_A is the compensating option price, an ex ante measure of damages, based on the utility achieved without risk, on the left-hand side. It is subscripted A (for ex ante) to distinguish it from a welfare measure under certainty. This is a standard definition of the compensating version of option price. (Compare this with Smith [1985], equation [1].)

Unfortunately, we are able only to approximate the welfare effect, as in expression (6), by the predicted price change. A reasonable approximation is

$$cv \approx h(z,1) - h(z,\pi), \qquad (10)$$

which is the predicted price differential from π (the probability of a desirable state) to 1.

The role of perceptions of risk is evident in the housing market. The function of opinions and the dispersal of information ought to be an integral part of modeling the hedonic price function. When there is publicity about hazardous contamination, opinions about risks are likely to change dramatically. In a typical case of release of hazardous substances, a good deal of public discussion takes place about the severity of the objective risk. It is reasonable to expect some disparity among scientists' estimates of objective risks. Such discussions may cause buyers to form estimates of subjective risk that substantially exceed the objective risk. (This would be consistent with results from psychological research, which

---

[5]There are some subtle welfare problems here. Note that expression (9) asks for the cv, the compensation required to accept the health risk $1 - \pi$. Alternatively, the amount one would pay to avoid the health risk is defined by the option price

$$u_1 (y - h - op, z) = \pi u_1 (y - h, z) + (1 - \pi) u_2 (y - h, z),$$

which is precisely the definition of option price given by Smith (1985). With approximate constant marginal utility of income in state 1, this becomes

$$u_1 (\cdot) - \lambda_1 op = \pi[u_1 (\cdot) - u_2 (\cdot)] + u_2 (\cdot).$$

Then solving for op implies

$$op = (1 - \pi) [u_1 (\cdot) - u_2 (\cdot)]/\lambda_1,$$

the expected difference in the utility levels, converted to dollars by the (assumed constant) marginal utility of state 1. The explicit value of cv_A in expression (9) is $cv_A = (1 - \pi) (u_1 - u_2)/E\lambda$. It is traditionally assumed that $\lambda_1 > \lambda_2$, that is, the marginal utility of income in the healthy state exceeds that of the unhealthy state, in which case op would be less than cv_A. Viscusi and Evans (1988) argue that the relation of λ_1 and λ_2 ought to be determined empirically.

suggests that some people overestimate the risks from low-probability events with severe outcomes. For examples and references, see Schulze and coauthors [1986].) At any rate, buyers and sellers in a housing market are likely to have perceptions of risk different from the best (or consensus) scientific estimates of risk. And estimation of the hedonic function ought to reflect at least the recent evolution of this function.[6]

In their state of relative ignorance about the objective risk, market participants must find indicators of the hazardous substance. One approach commonly taken is to equate distance from the site of the hazardous release with reduction in risk. This approach, originally investigated by Mitchell (1980), is supported in the results of Smith and Desvousges (1986b), who find through contingent valuation evidence of willingness to pay more for a house farther from a hazardous facility. However, Smith, Desvousges, and Freeman (1985, chapter 15) show that respondents have some difficulty in converting distance into risk. Thus, the assumption that people can reduce risk by purchasing houses farther from an injured resource has limited empirical support. Pursuing this approach, one can suppose that $1 - \pi$, the probability of being exposed to hazardous substances, is related to distance in a negative way (where s is distance):

$$\partial[1 - \pi(s)]/\partial s = -\pi'(s) < 0$$

or

$$\pi'(s) > 0.$$

This is perception of risk from hazardous substances. It seems plausible that $\pi(s)$ varies across households; people perceive the impact of distance on risk differently, depending perhaps on their own characteristics, such as health and education. See Smith, Desvousges, and Freeman (1985, chapter 15) for a lengthy discussion of this issue. But for the purposes of this analysis, $\pi(s)$ is assumed to be the same for all households. Basically, the risk–distance relationship must be established by a plausible story or anecdotal evidence, or perhaps contingent valuation work. It cannot be established solely by evidence from the hedonic price function.

With this risk–distance tradeoff, the buyer's problem would be to maximize the expected utility of owning the house:

$$\max_{s,z} \pi(s)u_1\{y_1 - h[z,\pi(s)],z\} + [1 - \pi(s)]u_2\{y_2 - h[z,\pi(s)],z\}. \qquad (11)$$

---

[6]Schulze and coauthors (1986) make a careful analysis of the role of subjective perceptions in determining housing prices for the hazardous waste site in Monterey Park, Los Angeles.

As above, π, the risk of not being exposed, increases with distance; $\pi'(s) > 0$: the farther the distance from the site, the lower the risk. Optimal choice of distance implies

$$\partial h/\partial s = [(u_1 - u_2)/E\lambda]\partial \pi/\partial s, \qquad (12)$$

which is analogous to equation (8) with a change in variable from π to s. The housing price changes with distance from the contaminated resource only because subjective risk changes:

$$\partial h/\partial s = \frac{\partial h}{\partial \pi} \frac{\partial \pi}{\partial s},$$

so that in equilibrium, equation (12) can be written

$$\partial h/\partial \pi = (u_1 - u_2)/E\lambda,$$

by dividing each side by $\partial \pi/\partial s$. This is the same as equation (8), which arose from the relevant problem, the optimal choice of π, not distance. Consequently, when the choice involves the probability of exposure only, and one uses a proxy for this probability, then the model implies the correct calculation. This conclusion does not change if the function $\pi(s)$ varies across individuals. For welfare measures, suppose $\hat{s}$ reduces the perceived risk to zero. The approximate welfare loss from the hazardous release analogous to expression (10) is

$$cv \approx h(z,\hat{s}) - h(z,s). \qquad (13)$$

When distance has direct effects on utility as well as changing the probability of exposure, the effects are confounded in the hedonic gradient. Other effects of distance would depend on the nature of the resource injured by the release. Distance from a landfill would increase utility, as the home would be further from local noise. But if the resource were an otherwise attractive body of water, then distance would have a negative effect. In cases in which distance has a direct effect, the utility function for state i becomes

$$u = u_i(y,z,s).$$

The hedonic price equation becomes

$$p = h^*[z,\pi(s),s] = h(z,s). \qquad (14)$$

Then the household's equilibrium condition is

$$\partial h/\partial s = [(u_1 - u_2)/E\lambda]\partial \pi/\partial s + \frac{E\partial u/\partial s}{E\lambda}. \qquad (15)$$

$E\partial u/\partial s$ is negative for an amenity and positive for a disamenity.

When distance from the injured resource has a direct effect on utility, the damage calculation becomes more complicated. In essence, one must subtract the direct positive or negative effects of distance. The ex ante welfare effect (cv_A) of the hazardous release *only* is implicitly defined as

$$u_1[y - h(z,s),z,s] = \pi u_1[y - h(z,s) + cv_A,z,s] \\ + (1 - \pi)u_2[y - h(z,s) + cv_A,z,s].$$

Unfortunately, the hedonic price function alone does not give enough information to separate the nonrisk amenities or disamenities from the risk. The predicted hedonic price change will overestimate the desired welfare approximation for positive amenities and underestimate for negative amenities. Consequently, with sufficient prior information that distance is an important factor independent of the effect of risk, complete damage assessment requires that one find not the effect of distance, but how the effect of distance changes with information about the release of hazardous materials. If we calculate $\partial h/\partial s$ before the dispersal of information about the hazardous release, we will approximate the expected locational effects from before the presence of risk. Also, a significant burden is placed on the researcher to account for the effects of distance.

Among the many practical problems with hedonic price functions, the separating out of effects of different attributes is paramount. One variant of the hedonic model that eliminates much of the collinearity among attributes (the source of imprecise parameter estimates) is the repeat sale technique. This technique, adapted by Palmquist (1982) for environmental variables such as exposure to hazardous substances, uses observations on sales of houses that have been sold more than once. It allows the exclusion of all housing attributes that have not changed between the two sale dates. For example, suppose that the original hedonic price function in year t is

$$p^{it} = h(z^i)B(t)\exp(\gamma s),$$

where $B(t)$ is a parametric function of time and γ is a scalar, both to be estimated. Then the log of the price relative is

$$\ln(p^{it}/p^{it'}) = \ln[B(t)/B(t')] + \gamma s.$$

Under appropriate assumptions about errors, one can estimate γ and the assumed impacts of distance on risk and of risk on housing prices.

Even with the traditional hedonic model, there is growing evidence of the effects of proximity to natural or man-made risk on housing prices. Evidence stems from studies that vary considerably in the degree to which they deal with threats to life, health, and property. Floods are more a threat to property than to health and life. Earthquakes and nuclear power plant accidents are a threat to both health and property. In housing markets, hazardous substance releases are a threat to health. All of these settings provide the opportunity for disastrous but uncertain events to be capitalized in housing prices. But it is reasonable to believe that opinions about potential health threats would be more diverse than opinions about earthquakes or floods, so that evidence on the situations involving only health threats would be less convincing in the context of CERCLA.

Table 8-1 summarizes the evidence, from a number of recent studies, in support of the idea that risks to life and property are capitalized in housing markets. Each of the studies takes into account the importance of information in the formation of perceptions, and most of the studies attempt to show the effect of timing or a particularly important piece of news on the hedonic function. Brookshire and coauthors (1985) show that location in a designated earthquake zone has a negative impact on housing prices only after the zone is designated. Kohlhase (forthcoming) shows that distance from the nearest hazardous waste facility has a positive impact on housing prices in an equation using sales observations after publicity about the facilities. Baker (1986) gives evidence for structural change in the hedonic price equation for housing sales taking place after the Bhopal, India, tragedy in 1984. However, she also finds that the impact of proximity to a chemical plant declined after the Bhopal incident. Further, she does not correct for temporal housing price movements that might have resulted from inflationary pressures, so that the effect of Bhopal is mixed with price changes over time. Adler and coauthors (1982) find no impact of location near a waste facility in Andover, Minn., and a limited effect of distance from a facility in Pleasant Plains, N.J., after publicity about contamination at the site. MacDonald, Murdoch, and White (1987) estimate the effect of location on a flood plain. Their results show the negative effect on price of location in an area rated as having a high flood threat.

Schulze and coauthors (1986) provide a valuable study of three housing markets near hazardous waste sites. In the first two cases, there was evidence that proximity to the sites depressed housing prices. While the sample sizes were not large (fewer than 200 houses in each case), both timing and distance seemed important. In the third case, a municipal landfill, the authors did not find a significant negative effect of location

Table 8-1. Housing Market Studies of Health and Property Risks

Study	Type of threat	Location	Proxy for risk	Evidence of effect
Adler and coauthors (1982)	Hazardous landfills	Andover, Minn.	Stepped function of distance	No?
Baker (1986)	Potentially hazardous production facilities (chemical plants)	Kanawha River, W. Va.	Natural log of distance to nearest plant; zonal dummy	Yes
Brookshire and coauthors (1985)	Earthquake	Los Angeles, Calif. San Francisco, Calif.	Dummy variables for location in zone	No in 1972 Yes in 1978
Gamble and Downing (1982)	Nuclear power plants	Plymouth, Mass. Waterford, Conn. Lacey Township, N.J. Rochester, N.Y.	Distance to plants; dummy for visibility of plant	No
Kohlhase (forthcoming)	Hazardous waste sites	Houston, Tex.	Quadratic function of distance to nearest site	Yes in 1980 and 1985 No in 1976
McDonald, Murdock, and White (1987)	Flooding	Monroe, La.	Dummy variable for location in flood zone	Yes
Michaels, Smith, and Harrison (1987)	Hazardous waste sites	Submarkets in suburban Boston	Distance to nearest site	Slight
Nelson (1981)	Nuclear power plant	Harrisburg, Pa.	Distance zones	No
Schulze and coauthors (1986)	Hazardous waste sites	Three housing markets in urban areas[a]	Distance zones; inverse function of distance from sites	Yes

[a] The locations are not given because of pending legal action.

near the site, despite the fact that a methane gas explosion destroyed a house near the site. Schulze and coauthors explain the absence of a depressing effect by suggesting that location closer to the site had an offsetting (positive) effect of being farther from the city. The absence of negative effect can also be explained by the city's acceptance of liability.

Surprisingly, two studies show the absence of an effect from nuclear power plants. Nelson (1981), using limited data on the surrounding housing markets, finds no effect on prices from the Three Mile Island accident. Gamble and Downing (1982) show results for four communities in the northeastern United States. In each of the housing markets, visibility of a nuclear plant (0,1 variable, taking 1 for visible nuclear plant, 0 for not visible) and distance to a nuclear power plant were not significant determinants of housing prices. Further, the authors are not able to show a significant shift in the marginal effect of distance from the nuclear plant after the Three Mile Island nuclear accident.

Michaels, Smith, and Harrison (1987) show only limited evidence of effect owing to location near a hazardous waste facility. They allow their models to respond differently before and after publicity concerning a hazardous waste facility. However, the basic approach of their paper suggests caution in interpreting results from other models. Their approach employs market segmentation prior to estimation. The market segmentation involved subdividing houses in a large market into distinct submarkets, which may not have been geographically contiguous. Houses in eighty-five towns of suburban Boston were classified into four distinct submarkets. Their segmentation was based on realtors' suggestions, and holds up statistically. It is not clear how distance to a hazardous facility would show up in an incorrectly pooled model.

An issue raised implicitly by Michaels, Smith, and Harrison is the extent of the market in hedonic models. Their work carefully lays out the nature of a housing market. Several of the studies cited in table 8-1 analyze houses in the vicinity of the potential threat, but do not attempt to determine whether the market extends beyond the vicinity analyzed. Care in defining a housing market can be illustrated by an example involving nuclear power plants: analyzing sales in the immediate vicinity of such a plant might not capture an impact on housing prices if people believe that the principal threat is from an explosion that would devastate or contaminate all houses within twenty miles. Both the studies by Adler and coauthors (1982) and Schulze and coauthors (1986) examine sales in the immediate vicinity of the hazardous facility, possibly truncating the housing market and obscuring the effects of distance from the facility on housing prices.

Hedonic price functions estimated for damage assessment under CERCLA ought in principle to be able to calculate service flows in the contaminated and uncontaminated state of the resource. This characteristic would appear to make them suitable for calculating the service flow under full restoration of the resource. There is a catch here, however. Full restoration is defined by DOI guidelines as restoring the resource's physical service flow "without contamination." Yet in the housing market the market-clearing conditions are strongly dependent on perceptions of risk. To argue that households will perceive a resource as uncontaminated when it has been physically treated to relieve the risk of hazardous substances is to ignore the real and crucial role of perceptions. By itself, the hedonic model cannot predict when full restoration is achieved. This requires a more elaborate model of the evaluation of perceptions.

It is frequently argued that the housing market overreacts to news about the release of hazardous substances. This implies that the subjective risk initially exceeds the objective risk. Can this disparity persist over time? Several forces suggest that it cannot. First, there is ample evidence that people are less risk-averse toward threats with which they are more familiar. Hence, over time and with no new information about the objective risks, households' perception of risk may well decline. Second, new information may emerge. If perceptions of risk initially exceed the scientifically measured risks, each period in which no visible health effects occur may cause market participants to revise their subjective analysis of risks. This is speculation, but it suggests the need for investigation of the effects of information on the hedonic price function at different periods after publicity about contamination.

There is an ironic relationship between the success of Superfund as a remedial tool and the future effectiveness of the hedonic model in damage assessment. The hedonic model works because households act as if contamination is an exogenous event, like an earthquake, and as if it will persist. However, if Superfund is used to clean up hazardous waste sites, then households may discount the future risk by some subjective estimate of the likelihood that the site will be cleaned up. Kohlhase (forthcoming) uses this argument to explain the perverse effects of distance for the Harris-Farley site in Houston, Texas. And Gamble and Downing (1982) argue that houses in the vicinity of nuclear reactors do not sell for lower prices because households believe that the government will compensate them for damages. This response to Superfund would not eliminate damages; it would merely reduce the effectiveness of the hedonic model to measure them.

3.2   The Travel Cost Model.   The travel cost model is a method for valuing nonmarketed service flows. This model was developed precisely because resources producing these services were held in trust for the public. The model was originally developed for valuing access to natural resources, but its applications have evolved to include valuing the quality of resources.

The travel cost model is motivated by the necessity for an individual to visit a particular recreation site to enjoy its services. The cost of consuming services is equated with the cost of transporting oneself to the recreation site. Spatial variation in residences translates into variation in the cost of access to individual users. (See Desvousges and Skahen [1986]; McConnell [1985]; and Bockstael, Hanemann, and Strand [1986] for a detailed analysis of the travel cost model.) A brief exposition of the deterministic model follows. Later I examine conditions under uncertainty.

A consumer has preferences defined by $u(x,z,q)$, where x is a Hicksian bundle, $z = (z_1, \ldots, z_n)$ is a vector of visits to each of the n recreational sites, and $q = (q_1, \ldots, q_n)$ is a collection of m-dimensional vectors of the measurable or perceptible qualities of the recreational sites. That is, $q_i = (q_{i1}, \ldots, q_{im})$ is the consumer's perceptions of amenities of the ith site, including such things as crowd size, water quality, and noise level. The consumer maximizes

$$u(x,z,q) - \lambda(x + pz - y), \tag{16}$$

where the price of the Hicksian bundle is $1, p = (p_1, \ldots, p_n)$ is the vector of costs of access to the recreation sites, and y is money income. A critical element in the costs of access is the value of time. In writing the budget constraint for expression (16), I have substituted in the time constraint, assuming that leisure time can be traded off for work at a constant wage. Several other models can be equally justified. The problem of valuing time is a perennial research topic, and is not limited to CERCLA cases.

The first-order conditions highlight the problem of site choice. With choice variables constrained to be nonnegative, the conditions include

$$
\begin{aligned}
[u_i(z,x,q) - \lambda p_i]z_i &= 0 \\
z_i > 0 \rightarrow u_i - \lambda p_i &= 0 \\
u_i - \lambda p_i < 0 \rightarrow z_i &= 0
\end{aligned} \tag{17}
$$

In any given survey of a group of recreational sites, many people visit only one or two sites out of a larger set. Further, in a survey of the population, a significant proportion of people do not engage in various kinds of outdoor recreation. Consequently, it is appealing to imagine several different kinds of decisions: whether to participate in outdoor recreation, which site to visit, how frequently to visit chosen sites. Hence expression (17) shows the optimal condition for some positive trips and some zero trips. When the optimal quantity of trips to the ith site is positive, the Marshallian demand function can be written

$$z_i = f_i(p,q,y), \tag{18}$$

where the arguments of $f_i(p,q,y)$ exclude the prices and qualities of sites not visited. As a rough approximation, one may think of the travel cost method as estimating equation (18) by observing that spatial variations in the location of sites and residences of users and potential users generate variations in the effective cost per trip, p_i.

Welfare measures for changes in exogenous variables can be calculated from the parameters of equation (18). Consumer's surplus, or the value of access to the site, is

$$CS(p,q,y) = \int_{p_1}^{p_1^\infty} f_1(p,q,y)dp \qquad (19)$$

when p_1^∞ is the Marshallian choke price and other prices are suppressed. When some aspect of the quality of the site has diminished (q is reduced to q^*), the consumer's surplus of this change is given by

$$CS(p,q,y) - CS(p,q^*,y) = \int_{p_1}^{p_1^\infty} [f_1(p,q,y) - f_1(p,q^*,y)]dp. \qquad (20)$$

In general, for the rather modest income effects found in recreational demand models, the surplus measures are good approximations of the variational measures. (For price changes see Just, Hueth, and Schmitz [1983]. Although their reasoning is different, for quality changes see Bockstael and McConnell [1987]).

The practical problem of valuing changes in q arises in the estimation stage. In the case of quality variables that are site-specific, there is no variation of q across the sample. One way to treat this problem is to use the varying parameters model. In this model, one estimates demand functions for different sites. Then the parameters of those functions are regressed against measures of variation in water quality, which vary across sites. (See Smith and Desvousges [1985], Vaughan and Russell [1982], and Bockstael, McConnell, and Strand [1988] for applications.)

The use of the travel cost model to measure damages for CERCLA will depend on how the injury is transmitted to recreationists. When access is eliminated by regulation, damages per user are simply the lost value of access—equation (19). When quality changes for health or aesthetic reasons, damages per user are given by equation (20), where q_1 is perceived quality in the uncontaminated resource and q_1^* is perceived quality in the contaminated resource. In either case, the research must provide a plausible story to explain why the recreationists respond as they do.

The transmission of information about hazardous releases is likely to be more informal for recreational decisions than in the hedonic market because of the ease of adjusting to new information. Decisions modeled in the maximization problem (expression [16]) on an annual basis are actually made on a trip-by-trip basis, whereas in the hedonic case the decision modeled on an annual basis is more likely to be a multi-year decision. Further, the cost of the decision is much greater for the housing market than for the recreation market. When individuals adjust their decisions almost instantaneously, travel cost welfare measures may be considered ex post.

There are situations in which uncertainty is not resolved by visiting the site. The resource may be contaminated by a hazardous substance that the recreationist perceives in the form of uncertain quality. When the user visits a site but fears unknown effects, his decision can be modeled as expected utility maximization.

Welfare measurement when the consumer is uncertain about the effects is analogous to the certainty case. Imagine state-dependent functions, so that the choice problem, instead of expression (16), becomes

$$\max_{z,x} \pi u_1(z,x) + (1 - \pi)u_2(z,x) - \lambda[x + pz - y], \qquad (21)$$

where u_1 is the healthy utility function and π is the subjective probability of not having one's health impaired. Suppose the hazardous release occurs at site one. We assume weak complementarity, which in this context means that if an individual does not visit site one, there is no risk; therefore u_1 prevails.

The basic problem is to show that the change in welfare from a reduction in the probability from $1 - \pi$ to 0 can be approximated by the area under the ex ante demand curve. The indirect utility function that is the solution to expression (21) is

$$v(p,1 - \pi,y) = \max_{z,x} \pi u_1(z,x) + (1 - \pi)u_2(z,x) - \lambda(x + pz - y). \quad (22)$$

The indirect utility function depends on $1 - \pi$ because this is the perceived health risk. Let p^∞ be the vector of prices that sets the demand for site one to zero. The compensating variation for access to this site, which is approximated by the area under the demand curve, is implicitly given by cv_A^1 in the expression

$$v(p,1 - \pi,y) = v(p^\infty,1 - \pi,y + cv_A^1) = v_1(p^\infty,y + cv_A^1), \quad (23)$$

where v_1 is the indirect utility function that prevails when site one's demand is zero. The notation cv_A^1 denotes the ex ante value of access to site one. With λ_1 constant, we can approximate cv_A^1 as

$$cv_A^1(1 - \pi) = [v(p,1 - \pi,y) - v_1(p^\infty,y)]/\lambda_1. \qquad (24)$$

Two effects are mixed in $cv_A^1(1 - \pi)$: reduction in risk and loss of access. Of course, cv cannot be negative, for otherwise the optimizing individual would not visit the site. If we want to decompose the effects, we can show that

$$cv_A^1(0) - cv_A^1(1 - \pi) = \frac{E\lambda}{\lambda} cv_A^\pi,$$

so that we get the approximate welfare measure by looking at the change in the areas under demand curves.[7]

The need for a plausible story about the link from resource injury to behavioral change is evident from an expression for annual damages. In the notation of section 2:

$$D(t) = \sum_{i=1}^{n_u} \int_{p_i}^{p_i^\infty} f(p, q_i^u, y_i) dp$$

$$- \sum_{i=1}^{n_c} \int_{p_i}^{p_i^\infty} f(p, q_i^c, y_i) dp, \tag{25}$$

---

[7]The compensation for accepting risk $1 - \pi$ such that expected utility equals utility without risk is implicit in

$$v_1(p, y) = v(p, 1 - \pi, y + cv_A^\pi).$$

The left-hand side of the equation is the exact utility, given optimal choices based on no contamination. The right-hand side is the expected utility function based on problem (22). The cv can be approximated as

$$cv_A^\pi = [v_1(p, y) - v(p, 1 - \pi, y)]/E\lambda,$$

where $E\lambda = \partial v/\partial y$, the expected marginal utility of income. The compensation for access when perceived risk is zero is

$$cv_A^1(0) = [v_1(p, y) - v_1(p^\infty, y)]/\lambda_1.$$

We calculate the approximate change in areas under demand curves as

$$cv_A^1(0) - cv_A^1(1 - \pi) = \frac{E\lambda}{\lambda_1} cv_A^\pi.$$

Hence the difference in exact areas under demand curves is not exactly equal to the payment required to absorb the risk. The exact compensation required to accept risk π is cv_π. Depending on what happens to the utility function in each state ($E\lambda/\lambda_1 \geq$ or ≤ 1), the difference in areas under demand curves may overestimate or underestimate cv_π. Traditional arguments suggest that $\lambda_1 > \lambda_2$, implying that the approximate estimated value would be less than the true value. This problem in approximations is created not by holding to λ's constant, but by an unavoidable ambiguity in the reference level of well-being.

where, for individual i, $p_i^\infty =$ choke price, $p_i =$ current price, q_i^c, $q_i^u =$ perceived quality or risk, u stands for uncontaminated, c stands for contaminated, n_u is the number of users in the uncontaminated state, and n_c is the number of users in the contaminated state. The specific problem of proxies and the more general problem of the availability of data for the travel cost models in CERCLA cases are closely entwined.

Consider the use of proxies for q's. Basically, there are two ways to show quality shifts in a recreational demand function estimated from cross-sectional data. The first way is to use the varying parameters model, which relies on variations in measures of quality across sites. The second way is to use individuals' perceptions of the quality of the natural resource. While the correct measure of quality is that which is perceived by individuals, measures of perceptions typically are not available. Instead one may be tempted to use objective measures of quality (or contamination) and to apply these measures in a varying parameters model. But there are several problems with using the varying parameters model in this context. This model relies on variations in contamination across sites. And it assumes that there is some correspondence between perception of risk and objective measures of risk.

When only one survey is used, damage assessment requires that the proxies not only shift demand for known users, but also that they predict demand for potential users. Equation (25) shows damages to be the sum over users in the uncontaminated state at demands evaluated at q^u and the sum over users in the contaminated state at q^c. For example, if users are surveyed after the release of a hazardous substance, changes in q or its proxies must be used to predict n_u. When demands are fairly elastic, as they are likely to be for sites with many substitutes, estimating changes in the number of users is as important as estimating demand shifts for a given user. Predicting the number of users who enter or exit the market is likely to be one of the most severe problems.

An alternative to the use of proxies would be to estimate different equations in the contaminated and uncontaminated states of the resource. Suppose the uncontaminated observations are taken in year t and the contaminated observation in year τ. In the uncontaminated case, estimate

$$z_i^u = f^u(p_{it}, y_{it}),$$

where p is an appropriate vector of costs, y_i is a vector of determinants particular to the individual, and z_i^u is the level of trips by the ith individual to the site in its uncontaminated state. This demand function yields baseline service flows as required by CERCLA. Then estimate

$$z_i^c = f^c(p_{i\tau}, y_{i\tau}),$$

where now the level of trips to the contaminated site is estimated. This demand function will vary because of the perceptions of risk from the contamination and because the vector of other influences $y_{i\tau}$ has changed. A measure of annual damages analogous to equation (20) is

$$D(\tau) = \sum_{i=1}^{n_u} \int_{p_i}^{p_i^\infty} f^u(p,y_{i\tau})dp - \sum_{i=1}^{n_c} \int_{p_i}^{p_i^\infty} f^c(p,y_{i\tau})dp. \qquad (26)$$

This expression provides a reasonable way around the problem of explicit proxies, but it makes rather severe and unrealistic demands for data, especially data on the site in its uncontaminated state.

Without a direct way to shift demand curves, as implied by equation (20), CERCLA damage assessment implies a need for two systematic samples of households or users. These surveys must obtain the origin and destination of trips to the specific sites in the contaminated and uncontaminated states of the resource. These are two ways to get the uncontaminated state data. A researcher may have the good fortune to have available a survey taken prior to the release of the hazardous substance, or the researcher may design a survey to obtain information from the current population on past use of the site. Neither option is attractive. The first alternative seems unlikely because the travel cost data requirements usually necessitate surveys designed with the goal of estimating travel cost demand functions. Broad surveys of outdoor recreation typically lack the pattern of origin/destination data needed for the travel cost model.

The alternative approach for getting data on the uncontaminated state—relying on memory to reconstruct observations on trips to specific sites—suffers from several drawbacks. The time between the release of the hazardous substance and the conduct of such a survey is likely to be so long that people's recollections of trips to specific sites may be quite inaccurate. Hence, unless an accident occurs where a suitable survey of the uncontaminated natural resource exists, users of the travel cost method will be forced to rely on the memory of sampled individuals to construct information suitable to estimate baseline service flows.

When the release of a hazardous substance effectively removes access to the resource, data problems are simplified and the problems of perceptions eliminated. In that case, damages are calculated from equation (26) when f^c equals zero. Damages are simply the opportunity cost of operating the resource in its uncontaminated state, given current demand for access to the resource. The need for data is reduced to a sample of users of the resource in its uncontaminated state. However, if contamination has existed for long enough, there may be no way to estimate f^u using equation (26). It is not possible to use a model of behavior from data relating to the resource in its contaminated state. Even when one can make a good estimate of the value of access per user (for example, a unit-day value), the problem of estimating n_u, the extent of the market, persists.

Damage assessment under restoration for travel cost models is quite similar to the hedonic case. The difference between full physical restoration of a resource and the perception of full restoration is due primarily to the difficulty in individual's sensory perception of hazardous substances. People cannot discern directly whether a resource is contaminated, they know that scientists disagree about the level of contamination, and they cannot be immediately convinced by the bulk of sometimes conflicting scientific opinion that a resource is free of contamination. Thus, even though Department of the Interior guidelines assume that there is no continuing damage when full restoration occurs, this may be contrary to fact.

Damage assessment under restoration is closely linked to the revision of public perceptions. There is ample evidence that people will misestimate the objective risk from the release of a hazardous substance. And in the period immediately following publicity about the hazardous release, people's perceptions of risk induce behavioral changes and thus people incur damages. Will the perceptions of risk be revised? It is quite possible that they will be, but how, why, and the precise mechanism by which they will is unclear.

The evidence that recreational behavior responds to risk is limited. In a study of pheasant hunting in Oregon, Shulstad and Stoevner (1978) show that the number of hunters declined as news coverage of mercury contamination in pheasants increased. Further, there is only limited evidence that the travel cost model can capture the importance of site quality variables. Smith and Desvousges (1985) show systematic effects of variations in the mean and variance of dissolved oxygen, a good proxy for water quality, over a variety of recreational sites across the country. Bockstael, McConnell, and Strand (1988) use a measure of nitrogen and phosphorus to show how demand functions for boating and swimming shift in different parts of the Chesapeake Bay. While these studies show that recreationists respond to impaired water quality, they provide no evidence that recreationists respond differently to different pollutants.

The evidence of responses to risks similar to release of hazardous substances is weaker for recreational behavior, as modeled by the travel cost model, than for the housing market. Hedonic models not only give evidence of the negative effects of proxies for risk but also show how these effects change with new information. No such corroborative information is available for the travel cost model.

3.3 Hedonic and Travel Cost Measures of Damages: Is There Double-Counting? In damage assessment under CERCLA, both the hedonic model and the travel cost model are frequently used. In this section I address the issue of whether both models measure the same damages, leading to double-counting. This approach is similar in spirit to work by Rosen (1979) and Roback (1982), who integrate hedonic wage and housing markets.

Consider the housing price equilibrium in which people are willing to pay more for a house closer to a natural resource because it reduces travel cost. For simplicity, let utility depend only on the Hicksian bundle and visits to the resource in the uncontaminated state. When the resource becomes contaminated, distance to the resource has a direct impact on utility. Here for simplicity I abstract from uncertainty. Let utility be

$$u(x,z_1,s) = \begin{cases} u^0(x,z_1) \text{ in the uncontaminated case} \\ u^*(x,z_1,s) \text{ in the contaminated case} \end{cases}$$

When a site is contaminated, the direct effect of distance is positive because distance from the resource reduces risk.

The budget constraint is given by

$$y = p(s) + csz_1 + x, \tag{27}$$

where c is the cost per mile of travel, z_1 is the number of recreational visits to the natural resource, and y is money income. In effect, cs is the travel cost per trip.

The equilibrium conditions for the housing market/recreational demand in the uncontaminated state include

$$p'(s^0) = -cz_1^0, \tag{28}$$

$$cs^0 = u_{z1}^0(x_1^0,z_1^0)/u_y^0, \tag{29}$$

where the superscripts indicate uncontaminated conditions. The housing price increases with the proximity of the house to the natural resource because being in close proximity lowers the price of trips (cs) and hence increases the number of trips. Equation (28) shows the marginal value of distance to be the price of distance times the number of trips.

Suppose that we do not know the motivation for the effect of distance on the hedonic price, except that it must be in the utility function. The welfare effect of increasing distance, holding income and the budget constraint constant, would be calculated in the standard hedonic model as

$$\int_{s^0}^{s^\infty} \frac{\partial u/\partial s}{u_y} \, ds = \text{area under marginal bid for the distance amenity,} \tag{30}$$

where s^∞ is the distance at which the quantity demanded of trips goes to zero $[z_1(cs^\infty) = 0]$. This, in the standard model, is the welfare effect of distance as it is approximated by the marginal price on the left-hand side of equation (28). What if distance serves only to change travel costs, as equation (29) implies? Then instead of expression (30), we get

$$- \int_{s^0}^{s^\infty} cz_1(cs)ds = \text{area under marginal bid for } z_1.$$

Now, if we change variables from distance to price $(dp = cds)$, this becomes

$$- \int_{s^0}^{s^\infty} cz_1(cs)ds = - \int_{p^0}^{p^\infty} z_1^0(p)dp. \tag{31}$$

The last expression is just the negative of willingness to pay for access to the resource for recreational purposes. Therefore, in a very simple model, when the motive for living close to the natural resource is simply the reduction in travel costs, the hedonic model and the travel cost model give the same answer. There is complete double-counting for such individuals.

Now consider the case in which the resource is contaminated. All else being equal, households prefer to live farther from the resource because they want to reduce perceived risks. And they have a diminished desire to live close to the resource for the sake of travel costs because the contamination has reduced their demand for trips to the natural resource. The utility function becomes $u = u^*(x, z_1, s)$. The budget constraint is the same. The equilibrium conditions become

$$p'(s) = u_s^*(x^*, z_1^*, s)/u_y^* - cz_1^*, \tag{32}$$
$$cs = u_{z1}^*(\cdot)/u_y^*.$$

Now the distance gradient represents two offsetting effects: higher travel costs and lower risks. Assuming s^∞ and p^∞ to remain unchanged, we find the welfare effects of distance from expression (30) as

area under marginal bid for the distance amenity =

$$\int_{s^0}^{s^\infty} \frac{\partial u^*/\partial s}{u_y^*}ds - \int_{s^0}^{s^\infty} cz_1^*(cs)ds = \int_{s^0}^{s^\infty} \frac{\partial u^*/\partial s}{u_y^*}ds - \int_{p^0}^{p^\infty} z_1^*(p)dp. \tag{33}$$

If we were able to measure complete welfare effects from utility function parameters, we would find that the welfare effects of distance are composed of the area under the travel cost demand curve plus the willingness to pay to reduce risk to zero, in a deterministic framework.

We can view equation (31) as the welfare effects of distance before contamination and equation (33) as the welfare effects after contamination. The difference between equations (31) and (33) is the damage from the release of the hazardous substance. Subtracting equation (31) from equation (33) yields

$$\int_{p^0}^{p^\infty} [z_1^0(p) - z_1^*(p)]dp \; - \; \int_{s^0}^{s^\infty} \frac{\partial u^*/\partial s}{u_y^*} ds$$

= change in the area under the demand for trips + willingness to pay to reduce risk.

Consequently, as a rough approximation one can argue that when distance proxies for risk, the distance variable in the hedonic model measures two effects brought about by a reduction in risk: the gain in consumer's surplus related to recreation and the other gain in well-being. A correct application of the hedonic model, therefore, is more general than the travel cost model in that it includes the travel cost measure of consumer's surplus.

In the hedonic model, we cannot measure exact welfare effects because we cannot identify the parameters of the utility function. Rather, we use the slope of the hedonic function, which equals the marginal bid in equilibrium. Extrapolating that slope gives an approximation of welfare effects. In this simple model one can measure the effects of hazardous releases, both on the demand for recreation and on willingness to pay to avoid risks, as the change in the welfare effects of distance on the housing price. This result must be hedged in several ways. When the budget constraint is nonlinear, as parts of it will be in the hedonic case, the standard Marshallian travel cost demand curve will not exist. These results are based on marginal bid functions. The results are based on a deterministic model, which does not account for risk. The model as constructed is a one-period model. In practice, the hedonic price would include the capitalized value of recreational services. Finally, demand for the resource for recreational purposes may emanate from residential areas that are not at risk from the hazardous substance and therefore will not be covered by a study of housing markets.

3.4 Random Utility Model. The random utility model of recreational behavior has been increasingly suggested as a substitute for the travel cost model (see Morey, Shaw, and Rowe [1991]; Bockstael, Hanemann, and Kling [1987]). This model provides a utility-based approach to analyzing choice among a set of sites. The model can be motivated by the predominance of corner solutions for any set of recreational sites—that is, when a person visits only a few of many available sites. In a multiple-site setting the random utility model is well suited for estimating substitutability among sites, especially when measures of attributes of different sites are available. The model can also be used in a single-site setting. The strength of the random utility model is its ability to assess changes in measurable attributes among sites. However, because it does not stem from a fully utility-theoretic model of quantity choice, the random utility model cannot address the issue of the quantity demanded of trips. It is therefore less well suited for answering questions about the value of access or changes in the site characteristics, which would induce large changes in the quantity demand of trips.

In principle, one uses the random utility model to calculate damages in the same way one uses the travel cost model. Damages per individual user are calculated as the value of access before and after the release of the hazardous substance. Individual damages are then summed across all potential users. Because the principles are the same, I concentrate in this section on the distinctive features of the random utility model.

While there are different ways of viewing the random utility model, it assumes that the individual chooses among a set of alternatives with known characteristics. The individual's decisions are deterministic to himself, random to the observer. Let

$$v_j(y - p_j, q_j) = u_j(y - p_j, q_j) + \epsilon_j$$

be the (indirect) utility achieved by choosing alternative j, where v_j is the utility known to the individual, u_j is its deterministic part known to observers, and ϵ_j is a random error. This is what Hanemann (1982) calls a budget-constrained random utility model. The probability that an individual t will choose alternative k among m alternatives is

$$\text{Prob (choose } k) = \text{Prob}(v_{kt} > v_{1t}, v_{kt} > v_{2t}, \ldots, v_{kt} > v_{mt}), \quad (34)$$

when there are m alternatives. One may make various assumptions about the cumulative distribution function in equation (34). Estimation and welfare properties are well worked out for the independent logit and the standard generalized extreme value. For example, when utility for the kth alternative is

$$v_{kt} = a_1(p_{kt} - y_t) + a_2 q_{kt} + \epsilon_{kt} \quad (35)$$

and the $\mu_{jt} = \epsilon_{jt} - \epsilon_{it}$ are distributed as independent logits, one estimates a_1 and a_2 by maximizing the log likelihood function for a sample of n individuals

$$l(a_1, a_2; x, p, q) =$$
$$-\sum_{t=1}^{n} \sum_{j=1}^{m} x_{jt} \ln \left\{ \sum_{j=1}^{m} \exp[a_1(p_{jt} - p_{it}) + a_2(q_{jt} - q_{it})] \right\}, \quad (36)$$

where t indexes the individual, and $x_{jt} = 1$ if the individual chooses the jth alternative, 0 otherwise. This highly simplified likelihood function illustrates the basic driving force of the random utility model: the difference in deterministic utility across alternatives. Hence, with a linear utility function, the difference in prices and qualities makes the model work. In this model, because the marginal utility of income is constant, the choice among alternatives is not influenced by income.

Welfare calculations in this model can show two effects: the welfare effect of changing a site characteristic (p_j or q_j) and the welfare effect of eliminating the site (see Hanemann [1982]). But each effect is a per-choice occasion measure. That is, it measures the welfare efforts for each occasion that a trip is taken. We can use the formula for calculating the compensating variation for an increase in q_j for individual t. This gives us the increased willingness to pay per trip, conditioned on taking a trip. To get the annual measures, we must multiply by the annual number of trips the individual has taken. The random utility model per se does not provide a utility-theoretic approach to determining the choice of the number of trips per year, but Bockstael, Hanemann, and Kling (1987) have a good intuitive approach for determining the number of trips. They estimate the total number of trips to all sites as a function of the inclusive price, among other things. The inclusive price is a probability-weighted average of indirect utilities from all sites. When conditions of access at one of the sites change, the inclusive price changes and induces change in the demand for total trips to all sites.

The role of perceptions in the random utility model is similar to its role in the travel cost model and the hedonic model. People base their behavior on how they perceive the site. There is no difference in principle in how information flows, nor is there a market to signal incorrect information. Further, because the basic model addresses each choice, the welfare measures are ex post in the sense that the individual is never more than one trip away from revision of perceptions. That is, an individual has full knowledge of site attributes, which can be perceived and which do not change over the season. Hence, choices made throughout the season will be fully informed choices. However, since many hazardous substances are imperceptible, the greater uncertainty will remain. The random utility model is typically risk-neutral, in the sense that the decision maker makes choices based on known preferences with known arguments. This could be modified if one had measures of different moments of subjective risk by alternatives—a fairly severe requirement.

The random utility model can be used for damage assessment under CERCLA in three different ways. First, in principle one could let q_j be a measure of the perceived risk from a hazardous waste release at site j. After publicity, one could determine new levels of perceived risk and then calculate the implied welfare effects of changes in risks. Second, one could estimate two random utility models, much as equation (26) shows two travel cost models. From each model one could calculate the implied value of access per trip. The difference in the value of access, conditioned on the number of trips, yields the damage per individual from the release of hazardous substances. A third approach assumes the release of hazardous substances renders the site unusable. In this approach, one counts as the damage the value of access before the release of the hazardous substance.

The first approach is the least likely to succeed. Measures of subjective risk are not easy to conceive, much less execute. And because the model works off of differences in q's (as equation [36] shows), in this case one would need to know each individual's numerical estimate of subjective risk for each site. It is more likely that one would use the random utility model in an uncontaminated setting to calculate the value of access, and simply call this value the damage. The efficacy of this approach depends on the number of sites in the model and the likelihood that the number of trips remains constant. When the number of alternatives is relatively small and the alternatives are located not too far apart, it seems probable that users will be induced to change their trips.

The data requirements for estimating in the random utility model are somewhat more severe than in the travel cost model. In the random utility model, one must have some information on all sites. For example, one might have the destination of a sampled trip and the distribution of total trips in a region among sites (see Morey, Shaw, and Rowe [1991]). Or one could use the total trips per user and their distribution among alternatives (see Bockstael, McConnell, and Strand [1988]). In either case, the demands are greater than for a single-site travel cost demand model.

The single-site random utility model is simpler in its data requirements and execution. This model assumes that at each choice, the person chooses whether or not to visit the site, based on the indirect utility attained by visiting the site. It is essentially another way of modeling the choice of a site, and hence uses the same information as a single-site travel cost demand model. It can be used to calculate damages in two ways. First, two different models can be estimated, one in the uncontaminated situation and one in the contaminated situation. Then the damages are calculated by the difference in the value of access under the two circumstances. Second, when the hazardous release is sufficiently severe to eliminate access, damages can be calculated from the forgone value of access in the uncontaminated case.

3.5   The Averting Behavior Model. In some cases, households can take defensive measures to avoid the perceived effects of hazardous substances. When these measures provide no utility per se but are merely carried out to prevent exposure to contaminants, they may leave footprints that can help in assessing damages. The averting behavior model has been developed in concept (see Courant and Porter [1981]) and applied to risky situations involving potential health impairment (Berger and coauthors [1986]). Smith and Desvousges (1986a) have found empirical evidence of averting behavior in the control of hazardous substances. For example, they document the use of bottled water by households that fear groundwater contamination from hazardous waste sites.

The use of data on averting behavior to help measure damages under CERCLA seems appropriate when households take action to avoid perceived risk, as in the Smith and Desvousges (1986a) example. Consider a simple model in which a household divides income between e, a good or service that averts the risk, and x, a Hicksian bundle. Households face the probability π of having no effect and $1 - \pi$ of sustaining an injury from the contamination. By purchasing more e, households can increase π. Households maximize expected utility by spending income on x and e:

$$\max \pi(e)u_1(z) + [1 - \pi(e)]u_2(z) - \lambda(p_e e + z - y), \tag{37}$$

where p_e is the price of the averting good, u_1 is the preference function when there is no effect, and u_2 is the preference function when there is an effect from the hazardous substance. Optimal expenditure on averting goods requires

$$\pi'(e)(u_1 - u_2)/\lambda = p_e. \tag{38}$$

This expression can be used to approximate the compensation that would have to be paid to consumers to get them to accept the risk. Let cv_A be this amount. It is defined implicitly as:

$$u_1(z) = \pi u_1(y + cv_A) + (1 - \pi)u_2(y + cv_A). \tag{39}$$

We can approximate cv as

$$cv_A = (1 - \pi)(u_1 - u_2)/E\lambda, \tag{40}$$

where $E\lambda = \pi \partial u_1/\partial y + (1 - \pi)\partial u_2/\partial y$. Here cv equals the probability of the undesirable outcome times the loss in utility if that outcome occurs, normalized by the expected marginal utility of income.

Equation (38) can help in the calculation of the value of cv_A in equation (40). Let e^* be the optimal value of averting goods and suppose that risk is completely averted, so that $\pi(e^*) = 1$. The area under the marginal value function in equation (38), holding z constant, is

$$\int_0^{e^*} \pi'(e)(u_1 - u_2)/E\lambda de = (1 - \pi)(u_1 - u_2)/E\lambda \approx cv_A.$$

Consequently, the marginal value function can give an approximate welfare measure. This is a nice result, but it requires that one observe variation in the price of averting goods. Additional work by Berger and coauthors (1986) and by Dickie and coauthors (1986) has expanded the way in which averting expenditures can be used to calculate welfare effects.

Welfare measures developed from averting behavior models have personal discount factors embodied in them when the good purchased is a capital good. Consider an air conditioner purchased to avert contaminated air. The purchaser considers, at least implicitly, the utility of the service flow over the life of the air conditioner. One must use caution in discounting welfare measures from averting models.

Given the appropriate kind of contamination, the averting behavior method is a reasonable tool for calculating damages. And while there are significant hurdles for the measurement of damages, there is good evidence that averting behavior is a relevant concept. The hurdles for welfare measurement from the averting behavior model, in addition to the typical absence of price variation, pertain to motives and effectiveness. When households get direct utility from the purchase of averting goods, the marginal value function will have a direct utility effect, and more will be included in the method than reduction in risk. Also, it may not be feasible for the household to reduce the risk to zero. Then the area under the marginal value function will fall short of the compensating variation.

4.   CONCLUSION

This chapter has explained and criticized the use of indirect methods for measuring damages in CERCLA cases. Much of the discussion has focused on the difficulties of using indirect models. Lest the reader come away feeling as though damage assessment is too difficult to warrant the expense, in this conclusion I gauge the strengths of the models. Finally, I suggest some areas of research that might help deal with damage assessment under CERCLA.

The strength of indirect methods lies in their reliance on actual behavior. Of the methods discussed, the hedonic method is most subject to the rigors of the market and seems the most likely to reflect informed optimizing behavior. Further, the very formality of the contract in a housing transaction ensures accurate observations on the house price and the attributes of the house. Consequently, the hedonic model seems well suited to approximating the damages associated with releases of hazardous substances. Because the hedonic model relies on a distance-to-risk transfer function not testable within the hedonic model, the plausibility of the model can be greatly enhanced by additional information on this link.

While the travel cost model and its variants are estimated from observations on actual behavior, their attractiveness is attenuated in several ways. First, observations are typically filtered through the memory of the respondent, making them less accurate than housing market observations. Second, the successful use of the travel cost model requires not simply that the model itself reflect the demand for services of the public natural resource, but that the model accurately capture the change in demand for the service after the resource is injured by the release of the hazardous substance. Despite these difficulties, a carefully planned and executed study can be expected to provide plausible results for damage assessment.

The averting behavior model has a special appeal because behavior may be directly linked to the release of the hazardous substance. Consequently, researchers need not make as many assumptions about the link from resource injury to behavioral change in order to motivate the model. The principal difficulty with this model is that to convert it to an approximate welfare measure, researchers must have variations in the price of averting goods.

Thus, despite the ample criticisms heaped on these methods throughout this chapter, care in study design and execution can provide respectable numbers for damage assessment. However, successful work on several research issues could considerably enhance the usefulness of indirect methods for damage assessment. The following issues seem especially important.

4.1 Risk and Behavior Toward Risk. It is in the nature of hazardous materials that potential health effects are not perceptible by people in the ordinary course of daily life; thus, uncertainty surrounds these threats. There are a variety of uncertainties: whether there is contamination, whether there is potential for human intake given contamination, whether there is a significant health risk given intake, and so on. To understand behavior in the context of the release of hazardous materials is to understand risk. Economists have recently begun substantial explorations of behavior toward risk, especially environmental risk. Yet much remains to be discovered.

Conceptually, the introduction of risk into the hedonic model is reasonably complete. Further, there is some evidence that this method can detect behavior toward risk. But a variety of interesting questions present themselves. In the studies cited in table 8-1, the potential exists for distance to represent other variables as well as risk from the release of hazardous substances. The fact that distance from a hazardous waste site becomes more negatively correlated with housing prices after information has spread about the site does not by itself provide evidence of damage. Further exploration of local housing markets is needed to help explain the locational effects of hazardous wastes.

In models of recreational demand, including random utility models, uncertainty has been ignored. This is so despite the attention given to option value and option price in almost the same literature. As has been amply demonstrated (Smith [1983 and 1987]; Helms [1985]), the use of option value is a quixotic attempt to mix preferences toward risk and deterministic welfare measures. This is obvious when one starts with a recreational demand problem that involves behavior toward risk. For the demand for recreational sites, the full panoply of research is needed, from completing the basic models to demonstrating that these models allow the estimation of risk effects to the full calculation of welfare effects. This is necessary both for travel cost demand models and random utility models. Larson (1988) has begun work on this problem.

4.2   The Revision of Subjective Risk. A corollary of the use of data on behavior motivated by perceived risk is that perceptions will likely be revised. People are unable to make accurate assessments of the risks they face, but research and experience suggest that they will become less averse as they become more familiar with the risk. But it is necessary to be precise about the model that leads to the revision of perceptions about risk and how this model can be estimated. Work by Viscusi and O'Connor (1984) and Viscusi (1987) illustrates models of the revision of perceptions of risk.

4.3   Double-Counting. Stylized models in this paper and basic intuition suggest that double-counting may be a problem, especially when hazardous substances are released into a natural resource that has recreational value. This area must be investigated more fully. Double-counting is also relevant when averting behavior is present. While determination of the magnitude of double-counting is an empirical problem and depends on the particular case at hand, some basic theoretical work is needed to establish the conditions for its existence.

4.4   Absence of Data. From the various CERCLA cases now being processed, it is evident that one of the biggest problems facing researchers is the absence of data, both baseline use data and contaminated site use data. If the hazardous substance was released a long time in the past, there may be no observed use in the baseline case. If the release is recent but relatively severe, there may be no observations on behavior toward the contaminated resource. In any case, where no data are available, it would help greatly to be able to use models that were estimated in other locations. This involves a study of how model results can be transferred. Ground-breaking work by Smith and Kaoru (1991) provides guidance on the problem of per-user benefits transfer for travel cost models. But even with good estimates of per-user benefits, the problem of calculating the extent of the market in the absence of good data remains.

REFERENCES

Adler, K. J., R. C. Anderson, Z. Cook, R. C. Dower, and A. R. Ferguson. 1982. "The Benefits of Regulating Hazardous Waste Disposal: Land Values as an Estimator," research report, Public Interest Economics Center, Washington, D.C.

Baker, M. D. 1986. "Property Values and Potentially Hazardous Production Facilities: A Case Study of the Kanawha Valley, West Virginia," Ph.D. dissertation, Florida State University.

Bartik, T. J. 1988. "Measuring the Benefits of Amenity Improvements in Hedonic Price Models," *Land Economics* 64, pp. 172–183.

Bartik, T. J., and V. Kerry Smith. 1987. "Urban Amenities and Public Policy," pp. 1207–1254 in *Handbook of Regional and Urban Economics*, vol. 2, edited by E. S. Mills. Amsterdam: Elsevier.

Berger, M., G. Blomquist, D. Keukel, and G. Tolley. 1986. "Valuing Changes in Health Risks: A Comparison of Alternative Measures," *Southern Economic Journal* 52, pp. 967–984.

Bockstael, Nancy E., W. Michael Hanemann, and Catherine L. Kling. 1987. "Estimating the Value of Water Quality Improvements in a Recreational Demand Framework," *Water Resources Research* 23 (5), pp. 951–960.

Bockstael, Nancy E., W. Michael Hanemann, and Ivar E. Strand. 1986. "Measuring the Benefits of Water Quality Improvements Using Recreational Demand Models," in *Benefit Analysis Using Indirect or Imputed Market Methods*, vol. 2. U.S. Environmental Protection Agency Cooperative Agreement #811043-01-0 with the University of Maryland, College Park, Md.

Bockstael, Nancy E., and Kenneth E. McConnell. 1987. "Welfare Effects of Quality Changes: A Synthesis," working paper, Department of Agricultural and Resource Economics, University of Maryland, College Park, Md.

Bockstael, Nancy E., Kenneth E. McConnell, and Ivar E. Strand. 1988. "Benefits from Improvements in Chesapeake Bay Water Quality," in *Benefit Analysis Using Indirect or Imputed Market Methods*, vol. 2. U.S. Environmental Protection Agency Cooperative Agreement #811043-01-0 with the University of Maryland, College Park, Md.

Brookshire, David S., Mark A. Thayer, John Tschirhart, and William D. Schulze. 1985. "A Test of the Expected Utility Model: Evidence from Earthquake Risks," *Journal of Political Economy* 93 (2), pp. 369–389.

Courant, P., and R. Porter. 1981. "Averting Behavior and the Cost of Pollution," *Journal of Environmental and Economic Management* 8, pp. 321–329.

Cropper, Maureen L., Leland B. Deck, and Kenneth E. McConnell. 1988. "On the Choice of Functional Form for Hedonic Price Equations," *Review of Economics and Statistics* 70, pp. 668–675.

Desvousges, William H., and V. A. Skahen. 1986. "Techniques to Measure Damages to Natural Resources," final report prepared for CERCLA 301 Task Force, U.S. Department of the Interior. Research Triangle Park, N.C.: Research Triangle Institute.

Dickie, M., S. Gerhing, W. Schulze, A. Coulson, and D. Tashkent. 1986. "Value of Symptoms of Ozone Exposure: An Application of the Averting Behavior Method," U.S. Environmental Protection Agency Cooperative Agreement Report CR-812054-01-2.

Foster, W., and R. E. Just. 1989. "Measuring Welfare Effects of Product Contamination with Consumer Uncertainty," *Journal of Environmental Economics and Management* 17, pp. 266–283.

Freeman, A. Myrick III. 1979. *The Benefits of Environmental Improvements: Theory and Practice*. Baltimore, Md.: The Johns Hopkins University Press for Resources for the Future.

Gamble, H. B., and R. H. Downing. 1982. "Effects of Nuclear Power Plants on Residential Property Values," *Journal of Regional Science* 22, pp. 457–478.

Hanemann, W. Michael. 1982. "Applied Welfare Analysis with Qualitative Response Models," working paper no. 241, Giannini Foundation of Agricultural Economics, University of California, Berkeley, Calif.

Helms, L. J. 1985. "Expected Consumer's Surplus and the Welfare Effects of Price Stabilization," *International Economic Review* 26 (3), pp. 603–617.

Just, R. E., D. Hueth, and A. Schmitz. 1983. *Welfare Economics and Public Policy*. Englewood Cliffs, N.J.: Prentice-Hall.

Kanemoto, Y. 1988. "Hedonic Prices and the Benefits of Public Projects," *Econometrica* 56, pp. 981–989.

Kohlhase, J. E. Forthcoming. "The Impact of Toxic Waste Sites on Housing Values," working paper, Economics Department, University of Houston, Houston, Tex.

Kopp, Raymond J., and V. Kerry Smith. 1987. "Can Natural Resource Damage Assessments Be Performed? A Summary of the Economic Issues," Discussion Paper QE88-03, Quality of the Environment Division. Washington, D.C.: Resources for the Future.

Larson, D. M. 1988. "Quality, Risk, and Welfare Measurement: Theory and Applications to Natural Resources," Ph.D. dissertation, Department of Agricultural and Resource Economics, University of Maryland, College Park, Md.

Lipton, D. W. 1986. "The Resurgence of the U.S. Swordfish Market," *Marine Fisheries Review* 48, pp. 24–27.

McConnell, Kenneth E. 1985. "Economics of Outdoor Recreation," in *Handbook of Natural Resource and Energy Economics*, vol. 2, edited by Allen V. Kneese and James L. Sweeney. Amsterdam: Elsevier.

McDonald, D. N., J. C. Murdoch, and H. L. White. 1987. "Hazards and Insurance in Housing," *Land Economics* 63, pp. 361–371.

Michaels, R. G., V. K. Smith, and D. Harrison, Jr. 1987. "Market Segmentation and Valuing Amenities with Hedonic Models: The Case of Hazardous Waste Sites," working paper, Department of Economics, North Carolina State University, Raleigh, N.C.

Mitchell, Robert Cameron. 1980. "Patterns and Determinants of Aversion to the Local Siting of Industrial, Energy and Hazardous Waste Dump Facilities by the General Public," unpublished paper, Resources for the Future.

Morey, E. R., D. Shaw, and R. D. Rowe. 1991. "A Discrete Choice Model of Recreational Participation, Site Choice and Activity Valuation When Complete Trip Data Are Not Available," *Journal of Environmental Economics and Management* 20, pp. 181–201.

Nelson, J. P. 1981. "Three Mile Island and Residential Property Values," *Land Economics* 57, pp. 363–372.

Palmquist, Raymond B. 1982. "Measuring Environmental Effects on Property Values without Hedonic Regressions," *Journal of Urban Economics* 11, pp. 333–347.

Roback, Jennifer. 1982. "Wages, Rents, and the Quality of Life," *Journal of Political Economy* 90 (6), pp. 1257–1278.

Rosen, Sherwin. 1974. "Hedonic Prices and Implicit Markets: Product Differentiation in Price Competition," *Journal of Political Economy* 82, pp. 34–55.

Rosen, Sherwin. 1979. "Wage-Based Indexes of Urban Quality of Life," in *Current Issues in Urban Economics*, edited by P. Mieszkowski, and M. Straszheim. Baltimore, Md.: The Johns Hopkins University Press.

Schulze, W., G. McClelland, B. Hurd, and J. Smith. 1986. "Improving Accuracy and Reducing Costs of Environmental Benefit Assessments. IV. A Case Study of Hazardous Waste Sites: Perspectives from Economics and Psychology," U.S. Environmental Protection Agency Cooperative Agreement CR-812054-02-1.

Shulstad, R. N., and H. H. Stoevner. 1978. "The Effects of Mercury Contamination in Pheasants on the Value of Pheasant Hunting in Oregon," *Land Economics* 54, pp. 39–49.

Smith, V. Kerry. 1983. "Option Value: A Conceptual Overview," *Southern Economic Journal* 49 (4), pp. 654–668.

Smith, V. Kerry. 1985. "Supply Uncertainty, Option Price, and Indirect Benefit Estimation," *Land Economics* 61 (3), pp. 303–308.

Smith, V. Kerry. 1987. "Uncertainty, Benefit-Cost Analysis, and the Treatment of Option Value," *Journal of Environmental Economics and Management* 14 (3), pp. 283–292.

Smith, V. Kerry, and William H. Desvousges. 1985. "The Generalized Travel Cost Model and Water Quality Benefits: A Reconsideration," *Southern Economic Journal* 51, pp. 371–381.

Smith, V. Kerry, and William H. Desvousges. 1986a. "Averting Behavior: Does It Exist?" *Economics Letters* 20, pp. 291–296.

Smith, V. Kerry, and William H. Desvousges. 1986b. "The Value of Avoiding a LULU: Hazardous Waste Disposal Sites," *Review of Economics and Statistics* 68, pp. 293–299.

Smith, V. Kerry, William H. Desvousges, and A. Myrick Freeman III. 1985. "Valuing Changes in Hazardous Waste Risks: A Contingent Valuation Analysis," vol. 1, draft interim report, U.S. Environmental Protection Agency Cooperative Agreement CR-811075.

Smith, V. Kerry, and Y. Kaoru. 1991. "Signals or Noise: Explaining the Variation in Environmental Benefit Estimates," *American Journal of Agricultural Economics* 72, pp. 419–433.

Swartz, D., and I. E. Strand. 1981. "Avoidance Costs Associated with Imperfect Information," *Land Economics* 57, pp. 139–150.

Vaughan, W. J., and C. S. Russell. 1982. "Valuing a Fishing Day: An Application of a Systematic Varying Parameter Model," *Land Economics* 58, pp. 450–463.

Viscusi, W. Kip. 1987. "Prospective Reference Theory: Toward an Explanation of the Paradoxes," paper presented at American Economic Association annual meeting.

Viscusi, W. Kip, and W. N. Evans. 1988. "Utility Functions That Are Dependent on One's Health Status: Estimates and Economic Implications," working paper, Economics Department, University of Maryland, College Park, Md.

Viscusi, W. Kip, and Charles J. O'Connor. 1984. "Adaptive Responses to Chemical Labeling: Are Workers Bayesian Decision Makers?" *The American Economic Review* 74, pp. 942–956.

9
Assessing Natural Resource Damages with Indirect Methods: Comments on Chapter 8

Robert Mendelsohn

1. INHERENT ADVANTAGE OF INDIRECT METHODS

Kenneth E. McConnell, in chapter 8 of this volume, offers a comprehensive review of indirect (revealed preference) methods as they may be applied to measuring natural resource damages from hazardous waste emissions. However, in his desire to merely present and not advocate indirect methods, he may inadvertently undersell the use of indirect methods for valuation of damages. In this chapter, I admittedly advocate the use of indirect methods because, in my opinion, they provide a more defensible and plausible measure of damages than do alternative valuation techniques.

One of the basic premises of economics is that it studies the behavior of economic agents. In contrast to other disciplines such as sociology and psychology, which are often interested in attitudes, the concern of economists has tended to be strictly behavioral. Thus, one advantage of indirect methods is that they rely upon an economic literature that extends far beyond the valuation of environmental goods. In addition, revealed preference values are less subject to bias than are attitudinal approaches. They are determined by what people do, not what they say. Indirect methods are therefore not influenced by many of the distortions that can affect attitudinal responses.

2. MEASURING BEHAVIOR

The best measure of the value of goods in modern market societies is the market price of traded goods. These prices reflect accepted transactions for familiar goods, as well as repeated experience. Economic approaches to valuing goods under these conditions have been studied for centuries and are well developed. Unfortunately, traditional methods of valuation through market prices and demand functions cannot always be directly applied in resource assessment examples because the resources themselves are not bought and sold in markets.

Valuation of nonmarket goods such as the damage from pollution consequently requires more ingenious approaches. In this case, we are looking for behavior that suggests the value of the affected resource. Specifically, we are looking for examples in which citizens expend valuable assets in the use of affected resources. These expenditures or costs can act as shadow prices. By carefully studying such expenditures, we can infer the value users place on the resource. McConnell identifies three types of expenditures from which behavioral values can be elicited: housing expenditures, travel costs, and averting costs. Another important factor is wages from employment.

3.   INTERTEMPORAL EVIDENCE

One of the central issues in hazardous waste measurement is how to isolate the variable that measures damage from confounding influences (unwanted variation). Unlike controlled scientific experiments, where by design the variable of interest is kept orthogonal from other influences, natural experiments must cope with correlated confounding effects. For example, a cross-sectional study of homes near a waste site must deal with the fact that most waste sites are located in industrial areas, which already have certain disamenities. The effects of the disamenities must be separated from the effects of pollution. A cross-sectional study of recreation destinations must also deal with confounding factors that may be correlated with pollution or environmental quality. For example, remote sites may have less pollution, but they may also have more natural amenities than sites near cities. These spatially correlated factors must be separated in the analysis in order to achieve an unbiased measure of the resource price gradient.

One powerful way to separate hazardous waste effects from spatially correlated variables is to take advantage of intertemporal variation. The discovery of many hazardous waste problems tends to be sudden and recent. By comparing behavior before and after pollution is known, it is possible to isolate the pollution effects from other spatially correlated factors. This is an especially attractive option with respect to housing studies, which can take advantage of permanent sales records to reconstruct information about prices before the pollution occurred. Given that many sales prices are now routinely computerized for real estate purposes, it can be a relatively inexpensive effort to maintain sales records of all residential areas near potential hazardous waste sites. If a hazardous waste problem then occurs, one can compare the before and after housing prices to determine the magnitude of the impact. Fragile environments that are likely to be affected by hazardous waste spills can also be analyzed, using travel cost techniques to establish baseline values. Once waste problems become evident, additional studies can be performed and the results compared. The development of such an intertemporal database could provide powerful empirical support for future measurements of natural resource damage.

Although McConnell discusses the use of the repeat sale technique in his section on hedonics, repeat sales have little to do with the hedonic method. Unlike the hedonic technique, which attempts to measure the value of a component by comparing houses with and without each feature, the repeat sale approach measures a property before and after an environmental change occurs. The repeat sale approach consequently does not require the exhaustive list of housing characteristics that are a part of hedonics. Housing qualities are controlled by comparing the sales value of the same property before and after the environmental change. First suggested by Lind (1973), this technique was advanced by Palmquist (1982) to measure the value of noise from a new highway.

Mendelsohn and coauthors (1992) further adapted the technique to measure the damage from a newly discovered hazardous waste site. Housing prices are expected to fall if a home happens to be near a hazardous site and if the home sells before and after the site becomes known as dangerous. Houses that are not near the site can serve as controls. Sales that occur either entirely before the pollution is known or entirely after it is known also serve as controls. This technique combines both intertemporal and cross-sectional evidence in a powerful panel approach.

4. WELFARE VALUATION

One advantage of the repeat sale method is that it can yield unbiased estimates of the damage from a hazardous waste site. As noted by Polinsky and Shavell (1975, 1976), if an environmental change occurs throughout a housing market, changes in housing values (rents) will underestimate the loss in welfare. However, when the pollution affects only a small part of the market, the bias approaches zero. Since many hazardous waste pollution problems tend to be localized, the repeat sale approach tends to provide unbiased welfare measures of the residential impacts of hazardous waste problems.

In contrast, the hedonic approach consistently underestimates the welfare value of proximity to a hazardous site. McConnell argues that the value of a change from a contaminated environment of quality $z(0)$ to an uncontaminated setting of level $z(1)$ can be approximated by

$$CV = \int_{Z(0)}^{Z(1)} p(Z)dZ, \tag{1}$$

where $p(Z)$ is the marginal hedonic price function. The hedonic price function, however, is not a demand function so equation (1) is not a direct measure of consumer surplus. All we know about the hedonic price function $p(Z)$ is that it is more concave than $h(Z)$, the demand function for Z. Consequently, the correct measure of consumer surplus CS is

$$CS = \int_{Z(0)}^{Z(1)} h(Z)dZ. \tag{2}$$

The correct measure (equation [2]) of damages is greater in magnitude than the McConnell measure (equation [1]) and the difference between the two can be very large. The integral of the hedonic price function is a poor measure of welfare, as has been widely noted in the literature (see Freeman [1979] for a review). The fact that hazardous waste sites may affect only a small part of the market makes no difference as long as a gradient is used for valuation.

To value nonmarginal changes in environmental quality using the hedonic technique, one must estimate the demand function for Z, not just the price. However, this introduces severe pressure on estimation as it is often difficult to observe more than one market. For example, most hedonic studies are limited to just one housing market. Although hedonic supply and demand functions can be estimated using single-market data, the underlying assumptions needed to justify such an analysis are usually untenable (see Mendelsohn [1984]). The only reliable attempts to measure hedonic structural equations have consequently relied on multiple markets (see Witte, Sumka, and Erekson [1979]; Brown and Mendelsohn [1984]; and Palmquist [1984]). This again reveals an advantage of the repeat sale approach, which provides accurate measures of even large changes of pollution levels.

5. SUBJECTIVE DAMAGES

Among the issues raised by McConnell's chapter is the potential for discrepancy between expert opinion and popular beliefs concerning cause and effect. For example, the pollution of a certain part of an estuary may cause some people to believe that larger areas have been damaged, even though there is no evidence to that effect. McConnell argues that such "subjective" damages are legitimate damages under the Comprehensive Environmental Response, Compensation, and Liability Act of 1980 because resource users behave as though there is a loss. It is not clear, however, that society should demand compensation from a firm for damages that a reasonable individual would regard as irrelevant. Subjective risks should probably be limited by some rule of reasonableness.

Suppose, for example, that demand for tuna falls because high levels of mercury are found in a few cans of tuna near a smelter. Then suppose that later it is revealed that these high levels of mercury are in all fish and are not related to the smelter. Should the observed reduction in demand for tuna be counted as a resource damage? It is not obvious. In contrast, suppose that a toxic but hard-to-detect pollutant is dumped in an estuary and scientists are having trouble measuring where in the estuary the pollutant has travelled. Suppose there is then a widespread reduction in use throughout the estuary. Even if it is unlikely that the entire estuary is polluted, the reduced demand for the entire estuary would seem a reasonable damage in this case because it is plausible that each specific area is damaged.

6.   RECREATION

McConnell perhaps spends too much time discussing the generalized travel cost method and not enough time discussing alternative travel cost models. Although the generalized travel cost model is ideally suited to model travel cost behavior before and after a pollution event, it is frequently applied using only cross-sectional data. Because the model does a poor job of controlling substitute sites, these cross-sectional applications are not clearly appropriate.

There are now several alternative travel cost methods that value site characteristics in addition to generalized travel cost: discrete choice, demand system, and hedonic travel cost. Although McConnell discusses the discrete choice approach, he overlooks the demand system and hedonic travel cost methods. The demand system approach has been pioneered by Morey (1984) and has been successfully applied in valuing the characteristics of ski sites. The hedonic travel cost method has been successfully applied in valuing a number of site attributes, including the value of old-growth forest and clear-cut forest (Englin and Mendelsohn [1991]), fish density (Brown and Mendelsohn [1984]), and deer density (Mendelsohn [1984]). Although pollution itself has not been included as a site characteristic in such valuations, it is often possible to link pollution with changes in site characteristics that matter to people. Estimating the values of the characteristics of sites that may be pollution-sensitive can therefore lead to useful measures of recreational losses from pollution.

7. CONCLUSION

Revealed preference techniques—indirect methods—have been used extensively to value the environment. Unlike attitudinal approaches, these techniques tend not to entail problems of potential bias on the part of individuals or researchers holding strong opinions. Further, unlike attitudinal approaches, revealed preference techniques are not encumbered by hypothetical questions that may not fully capture real choices. However, as with attitudinal approaches, more research must be devoted to revealed preference methods in order to increase their reliability and soundness. All available valuation techniques must be corroborated and confirmed by repeated applications and methodological development. With this increased effort, dependable, defendable measures of environmental damage will soon be commonplace.

REFERENCES

Brown, G., and R. Mendelsohn. 1984. "The Hedonic Travel Cost Method," *Review of Economics and Statistics* 66, pp. 427–433.

Englin, J., and R. Mendelsohn. 1991. "A Hedonic Travel Cost Analysis for Valuation of Multiple Components of Site Quality: The Recreation Value of Forest Management," *Journal of Environmental Economics and Management* 21 (November), pp. 225–290.

Freeman, A. Myrick III. 1979. *The Benefits of Environmental Improvement: Theory and Practice*. Baltimore, Md.: The Johns Hopkins University Press for Resources for the Future.

Lind, R. 1973. "Spatial Equilibrium, the Theory of Rents, and the Measurement of Benefits from Public Programs," *Quarterly Journal of Economics* 87, pp. 188–207.

Mendelsohn, R. 1984. "An Application of the Hedonic Travel Cost Framework for Recreation Modeling to the Valuation of Deer," in *Advances in Applied Microeconomics*, vol. 3, edited by V. K. Smith and A. D. Witte, pp. 89–101.

Mendelsohn, R., D. Hellerstein, M. Hugnenin, R. Unsworth, and R. Brazee. 1992. "Measuring Hazardous Waste Damages with Panel Models," *Journal of Economics and Management* 22 (May), pp. 259–271.

Morey, E. 1984. "The Choice of Ski Areas: Estimation of a Generalized CES Preference Ordering with Characteristics," *Review of Economics and Statistics* 66, pp. 584–590.

Palmquist, R. 1982. "Measuring Environmental Effects on Property Values Without Hedonic Regressions," *Journal of Urban Economics* 11, pp. 333–347.

Palmquist, R. 1984. "The Demand for Housing Characteristics: Reconciling Theory and Estimation," *Review of Economics and Statistics* 66, pp. 394–404.

Polinsky, M., and S. Shavell. 1975. "The Air Pollution and Property Value Debate," *Review of Economics and Statistics* 57, pp. 100–104.

Polinsky, M., and S. Shavell. 1976. "Amenities and Property Values in a Model of an Urban Area," *Journal of Public Economics* 5, pp. 119–129.

Witte, A., H. Sumka, and H. Erekson. 1979. "An Estimation of a Structural Hedonic Price Model of the Housing Market: An Application of Rosen's Theory of Implicit Markets," *Econometrica* 46, pp. 1151–1173.

10

Use of Direct Methods
for Valuing
Natural Resource Damages

William D. Schulze

1. INTRODUCTION

Damages to a natural resource can be defined as the sum of losses in use and nonuse values resulting from injury to the quantity or quality of service flows of the natural resource. The direct method of assessing damages—asking beneficiaries of a natural resource to indicate the values they place on hypothetical changes in service flows—has a number of distinct advantages. The first advantage is that indirect methods (such as the property value approach) can only measure use values, while the direct approach in the form of the contingent valuation (CV) method can measure both use values and nonuse values. However, this is not so for the alternative version of the direct method—the contingent behavior (CB) method. The CB method asks survey respondents for hypothetical adjustments in behavior in response to changes in the service flows of a natural resource and therefore suffers the same limitation as indirect methods in this regard.

The CV method itself and its ability to measure nonuse value has recently been a source of controversy in the federal courts. States, industry, and environmental groups were involved as petitioners or intervenors in a lawsuit brought against the Department of the Interior (DOI) concerning regulations issued for conducting damage assessments under the Com-

Although the views expressed here are the sole responsibility of the author, the conceptual framework presented is the result of collaborative research with Gary H. McClelland of the Department of Psychology, University of Colorado, and with Robert D. Rowe of RCG/Hagler, Bailly, Inc. The author is grateful for comments on an earlier draft from Raymond J. Kopp and V. Kerry Smith, and from several anonymous reviewers. Thanks go to Melinda Berg and Rebecca Boyce for research assistance and manuscript preparation.

prehensive Environmental Response, Compensation, and Liability Act of 1980 (CERCLA).[1] States and environmental groups argued that the DOI regulations inappropriately limited the use of the CV method, consequently excluding nonuse values from damage assessments. Industry argued that contingent valuation was a new and unproven methodology and that nonuse values, especially when measured by the CV method, were inappropriate for damage assessments. The judge, after reviewing the economics literature on resource valuation, concluded that nonuse values should be included in damage assessments and that direct methods, with their long history of acceptance in the field of economics, were comparable in acceptance to indirect methods.[2]

The second advantage of the direct method is that it has forced environmental economists to become proficient at collecting primary data. In many cases no data or only poor-quality data are available to estimate values through the indirect method. While collection of contingent values through implementation of a survey solves the overall problem of obtaining use and nonuse values, the implementation of the survey also provides an opportunity to collect data necessary to implement indirect valuation methods. For example, Rowe and Schulze (1987), in a damage assessment of the Eagle Mine conducted for the CERCLA Division of the Colorado Department of Law, collected contingent value data, contingent behavior data on visitation, and actual data on property values for use in an indirect valuation study. The three approaches gave similar estimates of use value for local natural resource damages, strengthening the argument that the damage estimates were robust.

Some of the disadvantages of the direct method are as follows. First, values obtained through the direct method are hypothetical. One must ask: How large are the biases associated with hypothetical values as opposed to actual market values? Under what circumstances do significant biases occur? Can hypothetical bias be eliminated through survey design or data analysis?

Second, the direct method encourages the unfortunate tendency in the uninformed to consider themselves experts in survey design. The problem arises because nonexperts, who would never consider challenging an econometrician's specifications of a property value equation, are able to read and answer a survey themselves and therefore feel free to express opinions on wording, survey implementation, and the like. An example will make clear the inadvisability of giving weight to the views of nonexperts. Some years ago a group of naive economists, who shall

---

[1]42 U.S.C. 9601-9675.

[2]*Ohio v. The United States Department of the Interior*, 880, F.2d 432 (D.C. Cir. 1989).

remain nameless, conducted a mail survey without taking into consideration the enormous body of research that was available on mail survey design and implementation. The resulting response rate was about 15 percent. Properly designed and implemented mail surveys obtain response rates of 70 to 80 percent. However, obtaining this result requires attention to matters as subtle as stamping rather than franking envelopes, hand-signing rather than machine-signing the cover letter, and organizing the questionnaire so that lengthy blocks of text are broken up by questions.

Two recent books provide complete documentation of research on, and applications of, the CV method. The first, *Valuing Environmental Goods: Assessment of the Contingent Valuation Method,* by Cummings, Brookshire, and Schulze (1986), provides a state-of-the-art assessment of the CV method based on an EPA-sponsored conference held in Palo Alto in 1984. This volume includes papers by other researchers and an overall assessment of the method by several prominent social scientists. As an assessment, the volume does not provide direct guidance on how to design and implement the CV method. The second book, *Using Surveys to Value Public Goods: The Contingent Valuation Method,* by Mitchell and Carson (1989), provides precisely this type of guidance in a volume that updates the work of Cummings, Brookshire, and Schulze several years later. Both of these works reach an essentially similar conclusion: the CV method has been demonstrated to provide credible value estimates for many categories of commodities in a wide variety of situations, but uncertainty remains as to the accuracy of the method (or perhaps of any method) for some commodities and under some circumstances.

Given the availability of these two volumes, it is not the purpose of this chapter to provide a comprehensive review of the CV method, but rather to update the evidence and conclusions of these volumes concerning the applicability and reliability of the method for natural resource damage assessments. This chapter summarizes new and relevant research into the method and applies what is known about the method to the specific commodities, situations, and types of values appropriate to assessing natural resource damages.

The chapter is organized as follows. Section 2 describes the CV method and summarizes the major concerns that have been raised about using the method. Following sections describe new research into these concerns both in the field and in the laboratory: section 3 discusses the role of context or framing in the value formation process; section 4 treats problems raised in attempting to value uncertain outcomes; section 5 examines the disparity between willingness-to-pay and willingness-to-accept measures of value; and section 6 discusses issues that arise in survey design, implementation, and data analysis. Section 7 presents conclusions and recommendations concerning application of the CV method.

2. THE DIRECT METHOD AND MAJOR CONCERNS
ABOUT ITS USE

The contingent valuation method was originally developed by Davis (1963) and refined by Randall, Ives, and Eastman (1974). In the context of natural resource damages, the CV method employs survey questions that rely on a hypothetical market or payment mechanism to capture the values of the service flows of a natural resource. Thus respondents are asked, for example, how much more they would pay in the form of higher taxes, higher prices for goods and services, or possibly higher entrance fees to obtain improved service flows. Alternatively, in the contingent behavior method respondents are asked how they would change their behavior in response to the improvement in service flows. The most common examples of behaviors are voting and recreation visitation (see Mitchell and Carson [1989]).

Both the CV method and the CB method require that the nature of the changes in the level of flows, or of the quality of those flows, be clearly understood by respondents. In other words, the good to be valued must be clearly defined. If respondents are very familiar with the good and have already made behavioral adjustments in response to the level of its provision, the burden on the survey design of specifying the commodity is lessened. For example, Rowe and Schulze (1987), in developing local damages for contamination by the Eagle Mine of the Eagle River near Vail, Colorado, had little difficulty in describing contamination. A four-mile stretch of the river was vividly discolored with red-stained rocks along the shore (the stains were caused by acid drainings). Local residents refused to use this stretch of the river for recreation or fishing. Conditions both upstream and downstream (after the confluence with another stream) were much better and provided a vivid contrast to the contaminated stretch. On the other hand, invisible contamination of groundwater is much more difficult to describe; therefore, a much greater burden is placed on the survey to define the good to be valued.

Three states (conditions) of the natural resource are relevant in defining the commodity to be valued for CERCLA damages: (1) the pre-physical injury or baseline state, (2) the unremediated or current state, and (3) the post-remediation state. If current damages are to be measured, the commodity must be defined as obtaining state 1 as opposed to state 2. If residual damages after remediation are to be measured, then the commodity must be defined as obtaining state 3 as opposed to state 1. Since CERCLA provides only for the payment of residual damages, the latter measure is the appropriate one. However, the residual damage measure has several clear disadvantages if it is used to define the commodity in a contingent valuation study. First, since neither state 1 nor state 3 currently exists, the survey must get respondents to provide a value for a change between two currently nonexistent states. This has never been tried in a CV study to the author's knowledge but would, if attempted, place a large cognitive burden on the respondent. Second, damages for CERCLA must often be measured before a final remedy has been determined. Thus, state 3 will often be unknown at the time the CV method is implemented. What has been done in recent CERCLA cases is to apply the CV method to measure current damages and then adjust those damages downward to account for the extent of remediation in calculating approximate residual damages for various proposed remedies. Thus, for example, a particular remedy that is 98 percent effective may reduce the discounted present value of damages (based on an extrapolation of current damage into the future) from $100 million to a discounted present value of residual damage of $2 million.

Another issue in the definition of the commodity is whether the commodity should be defined in terms of the physical state of the natural resource or in terms of the service flows of the natural resource. This issue is made more difficult by the possibility that, in attempting to describe the service flows in detail, the survey instrument may bias the perception of those flows. If respondents have their own perceptions of the loss in current service flows, then the burden on the survey instrument is small and the change in service flows need not be specified in addition to the physical injury. However, in more complex cases where scientific issues are involved, it may be better to explain the change in service flows to respondents.

When the commodity is defined, one must specify some hypothetical method of payment (such as a tax or entrance fee) if willingness to pay (WTP) is to be measured, or some method of compensation if willingness to accept (WTA) is to be measured. Cummings, Brookshire, and Schulze (1986) and Mitchell and Carson (1989) review the mixed evidence on this subject. If some unpopular payment vehicle is chosen, a downward bias will possibly result. Realism in the choice of vehicle is obviously desirable as well, since a mix of higher prices and taxes is often appropriate and has invoked relatively few protest responses. One example of a mechanism that could invoke vehicle bias is a cleanup fund built with money from respondents, in which the money would be paid directly to the operators of the site or to a government agency that local residents distrust.[3]

Compensation questions that elicit WTA have generally avoided a specific vehicle, since plausible vehicles that do not encourage strategic

---

[3]McClelland, Schulze, and Hurd (1987) found that among involved parties near a hazardous waste site, the Environmental Protection Agency and the operator were both viewed with distrust, as compared with local governments, citizens groups, and the like.

bias (possibly producing large values) are difficult to construct. WTP questions generally have not seemed to invoke large bids as a strategic response; rather, they seem to encourage zero bids. Respondents argue, "I'm not responsible, I should not have to pay." WTA questions such as "How much, at a minimum, should your family be compensated in the form of a cash settlement by corporation X for having lived near their hazardous waste site?" may encourage strategic responses.

A real question exists as to the relative magnitudes of WTP and WTA. For example, McClelland, Schulze, and Hurd (1987) found that WTP exceeded WTA for risk from a contaminated landfill by one order of magnitude. Because the site was surrounded by homes and because residents were aware of property value effects, a unique opportunity was present to define WTA and WTP measures in terms of changes in monthly payments for an identical home with and without such a site. This particular WTA question did not seem to invoke strategic responses. Since a WTA measure is technically the appropriate welfare measure for valuing residual natural resource damages under CERCLA, this large disparity between WTA and WTP is of some importance and will be discussed at length below. The recent literature in experimental economics and psychology will provide most of our understanding.

The final element in the design of a CV question is the method for collecting the hypothetical bid (in the case of WTP) or offer (in the case of WTA). Randall, Ives, and Eastman (1974) used an iterative bidding method in which respondents were asked if they would pay a stated amount and the amount was subsequently increased (or decreased) in prespecified intervals until the respondent refused (or agreed) to pay. This technique has been demonstrated to be subject to starting-point bias, which, however, can be fairly easily removed by a method described by Thayer (1981).

On the other hand, the iterative bidding procedure has been demonstrated to be of doubtful validity in several controlled laboratory experiments in which a priori hypothetical values were compared to the value of goods actually purchased in competitive auctions (see Coursey, Hovis, and Schulze [1987] and McClelland, Schulze, and Hurd [1987]). In these experiments, hypothetical values obtained by directly asking for the maximum willingness to pay corresponded closely with actual auction values. Iterative hypothetical bidding in the Coursey, Hovis, and Schulze experiment actually produced excess bids as compared to actual auction values. In CV surveys, values from respondents may (without iterative bidding) be obtained by asking for a stated or written dollar value or by having respondents choose from a list of values. If a list of values is provided (and such a list seems to assist respondents by indicating that "to the penny" precision is not required in answering), it is important that the range of values in no way constrains the choice. In a number of studies de facto trimming of high bids occurred because an upper bound in the list of values was set too low.

Although sampling issues will not be discussed further in this chapter, the issue of determining the size of the market for the injured natural resource can greatly affect estimated damages. It is not difficult to assess the market area for sampling use values since one can readily identify users. However, bequest and existence values may extend far beyond the market arca for usc and option values. Preliminary sampling by use of an abbreviated mail or telephone survey may be helpful in identifying the market area in which these values are relevant.

Use of the CB method has increased dramatically in the last several years. Mitchell and Carson (1989) argue that a yes or no question about how respondents would vote in a referendum that poses a specific cost to voters for a carefully specified commodity, is much easier for respondents to answer. The problem with this approach is that data analysis becomes much more difficult, and a much larger sample size is required to estimate willingness to pay. Multiple surveys, postulating different costs for the same level of provision of the commodity, must be used. Mitchell and Carson (1989) modified the referendum approach such that if respondents would consider voting "yes" to the referendum they would then be asked to state the largest cost they would accept before switching their vote to a "no." Thus, Mitchell and Carson have abandoned the CB method in favor of the CV method, but have retained the voting context.

It should again be noted that the CB method cannot estimate nonuse values and requires the additional assumptions and econometric procedures associated with the indirect method. In other words, the CB method collects hypothetical data for use in an indirect market study and so inherits all of the difficulties of data analysis described by Kenneth E. McConnell in chapter 8.

Why, then, might one wish to use the CB method in a natural resource damage assessment? To begin with, once the change in level of service flows of a natural resource has been specified by asking a CV question, it is easy to ask an additional question about changes in behavior. Analysis of choices such as referendum votes can provide important additional support in damage assessments. Psychologists argue that different ways of framing a decision can bias the outcome, a phenomenon that in this application is known as response mode bias. An example of response mode bias is the well-known preference-reversal phenomenon. Since this is likely to be a point of attack on the CV method, demonstrating that similar preferences are implied by stated money values and stated choices will demonstrate the robustness of damage assessments.

Loomis (1990) has recently demonstrated the comparability of the CV and CB methods in a state-of-the-art application of the CB method. Important theoretical and econometric advances have been motivated by the inherent difficulty in obtaining willingness-to-pay estimates from behavioral-choice data. Such estimates are made possible only by specifying a particular functional form for the random utility function implicitly or explicitly used in the econometric analysis. Cameron and James (1987) have argued that the random utility approach developed by Hanemann (1984) is not necessary to estimate WTP. However, McConnell (1990) has shown that the models used by Cameron and James and by Hanemann are dual.

Having described the core aspects of the direct method, we now turn to a discussion of remaining concerns about application of the CV method. In their state-of-the-art assessment, Cummings, Brookshire, and Schulze (1986) followed concepts of accuracy drawn from measurement in the physical sciences and arrived at four reference operating conditions (ROCs). These ROCs would in their view (which was based on an extensive review of the evidence) assure that the CV method could achieve levels of accuracy comparable to ordinary measurement of market demand. The reference operating conditions are as follows:

(1) Subjects must understand (be familiar with) the commodity to be valued.
(2) Subjects must have previously had (or be allowed to obtain), valuation and choice experience with respect to consumption levels of the commodity.
(3) There must be little uncertainty.
(4) Willingness to pay measures, not willingness to accept measures, must be elicited.

Obviously these conditions are stringent, so stringent that the usefulness of the method would, if the ROCs were strictly followed, be limited to mixed public/private goods traded in existing markets. Cummings, Brookshire, and Schulze (1986) proposed these conditions not as functional limits to the method, but rather as factors to be considered in evaluating the reliability of a particular application and as guidelines for future research, both in the experimental laboratory and in the field. The question becomes to what degree each of these conditions can be relaxed while still achieving acceptable levels of accuracy. As we will see, ROCs 3 and 4 actually relate more to potential difficulties with subjective expected utility theory (see Machina [1987]) than to problems with the CV method itself. I argue in section 3 that these ROCs may, in fact, be inappropriate.

Section 3 considers ROCs 1 and 2 together under the framework of context and value formation. It is argued that ROCs 1 and 2 should be combined into a generalized concern over context and value formation, which provides a conceptual basis both for evaluating the accuracy of the CV method and for many details of survey design. ROCs 3 and 4 are treated separately, followed by a discussion of issues that arise in survey design and implementation.

3. CONTEXT AND VALUE FORMATION

Reference operating conditions 1 and 2—familiarity with the commodity and valuation and choice experience—are both satisfied if a consumer has made choices between alternative levels of service flows of a natural resource. Thus, in choosing to fish or recreate in an uncontaminated portion of the Eagle River, which in many cases involved extra driving distance with less convenient access (Rowe and Schulze [1987]), local residents of the Vail, Colorado, area presumably had formed some value for improved service flows. Schuman and Presser (1981), in their study of question form, wording, and context in survey research, introduce the concept of crystallization of attitudes. They define crystallized attitudes as "those that exist independently of our measurement, and that when appropriately measured show high reliability" (Schuman and Presser [1981], p. 27).

It is likely that the same concept would be highly useful for the CV method, since we can define crystallized values as those that exist independently of our measurement and that when appropriately measured show high reliability. For example, values obtained from local residents for damages from the Eagle Mine proved to be surprisingly robust to differences in survey design. Rowe and Schulze (1987) employed two kinds of surveys to estimate local use and local and regional nonuse values: a local survey in Eagle County specific to the Eagle Mine and a very different statewide survey covering many hazardous waste sites in Colorado. The local and statewide survey responses, when analyzed for local damages to residents of Eagle County, provided nearly identical value estimates. In other words, values for fishing, sightseeing, and other uses of the river were crystallized and not sensitive to the details of the survey design. In some sense, because values were crystallized, local respondents in answering the CV questions knew the answers rather than having to work them out.

The sensitivity of hypothetical responses to small details of wording, information provided, ordering of information, ordering of questions, and the like can be summarized in the concept of context. Psychologists argue that context effects do not arise as a problem peculiar to survey design but rather as a fundamental issue in choice or decision theory (see, for example, Tversky and Sattath [1979] and Tversky and Kahneman [1981]). Minor and seemingly irrelevant changes in the context or framing of actual decisions have been repeatedly shown in psychology experiments to have great impact on outcomes. If the decision has been made, one can ask ex post what the decision was and presumably ask for any values involved in the decision. However, if the decision has not yet been made, if values are not crystallized, then context effects within the survey can easily bias values obtained unless the context precisely matches the real situation.

The source of context effects can be illustrated by difficulties that have arisen in artificial intelligence (AI) research. Consider the problem of programming a computer to respond appropriately, as would a human being, to a command given in conversational English. The computer might well take everything said to it literally or confuse possible alternative meanings. To solve this problem AI researchers have turned to a cognitive model developed by Roger Shank that supposes that key words in a message invoke a mental script that incorporates or guides the appropriate response. (For a nontechnical description, see Rose [1985].) Shank argues that few messages are likely to be sufficiently complete so as to be understood or to allow proper action to be taken without reference to such a script. The script serves to fill in missing information in the message. Such scripts are of course based on memories and incorrect scripts may be employed by mistake.

AI researchers often use examples drawn from the former George Burns and Gracie Allen show to illustrate such cognitive errors. For example, in one show Blanche, the next-door neighbor, comes in and finds flowers all around the room. Blanche asks Gracie where she got them, and Gracie explains that Helen was in the hospital. Since George told Gracie to visit the hospital and "take her flowers," Gracie did just that (when Helen wasn't looking) and brought them home. The explanation for this error in understanding is that Gracie lacked the appropriate script to refer to in trying to understand George's instructions to "take her flowers." The appropriate script, of course, says that when going to visit someone in the hospital one normally brings flowers.

Clearly, in a survey asking for contingent values, context effects can occur because words, information, even inclusion of irrelevant alternatives, can call up different scripts that will influence choices. Of course, the clearer and more complete the message or question is, the more complete the context of the question will be and the less a respondent has to rely on scripts to fill in missing information. This seems to be the approach recommended by Fischhoff and Furby (1988) in their review of the CV method as applied to visibility valuation.

Several new studies provide substantial support for the notion of crystallized values presented above. In a contingent valuation study of the value of electric power service reliability (Doane and coauthors [1989]), residential customers were sent one of six versions of a mail survey. The surveys differed substantially in the amount and type of context provided, as well as in the way the value questions were asked. None of the survey variants produced statistically different values. This result is consistent with the argument that, if respondents are highly familiar with the commodity itself and can take private market actions with respect to the commodity (such as purchasing a backup generator to avoid the consequences of outages), context effects are likely to be unimportant. The one exception to this conclusion is that a substantial disparity with respect to WTA and WTP measures of value was found, a topic that will be taken up in section 5.

Another new study sheds light on context effects. Irwin and coauthors (1990) conducted a mail survey to attempt to value air quality improvements, employing eight versions that varied dramatically in the context provided, the form of value questions, and other such factors. Respondents are likely to have less familiarity with air quality issues than with power outages and have fewer market alternatives, so values are likely to be less crystallized. In fact, two of the survey designs produced statistically different values. However, the differences were relatively small, on the order of 30 percent. Few researchers would wish to claim that any valuation method has an accuracy better than plus-or-minus 30 percent, so, in the judgment of the authors (including several psychologists on the research team), values in this case were robust. It should be pointed out that the air quality problem studied, Denver's "brown cloud" air pollution, had received considerable local media attention, and a community consensus on control strategies, which was even endorsed by the local chamber of commerce, existed.

It is unfortunate that the strategy of employing multiple survey designs with widely varying contexts has not yet been applied in a natural resource damage estimation arising from CERCLA. It is not at all clear that other commodities such as cleanup of Superfund sites will be robust to changes in context. It should be noted that large sample sizes are required to show the impact of context effects because individual public good values vary widely. Thus, the large variance in CV responses requires very large sample sizes to show significant effects.

In summary, context effects are not likely to be a serious problem in the case of crystallized values. However, in cases where values are not crystallized, a much larger burden is placed on the survey design to provide a complete, realistic, and clear context for the formation of values.

4. VALUING UNCERTAIN OUTCOMES

Early contingent valuation studies undertaken to value damages of possible exposure to hazardous wastes all found very large damages relative to scientific estimates of the risks (see for example Burness and coauthors [1983]; Smith and Desvousges [1987]; and McClelland, Schulze, and Hurd [1987]). The initial reaction to these results was that something might be wrong with the method when applied in uncertain, or at least low-probability, situations. This concern was the source of reference operating condition 3. However, there is increasing evidence and acceptance that, in the general population, low-probability events are overweighted (Edwards [1962] and Kahneman and Tversky [1979]), or alternatively that individuals are oversensitive to small probabilities (Machina [1984 and 1987]). Expected utility theory supposes that people weight the utility outcomes of states of the world linearly in their probabilities of occurrence. Psychologists have modified expected utility theory to account for the excess concern that people seem to show for low-probability events by proposing that the utility outcomes are multiplied by a weighting function of the probabilities. Thus, where $U(Y_1)$ and $U(Y_2)$ are the utility outcomes of two states of the world with income levels Y_1 and Y_2 and odds p_1 and $p_2 = 1 - p_1$, expected utility theory proposes that people evaluate the possible outcomes as

$$p_1 U(Y_1) + p_2 U(Y_2). \tag{1}$$

In contrast, psychologists argue that a weighting function $\pi(p)$, which overweights low probabilities [$\pi(p) > p$ for small p], is essential to explain observed behavior, yielding

$$\pi(p_1)U(Y_1) + \pi(p_2)U(Y_2) \tag{2}$$

as the evaluation criterion (see Kahneman and Tversky [1979]).

Economists, responding to the same evidence, have attempted to maintain the property of stochastic dominance by proposing specific functional forms for generalized utility functions (forms that are not linear in the probabilities), so in general we would have:

$$U(p_1, p_2, Y_1, Y_2). \tag{3}$$

Oversensitivity to low probabilities is implied by the usual concept of an increasing marginal rate of substitution as a probability becomes small (see Machina [1984 and 1987]).

McClelland, Schulze, and Coursey (forthcoming) conducted a series of laboratory experiments to test whether hypothetical values contributed in and of themselves to this overweighting or oversensitivity to low-probability events or whether hypothetical values were good predictors of actual values as probabilities became small. In the experiment, insurance was sold to subjects in a competitive auction against odds ranging from 0.9 to 0.01 of a \$4 loss. The ratio of the mean bids to expected value is shown in figure 10-1 plotted against probability of loss. The ratio shown is the mean over subjects and over ten repeated rounds. Note the sharp increase in this ratio that occurs as the probability of loss drops below 0.1; the ratio rises to 2.5 at a probability of 0.01. Since the loss was held constant across probabilities in this experiment, McClelland, Schulze, and Coursey (forthcoming) in a second experiment raised the loss to \$40 but only with one probability of loss of 0.01. Again the mean of bids for insurance against the loss exceeded expected value. Thus, the actual bids submitted in a competitive auction support the notion of overweighting or oversensitivity to low probabilities. They also show that risk aversion in an expected utility model cannot explain observed results since the ratio of bids to expected values is about the same for the \$4 loss and the \$40 loss at 0.01 odds.

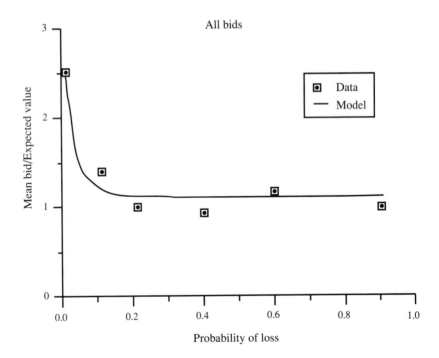

Figure 10-1. Ratio of mean bids to expected value, plotted over probability of loss

Figure 10-2 shows how the means of hypothetical bids compared with means of actual auction bids pooled across trials (shown in figure 10-1). Hypothetical mean bid divided by actual auction mean bid is shown on the vertical axis and probability of loss is shown on the horizontal axis. Hypothetical bids for insurance were collected from the inexperienced prior to the start of the experiment for all the probabilities used, and hypothetical bids were collected from the experienced before each probability was introduced. The inexperienced hypothetical bids collected at the start of the experiment clearly overestimate actual auction bids at low probabilities (since the ratio shown in figure 10-2 is greater than 1) and underestimate actual auction bids at high probabilities (since the ratio is less than 1). We have no explanation as to why inexperienced hypothetical bids at high probabilities show underweighting and actual auction bids do not. In contrast, however, experienced hypothetical bids, which were collected after actual auction experience at other probabilities, were good predictors of auction bids at probabilities of 0.2 and above.

Both inexperienced and experienced hypothetical bids are about twice actual auction bids at $p = 0.1$ and 0.01. We conjecture that the overestimation of hypothetical bids that occurs at low probabilities may be due to an incomplete gradient search for an optimal bid. In other words, individuals may start with the loss and work downward in search of an optimal bid. Since the distance between the loss and expected value is great at low probabilities, practice may increase the amount of downward adjustment that occurs, bringing bids closer to expected value. At the lower probabilities more search is required and both inexperienced and experienced hypothetical bids may represent the first iteration in the search process. In the second experiment, which is shown in figure 10-3, subjects began an actual auction at $p = 0.01$ with no prior laboratory experience of the auction procedure for this type of risk. If this hypothesis is correct, actual auction bids should start at very high values. From examination of figure 10-1, we see that actual auction bids are about two and a half times expected value at $p = 0.01$. From examination of figure 10-2, we see that hypothetical bids are about two times actual auction bids at $p = 0.01$. Thus, we might conjecture that completely inexperienced actual auction bids might be five times expected value. Since, from figure 10-3, we see that starting bids are about six times expected value, hypothetical bids might well be very good predictors of completely inexperienced auction behavior. Note in this context that all of the auction behavior in the first experiment described above was of the experienced type because the auctions began with four nonbinding practice trials.

Thus, the evidence from McClelland, Schulze, and Coursey (forthcoming) suggests that hypothetical values correspond fairly well to completely inexperienced auction values. However, from figure 10-3 it

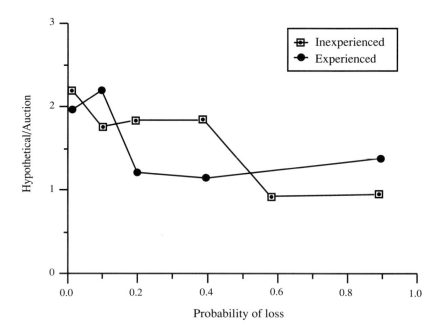

Figure 10-2. Hypothetical mean bids compared with actual auction bids, plotted over probability of loss

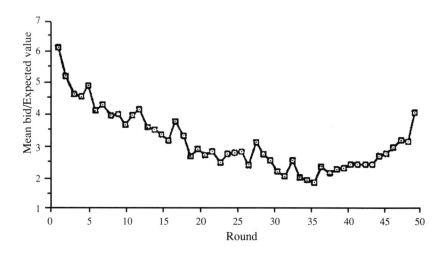

Figure 10-3. Relationship of mean bids to rounds of experience in an actual auction

appears that auction experience and benign experience seem to lower actual values (that is, subjects in a low-probability situation will likely accumulate many rounds of experience without suffering a loss). The question becomes: how much market/choice/benign experience do respondents have with low-probability risks such as those associated with natural resource damage? If such experience is negligible, then hypothetical values obtained by the contingent valuation method may be valid measures of the actual values that people hold. Contingent valuation may, from the perspective of economics, simply be the "bearer of bad news" concerning the extent to which people fear low-probability events.

5. WILLINGNESS TO PAY VERSUS WILLINGNESS TO ACCEPT

Early in the history of the contingent valuation method, Hammack and Brown (1974) noted a large disparity between willingness to pay and willingness to accept. Numerous field studies have repeated this finding (see Cummings, Brookshire, and Schulze [1986] for a summary). The disparity of WTA to WTP has ranged between a ratio of 2 to 1 and 10 to 1. This disparity has also been found in laboratory experiments. Knetsch and Sinden (1984) showed in a series of experiments that the willingness to accept required to buy back lottery tickets exceeded the willingness to pay for purchase of lottery tickets by a factor of about four to one. Although traditional analysis of welfare measures predicts that WTA may exceed WTP because of the income effect, it has generally been assumed by economists that, for commodities in which expenditures make up a small share of income (as certainly must be true in the laboratory), the difference between WTA and WTP should be negligible (Willig [1976]). Hanemann (1991) has demonstrated that WTA and WTP may differ substantially in a standard economic model of consumer choice when a public good is involved and substitutes for the commodity are unavailable. An extreme example of this phenomenon is the case in which an environmental good is a perfect complement to income. In this case, an L-shaped indifference curve yields WTA $\to \infty$ and WTP $\to 0$ for decreases and increases in the level of provision, respectively.

In contrast, psychologists argue that the disparity between WTA and WTP results from a difference in the way people treat gains and losses. A monetary loss from a reference point (which can be the current situation, a status quo, a norm, or an expectation) is argued to cause a much greater loss in utility than an equivalent monetary gain will cause a gain in utility. In effect, a kink forms in the utility function at the reference point. Because the left-hand derivative from the reference point exceeds the right-hand derivative, relative gains are valued differently from relative losses, leading to a difference in WTA and WTP. Note that the same change can be framed as a gain or a loss depending on the position of the reference point. Thus, if someone expects a 10 percent increase in salary and gets a 5 percent increase, a relative loss would have occurred. The kinked utility function described above has been formalized by Kahneman and Tversky (1979) in their prospect theory.

Coursey, Hovis, and Schulze (1987) demonstrated in another experiment that, where individuals were allowed to repeatedly submit bids to purchase one unit of a commodity or repeatedly submit offers to sell one unit of the same commodity in a competitive auction situation, WTA declined with market experience while WTP remained constant. At the point when the actual transaction occurred (either after a maximum of ten rounds or when a unanimous vote was obtained to end the bidding), offers in the WTA treatment were statistically similar to bids in the WTP treatment. Thus, the Coursey, Hovis, and Schulze (1987) results from a multiple-round competitive auction contrast sharply at the point where trade took place with the results of Knetsch and Sinden (1984) from a one-shot posted-offer market. However, initial bids or offers in the Coursey, Hovis, and Schulze experiments were consistent with the Knetsch and Sinden results of a large disparity between WTA and WTP.

In an experiment designed to explicitly test the hypothesis that at least part of the difference between WTA and WTP values is due to moral reasoning, Boyce and coauthors (forthcoming) compared bids or offers from subjects to purchase or sell back a small Norfolk Island pine tree suitable for use as a house plant. In one treatment the tree is killed if subjects do not retain possession of the tree and in another the fate of the tree is left undefined. The difference in values between these two treatments may capture some elements of nonuse value in that subjects have, by retaining possession of the tree, the opportunity to prevent the needless destruction of a living thing. The results show that values in the kill treatment exceed values in the no-kill treatment and that the disparity between offers (willingness to accept) and bids (willingness to pay) is much larger in the kill treatment. These results suggest that intrinsic values may be more completely captured by willingness to accept because subjects accept moral responsibility for allowing the death of the tree. In the case of willingness to pay, the experimenter is viewed as responsible for the death of the tree. The disparity found between these two measures of value may thus be associated with intrinsic value.

Boyce and coauthors (forthcoming) develop a model that accounts for the WTA/WTP disparity by assuming that subjects accept moral responsibility for preserving environmental commodities and incorporate existence value (or intrinsic value as they term the phenomenon) in a

WTA setting, but fail to completely incorporate existence value in a WTP setting. In particular, they argue as follows:

> Consider the case of the blue whale where Japanese whalers have driven the species to the edge of extinction. Clearly intrinsic values are of primary importance in this situation because option prices for use of the blue whale are likely to be trivial outside of Japan. If the public in the United States were asked to accept monetary compensation from Japan to allow final extinction to occur, very large WTA values might well be required because, in accepting money, the public would be accepting moral responsibility for the extinction of the species. In fact, many individuals might refuse any amount of money (WTA → ∞). On the other hand, if asked to pay the Japanese to induce them not to drive the blue whale to final extinction, many would respond that it is not their responsibility to preserve the blue whale since the Japanese are at fault. Thus, their WTP might well be zero. If this argument is correct, WTA measures intrinsic value while WTP only measures intrinsic value to the extent that consumers accept moral responsibility in a WTP context. (Boyce and coauthors [forthcoming])

A difficulty for the CV method arises from the results of these two experiments; it stems from the obvious direct analogy between natural resource damage and the WTA treatments. In the judgment on the Department of the Interior regulations discussed in the introduction to this chapter, exclusion of WTA values was cited as an example of an appropriate procedure. At the same time the judge ruled that nonuse values were appropriate. This may be a logically inconsistent viewpoint in that WTA values may be the proper measure of use and nonuse values. Thus, in a real-world setting where preservation of a natural resource is at stake, large compensatory demands motivated by moral reasoning may be the appropriate measure of natural resource damage in that slightly smaller offers of compensation would actually be refused. Knetsch (1990) has argued for the acceptance of WTA values where the property rights structure supports their use. Clearly, when public resources are damaged by private industry, as in most CERCLA cases, WTA values may be appropriate.

6.   SURVEY DESIGN, IMPLEMENTATION, AND DATA ANALYSIS

6.1   Survey Design. Two long-term studies have had a major impact on survey design. The first of these is summarized in a 1978 book by D. A. Dillman, *Mail and Telephone Surveys: The Total Design Method*. This book contains perhaps the most complete available discussion of issues in survey design, including highly detailed example surveys. It compiles a decade of careful research and is an invaluable aid for the economist unfamiliar with issues in survey design, including development of in-person interviews. One of the many subjects covered by Dillman is the role of the survey introduction. He has found that by avoiding long introductory blocks of text and replacing them with short questions that provide the same information on the purpose and nature of the survey, respondents are kept involved, which increases response rates. This approach is crucial in a mail survey but also has validity for in-person interviews. A brief review of existing CV instruments would show little attention paid to this point.

The second study is found in a 1981 book by H. Schuman and S. Presser, *Questions and Answers in Attitude Surveys: Experiments on Question Form, Wording and Context*. This book summarizes a lengthy research effort in which alternative question forms, wording, and contexts were added to existing survey designs to test the impact of varying these elements. While demonstrating the importance of context effects in general, Schuman and Presser also provide many examples in which context seems to matter little, leading in part to their concept of crystallized attitudes. However, summary questions seem most affected by context. Obviously, CV questions are likely to be "summary questions"; they will depend on the context established in the survey unless the question relates closely to existing behavior, in which case the "real world" rather than the survey may provide the necessary context. In consequence, Schuman and Presser suggest that important questions be developed in a pilot study using an open question form and then turned into closed questions based on responses. Although this is obviously difficult to do for a CV question, parts of CV questions such as "why did you bid zero" do lend themselves to an open form. Schuman and Presser (1981) also suggest that filtering out "don't know" responses is useful for obtaining informed opinion, but "basic values" are better obtained through use of standard unfiltered questions. A real dilemma exists in the CV method as to whether or not to force respondents to provide a value or allow a "don't know" response. Fischhoff and Furby (1988) suggest including a "don't know" response, but the research of Schuman and Presser argues otherwise.

6.2   Survey Implementation. The first decision to be made concerning survey implementation is whether to conduct in-person, self-administered, mail, or telephone interviews. Because of the complexity of the CV method in terms of defining the commodity, developing the appropriate context, and the like, telephone surveys may be inappropriate unless, for example, respondents have previously been mailed written material upon which to base their responses or are very familiar with the commodity to be valued. This generally leaves the researcher with a choice between in-person or mail surveys. Based on cost alone, the preference would obviously go toward mail surveys, which can include and have included full-color photographic representations of alternative levels of resource quality. However, response rates may suffer unless repeated mailings and reminders are utilized and compensation is paid to respondents.

In a study of the effect of compensation on response rates, six compensation schemes (including one that offered no compensation) were compared by Doane and coauthors (1989). Prior compensation of $2 worked as well as a priori compensation of $5 and as well as ex post compensation schemes of up to $10. All schemes using compensation generated response rates of about 80 percent, while the no-compensation approach yielded a response rate of just under 60 percent. It should be noted that the 60 percent response rate was itself exceptional, reflecting great care in survey design and implementation, so these figures represent the current upper bound for surveys of this type. Thus, if careful procedures are followed, nonresponse bias may not be a serious problem.

If problems do arise, telephone follow-up surveys of nonrespondents can be used to examine their characteristics and check for nonresponse bias. In-person, door-to-door methods may be superior in this respect since nonrespondents can be well documented. The major difficulty with in-person interviews is the problem of acquiescence, which is termed a "quagmire" by Schuman and Presser (1981). Unfortunately, there is strong evidence that the CV method is susceptible to having the responses influenced by the interviewer. Training of interviewers seems to help, but does not eliminate these effects (Schuman and Presser [1981]). Many anecdotes testify as to the systematic differences in values obtained by different interviewers in a variety of CV studies. However, these anecdotes have not found their way into the published literature on the direct method.

One exception is a paper by Dickie, Fisher, and Gerking (1987), which reports on a door-to-door study comparing hypothetical and actual sales of strawberries. Although they found essentially similar results for hypothetical versus actual sales of strawberries—a likely outcome since the context was precisely the same—they found substantial differences in sales performance for different interview teams. This result is important because it highlights the fact that the CV method is in some sense a matter of selling something to the respondent. Interviewer personality obviously plays a large role in making a hypothetical sale. The particular kind of training interviewers receive or fail to receive and any perceived goals that they may infer for the study may bias the results. Obviously self-administered or mail surveys avoid this difficulty, since responses will be based on the written material presented in or with the survey. Perhaps the best approach is a self-administered, in-person interview.

A final issue for all survey research is the problem of comprehension. Studies have shown that as much as one-third of the general population of the United States has problems related to literacy, language, or cognition. In laboratory decision-making experiments, psychologists have found that often 30 percent of the subjects are unable to make a decision (complete the task). Also in laboratory experiments, economists have found that about the same percentage of subjects appear to fail to understand the appropriate strategy for maximizing payoffs. Schuman and Presser (1981) extensively discuss the problem of respondents (termed "floaters") who give bizarre and inconsistent responses but who appear to be trying to respond to the questions asked to the best of their abilities. But Schuman and Presser indicate that no way has been found to pre-identify and re-move "floaters" from a sample population. Thus, removal of such re-spondents currently falls to data analysis. If respondents are literate in a foreign language the obvious solution is to use mail surveys written in that language or interviewers trained in that language. If a respondent is truly illiterate, the CV method will be very difficult to implement. Most de-scriptions of levels of commodity provision use ladders with written de-scriptions, and letters or numbers identifying steps or identifying photographs are embedded in written or oral questions.

Issues in sampling and methods of data collection are thoroughly covered in Dillman (1978) and Mitchell and Carson (1989).

6.3 Data Analysis. The frequency distribution of value responses to contingent valuation questions is almost always bimodal, showing one mode of zero values and another mode lying within a bell-shaped distribu-tion that often shows a thick upper tail. This distribution of values is obviously troublesome in that the validity of both zero and very large values is doubtful. Simple trimming of an equal proportion of low and high values makes little sense for a bimodal distribution. Reasonable procedures for eliminating suspect zero and large bids have, however, been developed in the absence of any theory to explain the source of such bids. Here I first briefly outline these strategies and then discuss alterna-tive theories of the formation of values, one based in economics and one based in psychology.

Suspect zero bids are best eliminated by asking an open-form ques-tion as to why the respondent refuses to pay. (Obviously, zero offers are not a problem in WTA questions.) Responses typically fall into four or five categories, which can then be broken down into protest bids and genuine zero bids. The problem with the genuine zero bids is that, when they are cross-checked against questions that ask whether the commodity in question is important or if it affects the respondent, further inconsistencies are revealed. For example, in a recent study of air pollution in the Denver area (Irwin and coauthors [1990]), essentially all zero bids failed a cross-check against a question that asked if air pollution was bothersome to respondents. Clearly, some threshold effect must be at work in generating zero bids.

Large bids have been eliminated through two methods. First, bids cannot exceed income in the case of WTP, so such bids can be readily disposed of. Judgment as to a cutoff point for the largest reasonable bid as a proportion of a respondent's income can also be utilized to eliminate large bids, but is an arbitrary approach. Second, an interesting approach that should be followed in future work has been employed by Smith and Desvousges (1987) in their CV study of the value of avoiding risks from exposure to hazardous wastes. They first use a probit equation to explain both protest and other zero bids, inherently allowing for some possible threshold effect. They then account for selection bias in estimating an explanatory model of positive bids. It would be useful to combine this approach with the procedure used to trim positive bids based on detecting outliers relative to an estimated model, as was done in earlier CV work on water quality (Desvousges, Smith, and Fisher [1987]). This would be a desirable approach if appropriate procedures could be developed.

A model of value formation may provide some guidance to appropriate procedures for dealing with zero and large values. Considerable evidence exists within the experimental economics literature that, in attempting to find the optimal response in a laboratory market setting, subjects engage in a gradient search similar to that employed to solve large nonlinear optimization problems (see for example Coursey and Mason [1987] and McClelland, Schulze, and Coursey [forthcoming]). Thus, one can imagine that a respondent who is asked for maximum willingness to pay will sequentially evaluate a series of bids B_i, $i = 1, \ldots, n$ according to the rule that

$$B_i - B_{i-1} = k \left[U(Y - B_{i-1}, X° + \Delta X) - U(Y, X°) \right],$$

where k is the adjustment parameter, $U(Y, X)$ is the utility of income Y, and X is the commodity to be valued. ΔX is the increment in the commodity for which the subject is bidding. This process will likely converge over infinite trials to satisfy $U(Y - B_n, X° + \Delta X) = U(Y, X)$. If n is less than ∞ then the true optimum will not be reached and B_n will be biased. The question is: how great is this bias in a survey as opposed to the real world (that is, is n smaller for a survey response than for a real decision?) and in what direction does the bias lie?

The direction of bias is likely to be determined by the starting point used for the gradient search. Starting points in actual computer solutions of nonlinear optimization problems are always arbitrary but generally satisfy the constraints, which in this case would be $0 \le B_o \le Y$. This suggests that the gradient search either starts at zero (if the respondent thinks the value is likely to be small) or at the budget level Y (or possibly at some large share of the budget allocated to the relevant commodity group). Thus, an incomplete gradient search will produce values that are either too small or too large. If a respondent thinks the value is small and starts at zero, even the first step in the search process may not be worthwhile, which would produce a large number of zero bids. Alternatively, respondents working down from a large value, if they are "lazy," will produce a thick tail.

An alternative model of the value formation process is available from psychology. This model does not assume optimizing behavior but rather focuses on describing the decision process as working through a preference tree that has probabilities attached to each branching point. The probabilities may be viewed as being context-dependent (see Tversky and Sattath [1979]).

Context dependence may be introduced into the gradient search model by assuming that the starting points or the utility function or both depend on context. Some field evidence exists to support the gradient search model. Brookshire and Coursey (1987) showed that in a hypothetical Smith public good auction held for placing trees in local parks, values changed over multiple rounds. Dickie and coauthors (1987) obtained many very large bids in a CV study of morbidity values and found that when such bids were challenged the thick upper tail of the distribution vanished in the revised bids. This suggests that some type of mechanism to induce repeated bidding (but not the iterative bidding procedure described in section 2) may be useful to force respondents to think more about the values, especially in cases where such values are not crystallized. Aspects of both the gradient search and preference tree models of consumer decision-making may prove to be valid.

7. CONCLUSION

Natural resource damages encompass many of the factors specified above that affect the accuracy of the CV method. It is the view of this author that the ROCs listed in section 2 collapse into the single issue of context and value formation. Further, ROCs 3 and 4 relating to uncertainty and the willingness-to-accept/willingness-to-pay disparity simply reflect widely recognized failures of the subjective expected utility model to explain human behavior, rather than any inherent problems with the CV method.

Thus, in evaluating the applicability of the CV method to the damage categories defined in the introduction to this chapter, it is readily apparent that, as one moves from use to nonuse values such as existence and bequest values, the "real world" progressively fails to provide the context necessary to yield precise value answers because no markets exist for bequest and existence values. It becomes less likely that respondents have gone through a relatively complete valuation process. To use the terminology of Schuman and Presser (1981), in terms of the survey design values are likely to be less crystallized and more context-dependent. This does not imply that valid values cannot be obtained for bequest and existence values. Rather, the burden on the survey design becomes greater both in terms of filling in a relatively complete context and leading respondents through a "natural" mental process to arrive at values.

However, no matter how carefully designed the survey, no matter how carefully implemented the research, a fundamental issue will separate plaintiffs and defendants in CERCLA natural resource damage cases. Plaintiffs will take the position that it is the perception of consumers that matters in deciding damages. In other words, if consumers are aware that a river is contaminated and choose not to fish, swim, or otherwise utilize the resource, an economic damage has occurred. Defendants will argue that the level of contamination is so low that no meaningful injury could possibly occur to users of the resource and that therefore the defendant should not have to pay damages for the incorrect beliefs of consumers. Consumers themselves might well respond that the public does not trust the scientific assessments of risk presented by the defendants (or for that matter by scientists in general) because health effects from toxic substances are long-term and poorly understood. The public would rather play it safe.

In essence, the argument can be reduced to one of consumer sovereignty. The core of the CV method is a direct assessment of consumer values, so a rejection of consumer sovereignty implies a rejection of the CV method. In this light, if one accepts that consumers overvalue or are oversensitive to low-probability events and that large WTA responses for toxic substances (which reflect consumer sovereignty and are the appropriate damage measure) are the result of affected decision-making, one can construct an argument to reject consumer sovereignty on the psychological grounds that consumers are especially prone to making cognitive errors in decisions regarding toxic substances. What is missing from the debate is a restatement of welfare economics that carefully considers cognitive errors and incomplete optimization.

REFERENCES

Boyce, R. R., T. Brown, G. H. McClelland, G. Peterson, and W. D. Schulze. Forthcoming. "An Experimental Examination of Intrinsic Environmental Values," *American Economic Review*.

Brookshire, D. S., and D. L. Coursey. 1987. "Measuring the Value of a Public Good: An Empirical Comparison of Elicitation Procedures," *American Economic Review* 77, pp. 555–566.

Burness, H. S., R. G. Cummings, A. F. Mehr, and K. S. Walbert. 1983. "Valuing Policies Which Reduce Environmental Risk," *Natural Resources Journal* 23(3), pp. 675–682.

Cameron, T. A., and M. James. 1987. "Efficient Estimation Methods for 'Closed-Ended' Contingent Valuation Surveys," *Review of Economic Statistics* 69, pp. 269–275.

Coursey, D. L., J. J. Hovis, and W. D. Schulze. 1987. "The Disparity Between Willingness to Accept and Willingness to Pay Measures of Value," *Quarterly Journal of Economics* 102(3), pp. 679–690.

Coursey, D. L., and C. F. Mason. 1987. "Investigations Concerning the Dynamics of Consumer Behavior in Uncertain Environments," *Economic Inquiry* 25, pp. 549–564.

Cummings, R. G., D. S. Brookshire, and W. D. Schulze. 1986. *Valuing Environmental Goods: Assessment of the Contingent Valuation Method*. Totowa, N.J.: Rowman & Allanheld.

Davis, R. K. 1963. "Recreational Planning as an Economic Problem," *Natural Resource Journal* 3(2), pp. 238–249.

Desvousges, W. H., V. K. Smith, and A. Fisher. 1987. "Option Price Estimates for Water Quality Improvements: A Contingent Valuation Study for the Monongahela River," *Journal of Environmental Economics and Management* 14(3), pp. 248–267.

Dickie, M., A. Fisher, and S. Gerking. 1987. "Market Transactions and Hypothetical Demand Data: A Comparative Study," *Journal of the American Statistical Association* 82(397), pp. 69–75.

Dickie, M., S. Gerking, G. H. McClelland, and W. D. Schulze. 1987. "Contingent Valuation: The Value Formation Process," manuscript, University of Wyoming.

Dillman, D. A. 1978. *Mail and Telephone Surveys: The Total Design Method*. New York: John Wiley & Sons.

Doane, M., G. H. McClelland, W. D. Schulze, and C. K. Woo. 1989. "The Value of Electrical Power Outages: A Contingent Valuation Study," report submitted to Niagara Mohawk Electric Power Company.

Edwards, W. 1962. "Subjective Probabilities Inferred from Decisions," *Psychological Review* 69, pp. 109–135.

Fischhoff, B., and L. Furby. 1988. "Measuring Values: A Conceptual Framework for Interpreting Transactions with Special Reference to Contingent Valuation of Visibility," *Journal of Risk and Uncertainty* 1, pp. 147–184.

Hammack, Judd, and Gardner M. Brown, Jr. 1974. *Waterfowl and Wetlands: Toward Bioeconomic Analysis*. Washington, D.C.: The Johns Hopkins University Press for Resources for the Future.

Hanemann, W. M. 1984. "Welfare Evaluations in Contingent Valuation Experiments with Discrete Responses," *American Journal of Agricultural Economics* 66, pp. 322–341.

Hanemann, W. M. 1991. "WTP and WTA: How Much Can They Differ?" *American Economic Review* 81, pp. 635–677.

Irwin, J. R., W. D. Schulze, G. McClelland, D. Waldman, D. Schenk, T. Stewart, L. Deck, P. Slovic, and M. Thayer. 1990. "Valuing Visibility: A Field Test of the Contingent Valuation Method," Environmental Protection Agency Cooperative Agreement No. CR-812054.

Kahneman, D., and A. Tversky. 1979. "Prospect Theory: An Analysis of Decision Under Risk," *Econometrica* 47(2), pp. 263–291.

Knetsch, J. L. 1990. "Environmental Policy Implications of Disparities between Willingness to Pay and Compensation Demanded Measures of Values," *Journal of Environmental Economics and Management* 18(3), pp. 227–237.

Knetsch, Jack L., and Jack A. Sinden. 1984. "Willingness to Pay and Compensation Demanded: Experimental Evidence of an Unexpected Disparity in Measures of Value," *Quarterly Journal of Economics* 94, pp. 507–521.

Loomis, J. B. 1990. "Comparative Reliability of the Dichotomous Choice and Open-Ended Contingent Valuation Techniques," *Journal of Environmental Economics and Management* 18(1), pp. 78–85.

Machina, M. J. 1984. "Generalized Expected Utility Analysis and the Nature of Observed Violations of the Independence Axiom." In *Foundations of Utility and Risk Theory with Applications*, edited by B. P. Stigum and F. Wenstop. np: D. Reidel Publishing Company.

Machina, M. J. 1987. "Choice Under Uncertainty: Problems Solved and Unsolved," *Economic Perspectives* 1(1), pp. 121–154.

McClelland, G. H., W. D. Schulze, and D. L. Coursey. Forthcoming. "Valuing Low Probability Hazards: Evidence for Bimodal Response to Low Probability Events," *Journal of Risk and Uncertainty*.

McClelland, G. H., W. D. Schulze, and B. Hurd. 1987. "A Case Study of a Hazardous Waste Site: Perspectives from Economics and Psychology," report prepared for the U.S. Environmental Protection Agency.

McConnell, K. E. 1990. "Models for Referendum Data: The Structure of Discrete Choice Models for Contingent Valuation," *Journal of Environmental Economics and Management*, 18(1), pp. 19–34.

Mitchell, Robert Cameron, and Richard T. Carson. 1989. *Using Surveys to Value Public Goods: The Contingent Valuation Method*. Washington, D.C.: Resources for the Future.

Morey, E. R., R. D. Rowe, and M. Watson. Forthcoming. "A Repeated Nested-Logit Model of Atlantic Salmon Fishing with Comparisons to Six Other Travel-Cost Models," *American Journal of Agricultural Economics*.

Randall, A., B. Ives, and C. Eastman. 1974. "Bidding Games for Valuation of Aesthetic Environmental Improvements," *Journal of Environmental Economics and Management* 1, pp. 132–149.

Rose, F. 1985. *An American Quest for Artificial Intelligence: Into the Heart of the Mind.* New York: Vintage Books.

Rowe, R. D., and W. D. Schulze. 1987. "Natural Resource Damages in the Colorado Mountains: The Case of the Eagle Mine," paper prepared for Association of Environmental and Resource Economists' session on Assessment of Natural Resource Damages, Allied Social Sciences Associations meeting, Chicago, Ill., December 28–30, 1987.

Schuman, H., and S. Presser. 1981. *Questions and Answers in Attitude Surveys: Experiments on Question Form, Wording and Context.* New York: Academic Press.

Smith, V. K., and W. H. Desvousges. 1987. "An Empirical Analysis of the Economic Value of Risk Changes," *Journal of Political Economy* 95, pp. 89–114.

Thayer, M. A. 1981. "Contingent Valuation Techniques for Assessing Environmental Impacts: Further Evidence," *Journal of Environmental Economics and Management* 8, pp. 27–44.

Tversky, A., and D. Kahneman. 1981. "The Framing of Decisions and the Psychology of Choice," *Science* 211, pp. 453–458.

Tversky, A., and S. Sattath. 1979. "Preference Trees," *Psychological Review* 86(6), pp. 542–573.

Willig, R. D. 1976. "Consumers' Surplus Without Apology," *American Economic Review* 66, pp. 589–597.

11

Contingent Valuation and the Legal Arena

Richard T. Carson and Robert Cameron Mitchell

1. INTRODUCTION

Is the contingent valuation (CV) method sufficiently mature and reliable to be used in natural resource damage litigation? That question fundamentally differs from the question: Does contingent valuation, in principle, work? The latter question must be answered in the affirmative. In chapter 10 of this volume William D. Schulze addresses the current state of the art of contingent valuation. Cummings, Brookshire, and Schulze (1986) and Mitchell and Carson (1989) discuss at some length how and why the CV method works. Since the *Ohio v. The United States Department of the Interior* decision in 1989,[1] the method's detractors have been in a much weaker position than they were during the initial formulation by the Department of the Interior (DOI) of rules for natural resource damage assessment under the Comprehensive Environmental Response, Compensation, and Liability Act of 1980 (CERCLA).[2] Hundreds of contingent valuation studies have now been completed, and the number of studies using contingent valuation is increasing at a more rapid rate than valuation studies using other nonmarket techniques.[3] If asked by a judge, an economist as an expert witness for either plaintiff or defendant would have to say that contingent valuation is now clearly a method that many experts routinely rely upon as a base for their judgments.

---

[1]880 F.2d 432 (D.C. Cir. 1989). The *Ohio* ruling by the D.C. Circuit Court is fairly unusual among federal circuit rulings in the depth of its consideration of an economic valuation technique.

[2]42 U.S.C. 9601–9675.

[3]Appendix A of Mitchell and Carson (1989) provides short summaries of more than one hundred of these studies.

The question of whether the CV method should be used in natural resource damage litigation is somewhat more difficult to answer. While successful CV studies are easy to find, the results of other contingent valuation studies seem implausible. This is to be expected. Any nascent methodology requires a certain amount of time to develop its basic operational principles. That period has passed for contingent valuation and a sizable corpus of information is available on contingent valuation techniques. However, the information is neither widely known nor widely disseminated among economists, for whom survey research is in general an unfamiliar or uncongenial way to gather data. Furthermore, these techniques are not yet routinely taught at the graduate level and contingent valuation, unlike many techniques of economic analysis, requires extensive practice. Contingent valuation is also susceptible to failure because of the great expense of conducting a CV study properly. Contingent valuation's apparent simplicity may lull the inexperienced into the belief that a study may be conducted cheaply with little development effort. An underfunded study is likely to be a poorly developed and poorly executed survey whose results lack reliability and validity.[4]

In any event, reliability and validity are relative concepts at best. A fair assessment of all nonmarket valuation techniques used during the last decade is that none of them automatically produce reliable and valid answers.[5] A certain amount of art is required to assess the value of a natural resource. For hedonic pricing and travel cost analysis, this art is shown primarily in econometric specification; for contingent valuation, it is shown largely in the form of wording of questions. In both cases the problem is that natural resources do not and cannot have a true value that is context-independent.[6] Unfortunately, this dependence is not comforting to those lawyers who expect economists to come up with *the* answer rather than *an* answer or, even worse, a range of answers. What the analyst can

---

[4]In the worse cases, failure is willfully courted by ignoring principles well established in the field. This failure is often used by the responsible party to claim that the method is fatally flawed.

[5]Opponents of nonmarket valuation and contingent valuation, in particular, use this assessment to argue that no attempt should be made by economists to value natural resource damages. Indeed, it is suggested in some quarters that nonmarket valuation should be left entirely to judge and jury, that values given to natural resources by resource economists are worse than useless—they are misleading. This suggestion—that a state-of-the-art nonmarket valuation study is not relevant—runs counter to common sense. Without such a study the fact-finder is left with only his own experience to help him determine the value of the resource.

[6]Economics as a profession is to a large degree based on the concepts of substitution effects and income effects that make all economic valuations context-specific. See Hoehn and Randall (1989) for a discussion of this issue as it applies to benefit-cost analysis.

do is eliminate or reduce many of the sources of uncertainty and, more important, explain to a lay audience the determinants of the range of estimates.

Preparing a contingent valuation study for a legal proceeding is a challenging task, in part because of the high standards of evidence that are likely to prevail in such a proceeding, in part because a judge or jury is more likely to understand the criticisms leveled against a contingent valuation study than the highly technical econometric criticisms likely to be raised against a travel cost or hedonic pricing analysis. However, the conceptual simplicity of contingent valuation is also an advantage, as its method of obtaining the valuation estimate may be much more intuitive to a judge or jury than are the other nonmarket techniques.

The issue remains whether the method can be applied to particular natural damage cases in such a way that its findings stand up in court. We agree with Schulze that the method can be so used provided suitable attention is devoted to the methodological challenges. Our disagreements with Schulze involve, for the most part, matters of emphasis.[7] For example, while we agree that the existence of crystallized opinions about the resource may facilitate the valuation effort, we add a couple of caveats. First, having direct experience with the amenity being valued does not necessarily imply that a respondent has a preexisting value for the amenity. Since the amenity is not bought or sold, the act of placing a dollar value on the resource may be unfamiliar, regardless of any extensive personal experience with the resource. Even if personal experience with the amenity aids the valuation process, it may also distort it. For example, personal experience may increase the likelihood of strategic behavior on the part of local residents who imagine that the survey will be used to impose costs on the corporate malefactor that they believe is responsible for the damage. We believe that the whole notion of reference operating conditions has clouded the key issues in contingent valuation without providing any useful guideposts for those evaluating a contingent valuation study.[8]

---

[7]One technical point over which we disagree with Schulze is on the ease of correcting for starting-point bias (see Carson, Casterline, and Mitchell [1985]). We also disagree with Schulze's view that in-person contingent valuation interviews are often strongly influenced by interviewer bias. We have seen no evidence of this phenomena with well-trained interviewers of the major survey organizations, nor does the survey literature suggest that we should. That we have so few disagreements of this sort with Schulze is one indication of how much the method has matured over the last ten years.

[8]The reference operating conditions arrived at by Cummings, Brookshire, and Schulze (1986) are as follows: (1) subjects must understand (be familiar with) the commodity to be valued; (2) subjects must have previously had (or be allowed to obtain) valuation and choice experience with respect to consumption levels of the commodity; (3) there must be little

In section 2 of this chapter we consider some aspects of natural resource damage cases that can make the design and implementation of a natural resource damages contingent valuation survey an exceptionally formidable task. We take as a given that the defense will attack the contingent valuation scenario in the plaintiff's survey as vague, will attack the depiction of the physical injury as more serious, permanent, or far-ranging that it is in actuality, or will suggest that the injury is due to a pollution source other than that for which the defendant is responsible.[9]

2. IMPLICATIONS OF NATURAL RESOURCE DAMAGE CASES FOR CONTINGENT VALUATION STUDIES

A contingent valuation scenario is of necessity an abstraction and a sim-plification of a very complicated situation. Most CV surveys to date have been restricted to a single environmental medium, either air, surface wa-ter, groundwater, or land, and often to a single pollutant. This restriction allows the researcher the maximum opportunity to inform the respondent about the situation without creating information overload. Natural re-source damage cases, such as the Eagle River case discussed by Raymond J. Kopp and V. Kerry Smith in chapter 7 of this volume, often involve multiple dimensions (such as the discoloration of a river and loss of a trout fishery), thereby complicating the task of communicating the nature of the good to the respondent. However, if the CV survey is to value only one of the several dimensions, the survey instrument must be designed to ensure that the respondents do not include some of the other dimensions in their willingness-to-pay (WTP) amounts. Getting a respondent to value only a single dimension is often a difficult task, in some cases perhaps an impos-sible task.

Another characteristic that makes damage estimates difficult is the site-specific nature of the physical injury. To place a dollar value on the injury, one must conceive of the natural environment in its pre-injury, or baseline, state and reconstruct the services it might have provided. The

---

uncertainty; and (4) willingness to pay measures, not willingness to accept measures, must be elicited. Schulze correctly notes that reference operating conditions 3 and 4 deal with issues not specific to contingent valuation. We would prefer to restate the first two reference operating conditions as saying that respondents should clearly understand what they are being asked to purchase, and should find the institutional/market structure in which that good will be provided to be plausible. Both of these notions make common sense.

[9]There are contingent valuation surveys against which the defense would be correct in making such attacks. It is incumbent upon the plaintiff's scientific experts to establish that the physical injury described in the plaintiff's contingent valuation scenario is not exaggerated.

CV scenario attempts to convey this information, but reading certain words to respondents does not necessarily mean that they will understand the words as intended. For example, if respondents lack personal experience with the site, the effort required to conceive how much and what quality of swimming experience the site would provide may tempt them to express a dollar value for a generalized site for a generalized cleanup. If the site is associated with such symbolically charged attributes as fishing, nature, toxic chemicals, wildlife, and the like, the image that people conceive may well have a higher value to them than the actual site-specific amenity they are intended to value (see Fischhoff and Furby [1988]).

Another frequent difficulty in damage assessment is the requirement that the valuation is of an injury to a natural environment that does not have implications for human health. Here the potential problem is that when respondents are told to value damages caused by toxic chemicals to aquatic species or groundwater resources, they may find it difficult to put aside health concerns. Even aesthetic impacts such as the discoloration of a river may evoke a feeling in some respondents that the situation must pose a health threat to humans. To the extent that respondents include health benefits in their value estimates, an upward bias will result. This problem is not limited to contingent valuation; travel cost analysis and hedonic pricing will suffer the same upward bias if people behave as if health effects are present. Contingent valuation raises the possibility that the dollar values that respondents give can be assigned to different motives in some unique and defensible way. Unfortunately, while economics has much to say about how people are willing to trade off dollars as a function of their preferences, the discipline has long disavowed any ability to answer questions as to why people have the preferences they do. Contingent valuation potentially has the ability to blur this distinction, but the legal arena is not the place to test the ability.

The original DOI rule effectively forced researchers into the business of determining motives by its dictum that, in most instances, only use values could be considered. This dictum put those engaging in contingent valuation in the position of either asking respondents to give only use values or asking for total value (the sum of use and nonuse values), and then separating out use values. Both approaches are usually doomed to failure. Respondents may not be capable of giving an amount that only includes use value, and any decomposition of total values must have a large degree of arbitrariness to it.[10] The problem is not with contingent valuation but rather with trying to measure only use value. Such a measurement is largely meaningless from the point of view of a natural re-

---

[10]Decomposing total value is difficult, like asking a person how much their car would be worth without a transmission, or their bread without a crust.

source damage assessment since total value, not use value, is the economic measure of the injury. The D.C. Circuit Court in *Ohio* ruled that the estimate of damages should include both use and nonuse values. This ruling eliminated one of the major impediments to the application of contingent valuation to natural resource damage assessment.

The defense is likely to argue that respondents to a CV survey engaged in strategic behavior. While strategic behavior is not likely to be a problem in a typical CV study (see Mitchell and Carson [1989]), it may be a problem in a study done for litigation. Here, familiarity with the site may create its own problem. The potential difficulty is that those who are familiar with the site, usually local residents, are also likely to be aware of who caused the damage and, possibly, that the government is pressing that party to pay for a cleanup. This knowledge sets the stage for possible strategic behavior. In some instances a closely related amenity for which strategic considerations do not loom as large should be valued instead.

Often no unambiguously correct solution is available for many of the design choices the CV researcher faces. Therefore, we advocate the use of an explicit design rule for making choices of questionnaire design such as the choice of the payment vehicle or the description of the damage. A conservative rule for the plaintiffs would be to make these decisions in such a way that if one reasonable choice about a scenario element would potentially increase the WTP amount and the other reasonable choice would potentially reduce it, the latter is chosen. For example, given a choice between asking for the WTP amount in the form of either a monthly or an annual payment, the annual payment would be preferred on the grounds that it maximizes the respondent's awareness of the financial implications of his dollar amounts and therefore, if anything, is likely to lower the amount.[11] The consistent application of this rule would result in an aggregate benefit estimate that can serve as a lower bound. Trustees for the resource would be well advised to adopt such a rule to enhance credibility of their CV estimates. Defendants may well be advised to follow the opposite tack in studies they commission.

3. DESIGN AND IMPLEMENTATION OF A VALID RESEARCH INSTRUMENT

The most important aspect of designing a valid and reliable contingent valuation study is to understand how and why the survey instrument works. Such an understanding generally cannot be acquired in a short

---

[11]In many instances it is both possible and desirable to make the respondent aware of his payment obligation on both a monthly and an annual basis.

period of time without great expense. Because of the difficulties of designing a valid research instrument, extensive preliminary research is necessary. This research will require some sort of qualitative field work, most likely using focus groups, to understand how people think about the resource and how they respond to scenario elements. Once a draft instrument is prepared, it must be tested until respondents find it understandable, plausible, and meaningful.

Increasingly, contingent valuation researchers are turning to discrete choice questions that ask for a yes or no answer to a specified dollar amount in order to simplify the respondent's cognitive task. When the amenity to be valued is close to a pure public good, this discrete choice question is often explicitly cast in a referendum context. These two features result in an incentive-compatible question. For this reason they simultaneously reduce the likelihood of strategic behavior and the impact of such behavior by any agent. Unfortunately, instead of eliciting actual valuation responses, such questions elicit only a discrete indicator of the agent's valuation. As long as the purpose is to estimate the distribution of economic valuation in the population of interest, this causes no problems because both the continuous and discrete valuation responses measure the same thing. Of course, discrete choice responses contain less information than the actual values elicited from the same sample of agents.[12] As a result, to achieve the same level of efficiency in estimating a summary statistic for the distribution, such as mean or median willingness to pay, this elicitation format requires either larger samples or much stronger statistical assumptions on the shape of the underlying distribution of values.[13]

In some circles, contingent valuation results have been characterized as vulnerable and as hearsay evidence because they are based on a survey of the public.[14] Contingent valuation surveys, however, are not different from non-CV surveys in this regard. Survey findings have long been accepted as evidence in courts provided they "meet the tests of necessity

---

[12]Cameron and Huppert (1989) show that the payment card, a method that appears to elicit an agent's actual willingness to pay, may be best thought of as eliciting willingness to pay lying in an interval between two amounts marked on the payment card. By analogy, their argument applies to the bidding game, and the direct question is undoubtedly subject to rounding behavior. (On the payment card and bidding game methods, see Mitchell and Carson [1989]). Thus, the difference between a discrete choice response and a so-called continuous response should be seen as a matter of degree—that is, the size of the interval in which the agent's willingness to pay lies.

[13]See Alberini and Carson (1990) for a discussion of optimal designs for discrete choice contingent valuation questions.

[14]Hearsay evidence in its simplest form is the recitation in court by one individual of statements made by another individual out of court. Such evidence is not admissible unless it qualifies as one of a number of exceptions.

and trustworthiness" (Federal Judicial Center, Board of Editors [1978], Section 2.712). Survey findings are frequently admitted into evidence in discrimination, antitrust, and product safety cases. The standard of evidence for surveys required in these cases is very strict, and few contingent valuation surveys to date have met them. The adversarial nature of litigation makes it imperative that the party conducting a CV survey for use in a natural resource damage case exercise extreme care in the design and execution of the survey.

The execution of a CV survey for use in a court case must meet the highest standards of survey research in order to withstand the attacks by the opposing side's experts. The sampling frame chosen, the training of the interviewers, the response rate, and the coding and data entry of the questionnaires will be attacked. As Zeisel (1978) has commented on presenting survey results as evidence: "The discovery of but one serious flaw may endanger the entire piece of evidence; the doctrine of *falsus in uno, falsus in omnibus* is sometimes the ground for not believing a witness's entire testimony if it is found to be untrue in a single instance, and such a flaw may also hurt the expert witness who presents the survey evidence" (p. 1119). Such a contingent valuation study would be costly to conduct: the sample would have to be carefully selected using a probability-based sample design; the sample size would have to be quite large; and each step of the research process would have to be meticulously documented. A widely respected survey firm should be retained to draw the sample and administer the survey. Devoting a great deal of resources to executing the survey does not usually result in estimates greatly different from those obtained in the much less expensive survey execution typical of policy studies, but the risk of obtaining a grossly aberrant estimate is much less and the courts appear to place great weight on minimizing such a possibility. Contingent valuation researchers are well advised to refuse to conduct a survey "on the cheap" if they are expected to defend the results in court.

In particular, we believe that mail surveys of the general public, while the least expensive method of survey administration, may be particularly difficult to defend in a natural resource damage case.[15] Besides having greater vulnerability to strategic behavior, mail surveys have two

---

[15]This statement should not be taken to apply to an ex ante contingent valuation mail survey conducted for a government agency and extensively used for policy purposes by the agency before the natural resource damage occurs. In such a case it can be argued that the agency was explicitly making decisions about the resource on the basis of the valuation indicated by the contingent valuation study. The ideal situation would be for a trustee agency to have established the value of the resources entrusted to it in advance of any possible damage, using the highest-quality contingent valuation techniques.

additional problems. First, those who return the survey are self-selected from those who receive it. Because those who receive the survey can read the instrument before they decide whether to fill it out, those who decide not to return it may be disproportionately uninterested in the topic and thus likely to hold lower values for the damage than others with the same socioeconomic characteristics. Therefore, those who return the survey may not represent the true distribution of values in the sample frame. In-person and telephone surveys do not suffer from this problem because the decision whether to participate is usually made before the potential respondent becomes aware of the survey's subject matter.

The second problem is that mail surveys rely on the ability of the respondents to read and understand the description given in the scenario. This ability is questionable for a significant portion of the general public, as shown by the findings of the National Assessment of Educational Progress, which conducted a study of literacy among a national sample of 3,600 young adults between the ages of 21 and 25. Among other findings, the study found that 6 percent were unable to read a short sports story in a newspaper, 20 percent could not read as well as the average eighth grader, and 37 percent could not present the main argument in a newspaper column (Kirsch and Jungeblut [1986]). These criticisms of mail surveys may not apply to mail surveys of specialized populations who enjoy higher than average levels of education and interest in the good being valued.

4.   CONCLUSION

The conceptual strategy of developing an appropriate CV survey involves the decisions made by the researcher about such matters as the resource to be valued, the magnitude of the physical injuries involved, the choice of property right structure, and the sampling frame. These decisions must be justified in terms of the facts of the situation, economic theory, and methodological appropriateness. In this light we wish to make three concluding comments on natural resource damage assessment in a legal setting. The first concerns the choice of the nonmarket valuation technique to be used. The second concerns the choice of the sampling frame—a problem that has received far too little attention. The third concerns the choice of willingness to pay versus willingness to accept as the measure of damages.

The concept of a hierarchy of methods for valuing a natural resource injury as embodied in the original Department of the Interior rules was fatally flawed. A technique preferred under the DOI hierarchy may be totally inappropriate for the situation at hand although it may have been feasible to implement. In other cases, more than one technique may be possible and estimates using more than one technique may be desirable. The court in *Ohio* rejected the DOI hierarchy and directed the agency to revise its rules accordingly. The new DOI rules should provide guidelines as to which techniques are appropriate in which situations rather than mandate a hierarchy of techniques to be used irrespective of the situation. The court's emphasis on total value and its explicit rejection of the proposition that only use values should be measured suggests that contingent valuation will be the technique of choice where nonuse values are important. In situations in which nonuse values predominate, contingent valuation may be the only appropriate valuation technique.

The issue of the sampling frame is important because the greater the population to which the survey estimates are extrapolated, the larger the benefit estimate is likely to be. Should only those who are familiar with the resource be enfranchised? Or should the franchise be extended to include those who lack familiarity with the resource but who have a stake in the damages because their state is the trustee? Because legitimate economic grounds support both approaches, policy guidance from the federal government would be most useful on this issue. The question of the appropriate market arises not only in natural resource cases but in other areas in which law and economics interface—in antitrust cases, for example.

The enabling legislation for the DOI natural resource damage rules clearly suggests a willingness-to-accept (WTA) valuation criterion, while the DOI rules call for the use of a willingness-to-pay criterion. The court addressed the issue of WTP versus WTA and upheld that part of the DOI rule that stated that WTP and not WTA should be measured. DOI's argument in favor of WTP was twofold: that theoretically little difference exists between WTP and WTA and that economists did not have techniques to accurately measure WTA. While the former argument has been shown to be false for the types of situations likely to characterize natural resource damage cases, the latter argument still holds true. In both contingent valuation surveys and experiments with actual money, WTP and WTA often differ radically; and none of the nonmarket valuation techniques at this point in time are capable of directly measuring WTA.

The use of WTP rather than WTA was previously justified by an appeal to Willig's (1976) results, which suggested that theoretically the difference between the two criteria should be small. Cognitive psychologists (Kahneman and Tversky [1979]) have presented theories explaining the large observed differences; and an economist (W. Michael Hanemann [1991]) has shown theoretically that for imposed quantity changes, such as natural resources injuries, the difference between WTP and WTA can be arbitrarily large. This is so because the difference depends on the ratio of income and substitution elasticities rather than on income elasticity alone, as under Willig's analysis of the difference between WTP and WTA measures for a price change.[16]

Whether the courts will uphold the use of WTP in a revised DOI rule in the face of substantial theoretical differences between WTP and WTA amounts remains to be seen. As a practical matter, WTP may be the only reliable measure achievable; and the courts may be willing to sustain the use of WTP merely on the grounds that is a reasonable implementation of congressional intent. Nevertheless, WTP is less than WTA. While this discrepancy will not disturb potentially responsible parties, neither will WTP fully compensate the public as Congress intended.

The power to remedy the situation lies in the hands of DOI in redrafting the natural resource assessment rules and ultimately in the hands of Congress. Economists cannot directly provide an estimate of the quantity desired by Congress. Economists can provide a lower-bound estimate of the desired quantity; the less unique the resource, the closer the WTP estimate will be to the desired WTA estimate. In some instances Hanemann's results may be used to estimate an agent's WTA amount from his WTP response to a contingent valuation survey. This would be the best solution from an economist's perspective. Another solution is allow courts the option of assessing punitive damages, a traditional remedy for an intentional breach of a property right.[17] However, punitive damages are normally reserved for intentionally unlawful behavior. Although one tends to think of the allocation of these costs to the potentially responsible parties as punishment, that allocation is instead merely a decision as to who should be the direct bearer of the burden. CERCLA is remedial by design, forcing those who profited from activities leading to the release of hazardous substances to bear the resultant costs to society. While DOI may seek to polish its justifications, it is left with only one solution—the current one, which does not strictly fulfill the statutory mandate for WTA. Unless Congress acts to correct this disparity, the issue will be handled by the courts in the current crop of post-*Ohio* cases.

---

[16]In most instances, the theories of the cognitive psychologists and Hanemann are observationally equivalent, with the psychologists' theories providing an explanation for the magnitude of an agent's perceived substitution elasticity, which drives Hanemann's results.

[17]The difference between WTP and WTA is one of property rights. In the case of injury to public resources, the difference is between whether the public should pay the firm not to pollute the public resource (WTP) or whether the firm should pay the public to be allowed to pollute the public resource (WTA).

REFERENCES

Alberini, Anna, and Richard T. Carson. 1990. "Choice of Thresholds for Efficient Binary Discrete Choice Estimation," Discussion Paper 90-34, Department of Economics, University of California, San Diego, Calif.

Cameron, Trudy A., and Daniel Huppert. 1989. "OLS vs. ML Estimation of Nonmarket Resource Values with Payment Card Interval Data," *Journal of Environmental Economics and Management* 17, pp. 230–246.

Carson, Richard T., Gary Casterline, and Robert Cameron Mitchell. 1985. "A Note on Testing and Correcting for Starting Point Bias in Contingent Valuation Surveys," Discussion Paper QE85-11, Quality of the Environment Division. Washington, D.C.: Resources for the Future.

Cummings, Ronald G., David S. Brookshire, and William G. Schulze. 1986. *Valuing Environmental Goods: An Assessment of the Contingent Valuation Method*. Totowa, N.J.: Rowman and Allenheld.

Federal Judicial Center, Board of Editors. 1978. *Manual for Complex Litigation*. Chicago, Ill.: Commerce Clearing House.

Fischhoff, B., and L. Furby. 1988. "Measuring Values: A Conceptual Framework for Interpreting Transactions with Special Reference to Contingent Valuation of Visibility," *Journal of Risk and Uncertainty* 1, pp. 147–184.

Hanemann, W. Michael. 1991. "WTP and WTA: How Much Can They Differ?" *American Economic Review* 81, pp. 635–647.

Hoehn, John, and Alan Randall. 1989. "Too Many Proposals Pass the Benefit Cost Test," *American Economic Review* 79, pp. 544–551.

Kahneman, D., and A. Tversky. 1979. "Prospect Theory: An Analysis of Decision Under Risk," *Econometrica* 47, pp. 263–291.

Kirsch, Irwin S., and Ann Jungeblut. 1986. "Literacy: Profiles of America's Young Adults," National Assessment of Educational Progress Report No. 16-P1-02. Princeton, N.J.: Educational Testing Service.

Mitchell, Robert Cameron, and Richard T. Carson. 1989. *Using Surveys to Value Public Goods: The Contingent Valuation Method*. Washington, D.C.: Resources for the Future.

Willig, R. D. 1976. "Consumers' Surplus Without Apology," *American Economic Review* 66, pp. 589–597.

Zeisel, H. 1978. "Statistics as Legal Evidence," in *The International Encyclopedia of Statistics*, edited by W. H. Kruskal and J. M. Tanur. New York: Free Press.

Part 3

Two Key Conceptual Dimensions of Damage Assessment

Introduction to Part 3:
The Roles of Time and
Nonuse Values in
Damage Assessment

Natural resource damage liability has changed the rules for those involved in activities that could (or did) result in releases of hazardous substances and oil. The collective description of the background, implementation, uniqueness, and measurement of this liability should now be clearer than it was at the beginning of our discussion. We believe that the effects of such liability on the direction of research in resource and environmental economics (and very likely on future policies) will be important. At our conference in June of 1988, two elements of natural resource damage liability were singled out for special attention. Since then, both court rulings and changes in the Department of the Interior rules have reinforced our decision that these elements—the role of time (especially discounting) and the definition and measurement of nonuse values—warranted special attention. They are discussed in the next two chapters.

The timing of releases of hazardous substances or oil and, in turn, the treatment of time as part of damage assessment have several important implications. First and perhaps most notably, the Comprehensive Environmental Response, Compensation, and Liability Act and the Superfund Amendments and Reauthorization Act established a retroactive liability: certain activities that were legal before 1980 can now be subject to natural resource damage liability. Moreover, before District Judge Young's decision in the *Acushnet River & New Bedford Harbor* case,[1] the damages from that liability (to the extent that injuries began before 1980 and continued after than date) could be accumulated during time when the liability had not yet been established. His decision clarifies whether damages can count before 1980. In chapter 12, Ralph C. d'Arge discusses the mechanism to be used in establishing liability—divisible or indivisible damages.

---

[1]District Court, District of Massachusetts, *Acushnet River & New Bedford Harbor: Proceedings Re Alleged PCB Pollution*, No. 83-3882-y, "Memorandum Concerning Natural Resource Damages Under CERCLA," District Judge Young, June 1989.

While Judge Young cites aesthetic injury as a potential example of an indivisible damage, he does not offer guidance as to whether this should be interpreted by the temporal pattern of the values lost. With use-related values, the benefits people receive are tied to their use of the resource. Consequently, a parallel can be expected between the temporal pattern of use and the corresponding pattern of use values. With nonuse values, this need not be the case. An episodic or short-term injury to a resource may imply very different damages for people than one that is long term or effectively irreversible. But the temporal pattern of realization of those losses may be quite similar to that in the use-value case, with the greatest loss experienced soon after the injury has occurred and is known. Does this mean that both types of injuries are divisible in time?

Natural resource damage liability acknowledges that resources are natural assets and that public agencies serve as trustees for these resources. As d'Arge observes, once the trustee knows the period of time over which to calculate past damages and knows the nature of the restoration plan that will determine the extent of future damages, the trustee must capitalize the past damages and discount the future damages. Early in this volume, Brown argued that there is no justification for differences in the conceptual bases applied in determining the rates to be used for capitalization and discounting. This does not mean that the numerical value of the rate actually used would be the same. If, for example, one accepts the real rate of interest as a measure of the public's rate of time preference, there is a simple distinction between capitalization and discounting. Capitalization refers to time intervals that have passed, while discounting refers to those in the future. For the former, we know what the real rates were, while for the latter we do not know with certainty how the rates might evolve. Of course, we should recognize that the conceptual rationale for using the real rate to describe how people evaluate tradeoffs over time usually argues that people's rate of time preferences remain relatively constant (given that the "representative" person's position in the life cycle is held constant), and that we should therefore expect relatively constant real rates in the future. However, as d'Arge acknowledges, economists are now reevaluating their conception of appropriate discount rates for public investment decisions, and we can expect their findings to influence how discounting is evaluated for damage assessment.

The second topic given special attention—nonuse values—has been described by many as "fuzzy" or "in flux" for all but the entrenched cognoscenti of resource valuation theory. A. Myrick Freeman, in chapter 13, systematically documents the definitions of components of nonuse value and describes the evolution of the literature. From the vantage of a clear taxonomy of the valuation concepts, he then discusses measurement, including what we can expect from indirect and direct methods as well as whether the existing literature has successfully measured nonuse value. He concludes by noting that the literature has not provided a basis for judging the relative size of use and nonuse value (and because this literature reflects research conducted prior to the current work supported by ongoing litigation, we do not know how the findings of this litigation-supported research would change his judgment). His chapter concludes with suggestions for future research, to which we turn in our closing chapter.

12
Marking Time with CERCLA: Assessing the Effect of Time on Damages from Hazardous Wastes
Ralph C. d'Arge

1. INTRODUCTION

The Comprehensive Environmental Response, Compensation, and Liability Act of 1980 (CERCLA),[1] and its reauthorizing amendments, the Superfund Amendments and Reauthorization Act of 1986 (SARA),[2] are among the most dramatic pieces of legislation regarding quantitative assessment of natural resource damages ever enacted in the United States. The sequence of events from legislatively defined mandates for damage assessments to development of rules by the Department of the Interior (DOI) on how to prepare such assessments, to court challenges, and ultimately to a decision by the U.S. Court of Appeals for the District of Columbia Circuit has required nearly a decade.[3] While a number of cases have been initiated under the statutes, revised DOI rules have not yet been

I wish to thank V. Kerry Smith, Raymond Kopp, Anthony Fisher, and A. M. Freeman III for comments on an earlier draft. The conclusions, opinions, and policy recommendations contained in this chapter are solely attributable to me.

[1]42 U.S.C. 9601–9675.

[2]Pub. L. No. 99-499, 100 Stat. 1613.

[3]Shortly after the DOI rules for type B assessments were issued, ten states, three environmental organizations, a chemical trade association, a manufacturing firm, and an electric utility petitioned for judicial review of the rules. These petitions were combined in one case: *Ohio v. The United States Department of the Interior*, 880 F.2d 432 (D.C. Cir. 1989). The case was presented before the District of Columbia Circuit Court of Appeals on February 22, 1989, and the court's ruling was issued on July 14, 1989.

issued and I anticipate that it will require more time and experience before the full process of natural resources damage assessment is understood, clarified, and made practicable by the courts. Potentially of greatest significance, the court of appeals decision has modified common tort law to include consideration of hazardous waste releases occurring years and decades ago and "harm to future" uses of the environment even when the identity of future damaged parties (much less the extent of individual damages) is unknown, and has widened the definition of loss beyond simple market price calculations (see Boland and Milliman [1987]).

A 1989 pretrial ruling by District Judge Young in *In re Acushnet River & New Bedford Harbor*—a case involving alleged polychlorinated biphenyl (PCB) contamination of a portion of New Bedford harbor in Massachusetts[4]—modified some of these issues by considering when recoverable damages begin and what classes of damages are recoverable at different points in time.[5] Specifically, Judge Young stated that "where natural resource damages are readily 'divisible' the sovereigns [trustees] cannot recover for such damages incurred prior to enactment [of CERCLA]" (Young, "Memorandum," p. 19). However, even with this ruling it is apparent that current statutes and decisions broaden the domain and time dimension of responsibility for hazardous waste releases and oil spills.

Historically, economists have utilized the framework of benefit-cost analysis for evaluating and assessing dollar losses and gains from public actions. The history of the implementation of benefit-cost analysis in public investment and regulatory evaluations is long and at times tortuous. These applications were primarily undertaken to assess the economic efficiency of projects (for example, whether the benefits would exceed the costs of building a new water storage reservoir), as opposed to providing a basis for estimating past and future societal losses from emissions of harmful substances. The guiding objective in such benefit-cost analysis was to evaluate an action that was potentially valuable to society in the present and future by comparing an estimate of the potential net benefits with the actual current costs of obtaining them. The comparison was between *potential* present and future net benefits and present costs.[6] The past, by definition, was excluded.

---

[4]722 F. Supp. 893, 897 (D. Mass. 1989).

[5]United States District Court, District of Massachusetts, *Acushnet River & New Bedford Harbor: Proceedings re Alleged PCB Pollution,* Civil Action, No. 83-3882-y, "Memorandum Concerning Natural Resource Damages under CERCLA," District Judge Young, June 7, 1989; hereafter cited as Young, "Memorandum."

[6]The terminology "potential net benefits" is deliberate. It implies that both future benefits and future costs are uncertain at the time of the decision. They are described as being compared with what is more certain—current costs. In actual practice all benefits are

Benefits accruing over future time were discounted relative to current benefits to reflect individuals' rate of time preference. People value dollars received at some future date less than they value dollars received today. A dollar of benefits received in one year would be worth only 90¢ a year later if the relevant discount rate was about 10 percent. While there are exceptions, especially for decisions involving time horizons extending over multiple generations, the discounting process of future net benefits relative to current values has been accepted by most economists as a meaningful and logical analytical tool (See Solow [1986], Spash and d'Arge [1989]).

Disagreement continues as to the appropriate rate of discount applicable under various circumstances. The major questions regarding the appropriate rate are: Are there social rates other than private, market-based rates, and if there are, how can they be measured? Should the opportunity cost of capital be utilized in lieu of a meaningful social rate, and if that cost is to be applied, how should it be measured? If there are recognizable structural failures in private capital markets, how should such imperfections influence the choice of a discount rate? If the funds used are drawn from different sectors of the economy, how can the differential impact on employment, consumption, investment, taxes, and growth be captured in adjustments to the appropriate rate? That is, if the opportunity cost of public investment varies in cost to the economy depending on origin of funds, how can this difference be imputed within the measurement of opportunity cost of public investments?[7] Can risk or uncertainty be adequately reflected by suitable adjustment of the discount rate, or is it better to modify the methods or measurement for each application? These and other related issues continue to provide grounds for disagreement among economists as to the appropriate discount rate(s) for evaluating future benefits and costs. Indeed, Lind (1990) has called for a reevaluation of discount rate policy. Lind argues that changes in the world economy, especially the international integration of capital markets, raise questions about earlier conclusions based on models that evaluate public investments in the context of a closed economy.

Similar issues undoubtedly will be confronted by the courts in evaluating future natural resource damages. But CERCLA introduces an added dimension to the traditional economic evaluation problem, namely,

---

combined and all costs are combined (with appropriate discounting). Nonetheless, in many project evaluations this approach led to comparison of known costs (because they were primarily incurred at the outset of a project) with uncertain future benefits.

[7]There is a substantial literature on these and related questions that considers the appropriate rate of societal discount and how to measure it. The reader is referred to the most complete discussion available in Lind and coauthors (1982). See especially chapters 2 and 3 of that book.

consistent evaluation of past as well as current and future damages. In this case, however, one must consider whether damages to natural resources are divisible or indivisible. If they are indivisible, one must consider how these damages will be measured. If they are divisible, past damages begin in 1980 (the date of enactment of CERCLA).

To deal consistently with the temporal dimensions of past and future damages requires the selection of a process for determining the discount rates appropriate to assessing past and future damages in some consistent metric. One such process would be to apply the same predetermined discount rate to both the past and the future. One can argue that such a "simple price of time" will adequately reflect current price and will not discriminate against either the past or future. Such an approach is likely to be more reasonable if the time frame is narrow. For example, if natural resource damages have occurred only in the past three years and will end in three more years, a single discount rate would seem most appropriate. However, if the damages extend five years into the future and extend back ten years into the past, a single discount rate may be less compelling. Further, there is no widely accepted theoretical economic model to deal with Judge Young's indivisible category of damages.

This introduction provides a framework for analyzing time discounting problems and possible solutions. Section 2 outlines the process of time discounting as stipulated in the provisions of CERCLA and SARA, the DOI rules, and the court of appeals decision. Section 2 also briefly analyzes the process and requirements stipulated by CERCLA for considering valuation of the past and future. Section 3 contains a brief ethical discussion examining CERCLA tradeoffs. Section 4 offers tentative policy and research recommendations along with several conclusions on the proper implementation of CERCLA damage assessments related to time.

2.   CERCLA APPLICATION OF TIME DISCOUNTING

How does CERCLA evaluate and extend the issues of appropriate time horizon and discount rates prescribed in economic analysis? To measure the current economic value of what was lost from injury to a natural resource, considering both services impaired in the past and those affected in the future, we must measure all past, current, and future damages, regardless of time of occurrence, and convert them to a present value utilizing an appropriate set of discount rates or time weights. A single discount rate is often selected as both a matter of convention and principle. A simple equation describes this conversion:

$$PV_n = \sum_{t=0}^{n-1} D_t (1 + r)^t + \sum_{t=n+1}^{\tau} F_t \left[\frac{1}{(1+r)^t} \right] + D_n, \qquad (1)$$

where past damages are capitalized forward to the present and future damages are discounted backward to the present, and both are added to current damages. D_t denotes damages occurring in the past at time t; F_t denotes damages occurring in the future at the time t; D_n denotes current damages; r is the preselected discount rate appropriate for both past and future damage evaluations; and PV_n denotes the present value of future and past sums. The relevant time horizon commences at time $t=0$ and ends at $t=\tau$. From the standpoint of economic analysis, the time at which damages should first be measured is when they first occurred, and consideration of the monetary value of damages should cease when loss in service stops.

How does the CERCLA process compare with this relatively straightforward economic accounting system? There are three major time-related issues: choice of discount rate, determination of the starting point when damages commenced, and determination of the future point at which damages are no longer evaluated. CERCLA, according to the U.S. Department of the Interior *Rules and Regulations* (hereafter referred to as the *Rules*), specifies that the appropriate real rate of discount is 10 percent.[8] This implies a monetary discount rate in excess of 13 percent per annum, if we assume 3 percent inflation. This greatly exceeds current long-term government bond yields in the 7.5 to 8.0 range.

The 10 percent real rate was one of the issues raised by the challenge to the DOI rules. The court's decision avoided the technical economic issues involved in selecting a discount rate and upheld the 10 percent requirement. The reasoning underlying this decision was that CERCLA requires a lump sum payment to cover future costs of restoration. Because this rate must consider market rates of return and inflation, the court found no grounds to challenge the 10 percent real requirement.

A further problem with this ordained discount rate is that it is inconsistent with other economic methodologies identified in CERCLA, including replacement cost and use value. Use values are to be measured by "diminution of the market price" in reasonably competitive markets.[9] Replacement cost is to be measured by the cost "to restore or replace the lost or disrupted [resource] services in a cost-effective manner."[10] Both of these values or costs are measured as outcomes of efficient competitive markets, yet the mandated discount rate is not. Thus, by definition

---

[8]51 *Federal Register* 27690 (August 1, 1986). *Rules and Regulations,* Final Rule, Natural Resource Damage Assessments. This rule is restated on page 27750. The citation is Office of Management and Budget Circular A-94, revised as the appropriate source for stipulating a 10 percent real rate.

[9]51 *Federal Register* 27691.

[10]51 *Federal Register* 27690.

CERCLA advocates the use of or mixing of competitive prices with a mandated price of time much different than the current competitive price. What does this two-price system do to damage assessments in a practical sense? Since the mandated real discount rate is almost double what it should be from a competitive pricing viewpoint, it strongly biases the economic evaluation toward overvaluing the past and ignoring the future. For example, the present value, using a 10 percent discount rate, of $1.00 in damages in 1980 is now $2.72, while the value of damages in 2020 of $2.72 is now approximately 14¢. Mechanically applying a high real discount rate makes future damages almost valueless in relation to historical damages. It may have influenced the "choice" of a real rate in practice. For example, in early analyses associated with *State of Colorado v. Idarado Mining Co.*,[11] much of the damage was asserted to have occurred in the past and a 10 percent rate was applied for part of the time for capitalization (see Bolland and Milliman [1986]). In contrast, in another case, where future impacts dominated the calculation of damages, a 3 percent real rate was selected (see Freeman [1988]). Such choices are likely to inflate the actual damage measures. A discount rate that exceeds the opportunity cost of capital tends to inflate past damages relative to future damages. A discount rate below the opportunity cost, alternatively, tends to inflate future damages relative to past damages. It is interesting to speculate whether some discount rate exists that effectively evaluates both past and future damages in an efficient and equitable manner. I am skeptical that such a single rate exists if for no other reason than that drifts in time preferences between generations will cause the correct rate to change.

A second problem in CERCLA is the selection of a date when damages commenced. These issues have been recast somewhat by Judge Young's decision in the *Acushnet River & New Bedford Harbor* case. According to the *Rules*, "recovery time" for the resource service flow injured by the release of hazardous substances must be calculated. Before Judge Young's decision there was some ambiguity as to when damage calculations should start. Except for damages occurring entirely prior to enactment of CERCLA in 1980, which are noncompensable under the statutes, one interpretation of the law would have held that damages began when the injury first occurred. Nonetheless, one can also find examples of confusion on this issue. Moreover, there appears to be substantial variation in the damage calculations in cases involving hazardous substances where the timing of initial releases and injury extends into the past. The only governing regulations in DOI's initial proposed rules were associated with situations in which damages occurred completely before 1980. For

---

[11]707 F. Supp. 1227 (D. Colo. 1989).

other situations, decisions on the starting dates appear to be based on what can be measured with "reasonable cost" together with a requirement of a "measurable adverse change to the resource"—that is, documented injuries. In most CERCLA cases I suspect that these two criteria would preclude compensation for past damages that occurred prior to scientific measurement or other reliable measures of reductions in service flows unless a low-cost way is discovered to accurately simulate the more distant past.

Judge Young's pretrial ruling *In re Acushnet* concerns the time period for the accrual of natural resource damages. At least two aspects of this decision are important to the definition of the time frame for damage assessment. First, Judge Young defined the "occurrence of damage" to coincide with additional expenses incurred by some party as a result of the injury caused by a release of hazardous substances. For example, Judge Young's memorandum specifically notes that it is important to distinguish between "damages" and "injury" to a natural resource and to define the term "occurred." One of the defendants argued that damages occur when injury occurs. Judge Young's memorandum explaining the decision rejects this interpretation, noting that

> . . . although no monetary impact due to PCB contamination of the mud at the bottom of the Harbor may have been felt until after enactment by a property owner, for example, when that owner incurred additional expenses during the building of a wharf due to the expense of disposing of contaminated dredge spoils, the "damages" had "wholly occurred" prior to enactment because the mud had become contaminated . . . i.e., the injury to the natural resource has occurred . . . prior to enactment. The Court rejects this view and holds that "damages" . . . i.e., the monetary quantification of the injury done to the natural resources . . . "occur" as a general rule when the property owner in this example, or some entity as a general rule, incurs expenses due to the injury to natural resources . . . i.e., when the owner seeks to develop the waterfront property. (Young, "Memorandum," pp. 12–13)

Judge Young's decision draws a distinction between "divisible" and "indivisible" damages. Divisible damages are capable of being estimated on a daily basis. He uses the example of the added expenses incurred by lobstermen in the form of fuel expenses, labor costs, and the like due to the longer trips required to avoid areas contaminated with PCBs. In such cases the trustees of the resource cannot recover divisible damages that occurred prior to enactment of CERCLA. Thus, for one component of damages the ambiguity about when to begin accruing damages is resolved.

For indivisible damages Judge Young's decision rules that

> In cases where the natural resource damage[s] are not divisible and the damages or the releases that caused the damages continued post-enactment [of CERCLA], the sovereigns [the trustees] can recover for such non-divisible damages in their entirety. (Young, "Memorandum," p. 20)

The third major time-related issue under CERCLA concerns the point at which damages are no longer evaluated. From the perspective of economic analysis, damages should be counted until they cease. Under CERCLA, this could be until unmitigated compensatory damages are paid to the trustee and/or restoration costs are incurred and restoration is finished. This time period could last from one to ten years. If irreversible or irreparable harm, such as PCB loadings in rivers or estuaries, has occurred, then the compensatory damages in the form or reduced service flows could continue almost indefinitely into the future. With a high discount rate, the value of distant irreversible damages would be exceedingly small in the present. For example, one thousand cancer deaths valued at $1 million each in one hundred years would be worth a total of $72,564 currently at a 10 percent real rate. If the public trustee calculates that damages will continue almost indefinitely into the future, it is in the trustee's interest to substantiate a very low discount rate.

Judge Young used the case of aesthetic injury to provide a possible example of an indivisible damage. The decision does not provide guidance on how to monetize injuries leading to indivisible damages. If the injuries initiate with the release and extend through the date of enactment, are not time-dated, but do lead to a stream of losses over time, should they be capitalized? This is the same question that faces all damage assessment for all classes of past damages prior to the judge's ruling. To the extent that there are substantial indivisible damages that nonetheless have annual monetary values, there will remain important issues about the implications of choosing a discount rate that functions as a rate both for capitalization (of past indivisible damages) and for discounting future damages in the absence of restoration of the resource to its baseline conditions.

In summary, CERCLA, the DOI rules, and the court of appeals decision all identify the appropriate real rate of discount to be 10 percent; nevertheless, to date there appears to have been some flexibility in the application of this rate in individual cases. It is important to recognize that many of these cases were initiated when the status of the DOI *Rules* and the court of appeals decision were not known. Now that the decision has returned the *Rules* to DOI for changes in some provisions and new proposed rules have been used, while no changes have been made in the treatment of the discount rate, it is not clear how damage assessments in future cases will deal with the discount rate. Judge Young's decision partly resolves the question of how far back the capitalization of past damages should go for those damages treated as divisible. It introduces a new set of issues associated with the classification of damages into the divisible and indivisible groups. These issues are relevant to the capitalization question because measurement of indivisible damages could well be argued to involve a stream of losses over time that do not relate to activities that are divisible over time. In such cases, the questions associated with selecting a rate for both capitalization of past and discounting of future damages remain important.

3.   ETHICS AND CERCLA DAMAGES

CERCLA, as applied to mining activities, imposes a relatively straightforward ethical criterion. This criterion is simply that the present is to compensate the future for the past. Restoration costs and some past damages will be paid in the present. The benefits of these expenditures will largely accrue to future generations, unless of course the courts decide to award damages to currently damaged private citizens. How fair is CERCLA to the various generations? It has been observed that different ethical criteria—such as those based on Rawls, Pareto, and utilitarianism—have distinctly different implications for the social rate of discount to be selected; that is, implementation of one ethical criterion will result in an implied social rate of discount while another will yield a distinctly different rate (see d'Arge, Schulze, and Brookshire [1982]). Thus, the choice of a social rate of discount depends on underlying ethical beliefs. Such a set of implicit beliefs is implied by the U.S. Department of the Interior's selection of a particular rate appropriate for past, present, and future damages. [12]

In recent years there has been substantial evidence that individuals have distinctly different private rates of discount depending on age, wealth, type of consumer or durable good purchased, and other factors (see Hausman [1979], Brookshire and coauthors [1979], and Case [1986]). There is also evidence that the desire or preference for valuing what happens to future generations emanates from a long list of individual motivations such as religious beliefs, ethical considerations, family

---

[12]The decision by DOI to opt for a 10 percent real rate implies that the past and present count a lot more than the future. If the future is perceived as being better off than the past or present, the DOI choice coincides with a Rawlsian ethic—that is, that the worst off should be made better off. However, if the future is perceived to be worse off than the present or past, the DOI has inadvertently opted for a Nietzchean ethic—that is, that the worst off should be made even worse off.

values, heritage-based beliefs, and just "doing what's right." If the motivations for values placed by present generations on the future and the past are highly diffuse across individuals, we should expect that their rates of time preference (or discount) reflecting these values will also be very different. For example, the subset of individuals who believe with great certainty that there will be no distant future because of nuclear war will have a distinctly different valuation than those who believe otherwise. Finally, if one accepts the idea that collective-choice rules or social welfare measures, inclusive of the social rate of discount, are made of nothing more than individual preferences, then imposing a single social rate of discount is either a dictatorial mandate or an inconsistent social policy.[13]

To restate this argument: individual discount rates are observed to be very different among individuals. Motivations for concern about the future are also observed to be very different. There is also a connection between individual rates of discount (valuing one's own time and assets) and an individual's social rate of discount (valuing society's time and assets); this is, I believe, a testable hypothesis. If the social rate of discount is determined solely by individuals' social rates, then there is likely to be no single social rate of discount, but rather an array of appropriate rates applicable to different groups, times, and types of commodities. There is some limited evidence of this likelihood in regard to ozone depletion and long-term depletion of oil reserves (see Brookshire and coauthors [1979] and Case [1986]).

I suspect that social rates of discount applicable to the past will differ strikingly from those for the future because of differences in fundamental human motivations. The past is history. No amount of wishful thinking or decisionmaking can change it. Thus, many ethical and religious beliefs are not highly motivating or even relevant. Some individuals, in a social sense, may value the past more than the present or future, but the norm is probably that the present is valued higher than the future, which is valued higher than the past.[14] Further, the appropriate real rates of discount should reflect these valuations, and both the future and past rates should be valued lower than the present. That is, a relatively low discount rate is implied if past damages are valued lower than current values. A higher discount rate is implied if future damages are valued lower than the present. And to value future damages higher than past damages, all else being the same, indicates that the discount rates are selected such that the

---

[13]On "natural" assumptions for collective choice rules, see Arrow (1951).

[14]I am suggesting here a definition of the social rate of discount that is very different from the one that evolves out of modern growth theory, where individual preferences are assumed to be identical or assumed away entirely and where a simple tradeoff relation exists between present and future consumption in a continuously existing society (see Dasgupta [1982]).

present value of past damages is smaller than the present value of future damages, for an identical amount of past and future damages.

In a highly informative paper, Talbot Page has argued that the discount rate question is fundamentally different than the question of intergenerational efficiency or equity (Page [1988]). He argues persuasively that questions on discount rates arise at three distinct levels: the level of estimating the feasible production and consumption set, the level of individual preference orderings, and the level of social choice rules inclusive of decisions affecting future generations. The arguments made above on the appropriateness of different discount rates are relevant only for Page's first two levels.

If one can accept, at least for the sake of argument, the tentative conclusion that different rates of discount are appropriate for damage assessment, then at least four distinct discount rates for CERCLA cases seem to naturally emerge. These four are identified as the distant past rate (r_{dp}), near past rate (r_{np}), near future rate (r_{nf}), and distant future rate (r_{df}). Treating each rate in real terms, we would anticipate that

$$r_{dp} \leq r_{np} \geq r_{nf} \geq r_{df} \qquad (2)$$

We should also anticipate that for intergenerational choice problems involving irreversibilities and no transfer payments or mechanisms for transfer, r_{df} would be exceedingly low, if not zero.[15] Except for the rate of inflation (which would be relevant for nominal versions of these rates), near-term future and near-term past discount rates should be similar in magnitude. However, if individuals tended to value even the near-term past at lower levels than they value the near-term future, we should anticipate that, in real terms, r_{nf} would be low, but r_{np} would be even lower.

What are the major determinants of the magnitude of these various discount rates? First, since we are typically examining damages to identifiable individuals rather than widely diffuse public benefits or costs, it appears that one important determinant of r, as identified earlier, is the individual or group being damaged. If damages occurred to some identifiable group in the near past and we desire to express that in terms of present value of damages to the group, the appropriate rate is their near-term discount rate. Likewise, for distant past damages, the appropriate rate is for those affected groups. Unfortunately, if this group lived in the distant past, it may be difficult, if not impossible, to even guess at a reasonable discount rate. In this case, perhaps the appropriate rate would be the present generation's social rate applied to the distant past. For near-term future damages, the desired rate would be the one for the damaged

---

[15]Mishan and Page (1982) have argued that ethically there are circumstances where future generations should be treated on an equal basis with the present.

group or individual. And the most appropriate measure of the rate for the distant future, since this is completely unknown, would be the present generation's preferences regarding distant future rates. The appropriate rate by time depends on a logical blending of the damaged group's rate of time preference with the present generation's preferences in valuing past and future natural resource damages.

I suspect that with normal private and public goods, and with natural resource damages to these commodities, the appropriate rate of discount will tend to remain the same as one moves toward the distant past and future. If the commodities damaged involve catastrophic effects on life, health, wealth, and ecosystems, the discount rates should tend to decrease, in terms of present preferences for the past and future (until they equal zero in some extreme cases).

In summary, different individual discount rates are readily observed. Different individual social rates of discount have also been observed, depending on the nature of future impact or the commodity. If societal rates of discount solely reflect individual social rates of discount, we should expect the societal rate also to vary. Thus, a constant social rate of discount applicable to both the past and the future is unlikely to truly represent societal preferences. Because natural resource damages are being assessed, it appears appropriate that the discount rate of the injured parties be employed where known. In the absence of this, a discount rate properly representing the present generation's preferences regarding the past and future, and differentiated by type of commodity, time horizon, and damage, must be analytically justified before application.

4.   RESEARCH AND POLICY RECOMMENDATIONS

The magnitude of natural resource damages, and thus the legal liability of firms for such damages, varies markedly depending on the discount rates and time horizons selected. Since economists have substantial difficulty agreeing on the appropriate rate of discount, the appropriate magnitude of actual future and past natural resource damages is difficult, if not impossible, to estimate. The differences in opinion among economists as to the appropriate discount rate has not lessened in recent years.[16] Further, questions remain regarding the treatment of temporal damages for indivisible categories of damage. It is also reasonable to expect that there will be considerable debate over what is and what is not a divisible damage in future CERCLA cases.

---

[16]For an overview, see articles contributed from Association of Environmental and Resource Economics meetings in the special March 1990 issue of the *Journal of Environmental Economics and Management*, vol. 18, part 2.

More generally, if economic damage measures and calculations are to be considered by the courts, the courts should insist on substantive proof of the accuracy of past and future damage estimates. Such proof would have to include convincing evidence documenting the past time horizon and the magnitude of past damages. There should be at least two independent approaches substantiating the magnitude of the estimate of past damages. For example, an estimate based on hedonic price could be compared with one based on contingent valuation. Consistency checks should also be performed. Thus if past estimated damages per capita exceed personal income per capita for a particular year, some doubts should arise as to the estimate's accuracy. It is also doubtful, except in unique cases, that environmentally based indivisible damages would extend back in time before the beginning of the general population's environmental awareness, say around 1967. Willingness-to-pay calculations for this early period should be significantly below those for the present, because of lower incomes and lower environmental awareness. Monetary damages and the discount rate should be treated consistently. If damages are estimated in current dollars, then the discount rate should be the nominal rate. When damages are measured in real terms, the real rate of discount is relevant.[17]

For future damages, again compelling independent evidence should be required to establish the existence of damages extending more than five years into the future. In some CERCLA cases where irreversibilities are not a fundamental problem, restoration can be essentially complete, or damages are totally reversible, the calculation of future damages is relatively straightforward. The appropriate rate of discount should be a real one and, if at all possible, should reflect the time preferences of those injured. For more extended damage assessments, detailed evidence on the probable accuracy of the damage estimates must be set forth. This should include economic evidence on the stability of future preferences and on the likelihood that prices used in estimating damages will remain relatively constant and that technological change is unlikely to substantially alter future damages. If uncertainty persists as to the magnitude of future damages, the courts may wish to consider the possibility of requiring an annual payment on damages, adjustable as evidence accumulates, rather than a lump sum payment at the conclusion of the trial. Such an annual payment would be derived from the court's best updated estimate of natu-

---

[17]It is interesting to note that Boland and Milliman (1987) appear to reverse this logic by utilizing a 2.5 percent rate for 1956–1975 and then a 10 percent rate thereafter. Such rates imply a negative real rate over some years, when inflation is considered. This is also true in the *New Bedford* case where in Judge Young's "Memorandum" a 3 percent rate is applied for the period 1980–1985. I am indebted to Dr. Ronald Cummings for this observation.

ral resource damages. Perhaps review and adjustment every five years would suffice until the courts are able to accurately assess remaining damages.

Past damages expressed in nominal terms can be assessed using monetary discount rates that are known today, because it can be observed how such rates reflect historical inflation rates. Future damages measured in real terms should be discounted with a real rate. Thus, logically the two rates can differ. At issue is consistent treatment of the effects of inflation and changing rates of time preference. An alternative equivalent strategy would be to use two distinct real rates—for the past, a rate that is lowered by the inflation rate, and for the future, a higher rate estimate based on anticipation of the real rate of time preference. For example, if the historical average inflation rate over the past damage time horizon was 5 percent, then the real rate of discount implied by using a 10 percent nominal discount rate is 5 percent. Thus, a 5 percent real discount rate is applied to the past. Use of a 10 percent nominal rate for the future would require that the damage estimates incorporate some assumed rate of increase in the general price level. The simplest way to avoid differences in nominal and real rates is for all past, present, and future damages to be expressed in real terms, commencing at the time damages are first assessed. For example, if natural resource damages commenced in 1956, then past, present, and future damages should be converted to present prices, and capitalized forward or discounted backward using a real rate of discount. The *Rules* currently do not specify this process, or when other procedures are to be used.

My final recommendation to the courts is that a variety of discount rates should be examined for estimating past and future natural resource damages separately. A relatively high rate will render substantial future damages almost valueless and a low rate will similarly undervalue distant past damages.

Court evaluation of economic principles and measurement techniques is often more exacting and demanding than are the requirements of referees of journal articles. If nothing else, CERCLA has raised a plethora of research questions that must be answered. Mistakes in logic or computation are not easily disposed of by publishing errata or contacting relevant parties. Errors in assessment cannot be dismissed as merely the fault of an errant graduate student when thousands or millions of dollars may change hands on the basis of the outcome. Economic research into nonmarket values, travel time values, or contingent valuation questioning procedures is no longer merely an intellectual exercise for researchers. Now such research must be responsive to the discipline of real markets designated through the adversarial process of the courtroom.

Among the important research questions confronting economics is the degree of uncertainty regarding past, present, and future environmental preferences. How have environmental preferences changed over time? Are individual, market-related discount rates appropriate for valuing past environmental damages? New experiments must be designed to yield compelling evidence on the accuracy of current nonmarket valuation techniques. Tests for the accuracy of these techniques must be devised, beyond those called for by the broad guidelines currently available in the literature. We must question whether the whole apparatus established for assessing benefits and costs of government investment programs is appropriately transferable, without substantive conceptual modification, to problems of public damage assessment, where conceptual or measurement errors can have serious implications for individual firms or citizens.

REFERENCES

Arrow, K. J. 1951. *Social Choice and Individual Values*. New York: John Wiley & Sons.

Boland, J. J., and J. W. Milliman. 1986. "Economic Damage Report: Idarado Mining and Milling Complex," report prepared for the State of Colorado.

Boland, J. J., and J. W. Milliman. 1987. "Overview of CERCLA Natural Resource Damage Procedures: Uses and Misuses of Economic Theory." Paper presented at the Joint Association of Environmental and Resource Economists–American Economic Association session, Chicago, Ill., December.

Brookshire, D. S., A. Randall, R. C. d'Arge, L. S. Eubanks, J. R. Stoll, T. D. Crocker, and S. Johnson. 1979. *Methodological Experiments in Valuing Wildlife: Phase 1 Interior Report*. University of Wyoming, Laramie, for the U.S. Fish and Wildlife Service.

Case, J. C. 1986. "Contributions to the Economics of Time Preferences," Ph.D. dissertation, University of Wyoming.

d'Arge, R., W. Schulze, and D. Brookshire. 1982. "Carbon Dioxide and Intergenerational Choice," *American Economic Review* 72 (3), pp. 251–256.

Dasgupta, P. 1982. "Resource Depletion, Research and Development, and the Social Rate of Discount." Chapter 8 in *Discounting for Time and Risk in Energy Policy*, edited by R. C. Lind. Baltimore: The Johns Hopkins University Press for Resources for the Future.

Freeman, A. M., III. 1988. "Assessing Damages to Marine Resources: PCBs in New Bedford Harbor." Paper presented at the Joint Association of Environmental and Resource Economists–American Economic Association session, Chicago, Ill. December 19.

Hausman, J. A. 1979. "Individual Discount Rates and the Purchase and Utilization of Energy-Using Durables," *Bell Journal of Economics* 10 (1), pp. 34–54.

Lind, R. C. 1990. "Reassessing the Government's Discount Rate Policy in Light of New Theory and Data in a World Economy With a High Degree of Capital Mobility," *Journal of Environmental Economics and Management* 18 (March), pp. S8–S28.

Lind, R. C., K. J. Arrow, G. R. Corey, P. Dasgupta, A. K. Sen, T. Stauffer, J. E. Stiglitz, J. A. Stockfisch, and R. Wilson. 1982. *Discounting for Time and Risk in Energy Policy*. Baltimore: The Johns Hopkins University Press for Resources for the Future.

Mishan, E., and T. Page. 1982. "The Methodology of Benefit-Cost Analysis with Particular Reference to the CFC Problem." In *The Economics of Managing Chlorofluorocarbons: Stratospheric Ozone and Climate Issues*, edited by J. H. Cumberland, J. R. Hibbs, and I. Hoch. Baltimore: The Johns Hopkins University Press for Resources for the Future.

Page, T. 1988. "Intergenerational Equity and the Social Rate of Discount." In *Environmental Resources and Applied Welfare Economics: Essays in Honor of John V. Krutilla*, edited by V. K. Smith. Washington, D.C.: Resources for the Future.

Sen, A. K. 1970. *Collective Choice and Social Welfare*. San Francisco: Holden-Day.

Solow, R. M. 1986. "On the Intergenerational Allocation of Natural Resources," *Scandinavian Journal of Economics* 88 (1), pp. 141–149.

Spash, C. L., and R. C. d'Arge. 1989. "The Greenhouse Effect and Intergenerational Transfers," *Energy Policy*, April 1989 special issue, pp. 88–96.

13

Nonuse Values in Natural Resource Damage Assessment

A. Myrick Freeman III

1. INTRODUCTION

The hypothesis that underlies this chapter is that people can place on natural resources monetary values that are independent of their present use of those resources. Thus, if human activities lower the quantity or quality of resources, people can experience losses. For example, people might experience a loss if they knew that the Grand Canyon had been flooded by a dam, even though they never expected to visit the canyon. Or people might be willing to pay to assure the survival of whales, eagles, or other endangered species, even though they never expect to see one of them. If people hold values of this sort and the resources are damaged, they have experienced an economic loss.

Natural resource values that are independent of people's present use of resources have been variously termed "existence values," "intrinsic values," "nonuser values," and "nonuse values." These values are said to arise from a variety of motives, including a desire to bequeath certain environmental resources to one's heirs or future generations, a sense of stewardship or responsibility for preserving certain features of natural resources, and a desire to preserve options for future use. The irreversibility of some environmental changes, such as extinction of a species or destruction of a unique scenic resource or ecological system, has been a key component in most discussions of nonuse value.

I think that a majority of economists working in the field of environmental and resource economics accept the concept of nonuse values, at

Research on this chapter was begun during my visiting appointment at the Robert M. LaFollette Institute for Public Affairs, University of Wisconsin, Madison. I am grateful to the institute for this support. I also acknowledge the helpful comments and suggestions of Raymond J. Kopp, V. Kerry Smith, and W. Michael Hanemann.

least in principle, and that many believe that nonuse values can be great in the aggregate, at least in some circumstances. Where nonuse values are significant, ignoring them in natural resource policymaking can lead to serious errors and resource misallocations. And failure to incorporate losses to nonuse values in natural resource damage assessments can defeat the purpose of assigning liability and collecting damages under the Comprehensive Environmental Response, Compensation, and Liability Act of 1980 (CERCLA).[1] Beyond this, however, I think there is very little agreement among economists as to terminology, definitions, what motivates people to hold nonuse values, and methods for measuring changes in these values empirically.

In this chapter I address five major topics related to the role of nonuse values in natural resource economics, and specifically address the assessment of damages to natural resources resulting from pollution and other human activities. In section 2, I review the concepts of nonuse values that have appeared in the literature. A number of different definitions and classifications of nonuse values have been offered. A brief review of how the questions of definition and classification have been treated in the literature will set the stage for section 3, which focuses on the development of a comprehensive framework for defining and measuring nonuse values.

Section 4 is concerned with the role of various types of uncertainty in the valuation of natural resources and specifically whether uncertainty can be viewed as a source of nonuse values, and if so, under what circumstances. In section 5, I explore the development of empirical techniques for the measurement of nonuse values, addressing the question of whether it is possible to derive measures of nonuse values from observations of individual behavior in a market setting in the same way that it is possible (at least in some circumstances) to do so for use values. I also consider the use of contingent valuation methods to estimate nonuse values.

In the concluding section, I briefly review the results of efforts to measure nonuse values in specific cases. The objective is to see whether the hypothesis of significant nonuse values is supported by the available empirical evidence. Several studies have reported nonuse values to be a very large percentage of total values (see Fisher and Raucher [1984] and Sutherland and Walsh [1985]). Do these studies offer reliable evidence in support of the hypothesis of significant nonuse values for natural resources?

2.   CONCEPTS OF USE AND NONUSE VALUES

In this section, I present a brief review of the various approaches to classifying values and the reasons offered in the literature for holding

---

[1]42 U.S.C. 9601–9675.

values that are independent of the use of a resource. There is no agreed-upon set of definitions, terms, and classifications concerning these values.

A typical approach in the literature is to distinguish between those who use the resource, for example by visiting a recreation site or observing a natural wildlife population, and those who do not. The values held by the latter group are termed nonuser values (see Fisher and Raucher [1984] and Greenley, Walsh, and Young [1981]). An alternative approach is to define use value as the economic value associated with the in situ use of the resource. Total value is an individual's willingness to pay to preserve or maintain the resource in its present state. If total value exceeds use value, the difference is variously termed "preservation value," "intrinsic value," "existence value," or "nonuse value." One feature of this latter approach is that it explicitly allows for the possibility that users as well as nonusers might hold values that are independent of the use of the resource.

Several authors have chosen one of the above terms to represent the whole of the difference between total value and use value and then identified various possible components of this total. For example, Fisher and Raucher (1984) use the term "intrinsic value" to refer to the aggregate, and they state that the total intrinsic value is the sum of option value, aesthetic value, existence value, and bequest value. Sutherland and Walsh (1985) use the term "preservation value" to refer to the aggregate, and they state that it is the sum of option, existence, and bequest values.

The variety of terms and concepts used in the literature can be explained at least in part by the fact that many authors have been concerned to explain why there may be nonuse values of various sorts. Thus they have discussed motivations and used different terms to describe the values associated with each possible reason for holding a nonuse value. For example, in justification of pure existence value, Krutilla suggests that "an option demand may exist . . . not only among persons currently and prospectively active in the market for the object of the demand, but among others who place a value on the mere existence of biological and/or geomorphological variety and its widespread distribution" (Krutilla [1967], p. 781). In an accompanying footnote, he also suggests that the "phenomenon discussed may have an exclusive sentimental basis, but if we consider the bequest motivation in economic behavior . . . it may be explained by an interest in preserving an option for one's heirs to view or use the object in question" (Krutilla [1967], p. 781, note). Later, Krutilla and Fisher wrote:

> In the case of existence value, we conceived of individuals valuing an environment regardless of the fact that they feel certain they will never demand in situ the services it provides . . . however, if we acknowledge that a bequest motivation

operates in individual utility-maximizing behavior . . . the existence value may be simply the value of preserving a peculiarly
remarkable environment for benefit of heirs. (Krutilla and
Fisher [1975], p. 124)

While Krutilla and Fisher offer a bequest motivation as one of several
possible explanations for a pure existence value, McConnell (1983) takes
a different point of view:

The notion that a good is valued only for its existence, that it
provides no in situ services, is far fetched. In most cases, resources are valued for their use. Existence value occurs only
insofar as bequest or altruistic notions prevail. We want resources there because they are valued by others of our own
generation or by our heirs. Thus use value is the ultimate goal of
preferences that yield existence demand, though the existence
and use may be experienced by different individuals. (McConnell [1983], p. 258)

It is also possible that people conceive what are essentially existence
values out of an ethical concern for the status of nonhuman species. While
ethical philosophers are not in agreement as to the validity and proper
form of such concerns, it is possible that some people hold such values
and are willing to commit resources on that basis (see Norton [1982],
Sagoff [1980], Rescher [1980], and VanDeVeer and Pierce [1986]).

I question the amount of attention given to the problem of motivations in the literature. Motivations do not play an important role in the
empirical analysis of the demand for market goods. There is little talk of
"prestige value" or "speed value" in the literature on the demand for
automobiles. So why should identifying and classifying motivations be
important in the case of nonuse values? Arguments about motivations
seem to be offered for the primary purpose of persuading the reader of the
plausibility of the hypothesis that nonuse values are positive. But the real
test of this hypothesis will come from the data. Rather than further debat-
ing definitions and possible motivations, I believe it would be more useful
to proceed with a test of the hypothesis that nonuse values (defined in a
way that makes testing of the hypothesis feasible) are positive. If the
evidence supports this hypothesis, then further research could be devoted
to testing hypotheses about the determinants (motivations) of the size of
nonuse values in different cases. But then the choice of terms and explanatory variables will be governed by what are empirically meaningful
distinctions.

Weisbrod (1964) first introduced the term "option value" into the literature of benefit-cost analysis. Option value is often classified as a nonuse
value (see Sutherland and Walsh [1985]). It is said to arise either when an

individual is uncertain that he will demand the use of a resource in the future or if he is faced with uncertainty about the future supply or availability of that resource. Weisbrod apparently viewed the existence of positive option value as intuitively obvious. More recent analyses have shown that option value as conventionally defined can be either positive or negative, depending on the particular circumstances (Schmalensee [1972], Bishop [1982], Smith [1983], and Freeman [1984b]). More important, these analyses have shown that what has been called option value is not really a separate component of value. Rather, option value is the algebraic difference between resource values defined from two different perspectives—an ex ante perspective yielding option price as the appropriate measure of value and an ex post perspective yielding expected consumer surplus as a value measure (Smith [1987a and 1987b]). The presence of uncertainty raises a quite different set of issues in resource valuation from the issues raised in the use-versus-nonuse benefit taxonomy. For this reason the role of uncertainty is treated in a separate section of this chapter.

A major issue in the literature on nonuse values is how to define the use that lies behind use value. The most common approach is to identify some market good or service that is a complement to the resource, as regards consumption, and to define and measure use in terms of the purchased quantity of this complementary good. If the resource is a park, the complementary good is the purchase of travel services to the park. Use of the resource is measured by number of trips purchased. However, this approach to defining use is clearly a simplification of a more complex reality. The physical proximity that one normally thinks of as being an essential part of use can exist independently of the purchase of a complementary good such as travel. For example, people who live within the natural range of an endangered species such as the bald eagle or peregrine falcon can view one of these birds and experience the utility and value associated with the sightings as an incidental part of their daily routine; there is no connection between that kind of use and any market good.

Some people have gone so far as to argue that some kinds of use do not require the physical proximity of the user to the resource. Randall and Stoll (1983), for example, argue that there can be offsite uses, which they label as "vicarious consumption." "Thus," they explain, "we consider the values generated by reading about Q [the resource] in a book or magazine, looking at it in photographic representations, for example, to be use values. Clearly our definition of use includes vicarious consumption" (Randall and Stoll [1983], p. 267). This is essentially what Boyle and Bishop (1987) choose to call indirect use value.

One problem with so-called vicarious uses is that the observable market transaction (for example, the purchase of a nature magazine) often entails the simultaneous or joint use of many environmental resources, so that allocation of the market transaction to specific resources is not possible. Furthermore, vicarious use has the odd feature that use can occur even though the resource no longer exists, as through the viewing of films and photographs. Also, where vicarious use involves information conveyed by photographs and the like, the public-good dimension of information seems likely to virtually destroy any meaningful relationship between observed market behavior and underlying values.

Finally, there is the question of whether the relevant distinction is between use and nonuse or whether it is more meaningful to distinguish between values to users and nonusers. I prefer the use-versus-nonuse distinction because it focuses on the presence or absence of activities involving the resource directly, rather than on the characteristics of the individuals holding the values. There is no logical reason why a user of a resource could not also hold values that are independent of that use and related to preservation, existence, or bequest motivations. By definition, nonusers of a resource can hold only nonuse values, but users may hold both use and nonuse values for a resource.

This discussion of the possible definitions of and motivations for various types of use and nonuse values is inconclusive. Definitions can be considered in part a matter of taste. A set of definitions can be considered useful if it furthers research objectives and leads to useful answers to meaningful questions and if the definitions are based on operationally meaningful distinctions. If, by definition, use values are limited to those associated with in situ use as measured by purchase of a complementary good, then this has the virtue of distinguishing between cases where use of a resource generates observable market data and cases where no meaningful data can be obtained by observing market transactions. However, if use value is defined in this way, then vicarious or indirect uses as well as what I would call incidental uses must be lumped together with the various types of nonuse values. On the positive side, as the theoretical analysis will show, when use is defined in terms of the consumption of a complementary good, there is a well-developed empirical methodology for estimating use values on the basis of observed market behavior. However, the values associated with incidental and vicarious uses share with nonuse values the characteristic that they probably can be measured only through some form of contingent valuation method.

3. A THEORETICAL FRAMEWORK

In this section I present a general model of individual preferences that does not distinguish between use and nonuse values. Such a distinction can only arise when one imposes additional structure on the individual's preferences by making assumptions. I then consider various ways of defining use and their implications for measuring use values as a separate category of value. I next impose additional structure on preferences to identify various forms of nonuse value. Finally, I take up some questions involving the temporal dimension of nonuse values.

Assume that an individual has a preference ordering over a vector of market goods X and some nonmarketed resource R. The individual has no control over the level of R, but takes it as given. R is taken here to be a scalar measure of some characteristic of the environment, such as the population or biomass of some species or the value of some parameter of water quality. In the abstract, R can represent a measure of either a quantity or a quality. The choice of a unit for measuring R has important implications for measurement in practice, but that issue is not addressed here. The assumption that the environmental resource can be described by a single attribute is clearly a simplification. A more realistic model would allow for simultaneous changes in two or more quantitative and/or qualitative characteristics of the resource, but the development of models incorporating more than one environmental characteristic is beyond the scope of this chapter.

The individual maximizes utility subject to the budget constraint given by prices P and income M. The standard measures of welfare change can be derived from the indirect utility function or the expenditure function, or both. The compensating surplus measure of welfare change CS is the difference between the two expenditure levels required to meet the initial level of utility given a change in R from R^1 to $R^2 < R^1$:

$$CS = E(P, R^1, U^1) - E(P, R^2, U^1) \qquad (1)$$

where U^1 is the solution to Max: $U(X, R^1)$ subject to $PX \leq M$. CS is negative for a reduction in R. Similar expressions can be found for the equivalent surplus (see Freeman [1979b and 1985a]). The derivative of the expenditure function with respect to R gives the compensated inverse demand function for R. If these inverse demand functions are known, the compensating and equivalent surpluses can be measured by integrating over the range of change for R. These are measures of total value and do not distinguish between use and nonuse values.

3.1   Weak Complementarity and Use Values. In order to deal with the distinction between use and nonuse values, it is necessary to give additional structure to the model by making some specific assumptions about the nature of preferences. The typical approach is to assume that use can be represented by the purchase of some market good x_1 such that use is defined to be zero when the individual's purchase of x_1 is zero (for examples, see Smith [1987a and 1987b] or McConnell [1983]). Market good x_1 could be a visit to a site for recreation, the rental of a boat for fishing, or the services of a guide for hunting or fishing. It is further assumed that R is an argument in the demand function for x_1 such that an increase in R increases the demand for x_1, all else being equal. However, R is assumed not to be an argument in the demand function for any other goods.

If the conditions for weak complementarity are satisfied, then the total damage associated with a decrease in R is reflected in the compensated demand function for x_1. Two conditions on the utility and demand functions must be satisfied in order to fit Mäler's (1974) definition of weak complementarity. First, there must be a value for p_1, designated as $p_1^*(R)$, such that the compensated demand for x_1 is zero: $x_1 = x_1(p_1^*(R), P, \ldots, R^1, U^1) = 0$. Second, at that price, the marginal utility or marginal welfare of changes in R must be zero. If these two conditions are satisfied, then the value of a decrease in R that shifts the individual's Hicks-compensated demand curve in to the left can be measured by the geometric areas between the two demand curves.[2]

The resource value measured in this way is a use value because it is associated with the use of the resource as measured by the consumption of x_1. The conditions of weak complementarity mean that the individual derives no utility from an increase in R when x_1 is zero—that is, the individual places no value on an increase in R when use is zero. If the second condition of weak complementarity does not hold, the area between the two demand curves is still a measure of use value. But, because the individual derives additional utility from an increase in R when x_1 (use) is zero, there is an additional nonuse value that is not reflected in the demand curves for x_1. If the first condition does not hold, there is no finite price that reduces use to zero, and there is no economically meaningful distinction between use and nonuse values.

3.2   Separability and Use Versus Nonuse Values. An alternative structure for preferences gives rise to a case in which all of the value of a change in R would be deemed a nonuse value, at least if use is defined as consumption of a complementary market good. Suppose that the utility function is strongly separable, with R being the single argument in one of the separable subsets (this is the "hopeless case" described in Freeman [1979b]. Changes in R have no effect on the demand functions for any market goods. And the utility associated with R is independent of the level of use of any market good. Use values as typically defined are therefore zero.

---

[2]See Bockstael, McConnell, and Strand (1991) for a discussion of some of the problems that arise when areas between ordinary (Marshallian) demand curves are used for the purpose of measuring the welfare value of changes in the quantity or quality of R.

But suppose that use is defined in terms of physical contact or proximity and that use is possible without the purchase of any complementary market good. One example of this would be a person who sees members of an endangered species as an incidental part of his or her daily activities. It might be reasonable to model this as a case of separable preferences, since R would not be an argument in any of the market goods demand functions. Given this conception of use, in this case there may be use values. But nothing can be inferred about these values from the demand curves from marketed goods. Thus estimation of this type of use value by indirect methods based on market data will not be possible.

3.3   The Household Production Framework and Types of Use Values.

The household production function provides a useful framework for thinking about how resources affect utility and welfare and what it means to assume that x_1 is a measure of the use of the resource. In the household production framework, the demand functions for market goods are derived demands. Assume that R is an input in the production of only one final commodity z_1. If x_1 is also an input in the production of z_1, then R will be an argument in the ordinary and compensated demand functions for x_1. If x_1 and R are the only inputs in z_1, then the value of R in producing z_1 will be reflected in the derived demand for x_1. If x_1 and R are both essential inputs, then the marginal product of each is zero if the other input is absent. A positive level of input for x_1 is required to utilize R in household production. This is equivalent to saying that the use of R, and hence its use value, is reflected in the level of x_1.

Bockstael and McConnell (1983) have shown that although in general it will not be possible to estimate the household production function from market data, it will still be possible to estimate the values of changes in R through their effects on the derived demand functions for market goods if the conditions of weak complementarity are satisfied. This analysis has shown that even if the conditions for weak complementarity are not satisfied, the use values of R can still be estimated by measuring areas between demand curves for market goods. Violation of the weak complementarity conditions means, in effect, that there are additional values over and above use values that are not reflected in the derived demands for market goods.

One of the advantages of thinking about resource values in the context of the household production framework is the light that it sheds on the nature of what have been called indirect or vicarious use values. It appears that there are two categories of indirect or vicarious values—those that derive from household production and those that derive from market production. If the vicarious use involves the viewing of home-produced films and photos, then the theory suggests that the place to look for measures of indirect use values is in the influence of R on the demands for other inputs in the production of films and photos. If there is a choke price for this indirect use, the use value of changes in R can be measured by areas between the demand curves for these other inputs in home production. Whether the effects of changes in R on the private goods demand functions are strong enough to be detected by ordinary econometric methods is an empirical question.

On the other hand, if indirect or vicarious use takes the form of the viewing of commercially produced films and television programs, or the reading of books and magazines, the source of value for R is in its influence either on the production function or the quality-differentiated demand functions for these marketed goods. If R is an argument in a production or cost function for a market good, then its role is analytically no different from that of air quality in the production of agricultural crops (Adams, Hamilton, and McCarl [1984]). There is a well-developed methodology for estimating the welfare value of changes in R (Freeman and Harrington [1990]). But it seems doubtful that a reduction in the availability of a specific resource would increase the cost of producing the editorial content of films, books, or magazines. So the empirical significance of this approach to measuring values of changes is in question.

It seems reasonable to assume that the demand for a specific magazine or television program will depend in part on the quality and information content of the material presented. But the link between changes in R and changes in the demand for information about a specific resource is complex and may not meet the requirements of the standard models for estimating welfare values from changes in demand. For example, a major pollution event that damages a unique or special resource system may increase the demand for information about the resource; and producers are likely to respond with more articles and programs about that resource. This would constitute an increase in vicarious use, but it could hardly be called a benefit resulting from the damage to the resource.

3.4   Defining Nonuse and Existence Values. In this section, I maintain the assumption that use of a resource is measured by the consumption of a market good x_1 and that x_1 and R are weak complements.[3] I show that within this framework use and nonuse values can be defined in a consistent manner that satisfies an adding-up condition. I also show that if there is some threshold for the resource, it is possible to define an existence value that is distinct from the nonuse value associated with increasing the quality or quantity of the resource above that threshold.

---

[3] I am grateful to W. Michael Hanemann for pointing out errors in an earlier draft of this section of this chapter.

I consider five specific cases that are distinguished by the way in which changes in R and p_1 affect the level of use as measured by x_1. In all of these cases, welfare measures are defined for decreases in R using the compensating surplus definition of welfare change. With appropriate modification, similar conclusions can be reached for increases in R or equivalent surplus measures of welfare change, or both.

Let $R^{\min}$ represent the minimum level of R at which it can be said that the resource exists and is available for use. $R^{\min}$ represents a threshold or minimum viable level of the resource. I begin by defining a range of values for R where the relationship between R and use as measured by x_1 at the current price of x_1 (p_1) has different characteristics depending on whether R is at or below this threshold. My purpose in defining this threshold is to show the distinction between the loss of nonuse values associated with the degradation of a resource that continues to exist and the loss associated with the destruction of a resource (the extinction of a species, the flooding of the Grand Canyon, or the clear-cutting of an old-growth redwood forest).

Assume that the choke price p_1^* is an increasing function of R when $R \geq R^{\min}$. Then:[4]

Condition I. For $0 \leq R < R^{\min}$,
$$x_1 = x_1(p_1, R, U^1) = 0$$
for all $p_1 \geq 0$.

Condition II. For $R \geq R^{\min}$
$$x_1 = x_1(p_1, R, U^1) > 0$$
for $0 \leq p_1 < p_1^*$, and
$$x_1 = x_1(p_1, R, U^1) = 0$$
for $p_1 \geq p_1^*$.

Condition I says that if the level of R is below the threshold, no use would occur even if use were free. This condition can be given a reasonable interpretation in the context of household production. Let utility be a function of commodities Z produced according to a household production function, where inputs include market goods X. Let z_1 (x_1, R) represent the household production function for one of these commodities. Also assume that R and x_1 are inputs in the production of only z_1. Condition I is equivalent to saying that R is an essential input in the production of z_1 and that $R^{\min}$ is the minimum level of R at which positive production of z_1 can be sustained. Thus if R is less than $R^{\min}$, z_1 must be zero and the derived demand for x_1 is zero at all non-negative prices.

---

[4]For notational simplicity, I suppress the term for all other prices.

Under condition II, R is sufficient to sustain production, so that at some non-negative prices for x_1 its demand is positive. The choke price can be interpreted as that price which raises the marginal cost of household production of z_1 to the point where the quantity demanded of z_1 falls to zero.

Let R^1 and R^2 represent the initial and final levels of the resource, with $R^1 > R^2$. We can distinguish between use value and nonuse value and between two forms of the latter that I will call simple nonuse value and pure existence value. The definitions of each form of value and their interrelationships are examined in the five cases that follow.

Case I. This case involves simple nonuse values. Let $p_1' > 0$ be the current market price for x_1. Let $R^1 > R^2 > R^{min}$. And suppose that at p_1' this individual's demand for x_1 is equal to zero both at R^1 and R^2. In other words, p_1' is above this individual's choke price for both R^1 and R^2. This individual is a nonuser of the resource both before and after the decrease in R. The value for the change in R is given by the difference before and after the change in R in the expenditure functions that are necessary to obtain the initial utility level, or

$$CS_N \equiv E(p_1', R^1, U^1) - E(p_1', R^2, U^1).$$

This corresponds to the measure of total value CS defined by equation (1). Note that since use would still be zero if p_1 fell to p_1^*, this can be rewritten as

$$CS_N = E(p_1^*, R^1, U^1) - E(p_1^*, R^2, U^1). \tag{2}$$

Of course, the loss in simple nonuse value as defined here could be either zero or negative, that being an empirical question.

Case II. If the market price for x_1 were to fall below the choke price, there would also be use value. Again, $R^1 > R^2 > R^{min}$. But for this individual, suppose that $p_1' < p_1^*$. The use value of the resource is measured by the increase in expenditure necessary to compensate for an increase in the price of x_1 that reduces the use of x_1 to zero. This value provides a dollar measure of the welfare change associated with the use that takes place at the existing price p_1'. The lost use value of a decrease from R^1 to R^2 is the decrease in the CS associated with x_1 when R changes—that is,

$$CS_U \equiv E(p_1^*, R^2, U^1) - E(p_1', R^2, U^1)$$
$$- E(p_1^*, R^1, U^1) + E(p_1', R^1, U^1). \tag{3}$$

CS_U can be defined only if there is a price that chokes off demand. CS_U is the area between the compensated demand curves for x_1 at the two levels of R.

Now define lost nonuse value, as in equation (2), as that change in expenditure which holds total utility constant, given that the price of visits is so high as to eliminate use of the site:

$$CS_N \equiv E(p_1^*, R^1, U^1) - E(p_1^*, R^2, U^1). \tag{4}$$

According to this definition, lost nonuse values can be negative for potential users and even for those who use the resource when p_1 is less than p_1^*.

A comparison of expressions (1), (3), and (4) shows that these values are related in the following way:

$$CS = CS_U + CS_N$$

$$\text{or} \quad CS = E(p_1^*, R^2, U^1) - E(p_1', R^2, U^1)$$
$$- E(p_1^*, R^1, U^1) + E(p_1', R^1, U^1)$$
$$+ E(p_1^*, R^1, U^1) - E(p_1^*, R^2, U^1)$$
$$= E(p_1', R^1, U^1) - E(p_1', R^2, U^1). \tag{5}$$

If the initial level of R and the price of x_1 are such that use is positive, and if nonuse value is defined in terms of the choke price for x_1 rather than the actual market price for x_1, then use, nonuse, and total values can be defined in a consistent manner that satisfies an adding-up condition. Also, if the conditions for weak complementarity are met, CS_N equals zero and CS_U equals total value CS.

Case III. Now let R^2 be less than R^{min} and R^1 be equal to R^{min}. Also, assume that at $R^1 = R^{min}$ the choke price is equal to the market price $(p_1' = p_1^*)$ so that $x_1(p_1', R^1, U^1) = x_1(p_1^*, R^1, U^1) = 0$.

From equation (1), the total value (loss) of the decrease from R^{min} to R^2 is

$$CS = E(p_1', R^{min}, U^1) - E(p_1', R^2, U^1) < 0. \tag{6}$$

Since $p_1' = p_1^*$, there is no use; so this is a form of nonuse value. Call this a pure existence value CS_E, since it stems from the resource falling below the existence threshold. In order to adequately capture the idea of the threshold and the impact of the loss of existence of the resource when R crosses the threshold, one must assume that the expenditure function is discontinuous in R at R^{min} and that the derivative of the expenditure function with respect to R is zero for $R < R^{min}$.

Case IV. Suppose that, at $R^{\min}$, $p_1' < p_1^*$. Now the change from R^1 to R^2 can cause losses to both pure existence and use values. The loss of value associated with losing the use made possible at the threshold is

$$CS_U = E(p_1', R^{\min}, U^1) - E(p_1^*, R^{\min}, U^1). \qquad (7)$$

The loss of existence value associated with falling below the threshold can be found by subtracting the lost use value (CS_U) from the total loss:

$$
\begin{aligned}
CS_E &= CS - CS_U \\
&= E(p_1', R^1, U^1) - E(p_1', R^2, U^1) \\
&\quad - E(p_1', R^{\min}, U^1) + E(p_1^*, R^{\min}, U^1) \\
&= E(p_1^*, R^{\min}, U^1) - E(p_1', R^2, U^1)
\end{aligned} \qquad (8)
$$

or, since $E(p_1', R^2, U^1) = E(p_1^*, R^2, U^1)$ when use is precluded by nonexistence,

$$CS_E = E(p_1^*, R^{\min}, U^1) - E(p_1^*, R^2, U^1). \qquad (9)$$

This shows that it is possible to define existence and use values in a consistent manner such that total value satisfies the adding-up condition. Also, if weak complementarity holds, CS_E is zero and total value equals CS_U.

Case V. Finally, consider the general case where $R^2 < R^{\min} < R^1$. There is a lost use value given by

$$CS_U = E(p_1', R^1, U^1) - E(p_1^*, R^1, U^1).$$

There is a lost nonuse value given by a revised version of expression (4) ($R^{\min}$ replaces R^2). And there is a lost existence value given by equation (8). These components of value satisfy the adding-up condition, as can be seen by substituting these expressions as follows and comparing the result with equation (1):

$$
\begin{aligned}
CS &= CS_U + CS_N + CS_E \\
&= E(p_1', R^1, U^1) - E(p_1^*, R^1, U^1) \\
&\quad + E(p_1^*, R^1, U^1) - E(p_1^*, R^{\min}, U^1) \\
&\quad + E(p_1^*, R^{\min}, U^1) - E(p_1', R^2, U^1) \\
&= E(p_1', R^1, U^1) - E(p_1', R^2, U^1).
\end{aligned}
$$

This analysis has shown that, in the general case in which there is a threshold value for R, the total value of a decrease in R that crosses that threshold is the sum of three components:

- a loss of use value because of crossing the threshold that makes use no longer possible;
- a loss of simple nonuse value associated with degradation of R down to the threshold; and
- a loss of pure existence value associated with falling below the threshold of existence.

These components of value can also be given an interpretation in the context of the household production framework, as follows.

- The first is a use component that is related to the marginal productivity of R in household production when R is greater than R^{min} and x_1 is greater than zero. This *use value* can be measured by the difference in consumer surpluses associated with use at the two levels of R.
- The second is a nonuse component that arises because x_1 is nonessential in the household production of z_1 and the marginal productivity of R is greater than zero when x_1 is equal to zero (provided that R is greater than R^{min}). This is a *nonuse value*.
- The third component relates to crossing the threshold for R and arises because R is an essential input in the household production of commodity z_1 such that the marginal productivity of x_1 in household production is zero when R is less than R^{min}. This is an *existence value*.

What I have been calling nonuse values in the first part of this chapter can now be defined more precisely. It is the sum of simple nonuse value and pure existence value. Although this analysis has shown that it is possible to distinguish between pure existence value and simple nonuse value in principle, it may be very difficult to do so in practice.

3.5   The Temporal Dimension of Nonuse Values. The focus of this section so far has been the structure of preferences in a static, timeless framework. I now take time explicitly into account, looking at both the nature of intertemporal preferences and the implications of different temporal patterns of changes in R.

The theory of preferences with which we have been working up to this point makes current-period utility a function only of the current-period consumption of marketed goods and services and environmental quality:

$$U_t = U_t(X_t, R_t) \tag{10}$$

where t indexes the period of time in question and X_t is a numeraire good with a unit price. In a model of lifetime utility an individual at any point in time would experience a level of lifetime utility from the goods and services and environmental quality he anticipates using over his remaining lifetime:

$$\overline{U} = \overline{U}(X, R) \tag{11}$$

where $X = X_1, \ldots, X_t, \ldots, X_T$ and $R = R_1, \ldots, R_t, \ldots, R_T$ and where T is the number of years of remaining life. For simplicity, this formulation implies that the individual gains no satisfaction from making a bequest to others at the end of his life. Also, in this analysis we abstract from all considerations of uncertainty concerning the future.

The existence of current-period preferences as described by equation (10) implies that the lifetime utility function (11) is separable—that is,

$$\overline{U} = \overline{U}[U_1(X_1, R_1), \ldots, U_t(X_t, R_t), \ldots, U_T(X_T, R_T)].$$

It is common to assume that this expression is additively separable and that the current-period utility function is the same for all periods. In other words,

$$\overline{U} = \sum_{t=1}^{T} \delta^t U(X_t, R_t)$$

where $U(\cdot)$ is invariant in t and δ^t is meant to capture the individual's time preference. I assume that the individual chooses a lifetime pattern of consumption X_t so as to maximize lifetime utility subject to a wealth constraint based on the known lifetime stream of income and the interest rate at which he can borrow or lend. The solution to this lifetime maximization problem yields the lifetime indirect utility function

$$\overline{V}(W, R)$$

where W is wealth or the present value of lifetime income stream.

Now consider a permanent reduction in R from R^1 to R^2 such that $R_t^2 < R_t^1$ for all t. The proper measure of the welfare is given by the compensating wealth payment that maintains lifetime utility. This is CW, which is the solution to

$$\overline{V}(W - CW, R^2) = \overline{V}(W, R^1).$$

Suppose first that weak complementarity holds so that only use value is lost. The lost use value for each period could be measured on the basis of each period's current utility function. The present value of the current-period lost use values would be given by

$$PV(CS) = \sum_{t=1}^{T} \frac{CS_t}{(1+r)^t}.$$

Following the analysis of Blackorby, Donaldson, and Moloney (1984), it can be shown that

$$|PV(CS)| \geq |CW|.$$

This result can be easily explained. If a sum equal to CS_t is paid to the individual in period t and spent by the individual in that period, then current-period utility is restored to its initial level and so is lifetime utility. But if the current-period marginal utility of consumption in t is affected by the change in R_t, then the first-order conditions for an optimum allocation of consumption over time will not be satisfied. The individual will wish to reallocate consumption across time through some pattern of additional borrowing and lending. This reallocation of consumption will increase utility. This means that a vector of smaller current-period payments would have been sufficient to fully compensate the individual. Similar conclusions will be reached if preferences are such that there are lost nonuse values as well as lost use values.

Now consider a temporary reduction in R—that is, assume $R_t^2 = R_t^1$ for some $1 < t \leq T$. This would likely result in lost use values. But would there also be lost nonuse values? There is nothing in the logic of the structure we have imposed on preferences up to this point that would preclude the existence of lost nonuse values. But the early literature on nonuse values emphasized irreversible change and the irreplaceability of natural assets as justifications for the presence of nonuse values (see Krutilla [1967] and Krutilla and Fisher [1975]). It seems to me that whether irreversibility or the irreplaceable character of a natural asset is a prerequisite for nonuse values is an open question that can only be settled on the basis of empirical evidence. This will probably prove to be an important issue in some natural resource damage cases involving long-term but perhaps not irreversible damage to special natural areas, such as Prince William Sound in Alaska.

3.6   Conclusions. In this section I have presented some results derived from one way of defining and modeling the use of a resource. I have shown that where there is a complementary market good that can be chosen to represent use, something about the value of the resource is revealed in the observable market demand for the complementary good. If the assumption of weak complementarity holds, then market demand information can reveal everything there is to know about the value of the resource. That is to say, value measures derived from market data reflect total value. If the conditions of weak complementarity do not hold, then there are other components of value that are not reflected in market demands. Also, there is a consistent way of distinguishing between pure

nonuse and existence values within this framework. But whether preferences actually take the form that leads to this distinction is an empirical
question.

If we adopt a broader concept of use based on physical proximity of
the individual to the resource we must confront the question of how to
model those uses that do not require purchase of a complementary good.
One possibility is that the requisite proximity is a characteristic of some of
the houses in a residential housing market. If that is the case, then hedonic
property value models can be used to learn something about that type of
use value. (For discussion of hedonic property value models, see Freeman
[1985a].) Similarly, if some jobs provide opportunities for incidental
viewing of peregrine falcons out of office windows, hedonic wage models
might be used to estimate this type of use value. But it is possible that
there are some types of incidental use that do not leave any traces in any
market behavior. If that is the case, the distinction between use and nonuse
values may well be irrelevant, since something other than indirect market-
based methods must be utilized to measure all values.

4.   UNCERTAINTY AND OPTION VALUE

Many of the taxonomies of benefits in the economics literature list option
value as one of the nonuse values. The purpose of this section is to review
the role of uncertainty in environmental valuation and to consider whether
it is correct to regard option value as a separate type of value.

There are two separate and distinct forms of uncertainty to be dealt
with in this section. The first is individual uncertainty; the second is
policy uncertainty. Individual uncertainty is that uncertainty faced by
individuals who are users or potential users of an environmental resource.
For example, individual users of a contaminated groundwater aquifer may
face a higher probability of cancer. Individuals may be uncertain as to
whether a particular unique and irreplaceable environmental resource will
be available for their use on some future date. And individuals may also
be uncertain as to whether they will actually want to use some environmental resource in the future. The term "option value," as originally
conceived, refers to the value to an uncertain demander of the elimination
of uncertainty about the availability of an environmental resource.

The second form of uncertainty is that faced by a public policymaker
who may be uncertain about the magnitudes of the benefits and costs of
the alternative policies he or she is contemplating. This form of uncertainty could arise because of inadequate scientific knowledge of the underlying physical and biological processes that influence the value of an
environmental resource to people. Or it could arise from lack of informa-

tion about the economic relationships and variables governing individuals' use of the environmental resource and the value they derive from it. Policy uncertainty is especially troublesome for decision makers when irreversible commitments must be made before the uncertainty is resolved. One example would be whether to convert a wilderness area to intensive forestry or mineral extraction when there is uncertainty as to the future benefit of preservation. One way that planners can respond to policy uncertainty is to seek to reduce the uncertainty by acquiring more information. The term "quasi-option value" refers to the increase in expected net benefits associated with deferring irreversible resource commitments until uncertainties are resolved.

4.1   Individual Uncertainty and Option Value. Individual uncertainty can take two forms. The first is uncertainty with respect to the existence or supply of the environmental resource. The second is uncertainty concerning the individual's demand for or value attached to an increase in R. Individuals could be uncertain about their demand for R due to uncertainty about their income, the prices of complementary or substitute goods, or their own preferences.[5]

The uncertain demander was the focus of attention of those developing the theory of option value. For the earliest writers (for example, Weisbrod [1964] and Cicchetti and Freeman [1971]), it seemed plausible that the uncertain demander would be willing to pay a little extra now over and above expected use value (the expected value of consumer surplus) to assure that the environmental resource would be available if it should turn out that his or her demand were positive. The maximum payment by the individual was assumed to be independent of the state of nature—that is, it was made before the resolution of uncertainty. This state-independent payment was termed "option price" (Cicchetti and Freeman [1971]) and the presumed excess of option price over expected consumer surplus was termed "option value." It was thought that, if possible, option value should be measured and added to expected consumer surplus in order to obtain the full measure of the value of providing an environmental service.

Unfortunately, further analysis showed that what was defined as option value in these models could be either positive or negative (Schmalensee [1972] and Bishop [1982]).[6] More recently, rigorous analysis of the theory of welfare change under uncertainty has shown that option value is

---

[5]Although the literature has treated option value as arising from potential future use, the analysis could also be applied to nonuse values in an uncertain world.

[6]For more recent analyses of the relationship between option price and expected consumer surplus under various conditions of both demand and supply uncertainty, see Freeman (1984b and 1985b), Wilman (1987), Hartman and Plummer (1987), and Johansson (1988).

not really a separate component of value. Rather, it is the difference between two perspectives on welfare measure—the ex ante perspective and the ex post perspective (Smith [1986 and 1987b]).

An ex ante perspective makes social welfare a function of the expected utilities of the individuals in society, while an ex post perspective makes social welfare equal to the expected value of the social welfares realized in alternative states of nature. Expected utility, which may reflect risk aversion, is the basis for ex ante welfare measurement. Option price is an ex ante measure since it is defined as that state-independent payment that makes the expected utility with the project just equal to the expected utility without the project. The expected value of consumer surplus is an ex post measure in that it focuses on the realized outcomes of policy choices.

The generally accepted view now is that the ex ante perspective is more appropriate for welfare analysis (see, for example, Graham [1981] and Smith [1986, 1987a, and 1987b]). Thus it is at best misleading to speak of option value as a separate category of nonuser values.

4.2   Policy Uncertainty and Quasi-Option Value. When decision makers are uncertain about the magnitude of the benefits and costs of alternative courses of action, decision rules and procedures should be modified to reflect this uncertainty. One possible modification entails altering the time sequence of choices so as to take advantage of information that might become available in the future. The term "quasi-option value" was coined by Arrow and Fisher (1974) to describe the welfare gain or benefit associated with delaying a decision when there is uncertainty about the payoffs of alternative choices and when at least one of the choices involves the irreversible commitment of resources. They showed that quasi-option value is not dependent on risk aversion. It can be present even when decision makers make choices on the basis of expectations of uncertain monetary benefits and costs.

Most of the literature on the role of this concept in environmental decision making has concluded that consideration of quasi-option value will lead to relatively less irreversible development and relatively more preservation of natural environments. However, the conclusion that there is a quasi-option value benefit to preserving a natural area or to delaying its development springs from a specific feature of the models used by Arrow and Fisher (1974), Krutilla and Fisher (1975), Conrad (1980), Miller and Lad (1984), Fisher and Hanemann (1987), and others. In these models quasi-option value stems from the value of the information gained by delaying an irreversible decision to develop a natural area. But it is not difficult to imagine situations in which the relevant information for guiding future decisions can be gained only by undertaking at least a little development now.[7] In such cases there can be positive quasi-option value to development, or, what is the same thing, a negative quasi-option value to preservation (Miller and Lad [1984] and Freeman [1984a]).

Whether quasi-option value exists or whether it is positive or negative for preservation depends on the nature of the uncertainty, the opportunities for gaining information, and the structure of the decision problem. Quasi-option value is not a component of the values individuals attach to resource changes. Even if individuals' utility functions were known, quasi-option value could not be estimated separately and added into a benefit-cost calculation. Rather it is a benefit of adopting better decision-making procedures. Its magnitude can only be revealed by comparing two strategies, one of which involves optimal sequential decision making to take advantage of information obtained by delaying irreversible resource commitments. The decision maker who knows how to use an optimal sequential decision-making strategy has no reason to calculate quasi-option value. The calculation would be redundant, since the best decision is already known.

4.3   Conclusions. It is at best misleading to consider option value and quasi-option value as separate categories of value. Quasi-option value does not relate at all to the values individuals place on resources. It is not a value that attaches to a specific resource. Rather, it is a social gain to be achieved by having planners adopt more sophisticated decision-making strategies in the face of their own uncertainty about policy variables. It does not relate to resource changes; it relates to changes in decision-making procedures.

The concept of option value does reflect individuals' valuation and does relate to resource changes. But it is not a separate component of value; rather, it is an algebraic difference between two measures based on different perspectives on valuation—an ex ante perspective focusing on option price and an ex post perspective focusing on realized surpluses. This option value can be either positive or negative depending on the particular structure of the uncertainty facing the individual.

5.   TOWARD MEASUREMENT

The question of how to measure nonuse values has two aspects. The first and more general aspect concerns measurement to test the hypothesis that

---

[7]For example, suppose there is uncertainty about the magnitude of a mineral or petroleum deposit underlying a wilderness area. Perhaps the only way the uncertainty about the magnitude of the benefits of development relative to preservation can be resolved is through exploratory drilling—that is, through a little development.

nonuse values are positive, to determine the magnitude of nonuse values, and to test hypotheses about which features of resources are likely to generate large nonuse values. The second aspect is whether (and if so how) to measure losses of nonuse values in the context of natural resource damage assessment. In this section, I address the broader question of measurement, leaving the question of measurement as part of natural resource damage assessment to the concluding section of the chapter.

The standard theory for measuring welfare changes was developed for the purpose of interpreting changes in the prices and quantities of goods purchased in markets. This theory has been extended in the past fifteen or so years to nonmarket or public goods such as environmental quality. And as I showed in section 3.4, this theory is applicable to nonuse as well as use values. This theory assumes that people have well-defined preferences over alternative bundles of consumption goods, including the quantities of nonmarket goods, and that people know their preferences. Also it assumes that these preferences have the property of substitutability—in other words, that preferences are nonlexicographic.

Although the assumption of substitutability is fundamental to the standard economic analysis of environmental and resource values, I frequently find resistance to this idea in discussions of resource policy issues with non-economists. A typical response is that the environment is too important, too special, to be treated like ordinary commodities such as bread or VCRs.

I make two points in response. First, there is an abundance of evidence that people do in fact behave as if substitutability were a characteristic of their preferences. That is, they display a willingness to make tradeoffs as revealed by such things as travel cost models of recreation demand and hedonic property value models (Freeman [1979b and 1982]). And second, I suspect that when some people say that they reject the assumption of substitutability, they may be expressing an ethically based attitude or sentiment about the general principles of environmental protection and preservation. This attitude is distinctly different from the economic notion of resource value or site-specific value. The problem for empirical research is that some measures of site- or resource-specific value, especially those derived from contingent valuation surveys, may incorporate expressions of general attitudes and therefore be inappropriate for specific resource management decision making or for damage assessment.

Any measurement technique should satisfy three criteria. First, the framework should be consistent with the standard economic theory of individual preferences and measurement of welfare changes, as reviewed in (for example) Freeman (1979b and 1985a). Second, the theoretical framework and measurement techniques derived from the framework should be capable, at least in principle, of reproducing what would be revealed as values by a well-functioning market for the resource, if such a market existed. Third, the theory and measurement techniques should be resource-specific—that is, they should refer to a specific site, species, ecological system, and so forth, rather than reflect general attitudes toward environmental protection and preservation. This last point is particularly important since it appears that the measurement of nonuse values will have to rely heavily on the contingent valuation method. Poorly designed contingent valuation questions may elicit general attitudes rather than the site- or resource-specific values needed for natural resource damage assessment or resource management decision making.

The empirical techniques for estimating individuals' resource values can be divided into two broad categories: indirect or market-based techniques that rely on the influence of the availability or quality of the resource on individuals' purchases of a market good; and direct methods that ask individuals to reveal values through responses to contingent choice, contingent activity, or contingent valuation questions (see Freeman [1979b] and chapter 8 by McConnell and chapter 10 by Schulze in this volume).

5.1 Can Indirect Methods Reveal Nonuse Values? It is usually argued that because indirect methods are based on the effect of the resource on purchases of a marketed good that is an indicator of use, they provide measures only of those use values linked to market goods. Thus, unless there is a market for the existence or preservation of a resource or for enhancing resource quality for nonusers, there will be no market transactions to reflect the nonuse values of individuals, and only direct methods of estimating nonuse values will be feasible. Also, because existence or preservation of a resource for nonusers has the properties of nonexcludability and nondepletability, we expect markets to fail to provide these services.

However, we do observe that environmental organizations undertake a variety of activities to protect and preserve natural environments.[8] Can we interpret individuals' contributions to these organizations as implicit purchases of environmental preservation and protection because of their nonuse values? For several reasons, I think that the answer is no. The economic data on the activities of these organizations cannot be relied upon as measures of nonuse values for policymaking purposes. In the following I discuss the range of these activities and what I think we can and cannot learn about values from them.

---

[8]See Mitchell (1979) for an insightful discussion of the activities of environmental lobby groups.

The activities of environmental organizations can be placed in one of two categories: direct provision of preservation through acquisition, and advocacy aimed at influencing public-sector provision of preservation. Organizations such as The Nature Conservancy accept private donations and use the funds to purchase lands with special ecological, geological, or scenic characteristics for the purpose of protection and preservation. Individuals' donations and dues paid to such organizations are manifestations of willingness to pay for preservation—that is, of nonuse values. But if "free-rider" behavior is significant, these donations would be only a lower bound of true aggregate willingness to pay for preservation. Furthermore, at least in some instances the lands acquired by such organizations are accessible to individual use. So individual donations could reflect a combination of use as well as nonuse values.

Many environmental organizations devote a substantial portion of their budgets to advocacy activities on behalf of environmental preservation in general and for policy actions to protect specific natural resources. Again, individuals' membership dues and donations in support of these activities reflect individuals' willingness to pay for nonuse values. But because of free-rider behavior, aggregate donations are likely to fall short of total willingness to pay for preservation. Also, the organizations undertaking these activities frequently have multiple purposes; they provide such services to members as magazines, other publications, and field trips. This means that only that portion of dues and donations supporting the incremental cost of advocacy to the organization is relevant for estimating nonuse values.

In the policymaking arena, another factor weakens the relationship between nonuse values and individual donations to support advocacy. This is the uncertainty concerning the outcome of the policy process and the contribution of advocacy activities to the desired outcome. A rational organization with limited resources would estimate the probabilities of successful advocacy as a function of the resource commitment for each specific issue, and would allocate resources across activities so as to maximize the expected value of the aggregate benefit of its activities. The observed allocation of advocacy resources across specific issues would reflect the interaction of the probabilities of a successful advocacy, the marginal productivity of advocacy in increasing the probability of success, and the value of success to the organization (Freeman [1969]).

It is reasonable to conclude that individuals' donations to environmental organizations involved in acquisition and advocacy do reflect willingness to pay for preservation and nonuse values. These activities provide evidence in support of the hypothesis of significant nonuse values. But for the reasons outlined here, aggregate nonuse values are likely to be larger, and perhaps very much larger, than observed acquisition and advocacy expenditures. Thus contingent valuation methods appear to be the only feasible approach to estimating nonuse values for policy purposes.

5.2   Contingent Valuation and Nonuse Values. There is now a substantial literature on the theory and practice of contingent valuation methods in natural resource valuation. This is not the place to attempt a review of this literature (for a review, see Mitchell and Carson [1989]). Here I wish only to summarize some of the key points concerning what the literature suggests about the design of instruments to estimate total values and nonuse values for natural resources and to draw on these key points to suggest some research strategies for testing hypotheses concerning nonuse values. In section 6, I will draw on these points in reviewing existing empirical estimates.

A conference organized by Cummings, Brookshire, and Schulze in 1984,[9] and reported in their 1986 book *Valuing Environmental Goods: An Assessment of the Contingent Valuation Method*, provided a comprehensive review of the state of the art and the issues involved in the design and interpretation of contingent valuation studies for resource valuation. On the basis of their review, Cummings, Brookshire, and Schulze suggested four reference operating conditions that must be satisfied for a contingent valuation study to be considered reliable. On the basis of their discussion and my own review of the state of the art (Freeman [1986]), I offer the following six characteristics of a reliable contingent valuation instrument for estimating nonuse values.

1. The instrument should clearly identify and accurately describe the specific resource to be valued.

2. The instrument should establish that the respondent is familiar with the resource in question. If the respondent has no knowledge of the important features of the resource in question, it is hard to see how he or she could hold significant nonuse values or experience loss of these values due to an injury to the resource. However, prior use is not necessary for an individual to have nonuse values. As Mitchell and Carson (1989) say, "direct prior experience is not essential for familiarity. Respondents who have never visited the Grand Canyon or seen a toxic waste dump may obtain considerable information about them from secondary sources" (p. 214). On the other hand, even for nonuse values it should be established that the respondents have actual prior knowledge of the resource in question; otherwise, their responses are likely to reflect only their general attitudes toward the problem, rather than being tied to the specific resource.

---

[9]The conference was held on July 2, 1984, in Palo Alto, California.

3. The instrument should clearly and accurately describe the change in the quality or availability of the resource that is being valued. The change should be described in terms that are meaningful to the individual.

4. To the extent possible, the change in the quality or availability of the resource being valued should be within the range of experience of respondents so they can be expected to have some familiarity with their preferences for the resource over the range in question. Clearly this criterion cannot be completely satisfied in the case of significant injury to major natural resource systems of the sort where nonuse values are likely to be significant. To the extent that the change being valued lies outside of an individual's range of experience, responses are likely to be less reliable. But even in such cases, reliability can be enhanced by increased effort to avoid implied value cues (Mitchell and Carson [1989], pp. 240–246). It may also be possible to increase reliability by increasing sample size (Freeman [1986] and Mitchell and Carson [1989]).

5. To the extent possible, the instrument should avoid questions framed in such a way as to link the survey instrument to current public controversies or political issues, so as to minimize the likelihood of strategic behavior, protest zeros, nonrespondents, and the expression of what Daniel Kahneman has called "ideological values" (in Cummings, Brookshire, and Schulze [1986], pp. 190–193). By this I mean values that simply reflect a willingness to support a "good cause" or general environmental preservation, rather than being attributable to the specific resource being valued. In some cases (for example, where nonusers are being asked about values) it may be desirable to test for the presence of ideological values. This could be done by altering certain features of the survey instrument for some subsets of the general sample. To the extent that mean or median expressed values are insensitive to relevant changes in the description of the resource being valued (for example, the magnitude or scope of the injury or the degree to which the resource in question is aggregated with other resources) or sensitive to irrelevant changes in the description of the resource or injury, doubt is cast on the validity of the survey responses.

6. The question format must be consistent with the theoretical framework being used to define use, nonuse, and existence values. Specifically, at least for users and potential users, the hypothetical conditions that preclude use must be specified when nonuse valuation questions are asked, and these conditions should be consistent with the model being used to define nonuse values.

The strategy chosen for the design of contingent valuation questions to elicit nonuse values depends in part on the purpose of the measurements. One possible purpose of measurement might be to determine a total value in order to guide a resource management decision or to collect damages under CERCLA. Alternatively, a purpose of the research might be to test hypotheses concerning use, nonuse, and existence values. If the objective is to obtain a measure of total value, a simple contingent valuation question may suffice. The distinctions among use and nonuse and existence values are not important for this purpose. If the objective is to test hypotheses, it is necessary to design the research strategy in a manner consistent with the theoretical framework and definitions adopted.

There are several alternative ways to structure questions to elicit nonuse values. Members of a sample group might be asked a total valuation question and then be asked to imagine themselves in a situation where the price of the use activity was so high as to preclude use.[10] Then they could be asked to state the amount they would be willing to pay for the change in the resource, given that their use had been precluded. A second approach would be to ask a total valuation question followed by a series of questions designed to determine respondents' present levels of use and their choke prices. The responses to the choke price questions could be analyzed to determine the implied use values. The difference between total values and use values could be interpreted as nonuse values. The results of these two approaches could then be compared to determine the consistency of the total valuations and implied nonuse values. A finding that the allocations between use and nonuse values were not consistent between the two approaches would suggest that implied allocations are sensitive to the question format and/or that respondents are not as used to thinking about the use/nonuse distinction as natural resource economists are.

Another approach would be to ask a sample of users of a resource a contingent activity question. They could be asked to report current levels of use and what these levels would become after some specified change in the resource. If respondents were also asked travel cost information, their actual demand curve and hypothetical demand curve for visits after the resource change could be estimated. The use value of the resource could be estimated by measuring the areas between the demand curves. (See McConnell and Morrison [1986] for an example of this approach to estimating use values.) Then respondents could also be asked a total willingness-to-pay question for the stated improvement in the resource. If total values exceeded total estimated values, the difference could be imputed to nonuse values.

As should be apparent, a problem that arises in all of these approaches to imputing nonuse values is that the imputation is based on the difference between two other values, both of which are measured with

---

[10]Alternatively, the sample group could be told that administrative regulation barred use in order to protect the resource. But this hypothetical situation would not be consistent with the definition of nonuse value developed above.

some unknown error. So, without some understanding of the error properties of the other measures, one cannot know whether the imputed value is simply the result of measurement error or is a true nonuse value.

Four additional issues concerning research study design deserve at least brief mention. The first issue, which applies only to studies designed to distinguish between use and nonuse values, is how use is to be defined and measured. This has been discussed above. The second issue concerns the definition and description of the resource to be valued. Resources have both quantitative and qualitative dimensions that can be affected by policy decisions or damaged by pollution events. Yet, in the theoretical discussion I assumed that the resource was measured in a single dimension. If the purpose of the empirical research is to estimate total values, then respondents must be given a clear description of the changes in all relevant dimensions of resource quantity and quality. The determination of what is relevant must come in part from the judgment of experienced researchers in this field and in part from research specifically designed to determine what characteristics of the resource are important to people. If the research is aimed at distinguishing between use and nonuse values through resort to weak complementarity, there are theoretical questions to be dealt with. The models for measuring welfare change based on weak complementarity have been developed for only one quantitative or qualitative characteristic that is complementary to the market good. Formal analysis with multiple characteristics has not as yet been carried out, as far as I know.

The third issue concerns the relevant population for sampling when nonuse values are involved. If the resource to be valued is in California, should the sample include East Coast residents? Or should it be limited to westerners or to California residents? Casting the sampling net too widely wastes scarce research resources; but important values may be missed if the geographic scope of the sample is too narrow. Even small average or per capita values can loom large when aggregated over a large population. Again, experience and the results of research designed specifically to shed light on this set of issues can help to guide research study design.

The fourth issue is the temporal framing of the contingent valuation question. This problem has two aspects. The first concerns the time dimension of the resource damage. Is it permanent? Or is restoration or recovery expected after some period of time? It is important that the contingent valuation question be clear about the temporal dimension of the damage to the resource. The second aspect concerns the temporal dimension of the value measure. In section 4, I showed that the correct welfare measure was the compensating change in wealth—that is, a "one-shot" payment. This amount would be elicited by asking individuals a lump sum or present value question. Some studies have asked respondents about their willingness to pay in equal annual payments over some specified time period—for example, five years. Studies of this sort are asking individuals to convert a present value question into an installment payment question; the individual is implicitly asked to carry out an annuitization calculation, which seems likely to reduce the reliability of responses.

6.   A REVIEW OF EMPIRICAL STUDIES

I have looked at over a dozen empirical studies of nonuse values, including studies of option, existence, and preservation values. They all provide at least some empirical support for the hypothesis that individuals hold values for some aspects of natural resources that are independent of their use of specific resources. These studies utilize a variety of approaches to estimate values for different characteristics of natural resources. It should be noted that I have not made a thorough search of the literature to identify all of the published empirical estimates, and that what follows is not a detailed or critical review of all of the theoretical and empirical aspects of those studies I have reviewed. Such a review is beyond the scope of this paper.

All of the studies cited here have been based on some variation of the contingent valuation method. These studies can be classified either according to the type of natural resource attribute they have valued or by the structure of the contingent valuation instrument and how nonuse values have been identified. These studies have been used to estimate values for specific locations or sites such as rivers and wilderness areas, individual characteristics of these sites such as water quality or visibility, and the preservation of viable populations of a number of species of fish, birds, and mammals. Table 13-1 lists the studies reviewed here, classified by the type of natural resource valued.

The most straightforward approach to estimating nonuse values is to ask total value questions about a resource to individuals who are unlikely to be users of that specific resource. One example of this approach is that of Samples, Dixon, and Gowen (1986). They asked students in a laboratory setting to state their total willingness to pay for the preservation of the humpback whale. Since most subjects were unlikely to ever observe members of this species, bids can be reasonably interpreted as being primarily if not wholly nonuse preservation values. Mean bids for different experimental groups ranged from $35 to $60. A major purpose of the experiment was to test the hypothesis that the type of information provided affected willingness to pay for preservation bids. The evidence supported this hypothesis both for the humpback whale bids and for other birds in a hypothetical setting.

Table 13-1. Studies Estimating Nonuse Values Classified by Type of Resource

1. *Sites of ecological or scientific importance*

   A. Walsh, Loomis, and Gillman (1984)

   > Resource: Wilderness areas in Colorado
   > Method: Respondents allocated total value to categories of nonuse values
   > Sample Size: 195

   B. Walsh, Sanders, and Loomis (1985)

   > Resource: Wild rivers in Colorado
   > Method: Respondents allocated total value to categories of nonuse values
   > Sample Size: 214

2. *Characteristics of specific sites*

   A. Schulze and Brookshire (1983)

   > Resource: Visibility at national parks in the Southwest
   > Method: Distinguished between users and nonusers in sample
   > Sample Size: 616

   B. Cronin (1982)

   > Resource: Water quality in the Potomac River
   > Method: Distinguished between users and nonusers in sample
   > Sample Size: 1,579

   C. Greenley, Walsh, and Young (1981)

   > Resource: Water quality in the South Platte River
   > Method: Distinguished between users and nonusers in sample
   > Sample Size: 202

   D. Desvousges, Smith, and, McGivney (1983)

   > Resource: Water quality in the Monongahela River
   > Method: Distinguished between users and nonusers in sample; respondents allocated total value to direct use and "other" categories; respondents were asked to state their preservation or existence value, excluding any use value
   > Sample Size: 211

   E. Sutherland and Walsh (1985)

   > Resource: Water quality in Flathead Lake, Montana
   > Method: Distinguished between users and nonusers in sample
   > Sample Size: 171

3. *Individual species*

   A. Brookshire, Eubanks, and Randall (1983)

   > Resource: Grizzly bear and bighorn sheep
   > Method: Distinguished between users and nonusers in sample
   > Sample Size: 1,743 grizzly bears and 1,858 bighorn sheep

(continued on next page)

293

Table 13-1.   (continued)

B.	Samples, Dixon, and Gowen (1986)
	Resource: Humpback whales
	Method: Sample limited to presumptive nonusers
	Sample Size: 228
C.	Hageman (1986)
	Resource: Blue and gray whales, bottle-nosed dolphins, sea otters, and sea lions
	Method: Respondents allocated total value to categories of nonuse values
	Sample Size: 180
D.	Boyle and Bishop (1987)
	Resource: Bald eagles and striped shiners
	Method: Sample limited to presumptive nonusers
	Sample Size: 1,215
E.	Bowker and Stoll (1988)
	Resource: Whooping cranes
	Method: Distinguished between users and nonusers in sample
	Sample Size: 741

A similar approach was employed by Boyle and Bishop (1987) to estimate the preservation values for bald eagles and striped shiners in Wisconsin. Wisconsin taxpayers were asked in a mail survey to indicate whether or not they would be willing to pay a stated fee to support a preservation fund for the species in question. In the case of bald eagles, some respondents were asked a total value question that included both use and nonuse values. Others were asked to state a value conditional on the assumption that the remoteness of the remaining bald eagle habitat would preclude their viewing bald eagles in the future even though the species was preserved. The latter value would include a pure existence value in my terminology. Since the striped shiner is a minnow with no recreational significance, these bids can be interpreted as nonuse values and would include a pure existence value. Mean values for the striped shiner were in the range of $4 to $6; means for bald eagles ranged from $10 to $75, depending on the type of question asked and whether the respondent was a contributor to the State Endangered Resources Donation Program.

A second approach is to ask individuals about their total value for the resource while distinguishing between users and nonusers in the sample. If all of the members of the nonuser portion of the sample are sure about being nonusers, the total values of this group must be nonuse values. On the other hand, if nonusers have some subjective non-zero probability of future use, their total values probably include some option price related to their uncertainty about future use, in other words an ex ante use value.

Two early examples of this approach are described in Fisher and Raucher (1984). These studies involved the salmon fishery in the Fraser

River Basin in British Columbia and fishing resources in the southeastern United States. The results suggest that nonusers may hold values for these resources in the range of 50 percent of the values held by users on a per capita basis.[11] These studies were used by Freeman (1979a) and others as the basis of estimates of aggregate nonuser values for U.S. water pollution control benefits. Other examples of this approach include Greenley, Walsh, and Young (1981); Bowker and Stoll (1988); Brookshire, Eubanks, and Randall (1983); Schulze and Brookshire (1983); and Cronin (1982). All of these studies show that individuals who say that they are not current users and/or do not expect to use the resource in the future may express substantial willingness to pay to preserve the resource either for others or for future generations. Several of these studies also find that current users say that they would be willing to pay something for preservation even if they do not expect to use the resource themselves in the future. These studies provide evidence that users can also hold nonuse values.

A third approach is to use a contingent valuation question to determine respondents' total values for the resource and then to ask respondents to allocate this total between use and various nonuse categories. This approach has been used in three different studies by a research team based at Colorado State University to estimate nonuse values for wilderness areas (Walsh, Loomis, and Gilman [1984]), wild rivers (Walsh, Sanders, and Loomis [1985]), and water quality in Flathead Lake, Montana (Sutherland and Walsh [1985]). In each case respondents were asked to allocate their total values among the categories of recreation use, option value, existence value, and bequest value. Use was defined as the right to visit the resource during the current year. Option value was the value of preserving the opportunity to visit the resource in some future year. (Note that this differs from the theoretical definition of option value. It is really an option price for future use.) Existence and bequest values were defined as knowing that the resource exists and knowing that future generations will have use of the resource. The sums of stated bequest and existence values ranged from 35 percent to 70 percent of total value, while option values were in the range of 15 percent to 20 percent of total value. Hageman (1986) obtained similar results with her allocation question involving values for several marine mammals (two species of whale, dolphins, sea lions, and sea otters). What is surprising about the results of these studies is that current use values are such a small proportion of the total stated values.

My principal criticism of this approach to determining nonuse value is that it does not provide a context for defining nonuse values and option

---

[11]As I showed in section 3.4, users' values could also include a nonuse value component.

value consistent with any set of theoretical definitions. For example, the definition adopted in this chapter for nonuse value is that it is a willingness to pay for the resource, assuming that the price of use is sufficiently high to choke off use. The studies cited here are not specific about what respondents are to assume about the conditions of access and why their use is hypothetically held to zero when they consider the nonuse components of their total bid.

Furthermore, since we have seen that option value is not really a separate category of value and can be either positive or negative, it is difficult to interpret the substantial positive option values that result from the allocation questions used in these studies. In the first question, respondents have been asked to state what is, in effect, an ex ante or option price form of value. Thus there is no theoretical justification for an allocation of some portion of that value to the category of option value. And if the allocation to option value has no theoretical justification, the allocations to the remaining value categories are also suspect because of the requirement that the percentage allocations add up to one. Respondents must have something quite different from our theoretical definition of option value in their minds when they make their allocations. But given the nature of the questions, we can only guess at what that is. Finally, when the definitions of the various nonuse categories are provided to respondents before they make their allocation, they may receive implied value cues from these definitions that encourage them to bias their value responses upward.

The last study to be discussed here utilized elements of both the second and third approaches described above. Desvousges, Smith, and McGivney (1983) used four different forms of a contingent valuation question to determine individuals' total willingness to pay for four different decrements and increments to water quality in the Monongahela River (see also Smith and Desvousges [1986]). The responses to these questions were option price or ex ante values. Responses were obtained from both users and nonusers of the river. Respondents were then asked to indicate what proportion of their option price was based on their actual use of the river. For most of the sixteen different combinations of water quality change and contingent valuation instrument, the reported use values were between 25 percent and 60 percent of the option price value, with some answers being even higher (up to 85 percent). Another question then asked explicitly for an existence or preservation value bid by stating, "We want you to think *only* in terms of this satisfaction which excludes any use by you of the river." The authors report that the mean responses to this question (averaged over the different contingent valuation instruments) "are quite comparable to the estimates for the option price. . . ." (Desvousges, Smith, and McGivney [1983], p. 5–32). The authors acknowledge that these responses must be regarded as tentative since respondents were given no specific reason why they should imagine that their use of the river was held at zero.

This review of empirical studies leads me to the following conclusions. First, the positive responses in a variety of studies applying three different approaches to several types of resources provide substantial support for the hypothesis that nonuse values (as I have used the term in this chapter) are positive. Furthermore, when it is recognized that even small per capita nonuse values may be very large in the aggregate if they are held by a substantial fraction of the population, there is a real possibility that ignoring nonuse values could result in serious misallocation of resources.

Second, I cannot say anything about the likely magnitude of nonuse values relative to use values on the basis of the evidence contained in these studies. There are two reasons for this. The first is that all of the studies cited here rely on some form of contingent valuation instrument. Each of these studies would have to be carefully reviewed in order to reach some judgment as to the reliability of the instrument design, based on an application of the Cummings, Brookshire, and Schulze (1986) reference operating conditions or the six characteristics of a reliable contingent valuation instrument outlined above. That kind of careful review is beyond the scope of this chapter. It should be noted, however, that many of these studies were carried out in the early days of the development of the contingent valuation method, when the state of the art of instrument design was not nearly as well developed as I think it is now. The second reason for withholding judgment as to the magnitude of nonuse values is that many of the studies described here have not used definitions of nonuse values that are solidly based in individual preference theory. This is especially true where nonuse values have been elicited from users without specifying the conditions leading to nonuse and where supposed option values have been estimated. In a sense, there has been too much measurement without sufficient attention to the theoretical development of the concepts purported to be measured.

Third, I am skeptical of the large nonuse values for individuals reported in some studies, especially those resulting from allocation questions. At issue is whether the responses are measuring a true willingness to pay as defined in our basic theory of individual preferences or whether they are indicators of a general sentiment for environmental protection or preservation that is only imperfectly related to the willingness to commit resources in a true market or a quasi-market setting. I have a suspicion (but it is only a suspicion) that at least some of these studies are capturing general sentiments. If that is the case, then their data cannot be compared with real resource costs in making resource management decisions, nor can they be used as a basis for assessing damages in court cases. A major task for research is to seek ways to design questions that focus people's attention on specific resource issues in terms of marketlike transactions, and to minimize any tendency to use dollar bids to express general sentiments for environmental protection.

Fourth, several of the studies described here are particularly hard to interpret because of their treatment of uncertainty and option value. These studies have typically treated option value as a separate category of value and as a form of nonuse value. Besides being inconsistent with our current understanding of the role of uncertainty in resource valuation, the presence of questions related to option value probably contaminates the responses to existence and bequest value questions as well. This is especially true of studies that use the allocation approach to estimating nonuse value.

7. CONCLUSIONS, AND IMPLICATIONS FOR NATURAL RESOURCE DAMAGE ASSESSMENT

The major focus of this paper has been nonuse values in general, not on their specific role in natural resource damage assessment. It is time to address this question. One way to pose the issue is to ask whether nonuse values should be a part of natural resource damage assessments. In part, this is a legal question that I am not competent to answer. But from an economic perspective, I think the answer is yes. Nonuse values, like use values, have their basis in the theory of individual preferences and the measurement of welfare changes. According to theory, use values and nonuse values are additive. And in practice, the distinction between use values and nonuse values is blurry because of the different ways in which use can be defined and modeled. Also, since the evidence suggests that nonuse values can be large, at least in some circumstances, the objectives of any natural resource damage assessment process, whether they be efficiency based or equity based, would be poorly served if nonuse values were omitted from the analysis. Having said this, it must be acknowledged that nonuse values will prove difficult to measure. The state of the art is not well developed at this point. A number of questions regarding theory and measurement remain unresolved.

One of these questions is how to distinguish between use and nonuse values. The present practice is a consequence of how the field of natural resource valuation has evolved over time. Economists have devoted their energies to developing techniques for measuring particular pieces of the total value puzzle. The success of such a piecemeal strategy depends greatly on how we choose to break up the pieces. The easy pieces have been those associated with identifiable uses such as recreation. As more specific uses have been identified, modeled, and measured, the use-versus-nonuse distinction has seemed to take on some validity. And some attention has been devoted to the separate development of a theory of nonuse values.

But as I have tried to show in this chapter, the question of how to model nonuse values cannot be separated from that of modeling use values. The theory of economic welfare gives unambiguous guidance only on defining total values as compensating income changes for changes in the resource. The question of whether nonuse values, however defined, are positive or large takes on meaning only after some decision has been made about what use values measure, since nonuse value is simply total value minus whatever has been called use value.

Most of the theorizing on nonuse value starts by defining use in terms of observable market-related behavior—that is, the purchase of a complementary market good. This has been a useful strategy because of the availability of indirect methods for estimating values from observed market data. But it is not totally unfair to characterize this strategy as one of shaping the definitions to fit the available empirical methods and data. This problem cannot be avoided by declaring that the relevant distinction is between users and nonusers, since users cannot be identified until we have decided what activity it is that characterizes users.

I urge that we not accept uncritically the present conventions for distinguishing between use and nonuse values. Ultimately, for policy purposes or for determining compensation, we want to be able to measure total value. Any distinction between use and nonuse values is itself useful only if it helps in the task of measuring total values. To be fair, I think that the present convention has been useful because it makes possible the measurement of certain kinds of use values by invoking the weak complementarity model. But this is not the only way to look at the problem.

A second important question is, when are nonuse values likely to be important? The long literature on nonuse values emphasizes the uniqueness or specialness of the resource in question and the irreversibility of the loss or injury. For example, economists have suggested that there are important nonuse values in preserving the Grand Canyon in its natural state and in preventing the global or local extinction of species or the destruction of unique ecological communities. In contrast, resources such as ordinary streams or lakes or a subpopulation of a widely dispersed wildlife species are not likely to generate significant nonuse values because of the availability of close substitutes. Moreover, the literature does not suggest that nonuse values are likely to be important where recovery from an injury is quick and complete, either through natural processes or restoration. But there are problems in giving operational meaning to the idea of uniqueness. In economic terms, uniqueness would be reflected in the absence of substitutes and a low price elasticity of demand. This is an idea that comes from the literature on industrial economics. But there is no threshold on price elasticity that distinguishes between the presence or absence of close substitutes. Similarly, long-term injury with slow recovery could give rise to nonuse values that are of the same order of magnitude as those associated with irreversible injury.

A third question concerns the relevant population over which nonuse values should be estimated. I am not sure what can be said about this question until we know a lot more about what characteristics of resources are likely to give rise to significant nonuse values. Some resources such as the Amazon rain forest and African elephants may have worldwide significance, which implies that the relevant population is the world population. And one cannot rule out the possibility of regionally significant resources where important nonuse values are held only by people within that region. All that can be said now, I think, is that this is an important research question.

REFERENCES

Adams, Richard M., Scott A. Hamilton, and Bruce A. McCarl. 1984. *The Economic Effects of Ozone on Agriculture.* Corvallis, Oreg.: Environmental Research Laboratory, Environmental Protection Agency.

Arrow, Kenneth J., and Anthony C. Fisher. 1974. "Environmental Preservation, Uncertainty, and Irreversibility," *Quarterly Journal of Economics* 88(1), pp. 312–319.

Bishop, Richard C. 1982. "Option Value: An Exposition and Extension," *Land Economics* 58(1), pp. 1–15.

Blackorby, Charles, David Donaldson, and David Moloney. 1984. "Consumer's Surplus and Welfare Change in a Simple Dynamic Model," *Review of Economic Studies* 51(164), pp. 171–176.

Bockstael, Nancy E., and Kenneth E. McConnell. 1983. "Welfare Measurement in the Household Production Framework," *American Economic Review* 73(4), pp. 806–814.

Bockstael, Nancy E., Kenneth E. McConnell, and Ivar Strand. 1991. "Recreation." In *Measuring the Demand for Environmental Quality*, edited by John B. Braden and Charles D. Kolstad. Amsterdam: North-Holland.

Bowker, J. M., and John R. Stoll. 1988. "Use of Dichotomous Choice, Non-Market Methods to Value the Whooping Crane Resource," *American Journal of Agricultural Economics* 70(2), pp. 372–381.

Boyle, Keven J., and Richard C. Bishop. 1987. "Valuing Wildlife in Benefit-Cost Analyses: A Case Study Involving Endangered Species," *Water Resources Research* 23(5), pp. 943–950.

Brookshire, David S., Larry S. Eubanks, and Alan Randall. 1983. "Estimating Option Price and Existence Values for Wildlife Resources," *Land Economics* 59(1), pp. 1–15.

Cicchetti, Charles J., and A. Myrick Freeman III. 1971. "Option Demand and Consumer's Surplus: Further Comment," *Quarterly Journal of Economics* 85(3), pp. 528–539.

Conrad, Jon M. 1980. "Quasi-Option Value and the Expected Value of Information," *Quarterly Journal of Economics* 94(2), pp. 813–820.

Cronin, Francis J. 1982. *Valuing Non-Market Goods Through Contingent Markets*. Richland, Wash.: Pacific Northwest Laboratory.

Cummings, Ronald G., David S. Brookshire, and William D. Schulze. 1986. *Valuing Environmental Goods: An Assessment of the Contingent Valuation Method*. Totowa, N.J.: Rowman and Allanheld.

Desvousges, William H., V. Kerry Smith, and Matthew P. McGivney. 1983. *A Comparison of Alternative Approaches for Estimating Recreation and Related Benefits of Water Quality Improvements*. Washington, D.C.: Environmental Protection Agency.

Fisher, Ann, and Robert Raucher. 1984. "Intrinsic Benefits of Improved Water Quality: Conceptual and Empirical Perspectives." In *Advances in Applied Microeconomics*, edited by V. Kerry Smith and Ann Dryden Witte. Greenwich, Conn.: JAI Press.

Fisher, Anthony C., and W. Michael Hanemann. 1987. "Quasi-Option Value: Some Misconceptions Dispelled," *Journal of Environmental Economics and Management* 14(2), pp. 183–190.

Freeman, A. Myrick III. 1969. "Advocacy and Resource Allocation Decisions in the Public Sector," *Natural Resources Journal* 9(2), pp. 166–175.

Freeman, A. Myrick III. 1979a. *The Benefits of Air and Water Pollution Control: A Review and Synthesis of Recent Estimates*. Washington, D.C.: Council on Environmental Quality.

Freeman, A. Myrick III. 1979b. *The Benefits of Environmental Improvement: Theory and Practice*. Baltimore: The Johns Hopkins University Press for Resources for the Future.

Freeman, A. Myrick III. 1982. *Air and Water Pollution Control: A Benefit-Cost Assessment*. New York: John Wiley.

Freeman, A. Myrick III. 1984a. "The Quasi-Option Value of Irreversible Development," *Journal of Environmental Economics and Management* 11(3), pp. 292–295.

Freeman, A. Myrick III. 1984b. "The Sign and Size of Option Value," *Land Economics* 60(1), pp. 1–14.

Freeman, A. Myrick III. 1985a. "Methods for Assessing the Benefits of Environmental Programs," In *Handbook of Natural Resource and Energy Economics*, Vol. 1, edited by Allen V. Kneese and James L. Sweeney. Amsterdam: Elsevier Science Publishers.

Freeman, A. Myrick III. 1985b. "Supply Uncertainty, Option Price, and Option Value," *Land Economics* 61(2), pp. 176–181.

Freeman, A. Myrick III. 1986. "On Assessing the State of the Art of the Contingent Valuation Method of Valuing Environmental Changes." In *Valuing Environmental Goods: An Assessment of the Contingent Valuation Method*, edited by Ronald G. Cummings, David S. Brookshire, and William D. Schulze. Totowa, N.J.: Rowman and Allanheld.

Freeman, A. Myrick III, and Winston Harrington. 1990. "Measuring Welfare Values of Productivity Changes," *Southern Economic Journal* 57(1), pp. 892–904.

Graham, Daniel A. 1981. "Cost-Benefit Analysis Under Uncertainty," *American Economic Review* 71(4), pp. 715–725.

Greenley, Douglas A., Richard G. Walsh, and Robert A. Young. 1981. "Option Value: Empirical Evidence from a Case Study of Recreation and Water Quality," *Quarterly Journal of Economics* 96(4), pp. 657–673.

Hageman, Ronda K. 1986. "Economic Valuation of Marine Wildlife: Does Existence Value Exist?" Paper presented at the Association of Environmental and Resource Economists Workshop on Marine Pollution and Environmental Damage Assessment, Narragansett, R.I., June 5–6.

Hartman, Richard, and Mark Plummer. 1987. "Option Value Under Income and Price Uncertainty," *Journal of Environmental Economics and Management* 14(3), pp. 212–225.

Johansson, Per-Olov. 1988. "Option Value: Comment," *Land Economics* 64(1), pp. 86–87.

Krutilla, John V., 1967. "Conservation Reconsidered," *American Economic Review* 57(4), pp. 777–786.

Krutilla, John V., and Anthony C. Fisher. 1975. *The Economics of Natural Environments: Studies in the Valuation of Commodity and Amenity Resources*. Baltimore: The Johns Hopkins University Press.

Mäler, Karl Göran. 1974. *Environmental Economics: A Theoretical Inquiry.* Baltimore: The Johns Hopkins University Press.

McConnell, Kenneth E. 1983. "Existence and Bequest Value." In *Managing Air Quality and Scenic Resources at National Parks and Wilderness Areas*, edited by Robert D. Rowe and Lauraine G. Chestnut. Boulder, Colo.: Westview Press.

McConnell, Kenneth E., and Brian G. Morrison. 1986. *Assessment of Economic Damages to the Natural Resources of New Bedford Harbor: Damages to the Commercial Lobster Fishery*. Cambridge, Mass.: Industrial Economics, Inc.

Miller, Jon R., and Frank Lad. 1984. "Flexibility, Learning and Irreversibility in Environmental Decisions: A Bayesian Approach," *Journal of Environmental Economics and Management* 11(2), pp. 161–172.

Mitchell, Robert Cameron. 1979. "National Environmental Lobbies and the Apparent Illogic of Collective Action." In *Collective Action: Applications from Public Choice Theory*, edited by Clifford S. Russell. Baltimore: The Johns Hopkins University Press for Resources for the Future.

Mitchell, Robert Cameron, and Richard T. Carson. 1989. *Using Surveys to Value Public Goods: The Contingent Valuation Method*. Washington, D.C.: Resources for the Future.

Norton, Bryan G. 1982. "Environmental Ethics and Nonhuman Rights," *Environmental Ethics* 4, pp. 17–36.

Randall, Alan, and John R. Stoll. 1983. "Existence Value in a Total Valuation Framework." In *Managing Air Quality and Scenic Resources at National Parks and Wilderness Areas*, edited by Robert D. Rowe and Lauraine G. Chestnut. Boulder, Colo.: Westview Press.

Rescher, Nicholas. 1980. *Unpopular Essays on Technical Progress*. Pittsburgh: University of Pittsburgh Press.

Sagoff, Mark. 1980. "On the Preservation of Species," *Columbia Journal of Environmental Law* 7, pp. 33–67.

Samples, Karl C., John A. Dixon, and Marsha M. Gowen. 1986. "Information Disclosure and Endangered Species Valuation," *Land Economics* 62(3), pp. 306–312.

Schmalensee, Richard. 1972. "Option Demand and Consumer's Surplus: Valuing Price Changes Under Uncertainty," *American Economic Review* 62(5) pp. 813–824.

Schulze, William D., and David S. Brookshire. 1983. "The Economic Benefits of Preserving Visibility in the National Parklands of the Southwest," *Natural Resources Journal* 23(1), pp. 149–173.

Smith, V. Kerry. 1983. "Option Value: A Conceptual Overview," *Southern Economic Journal* 49(4), pp. 654–668.

Smith, V. Kerry. 1986. "Benefit Analysis for Natural Hazards," *Risk Analysis* 6(3), pp. 325–334.

Smith, V. Kerry. 1987a. "Non-Use Values in Benefit-Cost Analysis," *Southern Economic Journal* 54(1), pp. 19–26.

Smith, V. Kerry. 1987b. "Uncertainty, Benefit-Cost Analysis, and the Treatment of Option Value," *Journal of Environmental Economics and Management* 14(3), pp. 283–292.

Smith, V. Kerry, and William H. Desvousges. 1986. *Measuring Water Quality Benefits*. Norwell, Mass.: Kluwer-Nijhoff.

Sutherland, Ronald J., and Richard G. Walsh. 1985. "Effect of Distance on the Preservation Value of Water Quality," *Land Economics* 61(3), pp. 281–291.

VanDeVeer, Donald, and Christine Pierce. 1986. *People, Penguins, and Plastic Trees: Basic Issues in Environmental Ethics*. Belmont, Calif.: Wadsworth.

Walsh, Richard G., John B. Loomis, and Richard A. Gillman. 1984. "Valuing Option, Existence, and Bequest Demands for Wilderness," *Land Economics* 60(1), pp.14–29.

Walsh, Richard G., Larry D. Sanders, and John B. Loomis. 1985. *Wild and Scenic River Economics: Recreation Use and Preservation Values*. Englewood, Colo.: American Wilderness Alliance.

Weisbrod, Burton A. 1964. "Collective Consumption Services of Individual Consumption Goods," *Quarterly Journal of Economics* 77(3), pp. 71–77.

Wilman, Elizabeth A. 1987. "A Note on Supply-Side Option Value," *Land Economics* 63(2), pp. 284–289.

Part 4

Research Implications of Damage Assessment

14
Natural Resource Damage Assessment: The Road Ahead

Raymond J. Kopp and V. Kerry Smith

1. INTRODUCTION

The conference that initiated this volume attempted to offer insight into how nonmarket valuation could be used in the assessment of damages to natural resources. A research dialogue has subsequently developed among many of the authors of chapters in this volume and among many more of our colleagues engaged in actual damage assessments and other forms of nonmarket valuation. In our discussions in this final chapter we recognize the feedback that damage assessments are providing to the research undertaken in resource and environmental economics, and acknowledge some previously unrecognized assumptions underlying methods used in nonmarket valuation—assumptions that have been exposed by the harsh discipline of litigation.

Before discussing the effects of natural resource damage assessment on resource economics, policy reform, and interactions between science and economics, we are tempted to speculate on some related issues—in particular, the question of whether it is a desirable allocation of intellectual resources for senior economists to focus so much attention on natural resource damage assessment. At a time when funding for economic research, especially large-scale applied microeconomic analysis, has diminished, it can be said that damage assessments brought about by civil litigation have offered unprecedented opportunities to investigate aspects of consumer preferences that cannot be investigated by examining consumer decisions regarding marketed commodities. An initial reaction among some to this influx of resources and interest is to suggest that it may be diverting attention from more important national or global environmental issues. This reaction may indeed be correct; however, it is important to recognize that for the past decade (at least) research in resource and environmental economics has been influenced largely by two forces—the community of researchers and the research budgets of government mission-oriented funding agencies. It is probably not too outlandish to suggest that research agendas in the natural sciences are similarly driven by personalities and the desires of funding agencies. In the case of damage assessments, the personalities have remained the same but the agencies have changed.

It is noteworthy that until natural resource damages appeared on the boardroom agendas of private firms little interest in the economics of the environment generally and in the valuation of its services in particular had been expressed by these firms. If pushed, most business-based analysts probably would have described nonmarket values as intangible and incapable of monetization. However, liability for damage to natural assets has introduced firms to a new perspective; some businesses must deal with households as consumers of nonmarketed public goods in addition to normal private goods. This awareness on the part of business and government, combined with economists' enhanced ability to quantify the services of environmental resources and their values, has influenced efforts to introduce marketable incentives into environmental regulation and to introduce new forms of public policy such as environmental costing. Thus, when we consider the multiple uses of this research, increased attention along with the new perspective may well come to be regarded as a fortuitous development.

Of course, we will never know the results that "might have been" had other factors influenced the direction of research. But we can appraise periodically the learning and contributions that are being made and evaluate their relevance to other areas in resource economics. It is in this context, then, that we close the volume by summarizing the issues raised by our dialogue. Our review draws on the insights of the preceding chapters, their authors' research programs, and the research and insights of our colleagues. Section 2 considers the practice of damage assessment as a policy for both protecting environmental assets and addressing other types of environmental degradation. Section 3 describes some of the new economic questions being raised by damage assessment. The chapter closes, as we began, with speculation; in section 4 we conjecture about what might be next.

2.   NATURAL RESOURCE DAMAGE ASSESSMENT AS A POLICY

Most of the discussion in this volume has focused on valuing the services lost because of injuries to natural resources. The authors have accepted the legislative mandate that defines natural resource damage liability as a means to maintain a set of natural assets held in public trust as a kind of portfolio. Given the desire to maintain this endowment, they have considered whether it is possible to measure those asset values that the liability implies must be recovered. In this section, we consider natural resource damage assessment from a different perspective: How do analysts view it as a policy influencing waste generation, disposal, and cleanup? In answering this question, we evaluate natural resource damage assessment— or, more properly, the use of liability rules—as a policy for dealing with certain types of externalities. To accomplish this goal, we must consider the incentive effects and risk-sharing effects that the liability establishes. Releases of hazardous substances or oil that produce the liability are generally not deliberate. They are often unintended, stochastic outcomes of socially desirable activities. Thus, in this context, we are interested in how well liability rules induce those involved to control a damaging stochastic externality produced by otherwise desirable activities.

At the outset it is important to recognize that old sites where hazardous releases continue to injure natural resources are different from oil spills produced by current activities. For oil spills, where the event is also regarded as a stochastic externality but the liability is prospective (not retrospective), most economists would agree that full liability would be warranted for its incentive effects.[1] For old sites, decisions on waste disposal were made when the production processes generating them were under way. Several economists have argued that if natural resource injuries are due to these past decisions, incentive effects are irrelevant to an evaluation of liability rules. For example, Segerson (1989) observed:

> In analyzing the incentive effects of liability, it is important to distinguish between its retroactive and prospective application. The current emphasis of the Superfund program is on cleanup of contamination resulting from past activities. Since the actions responsible for the damages have already occurred, the retroactive application of strict liability for these damages has little incentive effect. (Segerson [1989], p. 2)

Consequently, in Segerson's view, analysis of liability rules with regard to old sites can largely ignore incentive effects and focus on optimal risk-sharing rules, which will be based on the degree of risk aversion of the parties involved.[2]

---

[1]By full liability we mean that the party responsible for the spill bears all the liability and that such liability is "strict" in a legal sense, meaning that it is not based on negligence but applies regardless of fault.

[2]Segerson's analysis assumes that we base the evaluation of policy instruments on the goal of maximizing the sum of expected utilities across the parties experiencing the risk. For additional support for this position, see Polinsky and Shavell's (1989) comments on the Department of the Interior rules.

Segerson argues that a full liability rule would be warranted with old sites only in the case of a risk-neutral potentially responsible party (PRP). When PRPs are risk-averse and have limited access to insurance, optimal risk sharing would involve their bearing some (but not all) of the risk associated with the damages. This would imply that cleanup costs, restoration costs, and lost economic value be paid by taxes on firms involved in activities producing the hazardous waste and by the PRPs at each site.[3] If we use these arguments, natural resource damages would not be sought entirely from the PRPs, but would be part of the total funds to be raised from taxes on all firms responsible for generating the wastes, regardless of whether they were involved in particular sites.

The above position assumes that natural resource damage liability for old sites does not have incentive effects. Retroactively establishing liability for actions regarded as legal at the time they were taken could create incentives for firms to review currently unregulated potential sources of injuries to natural resources more carefully. These reviews might involve substances not now regarded as hazardous. Of course, retroactive liability could also promote industrial restructuring to limit liability (as in the case, for example, of a single-truck or single-ship firm that transports hazardous substances, where restructuring would have the effect of lowering the firm's net worth and therefore the amount that could be recovered as a result of an accidental release). Unfortunately, we do not know of any evidence that either supports or denies the incentive effects of strict, joint, and several liability for natural resource damages, under the Comprehensive Environmental Response, Compensation and Liability Act of 1980 (CERCLA).[4] Abstract economic theory seems to suggest that there are no such incentive effects, yet those involved in actual site cleanups and litigation believe that incentives affecting future behavior have been created. This is certainly an area where more research is needed.

For the most part, analyses of liability incentives have focused on classes of activities, such as patterns of disposal of certain types of substances. However, there is another way in which liability may have incentive effects, a way that is not reflected in the Segerson or the earlier

---

[3]Currently the Superfund cannot be used for either litigation for natural resource damages or cleanup beyond that warranted by the health standard. Moreover, the fund is viewed as a "revolving" source of resources that is replenished when PRPs pay all the costs involved. The Segerson argument implies that most of the funds would come from taxes on the firms that produce (or produced) hazardous wastes as residuals. The reason for adding the requirement of past production is to avoid the incentive effects associated with defining a fixed standard of what constitutes a "current" producer by a time period and a size designation. Collection from both present and past producers would allow burden sharing among those firms whose past activities contributed to current problems.

[4]42 U.S.C. 9601–9675.

Shavell (1984) research. This involves establishing price signals for the services of nonmarketed resources. Because most of the initial literature on the economic effects of liability systems has focused on marketed goods and services, it has been taken as a given that the market prices would already be known. For most of the environmental services of natural assets this is not the case. Thus, the assessment of natural resource damages provides two types of messages simultaneously. It signals activities that may well be costly to firms and it identifies "prices" that courts have accepted for nonmarket services. This latter message is an effect that is not recognized in Segerson's analysis and is at least as important as the other effects of liability rules on future precautionary activities.

If we accept the argument that natural resource damage liability has incentive effects, we still must face problems with the liability system as it is currently evolving. All cases since the early 1980s involving large-scale damages to natural resources have been settled out of court. Moreover, there is casual evidence to suggest that negotiated settlements routinely involve amounts substantially below the trustee's estimate of damages. If the trustee's estimates of damages accurately measure the restoration costs and lost economic value, settlements substantially below this amount will not provide efficient incentives.[5] While one might argue that this is not true for cases involving retroactive liability, it is certainly true for cases involving prospective liability.[6] If liability for old sites does produce an incentive effect, settlement for less provides the wrong signal. Equally important, it does not serve the compensation objective of the legislation. If settlements do not provide sufficient resources to cover restoration costs and lost economic value, challenges seem to be inevitable.

If the current system leads to settlements far below the actual restoration cost and lost economic value, it fails to provide either compensation or incentives. We should consider the factors that cause these particular out-of-court settlements. The system seems to provide incentives for both trustees and PRPs to settle. In the case of trustees, resources for litigation are limited, and a large number of cases are subject to a statute of limitations. While litigation costs can be recovered if cases are won, the time horizon for any single case can be long and the outcome uncertain.

---

[5]If the settlements are kept secret, efficient incentives will not be provided even when the damage awards accurately reflect true social losses.

[6]Even if there are no incentive effects for the firms involved in a specific case brought about by the retroactive liability provisions, the settlement of these cases does have incentive effects due to the fact that the settlements have left "posted" prices for the damage to the natural resource. If an old mine case involving river contamination and lost recreational fishing settles out for a certain amount, then in future cases litigants and the courts will be tempted to begin from this established price.

Once the linkage of PRP to substance release to injury is established, the central issue of the amount of damage remains. At present, both sides behave as if they do not trust economic methods to measure the monetary values of losses associated with injuries to natural resources. Indeed, the court of appeals ruling, in *Ohio v. The United States Department of the Interior*,[7] attributed similar concerns to Congress in its specification of natural resource damage liability under CERCLA as justification for adopting restoration costs as the exclusive basis for natural resource damages. More specifically, the ruling observed that:

> Our reading of CERCLA does not attribute to Congress an irrational dislike of "efficiency"; rather it suggests that Congress was skeptical of the ability of human beings to measure the true "value" of a natural resource. Indeed, even the common law recognizes that restoration is the proper remedy for injury to property where measurement of damages by some other method will fail to compensate fully for the injury. Congress' refusal to view use value and restoration cost as having equal presumptive legitimacy merely recognizes that natural resources have value that is not readily measured by traditional means. (*Ohio*, pp. 51–52)

On the potentially responsible party's side, an out-of-court settlement avoids a precedent that could influence future awards.[8] For trustees, the absence of court decisions raises uncertainty over how judges (and possibly juries) will evaluate the methods used in nonmarket valuation and thus raises uncertainty about litigation. Moreover, for trustees, settlement means that some restoration can begin and that resources used to initiate current cases can be recovered to advance new cases that face a statute of limitations. While the actions of both groups are understandable, they do not respond to the objectives of maintaining natural assets, providing incentives for precautionary activities, or optimally allocating risk.

3. NATURAL RESOURCE DAMAGE ASSESSMENT AND RESEARCH ISSUES

Most damage assessments have been directed at the measurement of lost use and nonuse value attributable to injuries to specific natural resources. To our knowledge, these efforts have not resulted in the development of

---

[7] 880 F.2d 432 (D.C. Cir. 1989).

[8] Of course, it may be difficult to keep these settlements secret in cases that are well known to the public.

new methods for estimating the values of nonmarketed resources. However, they have expanded our understanding of the conceptual and practical issues raised in using present methods to value changes in the quality of environmental resources or in the services they provide, as documented in chapter 8 by Kenneth E. McConnell and chapter 10 by William D. Schulze.

3.1   Measuring the Services of Natural Assets. There is growing recognition that the indirect or revealed preference methods for valuing the services of nonmarket resources exploit connections between those services that are best treated as private commodities (even though they may not be available through conventional markets) and those that have public good characteristics (see Bockstael and McConnell [1991] and Smith [1991]). For example, the travel cost recreation demand model describes the demand for a commodity that has the characteristics of a private good—a recreational site's services. However, most recreation sites are public facilities and are managed as open-access resources with nominal entrance fees.[9]

In a different context, the hedonic property value model describes equilibrium prices for a set of heterogeneous private goods. Measures of environmental quality influence these prices when environmental attributes are among the location-specific amenities (or disamenities) a buyer acquires by purchasing a house. The quality of both the recreation site and the home's location may be influenced by levels of a public good such as a measure of environmental quality. This linkage suggests that damage assessments often concern themselves with using travel cost demand models to value what are represented as quality changes and not necessarily to value the services of a specific recreation site. For the hedonic model, this distinction is crucial. Under the Department of the Interior (DOI) rules, one does not seek to value private losses. Rather, one seeks to estimate people's implicit valuation of the quality attributes acquired by purchasing a home in a specific location. These characteristics, analysts argue, are among the services provided by the natural asset. One is not predicting new housing prices, but measuring how a market for these services would value them.

There is a subtle but important linkage in the terms we have been using to describe how indirect methods can be used to value natural assets. When discussing the public good services provided by these assets, we

---

[9]However, users can be excluded. When facilities reach their carrying capacity (at which point congestion effects become important), policies not based on price have been used to ration use. But these same levels of use could be achieved with price-based rationing.

have referred to them as services. But when we describe the methods for valuing them, we refer to them as quality measures. This is probably confusing. The distinction reflects the modeling strategy implied in each of the indirect methods. To use people's choices to reveal the value of these public good services, analysts have linked them to some observable commodity or action, with the public good services being treated as a measure of that commodity's quality. If we go further and assume that the quality (or services) and the good involved are weak complements, then the values for quality can be completely recovered from observable choices for the appropriable commodity. Thus, what is important about each of these methods is how the linkage is characterized, whether it is plausible, and whether it offers the only way or one of many ways of acquiring the public services of the resource in question.

An important choice must be made in describing the effects of an injury to a natural resource. Does the injury affect appropriable commodities such as visits to a recreation area? Does it influence the quality of visits? Or does it influence the public good services provided by the area with or without a visit? This description must be based on both the injury's physical characteristics and the way people perceive its effects. Moreover, the description influences what we attempt to value and therefore the modeling framework used to estimate the losses. For example, economists have less experience with valuing quality changes within the travel cost model than with valuing changes in terms of access to recreation sites. The record of consistent performance and increasing reliability shown by indirect methods relates to its performance in valuing recreation sites, not necessarily to valuing changes in their quality.[10] Similarly, the history of hedonic modeling largely stops at the point of demonstrating empirically that it is possible to measure the effects of site-specific amenities on housing prices without proceeding to the equally difficult task of repeating the applications over a wide range of environmental services (see Smith and Huang [1991]).

From the pattern of past research and the experience of recent damage assessments we can identify a discrepancy between recommendations and practice. Economists describing the tasks involved in damage assessment have argued that they must begin by specifying the services provided by the resource and connecting these services to injuries that are scientifically linked to the releases of hazardous waste or oil (see Desvousges,

---

[10]As Bockstael and McConnell (1991) demonstrate, the theory connecting Marshallian and Hicksian measures of quality change is more complex than that associated with price changes. The Smith and Kaoru (1990) overview of the factors influencing the travel cost model's estimates of consumer surplus involved attempts to measure the value of a recreation site's services, not quality changes at different types of sites.

Dunford, and Domanico [1989], as well as chapter 5 by Gardner Brown in this volume). Indeed, this message has been so clear that the proposed revisions to the DOI rules incorporate it as one of the first steps in natural resource damage assessment. The proposed rules describe the process of selecting alternatives for restoring the resource and estimating costs and losses during the recovery period in terms of these services, noting that:

> (i) In developing each of the possible alternatives, the authorized official shall list the proposed actions that would restore, rehabilitate, replace, and/or acquire the equivalent of the services provided by the injured natural resources that have been lost, and the period of time over which these services would continue to be lost.

> (ii) The authorized official shall identify services previously provided by the resource in its baseline condition in accordance with § 11.72 of this part [that is, the quantification phase-baseline services determination] and compare those services with services now provided by the injured resource. . . .[11]

Yet actually measuring these services and quantifying the connection between physical injuries and changes in the services flows is a daunting task requiring considerable research effort.

The quality measures used for travel cost and hedonic models are usually technical measures of pollution concentrations, such as measures of biochemical oxygen demand for water quality and ambient concentrations of particulate matter. The models assume that people act as if they knew these technical indexes and understood their implications for the quality of the services involved. Where the issues involved have been studied, research to date has suggested that the more complex the linkage between technical measures and perceptions, the less clear are the correspondences between the experts' technical measures and people's perceptions.[12]

The DOI rules focus all attention and resources in the injury determination phase on collecting information to measure the physical effects of releases on resources, rather than on making connections to people's perceptions of services. Equally important, experience in making the connections between technical measures and people's perceptions of services, as reported in the literature on nonmarket valuation, is insufficient. Indeed, without collecting new information trustees have little or no basis on

---

[11]56 *Federal Register* 19770 (April 29, 1991).

[12]See Brookshire and coauthors (1982) for the correspondence between photographic and technical measures of air quality, and Bockstael, McConnell, and Strand (1987) for the same in the case of water quality.

which to accomplish the tasks defined for them as part of an assessment plan. If we are to expect a service-oriented framework to be implemented, then a program of research is needed on measuring resource services and describing how the injuries produced by releases of oil or hazardous waste will affect them.

It may seem curious that so few attempts have been made to measure people's perceptions of environmental services when a broad consensus accepts a service orientation. Part of the problem arises because the "transactions" we seek to understand are outside markets. All we can observe are people's choices of the linked commodity. There is no process that assures we can measure the amount of the natural resource's services someone receives because he purchased this linked commodity. Often, professional realtors' estimates of price differentials due to specific amenities (or disamenities) closely approximate the findings derived in a hedonic model.[13] But this is not equivalent to measuring the amount of the service people receive with that purchase. Usually these cases involve locations that are easily classified into distinctive groups by such factors as level of smog, proximity to an earthquake fault line, or level of airport noise. In some cases, technical measures of the source of the external effect (such as concentrations of oxidants, severity of earthquake damage levels, or increased noise levels) are available. However, these technical indexes may not readily convert to how such "services" as clean air, low earthquake damage, or low noise level contribute to people's well-being. Moreover, the market (despite the ideal assumptions of the hedonic framework) may only distinguish discrete categories of impacts and not the continuous gradations assumed in theoretical treatments.

Thus we may be able to determine that people value avoiding disruptions to environmental services, but with hedonic or other indirect methods we may not be able to measure how these values change with the amount of disruption. To examine how these issues can arise in a damage assessment, consider the following example. Some people buy homes near a river that periodically experiences oil spills. They buy the house because the housing prices are lower than those of comparable homes on sections of the river that preclude the barge traffic that gives rise to the spills. We conclude that these buyers' valuations of the losses must be less

---

[13]d'Arge and Shogren (1989) compared the performance of hedonic property value models (based on assessed valuations as price measures), realtors' evaluations, and CVM responses. They also used realtors' evaluations to attempt to distinguish the differences in housing prices due to water quality differences in the lakes near two areas. More recently, Michaels and Smith (1990) used realtor evaluations to define sub-markets for hedonic estimation. They found the classifications were consistent across realtors and that treating the models as separate had a marked effect on the effects attributed to hazardous waste sites in Boston.

than the price differential available to them in the market. How much of the reduced services do they consume? We do not know, and multiple factors contribute to the difficulty of answering this question. In our example, what is available to people—and what we can observe—are homes that vary in proximity to two different kinds of river area. How does the distance from each river area to a house relate to the services a household derives from each river area? By comparing the two situations, what insight would be gained into the loss of services suffered by homeowners closer to the river area with the potential for spills?—a question of particular relevance. In each case, the housing decision provides homeowners with increased access and earlier use, factors that lower the cost of obtaining the services of the river in terms of time and travel costs. But unless visitation information is collected, we cannot know how much services may have been reduced. Moreover, our example exposes another problem: several indirect methods can capture parts of the same losses a household incurs from injuries to a natural resource; this would lead to double counting in the estimation of damages (see the discussion by McConnell in chapter 8 of the potential for overlaps between the travel cost and hedonic models in valuing cleanups).

It is important to recognize that these issues are not unique to non-marketed services, and that we are not much better off in trying to measure the services of any marketed capital asset. The theory underlying indexes of capacity utilization and the endogeneity of an asset's life remain active areas of research because few situations exist where we can observe simultaneously markets for assets and rental markets for their services. Thus the absence of service measures for natural assets is not a unique deficiency.[14] It does, however, suggest that more careful evaluation of existing information on measuring the services of conventional capital assets offers another potential research area that is stimulated by the needs of natural resource damage assessment.

3.2 Measuring Aggregate Use Values. Three decisions distinguish the strategies used in measuring use values for injured natural resources. We described the first decision in the previous section—whether the analysis views the injury as eliminating the resource's appropriable services or as changing its public good services, which are often represented as quality features. The second decision concerns how the model for measuring losses in use values incorporates substitute sites and their availability

---

[14]Environmental services are not the only publicly provided services that raise such issues. Decisions on highway programs and user taxes for highways provide another example. Indeed, one of the arguments for using a constant tax per gallon of fuel is that fuel consumption provides a reasonable proxy for one component of the use of highway services.

during the injured resource's recovery period. The third decision concerns the transition between individual and aggregate estimates of damage.

Each of these issues is treated differently for oil spills than for old hazardous waste sites. Resources impacted by spills often can experience natural recovery. This feature seems to be generally understood, at least since publicity about the oil spill from the *Exxon Valdez*. Indeed, because of such greater understanding, one might argue that the proposed revisions to DOI's regulations are designed to be more responsive to damage assessments for oil spills than for old sites involving releases of hazardous substances.[15] Injuries resulting from oil spills have a clearly identifiable starting point in time, and in the case of spills it is possible (at least in principle) to consider the resource's services under baseline or pre-spill conditions. With old hazardous waste sites, the time period of releases may extend so far into the past that defining services, specifying how the restored resource would relate to available substitutes (and even what those substitutes might be), and identifying the likely group of new users are all exceptionally difficult.

Damage assessment has effectively demonstrated a weakness in the research strategy for improving nonmarket valuation methods. Researchers have focused on pushing the analysis to a more micro level in order to avoid the problems posed by using aggregate data to represent an average or representative individual, and to reflect more adequately the heterogeneity in the user population's preferences. In the process, they have concentrated on the typical user's values rather than on how to identify those people who will become the typical users under specific conditions. In other words, how would the user group change with modifications in the quality of a resource's services?

The literature on industrial organization has been forced to address comparable issues when evaluating whether changes in market participants (usually suppliers) would affect the efficiency of the market in allocating the commodities involved. A conceptual distinction is drawn between the commodity and the geographic extent of the market. In the field of benefit analysis, defining the market for a commodity has been described as the problem of characterizing available substitutes, and defining the geographic extent of the market has been described as the problem of knowing whose values to aggregate.[16]

---

[15]These revisions seem to have been designed to focus on oil spills, which is difficult to explain given the mandate to prepare separate rules for oil spills stated in the Oil Pollution Act of 1990 (33 U.S.C. 2701 *et seq.*).

[16]If we examine the literature, most discussions contend that in estimating demand functions for a resource's services, accounting for substitutes will be important to avoid specification errors in the estimates, but not necessarily for benefit measurement (see

In damage assessment, the analyst makes the assumptions that incorporate substitution and aggregation questions by translating the injury into something that can be monetized. The analyst would ask, for example, does the injury eliminate the site's services, change quality at a given price, or differentially affect certain uses only? Elimination of services would be conveyed by a price change from baseline price to the choke price or price of a perfect substitute (as in the Eagle River case described in chapter 7). Quality change involves describing how quality would shift demand.[17]

One example establishing a linkage between quality and demand functions can be found in Smith, Desvousges, and Fisher's (1986) simple travel cost demand model. This model incorporates the effects of variations in water quality on recreational boating on the Monongahela River by treating visits to all locations along rivers around Pittsburgh as if they were to the same site and using measured differences in dissolved oxygen at the specific locations visited as proxy variables describing quality conditions. This last approach requires an ability to measure demands for activities at injured sites or to infer the shift in site demand due to the elimination of activities. These are fairly specific requirements that very few valuation applications have had to tackle with the level of detail required for litigation. As a result, we know little about the estimates' sensitivity to modeling judgments.[18] Nonetheless, some work has begun in which random utility models (RUMs) are used. The RUM framework treats an individual's site-selection decision as a comparison of distinctive bundles of characteristics. On each trip occasion the individual selects the site providing the greatest utility, given its access and quality conditions. Because the RUM model allows the analyst to introduce fairly specific changes in quality conditions, it has emerged as a preferred modeling

Bockstael and Kling [1988] and Kling [1989]). This conclusion, while technically correct under a narrow set of conditions, is not relevant to damage assessment. It relates to only one type of valuation task—measuring the consumer surplus gain (or loss) from a change in a commodity's price.

[17]This is the approach that McConnell (1986 and 1991) used to evaluate the performance of a contingent behavior model describing the recreational use values associated with cleaning up polychlorinated biphenyl (PCB) releases in New Bedford harbor in Massachusetts. On the basis of actual use patterns and using a random utility model describing selection decisions for beaches in the area, McConnell isolated an effect that he attributed to the location of beaches in zones known to have PCB concentrations. This proxy variable was used to represent people's perceptions of how contamination affected quality and their site-selection decisions.

[18]A recent comparison of conventional travel cost demand models to random utility and hedonic travel cost frameworks indicates rather large differences among the methods in the measures for the value of improving sport fishing quality (as represented by catch rates). See Smith and coauthors (1992).

framework when damage assessments are described as quality changes for recreational resources.[19]

While this type of innovation is a promising method for nonmarket valuation of quality changes, it does not resolve the two fundamental issues associated with defining the extent of the market. Random utility model specifications routinely deal with a user population and do not describe either the decision to participate or the level of participation in a season. Both factors contribute to what we have referred to as the geographic extent of the market. Equally important, they require in advance a definition of what constitutes an alternative choice. Welfare measures must consider all the alternative choices each individual evaluates, even though estimation may (because of the independence of irrelevant alternatives assumption) be limited to a subset.[20] This subset limitation is simply another version of the commodity extent of the market.

Decisions on both aspects of developing an aggregate estimate of use value will remain modeling judgments because they arise from fundamental questions in implementing consumer preference theory. We are not suggesting that further research will change this status. However, further research should be able to provide measures that can evaluate the quality of these judgments in specific cases. This is a goal that can be realized by research outside the limitations of a specific natural resource damage assessment case. Moreover, because the same issues arise in using benefit-cost analyses for public investment decisions and in evaluations of regulations, the resulting guidelines would have broad relevance to applied welfare economics.

3.3 Nonuse Values. Natural resource damage assessment has helped to clarify both conceptual and practical aspects of nonuse values. It is too early to know whether the research for large cases (such as that resulting from the *Exxon Valdez* oil spill) will contribute significantly to our ability to measure nonuse values. Judgment must await disclosure of research findings so that we can learn from the approaches taken by each side. In the interim, new research questions raised by this focused attention on nonuse values have direct implications for valuing a wide range of public goods. We will consider four aspects of this research—embedding, measurement strategies and contingent valuation, the timing of services and nonuse values, and the extent of the market for the services underlying

---

[19]For example, the Jones, Jester, and Sung (1989) analysis of fishing quality in Lake Michigan focused on the impacts of warnings about hazardous waste contamination at specific fish locations and used the flexibility of the RUM formulation to describe the consumer losses by eliminating sites from the choice set.

[20]See Smith and Kaoru (1990) for an evaluation of the implications of site definition for tests of irrelevant alternatives assumptions and for benefit measurement.

nonuse values. However, before turning to each of these questions, we must describe how the chronology of ideas on nonuse values has evolved since the beginning of research associated with damage assessments.

Prior to the early background reports on measuring natural resource damages, a consensus had emerged on how to classify the components of a resource's total value. As described by McConnell in chapter 8 and Freeman in chapter 13, this scheme requires that valuation measures begin by specifying how an individual's well-being will be described—by utility or expected utility. The latter introduces uncertainty into the individual's decision process, and with it the opportunity to consider whether the events at risk influence the marginal utility of income. When these influences exist, institutions allowing people to adjust to risk can be especially important to monetary measures of changes in well-being. Depending largely on how differences in the marginal utility of income are treated, it is possible to define a variety of monetary measures of changes in a person's well-being (see chapter 13 by Freeman for more details). The chapters in this volume, and the recent research their authors use in developing their synthesis, make an important contribution to the definition and measurement of nonuse values: an overall acceptance that option value is *not* a distinct component of the total value an individual might place on a resource. Option value is viewed instead as one method (and there are numerous others) for describing how behavioral responses to uncertainty influence monetary measures of changes in well-being (now measured by the expected utility). With this clarification, use and nonuse values can be assumed to arise when the individual's decision situation approximates conditions of certainty or when there are behaviorally relevant sources of uncertainty.[21]

Our selection of the term "nonuse value" rather than "existence value" is deliberate, and is a more direct by-product of the natural resource damage assessment process. When Krutilla (1967) introduced existence value, he was describing irreversible allocation decisions involving unique natural environments. His argument has been misinterpreted to imply that irreversibility and uniqueness are required for existence values (see Cummings [1989] and Cicchetti [1989] as examples). This is not so. Rather, Krutilla was simply arguing that existence

---

[21]This is about the stage that the discussion of use, option, and existence values had reached (at least in unpublished literature up to 1984) two years before the final DOI rules were issued, in which option value was incorrectly identified as a distinct component of value. Of course, discussions in some literature continued to maintain the inconsistency (see Cross [1989] as a notable example). While it took some time for the clarification of option value to be accepted among those working on damage assessment, it is now widely acknowledged. But it should not be regarded as a product of research stimulated by damage assessments.

values might be especially important in cases involving unique natural environments.

Today's literature has rediscovered McConnell's (1983) original insight—that existence values arise from services that correspond to what we specify in defining a pure public good. They do not require in situ presence. There are no ways to appropriate the services involved, so others cannot be precluded from enjoying them. Criticisms by Quiggin (1990) and Rosenthal and Nelson (1991) of the attempts to estimate existence values misinterpret this feature, judging it as a criticism of nonuse values when it actually provides insight into why these values arise. Moreover, there is no need to assume that services only have value when some allocation of the resource eliminates its public good services. As Freeman explains in chapter 13, nonuse values can arise from changes in the amount or quality of these services. The 1989 court of appeals ruling in *Ohio* used this type of reasoning to suggest that nonuse values arise from nonconsumptive (that is, nonappropriable) uses that do not require in situ presence.

In its proposed revisions to the type B rules, DOI offers the prospective trustee a dilemma. Nonuse values are now recognized (as the *Ohio* ruling required) as part of a resource's total value and are included in what the rules define as compensable values. Moreover, DOI acknowledges that the techniques included under the broad category of contingent valuation (CV) methods offer the only approaches currently available to measure nonuse values. Yet the rules require that any of the CV techniques be treated as a least reliable approach to estimating values. Thus, trustees must include values that cannot be measured in what DOI regards as reliable ways.

In chapter 10 William Schulze focuses on whether we can assume that people have crystallized values for the commodities (or services) whose values are to be estimated with CV methods. When they do not, he argues, the context established for the valuation questions will be important to the valuation responses. In the view of Fischhoff and Furby (1988) and Mitchell and Carson (1989), this argument implies that the framing of the questions for these cases will be more likely to influence the CV value estimates. While Schulze describes this as a limitation, when we compare Rowe and Schulze (1985) (which underlies the plaintiff's side of the Eagle River case described in chapter 7) to more recent surveys designed to value reductions in the air pollution associated with Denver's Brown Cloud experiment (see Irwin and coauthors [1990]), we would argue that such responses should increase, not decrease, confidence in the methodology. People are recognizing differences in these descriptions and responding to them. From the analyst's perspective, the differences in framing may not seem important. Our current conceptual treatment of people's reasons for valuing particular services may not explain their responses, but this does not necessarily mean that the responses are inappropriate or that they reflect methodological flaws. Instead, it may mean that analysts do not understand the commodities involved or the full conditions of access to them.

Damage assessment has focused attention on one aspect of framing— the embedding problem. In many respects, embedding is not a new issue. Cummings, Brookshire, and Schulze (1986) identified it as the part/whole problem in their effort to evaluate the CV method and prescribe guidelines for its use. The most direct statement of the issue (in the context of criticism of the CV method) is in Kahneman and Knetsch's (1991) suggestion that a well-formed set of values should be insensitive to whether we ask about the value of some commodity after progressively identifying it as a subcomponent of various sets of environmental commodities or ask about it directly. Kahneman and Knetsch would argue, for example, that the stated value of an improvement in water quality in a specific section of a river should not depend on whether we first ask about the value for improvements in water quality at all rivers and lakes and then ask about the value for improvement in one section of a river. Finding differences in the values reported by individuals after different sets of initial questions (that is, levels of embedding), Kahneman and Knetsch (1991) conclude that CV results are arbitrary.

It is not our intention to criticize here Kahneman and Knetsch's analyses or conclusions (for a critique, see Smith [1991] and Harrison [1992]). We cite their argument to highlight the need to consider the research issues raised by the embedding problem. The commodity definition implied by the sequence of questions in our river and lake example (or in the much more diverse cases used by Kahneman and Knetsch) implicitly imposes specific commodity-aggregation conditions on the target good for valuation. Do people perceive water quality in a particular section of the river as a part of a more aggregate service flow—water quality in all rivers and lakes? This specification, when combined with valuation questions, establishes levels for the intervening variables (quality in several other lakes) that the individual has implicitly purchased. As a set of conditioning variables, these levels will influence the value offered for changes in any particular resource's quality because some degree of substitution is likely among the alternatives.

One can think of embedding as contributing to a definition of the equivalent of a commodity extent of the market. How do we define what is to be changed? Do we recognize and identify the condition of substitute or complementary resources and "control" what people know about their quality and availability through the CV questions? Or do we simply elicit people's perceptions of the resource's availability after the fact and exert "control" through multivariate analysis of the responses? There are no unambiguous answers to these questions in the available literature, but several important insights are emerging. Questions do not control people's perceptions in the same way that laboratory experiments in the natural or economic sciences can control activities. Instead, questions present information that will influence people's perceptions. Any specification of the availability or quality of other resources is simply information that will be considered along with what respondents already know.

If a question's framing does not conform to the way people evaluate a resource's services, their responses may be affected. Equally important (when we are focusing on nonuse values), the elicitation of behavior or values with CV for in situ uses faces the same issues. Moreover, the discussion in much of the literature is not clear about treating these components jointly or separately. Bishop and Welsh (1991) and other conceptual reviewers (see Randall [1991]) argue that a total value orientation is the most appropriate perspective for the CV method because total value is what we should be measuring, and because people may not be able to separate values into components attributable to motives in a reliable way.

Damage assessment has focused attention on the tasks of allocating values across components—that is, use versus nonuse. Before DOI's proposed revisions to the type B rules, nonuse values could generally not be included in damage assessments (as Brown describes in chapter 5). Even the proposed revisions comment on the reliability of value estimates arising from such allocations. Under the DOI revisions, use values derived from CV estimates of total value are classified, on the basis of respondents' allocations of the total use and nonuse components, as least reliable estimates.

These issues raise the need for developing conceptual and empirical analyses that parallel the extensive work done on demand interrelationships between market commodities. Discussions of the role of separability in specifying commodity aggregates and the implications of substitution and complementarity relationships for demand measurement are completely analogous to the questions implied in embedding and allocation among resources that can be assumed to comprise the commodity extent of the market for an injured natural resource. Carson and Mitchell (1991) recently compared their contingent valuation estimates for the value of water quality improvements at all freshwater bodies with those produced by a specific study of water quality in one river basin, the Monongahela River (Smith and Desvousges [1986]). Both studies used the same vehicle to explain water quality improvements. Because the Carson and Mitchell study defined the commodity as water quality at all lakes, an improvement in it should have been more highly valued than improvement in a single-river system. This is precisely what Carson and Mitchell's analysis of the two studies' findings concludes. Of course, this does not tell us how respondents formed the equivalent of a commodity aggregate that corresponded (from their perspective) to all freshwater bodies in the United States. Each respondent implicitly defined his or her own set of substitute and complementary resources, considered the value of improving them, and then used that composite in responding to the survey questions. While Carson and Mitchell's study considered partial improvements, they found their valuation measure insensitive to fairly large departures from the goal of improvement at all sites. To some extent this observation reinforces the conjecture we posed in chapter 7: discontinuities are likely to occur when people convert physical changes in a resource into changes in their perceptions of the services derived from it.

While most discussions of nonuse values argue that changes in such values can only be measured with CV techniques, Larson (1990) has recently suggested that Neill's (1988) framework could be extended to derive estimates without the CV method. Larson suggested that by assuming that preferences are implicitly separable and that at least one commodity in a system has a Marshallian income slope that is independent of the resource's services, we can recover measures of the incremental value of a change in the services using estimates of that demand function. These estimates would be combined with knowledge of how the demand for other commodities in the implicitly separable group would change with changes in the services. Because this strategy does not require weak complementarity, Larson suggested that the value measure includes both use and nonuse values. To implement the strategy we must know in advance the commodity with the independence of the Marshallian income slope and be able to both specify the implicitly separable grouping and estimate the changes in quantities demanded for the components.

Implementation of this strategy will depend on our ability to observe differences in people's perceptions of a resource's services, and to consider those differences with analytical judgment and empirical tests of demand specification (including proxy measures for those services). Are these approaches inherently more reliable than the CV method? It is important to recognize that these approaches substitute a statistical link for observed behavior. We do not observe changes in the implicitly separable commodities arising from the services of the nonmarket good in a controlled setting. We separate these demands from influences other than natural resources, using multivariate statistical methods. Progress in measuring nonuse values might be made by moving beyond such either/or choices (as found in CV or in the extensive set of prior restrictions suggested by Larson) to joint strategies. We must formulate testable hypotheses, as the Larson analysis assumes, and build them into contingent valuation design. This would seem to be a reasonable strategy for improving the plausibility of the results because it tests both analysts' judgments and respondents' answers for mutual consistency.

In the preceding sections we have frequently discussed injuries to natural resources as if they resulted in permanent changes in the resource's services. In practical terms, we have assumed that the natural recovery period was exceptionally long, so the reduction in services, quality, or both would remain if there were no restoration efforts. This characterization does not fit all situations. In fact, it may not adequately represent most of them. This is especially true for oil spills. Suppose, for example, that we must evaluate the damages from an oil spill that kills five thousand marine waterfowl, several hundred marine mammals, and several thousand fish of various species. None of the species affected are endangered, and the injuries from our hypothesized spill would not destroy their populations. Assume further that the spill can be cleaned up to restore the coastal environment to its baseline condition.

This example poses a number of challenging problems for measuring damages based on use, and especially nonuse, values. For instance, in the case of use values, how do we evaluate the use value losses for short-term disruptions that may involve substitutions both to other resources and over time to the use of the injured resource? While we have little experience with measuring the losses due to temporal substitution, a more challenging issue arises in attempting to characterize the nonuse values associated with the losses of waterfowl, marine mammals, and fish.

Undoubtedly these impacts cause immediate losses that may well be significant reductions in well-being for some people, even though those people did not actively use the resources injured in any specific way. However, the losses may not be permanent, even if the affected species' populations never return to their original sizes. Adjustment, substitution, and accommodation over time may restore people's original level of well-being.

Evaluation of the loss in well-being from these impulse effects (short-term events) is one of the most challenging issues raised by natural resource damage assessment cases. Certainly there are numerous parallels, ranging from the most extreme situation of losing a member of one's family to the less painful experience of losing a treasured souvenir. The object is irreplaceable, and the reduction in well-being is genuine, but the sense of loss may not remain at the same level indefinitely. Clearly this will vary with the loss and the individual.

Are such losses beyond economic valuation? They are not beyond the scope of analysis in the context of describing people's motives for purchasing insurance. Indeed, the very definition used to identify irreplaceable commodities in Cook and Graham's (1977) classic analysis of the demand for insurance—how the Hicksian consumer surplus for the object changes with income—corresponds to the attribute Willig (1978) identified as linking Marshallian and Hicksian consumer surplus measures for quality, as well as to Larson's (1990) proposed technique for using indirect methods to measure the total value of nonmarketed resources. Thus, these losses can be valued. They are likely to be the very cases that will enhance our understanding of preferences to assure better appreciation of how longer-term, irreversible losses should be valued.

3.4   Extent of the Market. Once an injury to a natural resource is defined physically, the economist must make two strategic decisions. First, how is that injury to be represented in economic terms? And second, who cares about the changes it produces? These questions parallel the task of defining the commodity and the geographic extent of the market in microeconomic evaluations of industry structure for performance. In the language of the proposed revisions to DOI's rules, are the services lost a small fraction of a much larger quantity, presumed to be available because the injured resource is treated as if it had a large number of perfect substitutes? Or, in contrast, is the resource assumed to be unique, so the loss may well be a large fraction of the total supply available? These questions are widely recognized in nonmarket valuation, especially in applications involving recreation resources. Unfortunately, recognition does not mean that we have advanced as far as applied industrial organization in offering practical answers.

Like other issues, the extent-of-the-market issue is not unique to resource economics. Willig's (1991) overview of the U.S. Department of Justice's 1984 Merger Guidelines describes market delineation as an economic evaluation that identifies the "universe" over which concentration measures are calculated and, in turn, the "net efficiencies" of changes in market structure that would be measured. Residual demand analysis (an approach similar to that found in general equilibrium demand models) is one method for developing empirical information that contributes to the economic judgment required in objectively delineating markets (see Scheffman [1990]). Similar strategies may well be possible for determining the limits to the effective market for environmental resources. Development of some guidelines for classifying resources that generate significant use values at a regional level would be a desirable first step. Comparable valuations for resources associated with nonuse values will be essential to implement DOI's requirement for restoration and rehabilitation plans prior to the measurement of damages.

As we note in chapter 7 and as McConnell in chapter 8 and Freeman in chapter 13 observe, the specification of who cares (or the geographic extent of the market) is likely to be more important to estimating aggregate damages than is the modeling judgment underlying the measurement of typical per-household losses. The Eagle River case illustrates the impact of these assumptions especially well (see chapter 7). Unfortunately, the available literature offers little guidance on this issue. More than a decade ago, we proposed a simple test for travel cost models estimated with origin zone data (see Smith and Kopp [1980]). However, most practitioners argue the need for micro data, and the majority of the available data rely on intercept surveys. So the extent-of-the-market problem usually cannot be addressed. The old DOI rules did not appreciate the problem, while proposed rules seem to appreciate it but offer no guidance to resolving it. Instead, the proposed rules handle the problem by labeling some methods, notably CV-based questions, as least reliable in developing information that might be used to specify the geographic extent of the market. For example, the rules suggest that:

> When CV is used to quantify use values alone, the survey population would normally consist of actual users of the resource. Use value estimates based on general population surveys would be considered in the least reliable category when survey respondents are asked to allocate a portion of their bid to nonuse values.[22]

Thus we are left with an impossible task in dealing with old sites for which there are no records of past users. Nor can we use surveys to determine reliably how the site might change with restoration. Such an analysis would require using the CV method to elicit how people might alter their behavior.

Regardless of the proposed rules, there seems to be little alternative to using household surveys to define the people who care, both as prospective users and as holders of nonuse values. As Freeman observes in chapter 13, these are not separate people. Simple initial questions may identify people who would use a restored resource or care about the resource before proposing an economic choice (such as willingness to pay for improvements or amounts of use at a restored site). Such questions need not be analyzed or interpreted independently from follow-up questions involving economic choices. Indeed, research on nonmarket valuation seems to consistently suggest strategies that use theory to link responses across questions posed to surveyed respondents, whether the analysis is directed at using a revealed preference model with past decisions, CV questions, or some composite of the two.

Issues associated with the geographic extent of the market will, in some situations, require a noneconomic policy decision. For resources with international significance, where does the boundary of a market stop for damage calculations? With use values, it seems reasonable to include

---

[22]56 *Federal Register* 19762 (April 29, 1991).

all (domestic and international) uses, although the modeling might be done separately to account for differences in the nature of the trips and the relevant set of substitutes. With nonuse values, the geographic boundary probably will be taken to correspond to national boundaries, but there is nothing in the economic theory underlying our definition of the value of such resources as assets that implies this will be the case. Indeed, discussions of the value of tropical rain forests or endangered species in developing countries to people in developed economies present an analogous problem.

3.5   Benefits Transfer. Benefits transfer is commonplace in nearly all benefit-cost analyses. It is an estimate of the value people would place on a particular change when the circumstances conditioning that estimate correspond to specific policy scenarios that hold other economic conditions constant.[23] In spite of fairly widespread use of benefits transfer in policy analyses, little professional discussion is available on how it should be done or on the issues involved in developing transferable models.[24]

Because natural resource damage assessment imposes intense scrutiny on damage estimates, it focuses attention on the assumptions and practices used in benefits transfer. It also identifies new issues that arise in damage transfers that are unlikely to have been encountered in benefit analyses for other policy questions.

In the case of contingent valuation, one is offered the opportunity to internalize the transfer with individual respondents. That is, with a CV approach we could ask individuals about their behavior in response to a change that would correspond to restoring a resource to its baseline condition or to whatever situation is envisioned in the restoration and compensation plan. In doing so, we would leave to each respondent the process of connecting adjustments to current activities in response to the proposed change.

Restatement of the benefits transfer issue identifies a different type of research strategy—that of developing transferable models for valuation. One way to research this issue is to ask what the limits are to type A assessments that rely on computer-based models to calculate losses. This is an important research question. It may make sense, for example, to estimate functions describing individuals' losses from damages at a micro level, transfer those models, and focus attention in each case on evaluat-

---

[23]In contrast, a forecast would attempt to incorporate all potential policy and predicted changes into the evaluation. It would focus on something we could observe directly.

[24]The first discussion of benefits transfer as a process is developed in Freeman (1984). The March 1992 issue of *Water Resources Research* (volume 28, number 3) includes a set of conceptual papers reacting to benefit transfer analyses conducted by Desvousges, Naughton, and Parsons (1992) and Luken, Johnson, and Kibler (1992).

ing the geographic extent of the market. The best strategy probably will vary with the type of resource that is injured.

Moreover, in some situations, we may be able to develop baseline models to use in evaluating future injuries. This is especially true for oil spills.[25] In principle, such models offer the ability to observe pre-spill or baseline conditions. A research strategy could involve developing models and valuation estimates for those areas with heavy oil tanker traffic or production activities. Indeed, this may be one of the PRP research strategies to emerge from the *Exxon Valdez* case. While we do not want to overinterpret the potential implications of this process, such activities could themselves induce behavioral responses. Firms might redirect precautionary activities to protecting the most highly valued resources at the expense of less valued ones. This signaling capacity is exactly what is envisioned by Shavell's (1984) assumption that firms know the damage functions when liability is argued as a way to encourage efficient management of activities that may cause externalities. The need to develop an inventory of transferable models for future litigation may serve this purpose. The damage functions also suggest that if these estimates are developed by the plaintiffs' analysts, as through the National Oceanic and Atmospheric Administration's Damage Assessment Office, the estimates should be widely reviewed and made available as signals to potential PRPs about the consequences of avoiding releases.

There are additional reasons for encouraging research focused on transferrable models. Without such research we can expect transfers to take place by precedent rather than according to the best professional judgment. The January 24, 1991, ruling in the *State of Idaho v. Southern Refrigerated Transport* provides an example.[26] The ruling allowed some types of benefit transfers and not others. Damages sought in the case included losses of use and nonuse values (the latter identified as existence values) from injuries to a fishery because hazardous substances were released into the Little Salmon River. Several aspects of the decision illustrate the types of transfers evaluated and how they might influence future damage assessments.

The state sought to claim existence value for adult steelhead trout that did not return to the river because of injury from the spill. The state used a CV analysis performed by the Northwest Planning Council intended "to determine what individuals in the Northwest would be willing to pay in the form of increases to their power bill to double the runs of steelhead and salmon in the entire Columbia River Basin" (*State of Idaho*, p. 61). The

---

[25]In fact, the state of California is currently undertaking such a modeling exercise for coastal oil spills.

[26]U.S. District Court for the District of Idaho, Civil Action No. 88–1279.

court ruled that the study did not determine existence value for the injured fish with "any degree of certainty." It continued by noting that the decision did not reject existence value for the steelhead; rather, the plaintiff's study was found to be not legally sufficient to establish the value.

A second aspect of the ruling also relates to transfer practices. The decision rejected the estimated recreational value lost due to in-season closure of the Little Salmon River for two months. Again agreeing that the value existed, the decision held that the method selected failed to prove damages with "reasonable certainty." The argument used to support the conclusion parallels our discussions of the need to consider the commodity extent of the market in determining damages. The state of Idaho's analyst contended that consumers place a value on fishing the Little Salmon River over and above other fishing areas. However, the court identified the benefits transfer as a contradiction to this assumption, noting that while this was the assumption, the value was based on the value of fishing a similar area. The ruling continued, suggesting that:

> Because the two areas are substitutes, there can be no extra value attached to one or the other. If one site is closed, the consumers will simply go to the other site to fish. From the evidence presented, an inference could be drawn that perhaps some fishing trips were canceled when the season was closed. However, an equally plausible inference is that steelhead fishermen, being a particularly determined lot who fish in all types of weather conditions, merely traveled a few more miles to fish at an equally comparable location. Based on the record, the Court does not have sufficient evidence to establish a value for the lost fishing days, if any did in fact occur. (*State of Idaho*, p. 64)

The court demonstrated by its decision that consistency in the transfer assumptions will matter. The fact that two sites are substitutes does not mean that they are perfect substitutes or that they will have equal value. They may be at different locations. Those "few more miles" were an added cost, and they were the basis for the defendant's damage estimates in the Eagle River case. However, if the analyst implicitly assumes perfect substitution by transferring one site's demand to value another, then the court will require the analysis of damages to be consistent with that assumption.

4. WHITHER NATURAL RESOURCE DAMAGE ASSESSMENT?

Our discussion of natural resource damage liability began with Anderson in chapter 3 describing how it is consistent with a more general liability system. Moreover, as Breen's (1989) article (written since the circulation of an early draft of Anderson's chapter) suggests, we can interpret the CERCLA/SARA definition as the result of an evolving doctrine of natural resource damage liability that began with the Trans-Alaska Pipeline Authorization Act of 1973.[27] The court of appeals ruling on challenges to the DOI rules, together with the Oil Pollution Act of 1990, seems to have firmly established restoration costs as a basis for damage assessment. Both recognize that use and nonuse values will be lost during the recovery period for the resource. However, none of the rulings, legislation, or newly proposed DOI rules deal effectively with defining what constitutes restoration. In short, the rhetoric of DOI's proposed rules does not match the practical implementation of restoration planning. There is little or no correspondence between the ways injuries to natural resources are being measured and the requirements to specify economically meaningful definitions of how their services are affected by those injuries. Without this correspondence, the prospects of developing damage estimates consistent with a restoration and compensation determination plan (as DOI's proposed rules envision) are slim.

Unfortunately, from the perspective of the incentive effects of natural resource damage assessment as a policy, the DOI rules are so vague as to make it possible for trustees and potentially responsible parties to avoid the problem entirely. In short, the Department of the Interior has written new rules that prescribe a procedure that is impossible to monitor effectively. The loopholes appear in the ten factors that contribute to selecting alternatives for restoration, rehabilitation, replacement, and acquisition of equivalent resources and to evaluating whether the costs are grossly disproportionate in relation to natural resource damages. Natural resource damage assessment could follow along the path that the National Environmental Policy Act charted with environmental impact statements and establish procedural requirements that increase the information that must be assembled, without offering a mechanism to monitor whether and how it is used to inform decisions.[28] However, instead we delay decisions and increase bureaucratic and transaction costs for action, while having no assurance that the goals motivating these costs will be considered. But there is an important distinction to be made. Environmental impact statements are a part of the record underlying administrative rulemaking, while natural resource damage assessments are subject to litigation and therefore to more intense scrutiny. It is assumed that a judicial review will take place. If the practices described in these chapters continue to produce settlements before trials, then no mechanism will exist for monitoring the

---

[27]43 U.S.C. § 1653 (a) (1), (c)(1).

[28]42 U.S.C.A. 4321 et seq. § 102 (2)(c).

performance of what seem destined to be the procedural activities. Under these circumstances, both the compensation requirements that motivate natural resource damage liability and the incentive risk-sharing properties of this type of policy must be questioned.

Remedies for the situation will require reforms. A set of practical rules should be written to define explicit criteria for restoration, rehabilitation, and replacement, as well as to define what constitutes grossly disproportionate costs. These rules must recognize that the natural and economic sciences involved in natural resource damage assessment must work together as partners in valuing the services of natural assets, and that experience with the process will require modifying those practices over time. Because many court cases are likely to arise from oil spills, the future of natural resource damage assessment as an effective mechanism for responding to the goals identified in the legislation establishing natural resources as important public assets may well rest with the National Oceanic and Atmospheric Administration and the responses it makes in preparing new rules for such assessments.

REFERENCES

Bishop, Richard C., and Michael P. Welsh. 1991. "Assessment of the Potential for Non-Use Valuation Research Under the Glen Canyon Environmental Studies: Literature Review and a Study Prospectus," draft report prepared for Glen Canyon Studies. Madison, Wis.: HBRS, Inc.

Bockstael, Nancy E., and Catherine L. Kling. 1988. "Valuing Environmental Quality: Weak Complementarity with Sets of Goods," *American Journal of Agricultural Economics* 70 (August), pp. 654–662.

Bockstael, Nancy E., and Kenneth E. McConnell. 1991. "The Demand for Quality Differentiated Goods: A Synthesis," working paper, Department of Agricultural and Resource Economics, University of Maryland, College Park.

Bockstael, Nancy E., Kenneth E. McConnell, and Ivar E. Strand. 1987. "Benefits from Improvements in Chesapeake Bay Water Quality." In *Benefit Analysis Using Indirect or Imputed Market Methods*, Vol. 2. Report to the U.S. Environmental Protection Agency, EPA Contract CR-811043-01-0.

Breen, Barry. 1989. "Citizen Suits for Natural Resource Damages: Closing a Gap in Federal Environmental Law," *Wake Forest Law Review* 24, pp. 851–880.

Brookshire, David S., Mark A. Thayer, William D. Schulze, and Ralph C. d'Arge. 1982. "Valuing Public Goods: A Comparison of Survey and Hedonic Approaches," *American Economic Review* 72 (March), pp. 165–177.

Carson, Richard T., and Robert Cameron Mitchell. 1991. "The Value of Clean Water: The Public's Willingness to Pay for Boatable, Fishable and Swimmable Quality Water," unpublished paper, Department of Economics, University of California at San Diego.

Cicchetti, Charles J. 1989. "Comments on the U.S. Department of [the] Interior's Advanced Notice of Proposed Rulemaking 43 CFR Part 11 Natural Resource Damage Assessments."

Cook, Phillip J., and Daniel A. Graham. 1977. "The Demand for Insurance and Protection: The Case of Irreplaceable Commodities," *Quarterly Journal of Economics* 91 (February), pp. 143–156.

Cross, Frank B. 1989. "Natural Resource Damage Valuation," *Vanderbilt Law Review* 42 (March), pp. 270–341.

Cummings, Ronald G. 1989. Letter to the Office of Environmental Project Review, with comments concerning type B natural resource damage assessments, on behalf of ASARCO, the Idarado Mining Co., and the Newmont Mining Corporation, November 10, 1989.

Cummings, Ronald G., David S. Brookshire, and William D. Schulze. 1986. *Valuing Environmental Goods: An Assessment of the Contingent Valuation Method.* Totowa, N.J.: Rowman and Allanheld.

d'Arge, Ralph C., and Jason F. Shogren. 1989. "Non-market Asset Prices: A Comparison of Three Valuation Approaches." In *Valuation Methods and Policy Making in Environmental Economics*, edited by H. Folmer and E. van Ireland. Amsterdam: Elsevier.

Desvousges, William H., Richard W. Dunford, and Jean L. Domanico. 1989. "Measuring Natural Resource Damages: An Economic Appraisal," final report prepared for the American Petroleum Institute. RTI/3981-00-FR. Research Triangle Park, N.C.: Research Triangle Institute.

Desvousges, William H., Michael C. Naughton, and George R. Parsons. 1992. "Benefits Transfer: Conceptual Problems in Estimating Water Quality Benefits Using Existing Studies," *Water Resources Research* 28 (3), pp. 675–683.

Fischhoff, Baruch, and Lita Furby. 1988. "Measuring Values: A Conceptual Framework for Interpreting Transactions with Special Reference to Contingent Valuation of Visibility," *Journal of Risk and Uncertainty* 1 (June), pp. 147–184.

Freeman, A. Myrick, III. 1984. "On the Tactics of Benefit Estimation and Executive Order 12291." In *Environmental Policy Under Reagan's Executive Order: The Role of Benefit-cost Analysis*, edited by V. Kerry Smith, pp. 167–186. Chapel Hill, N.C.: University of North Carolina Press.

Harrison, Glenn W. 1992. "Valuing Public Goods with the Contingent Valuation Method: A Critique of Kahneman and Knetsch," *Journal of Environmental Economics and Management* 23 (3) (November).

Irwin, Julie R., William D. Schulze, Gary H. McClelland, Donald M. Waldman, David J. Schenk, and Leland G. Deck. 1990. "Survey Values for Public Goods: A Field Test of the Contingent Valuation Method," draft report, University of Colorado at Boulder.

Jones, Carol Adaire, Douglas B. Jester, and Yuc-sheng Sung. 1989. "Valuation of Changes in the Quality of Lake Michigan Recreational Fisheries," unpublished paper, School of Natural Resources, University of Michigan.

Kahneman, Daniel, and Jack L. Knetsch. 1991. "Valuing Public Goods: The Purchase of Moral Satisfaction," *Journal of Environmental Economics and Management* 22 (1), pp. 57–70.

Kling, Catherine L. 1989. "A Note on the Welfare Effects of Omitting Substitute Prices and Qualities from Travel Cost Models," *Land Economics* 65 (August), pp. 290–296.

Krutilla, John V. 1967. "Conservation Reconsidered," *American Economic Review* 47 (September), pp. 777–786.

Larson, Douglas M. 1990. "Measuring Willingness to Pay for Nonmarket Goods," paper presented at American Agricultural Economics Meetings, Vancouver, British Columbia.

Luken, Ralph A., F. Reed Johnson, and Virginia Kibler. 1992. "Benefits and Costs of Pulp and Paper Effluent Controls Under the Clean Water Act," *Water Resources Research* 28 (3), pp. 665–674.

McConnell, Kenneth E. 1983. "Existence and Bequest Value." In *Managing Air Quality and Scenic Resources at National Parks and Wilderness Areas*, edited by Robert P. Rowe and Lauraine G. Chestnut. Boulder, Colo.: Westview Press.

McConnell, Kenneth E. 1986. "The Damages to Recreational Activities from PCB's in the New Bedford Harbor," report prepared for National Oceanic and Atmospheric Administration with Industrial Economics, Inc.

McConnell, Kenneth E. 1991. Private correspondence with V. K. Smith, June 1991.

Michaels, R. Gregory, and V. Kerry Smith. 1990. "Market Segmentation and Valuing Amenities with Hedonic Models: The Case of Hazardous Waste Sites," *Journal of Urban Economics* 28, pp. 223–242.

Mitchell, Robert Cameron, and Richard T. Carson. 1989. "*Existence Values for Groundwater Protection*," draft final report to the U.S. Environmental Protection Agency, Cooperative Agreement No. CR814041-01.

Neill, Jon R. 1988. "Another Theorem on Using Market Demands to Determine Willingness to Pay for Nontraded Goods," *Journal of Environmental Economics and Management* 15, pp. 224–232.

Polinsky, A. Mitchell, and Steven Shavell. 1989. "Economic Analysis of Liability for Natural Resource Damages Caused by an Oil Spill," memorandum prepared for submission to the U.S. Department of the Interior.

Quiggin, John. 1990. "Do Existence Values Exist?" unpublished paper, Department of Agricultural and Resource Economics, University of Maryland.

Randall, Alan. 1991. "Nonuse Benefits." In *Measuring the Demand for Environmental Improvement*, edited by John B. Braden and Charles D. Kolstad. Amsterdam: North Holland.

Rosenthal, Donald H., and Robert H. Nelson. 1991. "Why Existence Value Should Not Be Used in Benefit-Cost Analysis," *Journal of Policy Analysis and Management* 11 (1), pp. 116–122.

Rowe, Robert D., and William D. Schulze. 1985. *Economic Assessment of Damage Related to the Eagle Mine Facility*. Boulder, Colo.: Energy and Resource Consultants, Inc.

Scheffman, David. 1990. *"Statistical Techniques for Market Delineation in Merger Analysis,"* unpublished paper presented at Allied Social Sciences meetings, Washington, D.C., December.

Segerson, Kathleen. 1989. "Risk and Incentives in the Financing of Hazardous Waste Cleanup," *Journal of Environmental Economics and Management* 16 (January), pp. 1–8.

Shavell, Steven. 1984. "Liability for Harm Versus Regulation of Safety," *Journal of Legal Studies* 8 (June), pp. 357–374.

Smith, V. Kerry. 1991. "Household Production Functions and Environmental Benefit Measurement." In *Measuring the Demand for Environmental Improvement*, edited by John Braden and Charles Kolstad. Amsterdam: North Holland.

Smith, V. Kerry, and William H. Desvousges. 1986. *Measuring Water Quality Benefits*. Boston: Kluwer-Nijhoff.

Smith, V. Kerry, and Ju Chin Huang. 1991. "Meta Analyses for Nonmarket Valuation: Hedonic Models and Air Quality," paper under revision, Resource and Environmental Economics Program, North Carolina State University.

Smith, V. Kerry, and Yoshiaki Kaoru. 1990. "Signals or Noise: Explaining the Variation in Recreation Benefit Estimates," *American Journal of Agricultural Economics* 72 (May), pp. 419–433.

Smith, V. Kerry, and Raymond J. Kopp. 1980. "The Spatial Limits of the Travel Cost Recreational Demand Model," *Land Economics* 56 (February), pp. 64–72.

Smith, V. Kerry, William H. Desvousges, and Ann Fisher. 1986. "A Comparison of Direct and Indirect Methods for Estimating Environmental Benefits," *American Journal of Agricultural Economics* 68 (May), pp. 280–289.

Smith, V. Kerry, Raymond B. Palmquist, Yoshiaki Kaoru, Jin Long Liu, and Paul M. Jakus. 1992. "A Comparative Evaluation of Travel Cost Methodologies for Valuing Quality in Marine Fishing: The Albemarle-Pamlico Estuary," Resource and Environmental Economics Program, North Carolina State University.

Willig, Robert D. 1978. "Incremental Consumer Surplus and Hedonic Price Adjustments," *Journal of Economic Theory* 17, pp. 227–253.

Willig, Robert D. 1991. "Merger Analysis, Industrial Organization Theory, and Merger Guidelines." In *Brookings Papers on Economic Activity, Microeconomics*, edited by M. N. Bailey and C. Winston. Washington, D.C.: The Brookings Institution.

GLOSSARY OF TERMS FOR NATURAL RESOURCE DAMAGE ASSESSMENT

This glossary is not intended to be definitive. Many of the terms have several, equally valid interpretations.

Asset   A resource capable of providing services over time.

Asset price   The one-time price of a commodity providing services over time.

Averting behavior   Any activity that people undertake to avoid or mitigate an external effect. With averting behavior, individuals undertake private actions to reduce adverse effects on them until the costs of these actions at the margin just equal the avoided losses from the external effects.

Bequest value   That component of the value of a natural resource that derives from an individual's desire to preserve the resource for the benefit of future generations.

CERCLA   Comprehensive Environmental Response, Compensation, and Liability Act of 1980. This legislation was the original Superfund law.

Choke price   The price at which there will be no more demand for the use of a resource.

Compensatory   Describes any act which involves payment to the owner(s) of a natural resource for the purpose of making amends for damage to that natural resource. The owner(s) may be private or public, the latter a **trustee** as representative of the public at large.

Consumer surplus   The excess in monetary value an individual would be willing to pay for a good over and above the total expenditures that would be made at a fixed price.

Contingent valuation   A valuation method that asks individuals for their values (in monetary units) for defined changes in the quantities or qualities of goods or services. Persons might be asked, for example, how much they would be willing to pay for the establishment of a new national park in the Great Basin area of the United States.

337

Damage   The amount of money sought by a federal or state agency, acting as **trustee,** as compensation for **injury** to, destruction of, or loss of natural resources, as set forth in section 107(a) or 111(b) of **CERCLA.**

Damage assessment   The use of valuation methods to assess damage to natural resources. An important benefit of damage assessment lies in the consistent and explicit application of theoretically grounded procedures for damage valuation. Under U.S. Department of the Interior rules, a specific comparison of natural resource restoration costs with replacement costs. (See also **Type A assessment, Type B assessment.**)

Discount rate   The rate at which future monetary values are converted into a current dollar measure.

Economic value   The monetary value for a good or service. In the context of a marketed good, economic value is the excess of individuals' total **willingness to pay** over the total cost of providing the good.

Ex ante valuation   In a natural resource context, an evaluation that must be made in advance of knowing all that would be relevant to decision making. Thus judgment must be made in the face of **uncertainty.** For example, the valuation of the environmental amenities of Alaska's Brooks Range is uncertain if individuals are not sure about the characteristics of the area's ecosystem, the pace of future development there, or their ability to make future visits to the range.

Existence value   That component of the value of a natural resource which derives solely from an individual's knowledge that the resource exists. For example, an individual may derive satisfaction purely from the knowledge that Alaska's Denali National Park exists, even if that person has never visited Denali and is sure that he or she will not do so in the future.

Expectations   Beliefs about how events that are uncertain will be resolved. Expectations concerning future resource supply and demand relate to the concept of ex ante resource valuation, and expectations may or may not be realized ex post.

Expected utility   When the outcome of an action is uncertain, and the possible outcomes involve different levels of **utility,** the expected utility of the action is the weighted sum of the utility levels of the possible outcomes. The weight for each of the possible utility levels is the probability that the associated outcome will result.

Ex post valuation In a natural resource context, an ex post valuation is made when there is no **uncertainty** regarding the events that can affect the benefits provided by the resource or the costs of taking specific actions. That is, an ex post valuation is made after the state of the world is known. For example, an individual would be able to value the benefits he would receive from a national park only if he knew (among many other factors) how many times he would visit the park and the kinds and degrees of satisfaction he would derive from each of those visits. Such information generally is known with certainty only after the individual has experienced the resource.

Hazardous waste Section 101(e) of **SARA** specifies that the term hazardous waste shall be defined as provided in Section 1004 of the Solid Waste Disposal Act: "A solid waste, or combination of solid wastes, which . . . may . . . (A) cause, or significantly contribute to an increase in mortality or an increase in serious irreversible, or incapacitating reversible, illness; or (B) pose a substantial present or potential hazard to human health or the environment when improperly treated, stored, transported, or disposed of, or otherwise managed." Under **CERCLA** and **SARA,** oil releases are treated similarly to hazardous wastes.

Hedonic model A modeling strategy for dealing with heterogeneous goods. The model assumes that these goods will be exchanged within a process that allows individuals to consider all possible types of the good and to select the one, given price that maximizes **utility.** A similar process for sellers would be assumed to be present. With this assumed process, the model permits the marginal value of a non-marketed resource to be computed from the prices for heterogeneous goods, provided the market prices are "connected to" the non-marketed good. For example, the marketed goods could be houses and the nonmarketed goods could be site-specific amenities.

Injury A measurable, adverse change, either long- or short-term, in the chemical or physical quality or the viability of a natural resource. Such injury may result either directly or indirectly from exposure to a discharge of oil or release of a hazardous substance, or exposure to a product of reactions resulting from the discharge of oil or release of a hazardous substance. As used in **damage assessments,** injury encompasses the terms "injury," "destruction," and "loss."

Natural resources As defined by Section 101 of **CERCLA,** "land, fish, wildlife, biota, air, water, ground water, drinking water supplies, and other such resources belonging to, managed by, held in trust by, appertaining to, or otherwise controlled by the United States . . . , any State or local government, any foreign government, (or) any Indian tribe . . . (or) . . . member of an Indian tribe."

Nonuse value That component of the value of a natural resource that does not derive from the in situ consumption of the resource.

Perceptions An individual's or a firm's interpretation of the conditions experienced by that individual or firm. In the context of a situation involving **risk,** the perception could be an individual's personal estimate of the probability of a specific undesirable outcome.

Producer surplus The incremental costs of producing specific goods or services associated with relaxing constraints on one or more fixed resources constraining production activities.

RCRA Resource Conservation and Recovery Act of 1983.

Real rate of interest The nominal interest rate adjusted for the expected rate of inflation. If the prevailing nominal rate of interest is 10 percent and the expected rate of inflation is 2 percent, then the real rate of interest equals 10 percent − 2 percent, or 8 percent.

Risk Risk arises when there exists some probability, greater than zero, that there will be some unfavorable outcome affecting individuals or firms. In the context of resource development, risk exists when there is some probability that a particular type of damage will result from development, or when there are a set of potentially harmful conditions, each with an associated probability. Risk is used in these circumstances to refer to the probability of undesirable outcomes. In a financial context, risk refers to the variation in outcomes against which one cannot insure.

SARA Superfund Amendments and Reauthorization Act of 1986. This Superfund legislation amended **CERCLA.**

Service flow A utility-generating or production-enhancing action that cannot be stored.

Social rate of discount The rate used to discount the future benefits and costs of public projects.

Time preference The attitude of individuals, firms, or society toward current sources of value in relationship to future sources of value.

Travel cost model A valuation approach which uses variations in the costs of travel to a recreational site, as well as variations in other expenditures, as implicit prices for site usage in order to estimate the demand for a particular recreational area. Such an approach can work because, for example, a household's costs of using a beach alongside the Chesapeake Bay vary depending on the household's location and its other characteristics.

Trustee An agent who holds the legal title to a natural resource and administers it for others' benefit. **SARA** designates specific agencies as trustees and describes mechanisms to assure coordination of federal and state trustees.

Type A assessment A **damage assessment** for a small incident of natural resource damage. Type A assessments do not call for a large amount of field study. In the context of marine environments, type A assessments require use of a U.S. Department of the Interior computer model.

Type B assessment A damage assessment for a large occurrence of natural resource damage. Type B assessments do necessitate a significant degree of field work.

Uncertainty There are multiple types of uncertainty. When uncertainty relates to measurement and estimation issues, it refers to the range of errors in the estimates of the parameters of interest. In the context of describing decisions by individuals or firms, it refers to circumstances in which these economic agents may not be sure of the market conditions, regulatory conditions, prices, and other conditions that they will face; consequently, their decisions will reflect some responses to this incomplete knowledge.

Use value The value that individuals attach to the in situ consumption of the services of a natural resource. For example, two important components of the use value of Colorado's Rocky Mountain National Park would be the value of hikes to the summit of Longs Peak and the value of fishing in Bear Lake.

Utility The welfare, or satisfaction, that an agent or group of agents derives from their use of a good or service or from the existence of that good or service, or from both.

Willingness to accept (WTA)   A monetary measure of compensation defined as the (minimum) amount that an individual would accept in place of having some amount of a commodity, or to experience a quality change (reduction) for a good. The use of this measure in **damage assessment** involves the implicit assumption that the public at large owns the resource in question.

Willingness to pay (WTP)   A monetary measure of the value of a change in the quantity or quality of a commodity measured as the (maximum) amount that an individual would pay to have the specified change. The use of this measure in **damage assessment** involves the implicit assumption that the public at large is not entitled to the services of the resource foreclosed by the damages.

Index